RUSSIAN OFFICIALDOM

RUSSIAN OFFICIALDOM

THE BUREAUCRATIZATION OF RUSSIAN SOCIETY FROM THE SEVENTEENTH TO THE TWENTIETH CENTURY

Edited by
Walter McKenzie Pintner
and
Don Karl Rowney

CONTRIBUTORS

Helju Aulik Bennett　　*Bruce W. Menning*
Robert O. Crummey　　*Daniel T. Orlovsky*
Robert V. Daniels　　*Walter M. Pintner*
Robert D. Givens　　*Borivoj Plavsic*
Brenda Meehan-Waters　　*Don Karl Rowney*
Stephen Sternheimer

THE UNIVERSITY OF NORTH CAROLINA PRESS

CHAPEL HILL

© 1980 The University of North Carolina Press
All rights reserved
Manufactured in the United States of America
Cloth edition ISBN 0-8078-1392-3
Paper edition ISBN 0-8078-4062-9
Library of Congress Catalog Card Number 79-14632

LIBRARY OF CONGRESS CATALOGING IN PUBLICATION DATA

Main entry under title:

Russian officialdom.

Bibliography: p.
Includes index.
1. Government executives—Russia—History—
Addresses, essays, lectures.   2. Russia—Officials and
employees—History—Addresses, essays, lectures.
I. Pintner, Walter McKenzie.   II. Rowney, Don
Karl, 1936–
JN6549.E9R87   354'.47'01   79-14632
ISBN 0-8078-1392-3
ISBN 0-8078-4062-9 pbk.

Contents

Tables

Glossary

The following list includes Russian terms used frequently in the text. Definitions are brief and necessarily imprecise because the Russian terms would not be used at all if there were an exact English equivalent. Singular forms are generally given here and will differ slightly from plural forms sometimes used in the appropriate context.

Boyar A member of the highest rank in the Duma of Boyars. More loosely, a high noble in pre-Petrine Russia.

Chin Rank, as applied to the hierarchy of titles created by Peter the Great, or to the parallel hierarchy of jobs. In pre-Petrine times, a social estate.

Chinoproizvodstvo The process of rising from personal rank to personal rank and from ranked job to ranked job.

Chinovnik An official in post-Petrine Russia, more precisely the "holder of a rank."

Deloproizvodstvo The conduct of affairs, or, more literally, the progress of paperwork.

D'iak A clerk in pre-Petrine Russia.

Duma A council.

Dumnyi d'iak A member of the lowest of the four ranks in the Duma of Boyars.

Dumnyi dvorianin A member of the third rank in the Duma of Boyars.

Dvorianin A noble.

Dvorianstvo The nobility.

Krug Cossack popular assembly.

Mestnichestvo The system of precedence ranking of high nobles by a combination of genealogical considerations and service precedents (abolished in 1682).

Okol'nichii A member of the second-highest rank in the Duma of Boyars.

Orden Ceremonial award.

Pod'iachii Junior clerk in pre-Petrine Russia.

Prikaz Chancery, agency of government in pre-Petrine Russia.

Prikaznye liudi The office workers in a *prikaz*.

Raznochintsy Persons of various class origin, those who do not easily fit into established legal categories.

Soslovie Estate or social class.

Stanitsa Cossack settlement.

Voevoda Originally a military commander, later a provincial governor.

Zemstvo Organs of local self-government in rural areas established in 1864.

Znat' The elite (literally, "the known").

Abbreviations Frequently Used

AMG   *Akty Moskovskogo gosudarstva (Acts of the Muscovite State.*
3 vols. St. Petersburg, 1890–1901.)

GPB   *Gosudarstvennaia publichnaia biblioteka imeni Saltykova-*
Shchedrina (Leningrad), Rukopisnyi otdel (Saltykov-
Shchedrin State Public Library, Leningrad, Manuscript
Division).

MVD   *Ministerstvo vnutrennikh del* (The Ministry of the Interior).

LOII   *Leningradskoe otdelenie instituta istorii SSSR, Akademii*
Nauk SSSR (Leningrad Division of the Institute of History
of the Academy of Sciences of the USSR).

PSZ   *Polnoe sobranie zakonov Rossiiskoi Imperii (The Complete*
Code of Laws of the Russian Empire). Issued in three series
covering the years 1649 to 1916.

RBS   *Russkii biograficheskii slovar' (Russian Biographical*
Dictionary. 25 vols. St. Petersburg, 1896–1918.)

TsGIA   *Tsentral'nyi gosudarstvennyi istoricheskii arkhiv* (Central
State Historical Archive, Leningrad, USSR.)

TsGADA *Tsentral'nyi gosudarstvennyi arkhiv drevnikh aktov* (Central
State Archive of Ancient Acts, Moscow, USSR.)

Citations to Soviet Archival Collections

The most commonly used form of archival citation is as follows: The name of the archive or its abbreviation, the "Fond" (Collection) number, "op." (*opis*, inventory) number, the year if needed (using "g." for *goda*, year), "d." (*delo*, item), number, and "fol." (folio, for the Russian *list*) number. Thus, for example, "TsGADA, Fond 100, op. 100, 1700g., d. 100, fols. 100–101."

Because of the diversity of archival materials and classification systems other notations are used where required.

Acknowledgments

Each contributor to this volume would wish us to acknowledge the support of those who assisted and supported him in his work if the space were available. However, we must confine ouselves to the considerable list who aided the project as a whole. The Russian Research Center at Harvard University, the Committee on Soviet Studies at Cornell University, and the Kennan Institute for Advanced Russian Studies provided facilities and generous hospitality for our three working conferences. The Research and Development Committee of the American Association for the Advancement of Slavic Studies gave us the financial support that made the final conference at the Kennan Institute possible. Bowling Green State University and Cornell University provided the secretarial and other assistance necessary to create a finished manuscript. The publication of this volume was assisted by a grant from the Hull Memorial Publication Fund of Cornell University.

From the beginning we have enjoyed the encouragement of Edward L. Keenan and S. Frederick Starr, without which it would have been difficult to complete the work. At various stages the manuscript has been read by John Armstrong, Dietrich Geyer, Alfred Rieber, T. H. Rigby, and Mack Walker and we have benefited greatly from their criticism. Most of the authors were enabled to pursue their research in the Soviet Union only through the support of the International Research and Exchanges Board or its predecessor, The Inter-University Committee on Travel Grants. Without the work of these agencies and the assistance of many Soviet institutions and individual scholars this study would have been inconceivable.

Above all the editors wish to acknowledge the support of the contributors. They came to our long and sometimes tedious conferences, often at their own expense, and made the project possible. If not a labor of love (who *loves* a bureaucrat?) it was at least an example of truly professional dedication.

Although the successive conferences produced general consensus on the major issues, each contributor remains solely responsible for his chapter and for that alone. The editors are jointly accountable for chapters one and fourteen and for the short introductions to each contribution.

W.M.P.
D.K.R.

[xvii]

RUSSIAN OFFICIALDOM

CHAPTER ONE

OFFICIALDOM AND BUREAUCRATIZATION: AN INTRODUCTION

Don Karl Rowney and Walter M. Pintner

This is a study of the civil officialdom, or officeholders, of the state administration of the Russian Empire and the Soviet Union. The work of eleven scholars is combined here in order to create an extensive and detailed history of Russian civil officialdom from the seventeenth century to our own times. In most studies of Russian and Soviet politics, government, and society, state functionaries are only a vague and undefined background to great events and the lives of great personages. In fact, in the normal order of things, it is the vaguely perceived officials who initiate, manage, and bring to fruition most governmental acts. Our aim is to make the Russian official a more distinct entity, to describe him not only as the law described him, but in terms of the society out of which he emerged, the qualifications he brought to his career, and the experience that rendered him ever more indispensable as government became more complex, more comprehensive, and, perhaps most important, as officialdom itself became more uniformly bureaucratized.

The volume is the product of several hands rather than one and it was conceived as such. One reason for this is that, collectively, it is an analysis of literally thousands of official careers across some thirty decades, nearly ten generations. Its purview comprehends the seventeenth century *d'iak* (clerk) and the twentieth century technocrat, the most powerful of high civil servants and their obscure subordinates in the centers of government and the provinces. Thus, each author brings a different perspective to the work as well as a different focus on the body of officialdom. The diversity of perspective and focus permits a variety of insight without sacrificing the continuity that emerges from the unity inherent in the subject.

The task that this study sets itself is of great importance, even if it may seem at first glance unglamorous and pedestrian. In pluralistic modern societies, the state apparatus, composed in the main of professional servants of the state, occupies a position of commanding importance linking together those who rule and those who are ruled. In Russia, the role of the official has been historically more important precisely because of the diminished or nonexistent role of institutions of power other than the state administration. Legislatures and political parties did not exist until the twentieth century and even then their appearance was short-lived. More important was the absence or limited role of "estates" in the sense of formally recognized segments of society with significant legal rights. These facts are well known and thus the importance of the official's role is taken as an axiom rather than a hypothesis in the present study. That is, the significance of state officialdom in Russia is taken for granted and the problem with which this study deals is to identify the many kinds of men who comprised Russian officialdom, and to explain how and why they achieved their positions and how their condition changed over time.

RUSSIAN GOVERNMENT AND THE ROLE OF OFFICIALDOM

Well before the birth of the first generation of officials studied in this book, the characteristic structure of Russian government was formed. The structure was one in which central political authority was paramount, dominating, at least formally or in theory, all regional and local centers. Central authority par excellence was represented in the person of the tsar or emperor. Those portions of state activity that did not involve the population directly (foreign affairs, waging war) were conducted by the tsar and his officials, military, civil, or religious. Activities that brought state servitors into contact with the population (tax collection, land settlement, regulation of commerce, law enforcement) were divided both territorially and functionally. In theory, and often in practice, regional and local administration was fully subordinate to the central authority of the tsar and his official servitors. The principal exceptions to this pattern of hierarchical subordination were ecclesiastical administration until the eighteenth century and the administration of rural estates until the mid-nineteenth century. Prior to the emancipation of the serfs in the 1860s, the state collected taxes and recruits for the army through the noble landlord who, in turn, usually dealt with the peasants through the village elder. Thus under normal circumstances the bulk of the Russian population had little direct contact with state officials, especially those appointed from St. Petersburg. The activities of state officials were concentrated in the two capitals, Moscow and St. Petersburg, and, from the late eighteenth century on, in an increasing number of provincial centers. In the nineteenth century the pattern changed even more. Those activities in which the central state apparatus was already engaged, such as tax collection and the regulation of commerce, expanded and new activities were added. The abolition of serfdom and the new formal administrative roles of the landed nobility is the best-known instance of the expansion of officialdom, but there were many others both before and after the 1860s. Indeed the mere fact of the doubling and redoubling of the Russian population in the eighteenth and nineteenth centuries accounted for growth in many areas of administration such as police, fiscal affairs, and public health. However, there was also an increase in the number of officials per inhabitant since the number of officials rose even more rapidly than the population of the empire.[1] What had been a small group of officials attendant on the tsar in the seventeenth century became an army of thousands in subsequent centuries as the empire expanded, provincial centers developed, and the government tried to do more things. It is important to emphasize that officialdom underwent an expansion of both numbers and roles over time. For almost forty decades the Russian official—ranked, compensated, and promoted by a system controlled by the central government—linked the diverse elements in Russian society to an increasingly dominant central authority. By the nineteenth century it was surely one of the largest such organizations in the world and, by the twentieth century, one of the longest-lived, with structures, functions and, in many cases, personnel surviving for some years following the holocaust of revolution.

PROBLEMS OF ANALYSIS AND CONCEPTION

Transmission versus Transformation

The most primitive conception of politics is one in which some agent or agents hold power, imposing it at will on others in society who are themselves powerless. Although political theorists and historians have quarrelled with the idea that this is so,[2] the Imperial Russian theory of government—the legal definitions of power and authority that lay

---

1. P. A. Zaionchkovskii puts the ratio of officials to Russian subjects in 1851 at 1 to 929; in 1897 he calculates it at 1 to 335. During the nineteenth century he estimates that the number of servitors increased seven times. See *Pravitel'stvennyi apparat samoderzhavnoi Rossii v XIXv.*, Moscow, 1978, p. 221.

2. George L. Yaney, "Bureaucracy and Freedom: N. M. Korkunov's Theory of the State," *American Historical Review*, 71 (January 1966): 468–86.

behind the exercise of imperial political power—seemed to conform to such a primitive conception.[3] Thus it is understandable, given the legal prescription and the actual structure of the state, that historians of Russia and the Soviet Union have sometimes subscribed to an essentially monolithic view of both the source and the exercise of political power in Russia. The historical record of Russian and Soviet politics has most often been that of political actions by the tiniest minority of persons who are defined as most powerful by the law. Such a power elite in the pre-Revolutionary period would include the tsar, certain members of the royal family, and the most visible of their immediate advisors and subordinates: the Filarets, Orlovs, Potemkins, Speranskiis, Arakcheevs, and Wittes. Often enough, the approach of historians and many political scientists to the Soviet era has also focused on the great men of power and, up to perhaps fifteen years ago, virtually no attention was paid to other elements in a political scheme of things.[4]

Of course this is not to say that there have only been historical studies of the tsar and his advisors in the pre-Revolutionary period. Studies of groups and group actions such as those of Marc Raeff, Terence Emmons, and Samuel Baron immediately come to mind.[5] Surely the importance of the groups studied in these works must rest on some assumptions about their importance in Russian politics. And to some extent they do, but the issue is somewhat skirted because the groups are treated as social, rather than political, or their role in politics is episodic and relevant to a specific political issue rather than consistently influential over time. In fact, there are few works one can readily cite that make explicit use of an idea of Russian politics in which other agents countervail, mitigate, or obstruct the power of the tsar, the first secretary of the Communist party, and their closest advisors.[6]

3. *Svod zakonov rossiiskoi imperii*, St. Petersburg, 1906. Vol. 1, Pt. 1, Articles 4–24.

4. John A. Armstrong's *Soviet Bureaucratic Elite: A Case Study of the Ukrainian Apparatus*, New York, 1959, is an early example of this reorientation. Others include Jerry Hough, *The Soviet Prefects: The Local Party Organs in Industrial Decision-Making*, Cambridge, Mass., 1969; and Jeremy Azrael, *Managerial Power and Soviet Politics*, Cambridge, Mass., 1966.

5. Marc Raeff, *Origins of the Russian Intelligentsia: The Eighteenth-Century Nobility*, New York, 1966; Terence Emmons, *The Russian Landed Gentry and the Peasant Emancipation of 1861*, Cambridge, 1968; Samuel H. Baron, "Who Were the Gosti?" *California Slavic Studies*, Berkeley, 1973, 7: 1–40.

6. Alfred J. Rieber, "The Moscow Entrepreneurial Group: The Emergence of a New Form in Autocratic Politics," *Jahrbücher für Geschichte Osteuropas* 25 (1977): 1–21, 174–99.

The present study reverses this pattern. Here the principal focus is on the main link between the decision makers and the society affected by the decision. For more than a generation it has been argued by an increasing number of social scientists that the official apparatus of government, conciliar bodies, the military, and the civil administration, have been far more than devices for transmitting policy from one level of government to another.[7] Transmission of policy undoubtedly occurs, but according to the research, the process also typically involves transformation, so that the ultimate effect of policy on society is often not what was originally intended by the decision makers.[8] It is the intervening officials upon whom this study focuses, the officialdom of Russia and the USSR as they emerge from the record of their public and private lives.

It is one thing to assert that officials play a role in both the transmission and the transformation of policy decisions. It is quite another to specify in any given case how this is done and to what extent the role is one of transmission or of transformation. To the extent that it succeeds in defining Russian officialdom and changing official roles, this study is intended to enlarge our understanding of the capacity of officialdom either to transform or simply to transmit policy.

Institutionalization

Political behavior as we are describing it here assumes an "institutional" approach by the political authority rather than something more informal. In the informal situation we would expect administration to consist simply of ad hoc solutions to specific problems. In the institutional situation revenue is generated by a regularly established administration for collection. Proceeds from the collection might fluctuate, but the process would be likely to be stable in that it would occur regularly, year after year. For the ad hoc solution of problems, officials, as we use the term here, do not exist. However, the combination of officials designated to certain tasks and the establishment on a regular basis of the tasks themselves through the authority of the

7. This literature is voluminous and growing all the time. Some oft-cited examples include: Max Weber, *The Theory of Social and Economic Organizations*, trans. A. M. Henderson and Talcott Parsons, ed. Talcott Parsons, New York, 1947; Talcott Parsons, *The Social System*, Glencoe, 1951; Amitai Etzioni, *A Comparative Analysis of Complex Organizations: On Power Involvement and Their Correlates*, New York, 1961; Phillip Selznik, *TVA and the Grassroots*, Berkeley, 1949.

8. George L. Yaney, "Concept of the Stolypin Land Reform," *Slavic Review* 23 (June 1964): 275–93.

sovereign constitutes the "institutional" approach to revenue raising. Although the present study begins in the early seventeenth century, it is noteworthy that we do not encounter a preinstitutional period, i.e. one that antedates officials. From our perspective there were always Russian officials interacting with Russian decision makers—the tsars and their immediate assistants always operated in an institutional framework. Therefore Peter I's Westernization of Russia, whatever it does consist in, does not consist in the institutionalization of policy implementation. To be sure, Peter extended and altered institutional structures and roles, but institutionalization as such exists clearly, formally, self-consciously in the seventeenth century. The political choices of tsars and first secretaries may be described and conceptualized in individualist, personal terms, but since the seventeenth century at least, they have always been implemented through, or around, institutions and officials. Often enough such choices have implied reorganization of institutions and their restaffing, or staffing new institutions afresh. In the case of Russia, moreover, the implications of political choices over the long run have included the extension of official institutions and officialdom as well as their organization. This is an obviously complex process: one that may place great strain on the limited educational, technical, and financial resources of a society which is poor, premodern, or in the process of modernization.[9]

Officials, Institutions, and Bureaucracy

If officials and the institutional approach to government extend back beyond the seventeenth century in Russia, what can it mean to speak of the bureaucratization of officialdom? As we tend to use the terms here, "official" means an appointee of some state institution while "bureaucrat" means something rather different. Let us begin with the concept of bureaucracy. Bureaucracy is used here to identify a type of institutional organization characteristic of—but not identical to—modern state administrations. There may (and do) exist major institutions in the twentieth century that are composed of officials but are not bureaucratic. The cabinets of most Western governments are illustrations of such institutions. The fact that, in the case of the United

---

9. Indeed, policy choices of certain kinds can easily put strain on these resources in industrial societies, as witness the consequences of major military efforts or, say, the United States space effort in the 1960s. In cases such as these we can speak of "distortions" of bureaucratic resources just as economists speak of distortions in the private and public sectors of the economy as a consequence of inflation.

Kingdom or the United States, these institutions do not enjoy the formal constitutional status of other institutions does not meaningfully limit their institutional standing or the official status of their appointees any more than does the fact that they are collegial bodies, composed of officials with roughly equal authority. Such institutions and officials are common enough, and it is of some interest to note that they are often political, or policy-making bodies whose incumbent officials have not risen through the ranks of the bureaucratic institutions that they individually command (e.g. the Department of Commerce), but owe their appointment to factors rather far removed from the bureaucracy.

Bureaucracy, then, is a technique of organization that may or may not be characteristic of a body of officials. The specific characteristics of bureaucracy that are relevant to the present study may best be understood if we attempt to characterize the process of bureaucratic formation, or bureaucratization. Bureaucratization is the formation of activities in an organization into compartments of activity that are separated from one another according to perceived differences in the formal objectives of participants in the activity, differences in the training or preparation of the participants, and differences in the career experiences of the participants. It is useful to note that we speak of "perceived" differences, since these are subject to change and, with them, what is thought to be a properly or rationally compartmentalized bureaucracy. Thus in the early nineteenth century, in many European countries, sanitation, public health, and police work were perceived to be aspects of the same official responsibilities and so were often grouped within the same institutional body under the authority of the same minister. The grouping and dividing of functions in a bureaucracy is typically expressed in legal statements that define the authority and responsibility of the institution and in the formulation of procedures which the institution is expected to use in discharging its responsibilities. In Russian, the formal procedure that is shaped within, and by, an institutional structure is called *deloproizvodstvo* ("the processing of affairs").

The definition of an institution's function seems to govern or control the concomitant definition of what constitutes adequate preparation and career experience of its officials. These definitions can be more or less narrow and technical. It is important to note, moreover, that while the definition of rational structure may be imposed on the bureaucratizing institution from without (e.g. by political policy makers), the institution or its officials can also establish "professional" criteria for the admittance and advancement of its own officials. In any event, one of the characteristics of bureaucratization in an institution is that officials are selected into, advanced, and selected out of the institution on the basis of their fulfilling certain requirements which are uniform for everyone and which usually have at least a nominal relationship to the tasks the official is expected to perform. In Russian, the procedure of passing an official through the ranks is called *chinoproizvodstvo* ("the processing of ranks").

In addition to compartmentalization on the basis of function, bureaucratization also typically consists in the subordination of specialized activities to hierarchies of decreasingly specialized, more or less formal, authorities. "Success" in a genuinely collegial body is principally associated with simple admittance to it, after which a greater or lesser degree of importance may be attained by a member through the manipulation of political or social relations that do not have very much to do with the special functions of the body. Success in a bureaucracy, however, is defined in terms of traveling through a hierarchy of more and more general and authoritative offices. The main criterion for selecting those who succeed is, nominally at least, demonstrated ability to perform appropriate institutional tasks. As we shall see, bureaucratic *chinoproizvodstvo* does not preclude the influence of social or political factors (like wealth and family connections) so important in determining status in a collegial body, but it does give scope to more uniform criteria that even the materially and socially impoverished can hope to satisfy and to which even the opulently rich must appear to conform.

Bureaucratization can thus be said to happen to an institution that is already in existence but organized in a different way. Institutions can be reorganized and thus bureaucratized. Individual officials and groups of officials can be disciplined to the special requirements (*deloproizvodstvo* and *chinoproizvodstvo*) of a bureaucratized organization and thus become bureaucratized. Societies, too, when more and more of their social, political, and economic functions are submitted to bureaucratic discipline, can be bureaucratized. Thus, we can speak of the bureaucratization of manufacturing, farming, and perhaps even sport. These activities may or may not be official, depending upon whether they are part of the activities of the state.

Bureaucratization and Law

Max Weber tended to discuss bureaucratization as though it were a uniform development that societies at certain stages of maturity would achieve. In particular he associated the development of large uniform societies, sharing in common social, economic, and political values and behavior, with the development of a true bureaucracy. For Weber, the achievement of bureaucracy included not only the rationalization of official functions and official statuses, but also the discipline of these activities and those of the entire society to an impartial body of law.[10] To the extent that Russia is an important example of bureaucratization, it is clear that the implication of Weber's typology is incorrect. In general, law and bureaucracy need not be linked as Weber thought they were. It is not merely that Weber's "ideal-types" of officials and organizations were not realized in detail in Russian-Soviet history; these are, after all, merely pure types, not empirical or historical phenomena, a disclaimer that Weber himself often makes.[11] The main problem with the Weberian conception of bureaucracy vis-à-vis the Russian reality is that in Russia the role of law has always been sharply circumscribed both for the society generally and within officialdom itself.

The creation of uniform social organizations is clearly one of the most common characteristics of modern industrial urban societies. Educational uniformity, uniform norms of public behavior, uniform language, social behavior, and so forth are achieved historically in a variety of ways depending upon the society in question. Among Western societies the formulation of socially acceptable custom and politically and economically necessary procedure into law has been commonly associated with the creation of such a society. In these cosmopolitan—"mobilized"—societies, the state was thought to be subject more to the impartial control of the law, a *Rechtsstaat*, than to the arbitrary and whimsical will of mortal men. In Russia such a *Rechtsstaat* never displaced the ultimate, absolute rule of a mortal man. The autocrats down to 1917 and the Party leaders after them did not shrink from the role of ultimate arbiter. The creation of uniform social structures in Russia is clearly the consequence of many trends of development from the seventeenth century onward but, just as clearly, in the absence of a *Rechtsstaat*, enormous segments of modern Russia have conformed to the bureaucratic state. The fact that such conformity comes finally to include important segments of political life prompts us to speak of an apotheosis of bureaucratic institutions, an ultrabureaucracy. Where once the modest task of officialdom was to transmit the wishes of the autocrat and his noble advisors to the society, the ultimate transformation has now taken place and politics itself has been bureaucratized.

10. Weber, *Theory of Social and Economic Organizations*, pp. 328–41.
11. For example, see Weber, *Theory of Social and Economic Organizations*, p. 329.

Social Characteristics

An officialdom cannot be created that has only a political or administrative life. Inevitably, the acquisition of money, power, and place in
government institutions results in the establishment of parallel social
characteristics that single out the officials from others in the society—
both their social inferiors and superiors. Moreover, it is clear that
officials are not chosen by the major decision makers at random, as it
were, from society at large. The need for both reliability and technique
in the exercise of administrative authority is always such as to cause
officials in even the most informal and primitive societies to be selected with some evidence of prejudice.[12] This evidence, of course, lies
in the fact that officials are typically anything but a microcosm of
society at large. The atypicality of officials in turn becomes one of the
principal arguments in favor of analyzing the demographic characteristics of civil servants, military officers, collegial advisory bodies, and
so on. What values, what social and economic resources, what patterns
of experience and expertise appear to be tapped in the formation of
any specific officer corps for higher civil service? To what extent do
these values, resources, and expertise accord with the explicit objectives of the decision makers in the formation of the corps? To what
extent do they reflect the intervention of senior members of the corps
itself in selecting (coopting) their juniors and successors? To what
extent do they simply reflect the fact that the objectives of decision
makers and the demands which they consequently impose on the
experience, expertise and, possibly, the loyalty of administering officials often outstrip the capacity of society—or of the privileged social
strata—to deliver replacements to fill vacated or new positions? On
the other hand, changing goals, changing technology, and changing
loyalties often create conditions in which too many officials—at least
too many of a certain kind—are present, and tend to hang on in the
system of government organization.

An important related issue is whether the creation of officialdom
produces social differentiation or whether the official group is a product or even a reflection of the social class. The present study cannot
answer that question in terms of ultimate origin, because even in
seventeenth-century Russia both officialdom and social differentiation
were already well developed. The essays in this volume deal with the
interaction of the two. In one way or another, state service was an

---

12. Lloyd A. Fallers, *Bantu Bureaucracy: A Study of Integration and Conflict in the Political
Institutions of an East African People*, 2nd ed., Cambridge, 1965, especially Chaps. 6 and 7.

important way for some individuals to gain admittance to more privileged levels of society, and at the same time men from the existing privileged groups filled most of the higher positions. The upper levels of society were used to having their sons serve. The question of whether officials simply implemented or modified institutional policy runs afoul of the extent to which the special interests of the servitors as a social class affected policy. The situation is especially complex in pre-Revolutionary Russia because of the multiple roles of the nobility as officials, landholders, and as the socially privileged class.

Formal Education and Other Forms of Socialization

The fact that officialdom necessarily exists in social dimensions in addition to institutional or political dimensions has other implications. One of the most important of these is that there must exist a social process whereby new generations are prepared to assume the roles held by an older generation. As time passes, beginning in the eighteenth century in Russia, the state, through formal institutions of learning, assumes a greater proportion of the responsibility for preparing the young to take the places of the old. Still, the influence of the family and the social environment in which the young mature continues to be important even as the role of the state increases,[13] underscoring the fact that reading, ciphering, the law, and other professional skills are only part of the socialization process of a new generation. Other elements such as general social behavior and networks of friends and relatives are important in determining career patterns, as are professional skills. Obviously the composition and the range of skills, training, and experience upon which the decision maker may call for implementing policy at any given moment are limited by the capacity of the provisioning society and the educational institutions to supply people so trained. They are also limited by the capacity of the institutions to absorb them as replacements for others who were differently trained or who were subject to a different, and now undesirable, range of experiences. Thus, if officialdom is going to change or be changed, the fact that officials are rooted in a social class must be confronted. New forms of training, however effective or ineffective, are time-consuming and probably socially disorganizing.

13. John A. Armstrong, *The European Administrative Elite.* Princeton, 1973, especially Chaps. 5 and 6.

Diversity within Officialdom

An additional complicating factor in understanding officialdom is its diversity. Up to this point, we have spoken of officialdom as though it were monolithic. Of course this is not, and never has been, the case. Even if we assert that the definition of an official is anyone compensated in some way by the state for the performance of an assigned, institutionalized function, that definition leaves the way open for variation within the type at any point in time and for great variation over time. Thus, we shall see that socially and professionally there is considerable variation in the case of Russian officialdom, from its top to its bottom, and from the seventeenth century to the twentieth. Several strata of officials emerge within the central bureaucracy, just as immense variations will be evident between the center and the provinces. Always present in some degree, the variation among officials because of professional specialization increases as does the state's reliance on technology and professional training in the nineteenth century. The "Russian official," thus, can refer to an illiterate policeman in 1900 who resided in some remote provincial town, but it also refers to Count N. S. Mordvinov, owner of hordes of serfs, inventor, and economist, who corresponded with Jeremy Bentham; the title refers to a civil engineer, builder of sanitary sewers, just as it refers to K. P. Pobedonostsev, keeper of the royal conscience in the 1880s and 1890s. The differences, as we shall see, cut across profession, career patterns, compensation and other emoluments, social background, and education. They are so great as to lead us to wonder whether there is any substance to a general definition of "official." The truth, surely, is that, while the legal definition of the terms "official," "bureaucrat," "ranking officer," and others may be relatively stable over time, the functional meaning of those terms in many cases has changed dramatically from the seventeenth to the twentieth century.

Change across Time

These threads of continuity and change are what finally lace together the several parts of this study. From the seventeenth century, at least, the central Russian government reserved certain social, economic, and political functions to officialdom and defined officialdom in certain ways. At the same time, there is a pattern of change over time, interweaving, as stimulants and products of change, government policy, technology, the distribution of wealth, status, and power. Policy change produces deliberate and unintended changes in officialdom, its makeup, and its distribution. These changes together, in turn, work change in the society at large, which may cause a fresh cycle of policy change. The patterns of change in officialdom—its makeup, distribution, and size—and the rhythm of that change—the time required for a change, say, in educational requirements or an expansion of the bureaucratic role to affect a substantial portion of officialdom— become indications for us of patterns and rhythms of change in policy, on the one hand, and social structure and function, on the other. The study of Russian officialdom is central to the study of Russian society. Though this study deals not at all with policy directly, it seems crucial to understand the composition, the social environment, and the characteristics of change over time of the officialdom if policy making and policy implementation are to be understood. Neither is this a study of Russian society as such. Yet in a society where so great a proportion of life is shaped by the official presence, it seems vital to have fixed clearly in mind the official role and the official physiognomy.

But there is more to be gained from such a study than a deeper and broader understanding of the past, however important that may be in itself. This introductory essay intimates, and the following chapters demonstrate, that there is a pattern of continuity amidst massive change. If the era of Catherine the Great was meaningful to understanding the era of Nicholas I, surely we do not have to wait a hundred years to discover that the officialdom of Nicholas II played its role in structuring and shaping the operation of Soviet officialdom in the time of Stalin and his successors. Of course, the revolutions of the twentieth century, the introduction of the ubiquitous commissar, massive urbanization, industrialization, and growth in both wealth and population have transformed the face of Russia. But what about the skeleton beneath? The assumptions about the role of officialdom in society and economy? The authority attaching to official status? The tendency for class structure and social status to be shaped by official status and roles and for these, in turn, to be shaped by class influence? Any generation, however revolutionary it may be, is always the child of the preceding generation. In this context paternity and childhood mean the transfer, over time, of values—assumptions, perspectives, goals, prejudices—and behavior, collectively, the way a given society tends to perform the most important tasks of feeding, clothing, defending, preserving order, accumulating wealth. The principal means available to any society to achieve this transfer are its fundamental and characteristic institutions, such as work institutions, educational institutions, military institutions, and governing institutions. In Russia, government has meant officialdom, and its progressive bureaucratization, as far back into the past as our collective vision enables us to penetrate. The definition—and, thus, the role of official institutions—has not changed to the present day. This fundamental continuity is the preoccupation of the present series of studies.

BASIC ORGANIZATION OF THE STUDY

The book is organized chronologically. The essays by Plavsic, Crummey, Meehan-Waters, and Givens cover the early modern period from before Peter I to the late eighteenth century. The studies by Menning, Pintner, Orlovsky and Bennett, extend from the mid-eighteenth to the late nineteenth century. The final decade of the empire and the Soviet period are treated by Rowney, Sternheimer, and Daniels. While this organization implies a straightforward series of surveys, each taking up where the other leaves off, the coverage, in fact, is considerably more complex. Although the work is a collective one, each author has maintained the individuality of his own approach. As the preceding brief survey of the subject of Russian officialdom indicates, there are many dimensions of the problem to be assessed, and each author has adopted his own method. Thus, the question of how Russian officialdom has changed across the span of several generations is dealt with in a major way by the collection of essays, rather than by each of them individually, and by the editors' commentary which introduces each chapter and which aims to keep the broad issues in focus. In the end, the most important changes and continuities in characteristics of Russian officialdom should be clear to the reader.

ANALYSIS OF STRUCTURE AND DISTRIBUTION OF PERSONNEL

Most of the essays (Plavsic, Crummey, Meehan-Waters, Pintner, Orlovsky, Rowney, and Daniels) take the central, or cosmopolitan, officialdom as their primary focus. This is as it should be. It has already been pointed out that, for most of the period in question, the bulk of official activity in Russia was concentrated in the urban centers, especially St. Petersburg and Moscow. On the other hand, as both Givens and Menning show, certain kinds of social and economic organization in the countryside were controlled by, and sustained, their own elites, which were also a quasi-officialdom. By the nineteenth century, the growth of rural offices—and, thus, of rural officialdom—

is increasingly important to the structure of the entire administration and the character of the officialdom. Thus Pintner deals in some detail with these local officials and with the important contrast between them and the officials of central agencies. Similarly, by the twentieth century the development of the economic, health, and educational administrations has produced massive growth in numbers and significance of local and regional officialdom, which is reflected in the data reviewed by Sternheimer.

Thus each of the essays can be distinguished by its chronological orientation and by whether it focuses on the central or provincial officialdom or both. In addition, the essays differ according to the kinds of officials they are primarily concerned with. Thus, Plavsic, Pintner, Orlovsky, Rowney, and Sternheimer each concentrate on what, in modern history, may be regarded as the primary type of official, the bureaucrat. The subjects of these analyses typically hold positions which, from a functional point of view, are rather clearly defined and which are hierarchically ordered. Crummey, Meehan-Waters, Menning, Givens, and Daniels deal with elite or superelite officials. That is, these essays focus on an officialdom whose primary role in the body politic was not traditionally as distinctly circumscribed as that of the bureaucrat and who, instead of being exactly fixed in an organizational hierarchy, was more frequently treated as an *aequus inter pares*, the member of a social or political collegium. What is striking here, of course, is the tendency of bureaucratic characteristics—especially uniform ranking and career development, and uniform organization and procedure—to encroach upon these collegial elites. This tendency, which begins with the "noble bureaucrats" of the eighteenth century, reaches its greatest extension and intensity with the emergence of informal yet clearly marked career paths through the bureaucracy to elite status in the Central Committee of today.

ANALYSIS OF CAREER AND DEMOGRAPHIC CHARACTERISTICS

Apart from whether the subjects of each essay were bureaucrats or counciliar elites, in a central or a provincial administration, the characteristics most essential to describing them, to assigning them a role or niche in both the social and the political-administrative systems of the country, are career and demographic variables. For the most part, career and demographic factors are used as the principal devices for

[18] *Don Karl Rowney, Walter M. Pintner*

evoking an image of Russian officialdom. Indeed, these factors are so crucial to the structure of the entire study that a kind of outline history of Russian officialdom may be discerned merely by summarizing the most important career and demographic characteristics used to describe Russian officialdom from the seventeenth century to the twentieth.

DEVELOPMENT OF THE PROJECT

The present study developed from the recognition some six years ago that a significant number of scholars in the United States were concerned with various aspects of the history of Russian officialdom in widely separated periods and that the information possessed by these individuals collectively greatly exceeded that available to any one researcher. Informal meetings, followed by a series of three annual working conferences (at Harvard and Cornell Universities and the Kennan Institute in Washington) convinced those involved that their individual and necessarily particular research would benefit not only from the comments and criticism of others, but from inclusion in a volume devoted to a common theme, one that flowed naturally from the existing interests of the participants. The division of labor is chronological, but each author has benefited from repeated discussion of similar problems in periods other than his own. The editors are convinced that a coherent progression emerges from the specialized discussions that follow, without destroying the variety of approach and illuminating detail of the individual contributions.

CHAPTER TWO

SEVENTEENTH-CENTURY CHANCERIES
AND THEIR STAFFS

Borivoj Plavsic

To Western visitors sixteenth and seventeenth-century Muscovy was a "rude and barbarous kingdom" because of marked differences in Russian social customs as compared with those familiar to the visitors. This view persists in much present-day scholarship.

Plavsic suggests that in terms of bureaucratic institutions and personnel, Muscovy had already established many of the structures and administrative practices that are associated with "modern" or "developed" governments. The chancery officials of the seventeenth century emerge as a body of trained, professional employees of the state's civil government. Equally, they emerge as a body of officials without land and of a social status distinctly inferior to the administrative-political elite discussed by Crummey in Chapter Three. Nevertheless, these career bureaucrats were not exclusively lowly clerks. They included a broad range of officially established ranks and a few influential officials who held positions comparable to those of the leading members of the landed military and civil servitors described in subsequent chapters.

Plavsic's work here introduces much new information about Russia's early professional bureaucrats, a group consistently overshadowed by the more prestigious and powerful boyar elite, both when they lived and, later, in historical accounts. However, in the long run—in the twelve or so generations surveyed in this book—it is the landed, socially prominent, aristocratic elites who will be obscured by the ever more numerous, more powerful lower class and classless bureaucrats. [THE EDITORS.]

During the two centuries preceding the reign of Peter the Great, the state of Muscovy expanded its boundaries in a truly spectacular manner and developed into an absolutist state par excellence. Some aspects of the Muscovite growth have been examined extensively, while others have received only erratic attention. It is to the latter of these categories that the study of the institutions and the officials who effected this growth belongs.[1]

Until Petrine times and the introduction of the Table of Ranks (1722), Muscovite Russia employed two clearly separate state servitor groups, one group's service based on noble birth, the other group's service based on administrative skill and experience. That some men of the first group, such as V. V. Golitsyn or A. L. Ordin-Nashchokin, did possess undeniably high competence in civil-administrative matters should not obscure the fact that this competence was not a prerequisite for an appointment to any high post. Below, we shall see that the opposite held true for the second group. This dichotomy poses the question, Who ruled and who governed? The studies of the first group by V. O. Kliuchevskii, Robert Crummey, Gustave Alef, and others provide only a part of the answer. Nominally, the tsar and the Council of the Boyars, and the council members as holders of various other high offices had a monopoly of decision making, but if we consider the role of the administrative decrees in all facets of the Russian national life, and the role of the professional administrators in both formulating and implementing these decrees, for the time being the question must remain an open one.

Each of the two groups played a key role in the development of the Russian state, and it is on the professional administrators, or more precisely the *prikaznye liudi*, that the present article will focus. The term means, literally, "chancery men," that is, employees of the *prikazy* (chanceries). The existence of the *prikaznye liudi* in the pre-Petrine Russia as a distinct and separate social group is widely recognized both in specialized literature and in general works. Yet, the *prikaznye liudi* are almost without exception bypassed in the analysis of the Muscovite society and their role in the government accorded but a fleeting mention. To date we lack a sufficient base for an analysis and understanding of the function and characteristics of the administrative apparatus and of the professional segment of the Russian officialdom before the Table of Ranks. To be sure, the field is not completely barren; the authors of many essays and monographs on individual *prikazy* have contributed much, and there are a few wide-ranging articles as well.[2]

---

1. Ironically, it is the earlier period that has been studied better despite the paucity of the source material. See especially N. P. Likhachev, *Razriadnye d'iaki XVI veka*, St. Petersburg, 1888, and A. K. Leont'ev, *Obrazovanie prikaznoi sistemy upravleniia v russkom gosudarstve*, Moscow, 1961.

2. The earliest period that has been studied in adequate breadth and depth is from the mid-eighteenth century. See S. M. Troitskii, *Russkii absoliutizm i dvorianstvo v XVIIIv. Formirovanie biurokratii*, Moscow, 1974. The literature on the single *prikazy* is too

Yet many students of Russia, both Soviet and Western, lack understanding of a number of the early period's salient qualities. This article's purpose is to outline the basic functional and social characteristics
and attributes of the *prikaznye liudi* prior to the Table of Ranks.

The prevalent view of the reign of Peter the Great, dating back to
the eighteenth century, is that Peter reformed the central government
on a rational organizational basis and made the state service and administration more efficient. The old overlapping jurisdiction of the
intractable *prikazy* was replaced by the new streamlined system of
colleges.[3] Merit, rather than birth, became the prime criterion for service and advancement. The Table of Ranks opened the career to talent
and provided an important avenue for upward social mobility. Now,
of course, no historical interpretation that has enjoyed popularity for
such a long time can be entirely without foundation. Yet it will be
argued here that the above view, at least as far as the administrative
institutions and their personnel are concerned, is but one of the many
myths surrounding the reign of Peter the Great. The traditional view
obscures the fact that there is good reason to believe that pre-Petrine
Russian administration was organized in a more modern manner than
it came to be after Peter's many "reforms." It is quite possible that

---

numerous to cite here. Probably the best example is S. Belokurov's *O Posol'skom prikaze,*
Moscow, 1906. The major articles on them include: S. K. Bogoiavlenskii, "Prikaznye
d'iaki XVII veka," *Istoricheskie zapiski,* 1: 220–39 (hereafter: Bogoiavlenskii, "D'iaki");
N. F. Demidova, "Biurokratizatsiia gosudarstvennogo apparata absoliutizma v XVII–
XVIIIvv.," *Absoliutizm v Rossii,* Moscow, 1964, pp. 206–42 (hereafter: Demidova,
"Biurokratizatsiia"), and "Prikaznye liudi XVII veka. Sotsial'nyi sostav i istochniki
formirovaniia," *Istoricheskie zapiski,* 90: 332–54 (hereafter: Demidova, "Prikaznye
liudi"); N. V. Ustiugov, "Tsentral'noe upravlenie. Prikazy," *Ocherki istorii SSSR. Period
feodalizma XVIIv.,* Moscow, 1955, pp. 366–84, and "Evoliutsiia prikaznogo stroia
russkogo gosudarstva v XVIIv.," *Absoliutism v Rossii,* Moscow, 1964.

3. There is no agreement among the scholars on the number of the *prikazy* in the
seventeenth century. S. K. Bogoiavlenskii lists 77 *prikazy* in *Prikaznye sud'i XVII veka,*
Moscow and Leningrad, 1946 (hereafter: Bogoiavlenskii, *Sud'i*), while Demidova enu-
merates 96 (N. F. Demidova, "Prikazy," *Sovetskaia istoricheskaia entsiklopediia,* Vol. 11,
cols. 560–66). We could add to their lists another 10 to 20 *prikazy,* including, for
example, the *Prikaz sysknogo Permskogo dela,* which existed for at least two years starting
with 1652, or the *Prikaz sbora soldatskogo stroia,* which was apparently formed in 1658
judging from the reassignments to it of several of the *pod'iachie* (junior clerks) of Land
Chancery (*Pomestnyi prikaz*). See A. A. Sokolova and A. K. fon Mekk, eds., *Raskhodnye
knigi i stolpy Pomestnogo prikaza,* Moscow, 1910, p. 277. I. K. Kirillov, statistician and the
senior secretary of the Senate in the closing years of Peter's reign, counted no less than
905 bureaus and offices (*kantseliariia i kontory*), any or all of which could have qualified
as a *prikaz.* See V. O. Kliuchevskii, "Kurs russkoi istorii," Pt. 4, *Sochineniia,* Moscow,
1958, 4: 195, 387.

in certain important respects seventeenth-century Russia had developed an administrative apparatus that was more "rationally bureaucratic" that those in seventeenth-century Western Europe. The discussion that follows of organization, training, accountability, promotion, and so forth will provide the basis for such a comparison. An examination of Western institutions, however, is beyond the scope of a short paper.

The seventeenth century witnessed an overall decline of the nobility (*dvorianstvo*) vis-à-vis the state, both de facto and de jure, as the state preempted even the last vestiges of independent presence of all the social classes and institutions. Accompanying the omnipresence of the autocracy was excessive regularization and "paperization"; one is very much tempted to write "bureaucratization." To survive and to prosper in an overly regularized society, the leading institutions and social groups needed both the state's benevolence and a level of competence in discharging responsibilities to the state that would make them indispensable. The nobility had benevolence, but not competence, neither military, technical, nor administrative. It is as an attempt to promote, nay to create, this competence that we must view much of Peter's activity. He wanted a strong Russian state, both internally and internationally, and to accomplish this he turned to the nobility as the only socially fit group.

In the past, nobles had fulfilled their obligatory state service through a multitude of haphazard ways. The length of service was not fixed. They could be serving in the military, in the court, in the administration. They could be, and were, transferred from one type of service to another, and consequently became jacks of all trades and masters of none. Even in the military the nobility was being superseded by either foreigners or by the Russians of inferior birth trained by the foreigners. It is clearly not by accident that nobles, even members of the oldest and of the best connected noble families, were never assigned to any civil administrative post alone, but always with the *prikaznye liudi*. Exactly what their respective roles were is still subject to dispute, or rather, is still not clear. Even at the sittings of the Council of the Boyars it was the *dumnyi d'iak* (a professional administrator and a member of the council), often referred to by the West European visitors aptly as "chancellor") who was charged with all substantive matters on the agenda, from putting them before the council to writing the final resolutions. However, if one considers the measures Peter took to upgrade the competence of the nobility, most tellingly the arbitrary and forcible assignments to acquire specialized education, one must conclude that the overall competence of the nobility was very low. It is then the social consideration, the determined effort to competitively integrate the nobility into all the branches of the state service, including civil, that was the reason behind the introduction of the Table of Ranks.

However disliked and opposed initially, the Table of Ranks did yield at least some of the results Peter expected from it. The cultural and competence level of the nobles did rise, and the eighteenth century is in retrospect viewed as the golden age of the Russian nobility. But the fusing of the two groups of servitors, the generally unmotivated high-born with mediocre skills and the low-born with good skills, dulled and decreased the overall quality of the Russian state administration. Under Peter, and after him, inertia, incompetence, corruption, and adhministrative confusion, are all increasingly evident. The post-Petrine Russian state administration may well be seen as dysfunctional.

ORGANIZATIONAL ASPECTS
OF ADMINISTRATIVE SERVICE

A prerequisite for any formal administrative organization is a perma-nent budget for a permanent staff. The existence of, and indeed the strict adherence to, the staff budget in pre-Petrine *prikazy* has some-how eluded the attention of modern scholars. Yet, there are published summaries of the annual budget of the Foreign Chancery going back to at least the reign of Fedor Ivanovich (1584–98), and the archives contain other similar and corroborative summaries. That all *prikazy* had similar staff budgets is evident from a multitude of sources.[4] Long before Peter, salary was the primary means of payment and support of the *prikaznye liudi*, and it is most puzzling that N. F. Demidova, the world's leading authority on the *prikazy*, should have misrepresented this key feature and one of the pivotal points in the development of the Russian bureaucracy:

---

4. Belokurov, *O Posol'skom prikaze*, pp. 131–41, and Tsentral'nyi gosudarstvennyi arkhiv drevnikh aktov (hereafter: TsGADA), Fond 138, 1645 g., No. 5; ibid., 1700 g., No. 33. Archival materials such as *Knigi moskovskogo stola* (TsGADA, Fond 210, Nos. 64, 70, etc.) run into hundreds of pages and contain nothing but the staff entitlements of virtually all the *prikazy* in given years. Recently published *Knigi moskovskikh prikazov v fondakh TsGADA. Opis'*, Moscow, 1972, based on only 5 *fondy* and encompassing only 14 *prikazy*, lists no less than 430 *prikhodo-raskhodnye knigi i stolbtsy* (annual account records of all cash received and disbursed) for the period 1614–1718, all of which are replete with information on entitlements and payments in cash to not only *prikaznye liudi*, but other ranks as well.

In 1714, with the abandonment of the practice of granting an estate [as a payment for state service] to all state servants, including the personnel of the *prikazy*, salary was introduced for the first time not as a supplement to payment in land but as an independent and sole reward for service. This led directly to an increased dependence of the officials on the central government. Another consequence of the same act was a discontinuation of the heretofore obligatory nexus between the civil service and the ownership of the land; this affected above all the lower ranking bureaucrats, and later on it carried over to the middling ranks.[5]

With regard to the entire professional administrative staff, that is, not only the junior staff but also the senior staff, Demidova is in error. The dependence of virtually the entire group on cash payments from the state was complete some decades before Peter and in no way changed in 1714. By the second half of the seventeenth century at the latest there was nothing like an "obligatory nexus" between the *prikaz* service and land ownership. In fact it was the land payment or ownership that was supplementary or incidental, not the salary.[6]

The staff budget was rarely exceeded. When a junior clerk petitioned for a raise, or reinstatement to the payroll after a period of service elsewhere, he was often, when funds were not available in the regular budget, granted the request but with a proviso that the money was not payable until funds did become available. So strict was the observance of the budgetary ceiling that there were cases when the full new regular entitlement was paid out "*v prikaz*," that is, as a bonus payment, distinctly separate from the funds for regular salaries.[7]

5. Demidova, "Biurokratizatsiia," pp. 229–30. Her statement is repeated virtually verbatim by S. M. Troitskii, *Russkii absoliutizm*, p. 254. Demidova's statement reflects not only her neglect of the staff budget, but also of a veritable sea of material with which she must be very familiar. The payrolls (*okladnye knigi* and *raskhodnye stolbtsy*, see above note 4) list the annual entitlements of all lower ranking *prikaznye liudi*, give the actual sums paid out, and bear the signature of the recipient. The entitlements of the *dumnye d'iaki* and the *d'iaki* are found in the *Boiarskie knigi* and *Boiarskie spiski* (TsGADA, Fond 210).

6. See below on the cash entitlements and on landholding of the *prikaznye liudi*, pp. 42–44.

7. To cite but a few examples. On 27 January 1649, one Zakhar Nikonov, a junior clerk in the Land Chancery (*Pomestnyi prikaz*), was granted a regular salary of 4 rubles with the stipulation that payment was not due until the regular budget would allow (*do ubylykh okladov*). Thus on the payday, March 23 of the same year, he was paid and signed for, the 4 rubles "*v prikaz, a ne v oklad*" (Sokolova and fon Mekk, *Raskhodnye knigi*, pp. 146, 150). In March 1700 several of the *pod'iachie* of the Foreign Chancery were receiving either a part or the entire entitlement outside the regular budget. Anisim

Another prerequisite for the functioning of a complex administrative organization is the existence of fully developed written rules of procedure and a hierarchical authority structure. The Muscovite state administration possessed both. The activity of each *prikaz* was regulated by its Administrative Manual. These manuals spelled out in the minutest detail who was to do what and how. In fact the administrative rules and directives were the law of the land. The Law Code of 1649, which remained in force until 1830, is nothing more than a compilation of these administrative manuals. No one who has consulted the recently published *Monuments of Russian Law* starting with the Code of 1497 can have any doubts about the existence of a most elaborate set of administrative directives covering every conceivable situation.[8] Wherever the situation arose for which the rules were either previously not set or were unavailable, the administrators would request and would be provided with the appropriate rules. The same *Monuments* testify to the existence of an elaborate set of injunctions to the administrators, noble or *prikaznye liudi*, demanding an impartial and expedient resolution of cases and tasks pending. Failing such performance, the administrators were subject to penalties of varying severity, from oral reprimand, fine, flogging, firing with the stipulation that the transgressor not be employed in any other administrative post ever, to the confiscation of property with exile. Capital punishment was applied only in the case of high treason. Furthermore, each *prikaz* maintained a daily Log or Records Book of all the business transacted.[9]

Each *prikaz* was headed by one or more "judges" (*sud'i*) to whom all official business was addressed and who acted as the ultimate arbitrators and supervisors of all *prikaz* activities. The *prikazy* varied widely in size and importance. The largest and the most important ones, such as Foreign, Interior and Military, and Land Chancery, usually had three to six *sud'i*. As a rule the *sud'i* were appointed from either the noble or the professional group, *prikaznye liudi*. However,

---

Shchukin, Lavrentii Protopopov, Andrei Eremeev, and Ivan Nebogatovo. TsGADA, Fond 138, 1700 g., No. 33, fols. 62, 64–65.

8. The administrative manuals were the *ustavnye knigi* (or *ukaznye knigi*). Four are published in Pt. 5, pp. 185–554, of *Pamiatniki russkogo prava*, 8 vols., Moscow, 1952–61 (hereafter PRP).

9. A number of these *zapisnye knigi* have been published. *Russkaia istoricheskaia biblioteka*, Vols. 9–11, St. Petersburg, 1884–89 (hereafter RIB), contains no less than ten *zapisnye knigi* of only one section, the "Moscow desk" (*Moskovskii stol*), of the Military and Interior Chancery (*Razriadnyi prikaz*) for diverse years between 1626 and 1679. More are available in print elsewhere and still more in the archives.

in the case of these three most important *prikazy* the *sud'i* were appointed almost exclusively from the professionals, the *prikaznye liudi*, throughout virtually their entire period of existence. We feel justified in inferring that the more complex and important the administrative post, and consequently the greater degree of competence required, the greater the role of the *prikaznye liudi*. Below the *sud'i* in the larger *prikazy* were the heads of departments or sections. These were generally junior clerks with substantial seniority who attended to and supervised all of the routine work. This work itself was done by the junior staff.[10] Only a minute portion of the business under the jurisdiction of a *prikaz* was decided in the Council of the Boyars on the appointed day of the week when that specific *prikaz* was assigned time to present its affairs to the council.[11]

Each *prikaz* had a clear-cut jurisdiction over certain matters or areas, and different departments within a *prikaz* were charged with just as clearly defined tasks. Over time this jurisdiction was of course subject to change, but was no less clear for that. Despite the opinion of some modern historians that the jurisdictions of different *prikazy* were "overlapping," in the seventeenth century neither the government nor its subjects had any doubt which *prikaz* was in charge of what.[12] It is true that there were instances of contested jurisdiction, but this is a phenomenon we still find in contemporary administrative structures,

10. The junior clerks, *pod'iachie*, were divided into four levels: senior (*starshei stat'i*), middle (*serednei stat'i*), junior (*mladshei stat'i*), and the *pod'iachie*-in-training (*neverstannye*, literally those "not on the payroll"). The total number of *pod'iachie* in Moscow was fluid and constantly growing. For example, in 1669–70 (in the seventeenth century the Russian calendar year began on September 1, and was counted "from the creation of the world," thus 1669–70 was actually the year 7178) the official central list that includes virtually all *prikazy* lists 45 *prikazy* with the total of 1,068 *pod'iachie*; of this number, 626 were on the payroll while 442 served without regular pay. (TsGADA, Fond 210, Knigi moskovskogo stola, No. 64, fols. 1–3, 127.) Five years later, in 1674–75, the official list shows a total of 1,458 *pod'iachie* in 48 *prikazy*, or 850 with salary and 608 without. (TsGADA, Knigi moskovskogo stola, No. 73, fols. 131–43.) The impressive 36.5 percent increase in the total does not necessarily reflect the true increase in the number of *pod'iachie* for any given year. Hundreds of them might have been on assignments in the provinces and not carried on the official lists, or hundreds of them might have been temporarily posted to Moscow, reflecting in either case particularly huge manpower demands of specific periodic tasks in which the administration was engaged.

11. TsGADA, Fond 210, Stolbtsy moskovskogo stola, No. 421, fol. 272; PSZ, Vol. 1, No. 460, p. 828, Vol. 2, No. 656, pp. 72–73.

12. N. V. Ustiugov, "Tsentral'noe upravlenie. Prikazy," p. 367; N. V. Riasanovsky, *A History of Russia*, 3rd ed., New York, 1977, p. 255. For clearly defined division of responsibilities of the five departments within the Foreign Chancery, see Belokurov, *O Posol'skom prikaze*, pp. 51–53. Similar divisions are evident in the desks (*stoly*) of the Land, and Interior and Military Chanceries, indeed in all of the more complex *prikazy*.

and it is not until the eighteenth century that there is in Russia what might be described as a state of severe administrative confusion. Witness the complaint of a provincial governor to the central government from 1737, where he stated that in one week his office received dozens and dozens of threatening requests and directives from fifty-four different central bureaus, without any regulatory foundations or regard for reason.[13]

The internal hierarchy within a *prikaz* was strictly observed. If we examine the successive annual rosters of any one *prikaz* we find that the hierarchical order was undisturbed. Considerable jumps in the hierarchical ladder occurred only after some special assignment outside regular posting. A junior clerk never skipped a rank, but this does not mean that some junior clerks did not advance faster than others. Not only was a strict hierarchy of offices observed, but junior officials were subject to strict supervision by their superiors and to control and inspections from outside as well as from within.[14]

WORKING CONDITIONS AND TRAINING

Both the work day and the work week were strictly fixed. The work day was twelve hours until 1680, when it was reduced to ten. Work conditions were rather taxing.[15] The *prikazy* were cramped, and space, as well as other amenities down to the quality of ink and quill, went with seniority. The lighting was poor and one can easily understand the almost obligatory reference to blindness in the petitions for retirement of those who spent the better part of half a century in such surroundings.

A substantial majority of the *prikaznye liudi*, including *d'iaki*, began

13. S. M. Troitskii, "Iz istorii sostavleniia biudzheta v Rossii v seredine XVIIIv.," *Istoricheskie zapiski*, 78: 196.

14. For evaluation by the senior *pod'iachie* of those assigned to serve under them, see Belokurov, *O Posol'skom prikaze*, pp. 163–64. The outside control was exercised by the *Tainyi prikaz* (Secret Chancery), the *Chelobitnyi prikaz* (Petitions Chancery), and various other temporary investigatory commissionlike *prikazy*.

15. One cannot hope to improve on the excellent description of working conditions by N. A. Baklanova, "Obstanovka moskovskikh prikazov v XVIIv.," *Trudy gosudarstvennogo istoricheskogo muzeia*, vypusk 3, Moscow, 1926, pp. 53–100. For the definition of the work period see: PSZ I, 1649, Vol. 1, No. 21, p. 222, and No. 237, p. 467; TsGADA, Fond 210, Stolbtsy moskovskogo stola, No. 301, fol. 56, published in *Akty moskovskogo gosudarstva*, (hereafter: AMG), Vol. 2 (St. Petersburg, 1894), p. 628 (1658); PSZ I, 1669, Vol. 1, Nos. 461, 462, p. 828; ibid., 1670, No. 477, p. 841; ibid., 1680, Vol. 2, No. 839, p. 281; etc.

their careers as *pod'iachie*-in-training. As in anything else in seventeenth-century Muscovy, to be hired one had to present a petition. As the host of observers and historians have pointed out, the *prikazy* were populated by members of the same families. If in the petition one was able to mention a relative in service, the request was as good as granted.[16] This points to the principle of nepotic cooptation as the basic avenue of recruitment. But since the administrative apparatus grew by leaps and bounds and since the administrative service was one of the best vehicles of upward social mobility, there had to be, of necessity, other ways of entering the service.

In times of acute personnel shortage, applicants from other, generally lower, social strata were admitted, but literacy was a prerequisite, thus the frequent comment on the back of the applications for admission, "To be hired, if qualified" (*Vziat' esli delu goden*). In light of the standing injunction and repeated efforts to limit access to service to the lower classes and to members of clerical families (see below), there is a rather telling statement of hiring criteria in 1656, after the plague had depleted the competent ranks: "To hire as *pod'iachii* anyone able to perform, regardless of social origin."[17] In rare instances competent individuals were hired directly as *d'iaki*, and even as *dumnye d'iaki*, and these exceptions are accounted for rather easily.[18] Some were transferees from merchant status whose prior experience in financial matters was apparently needed and all that was required. These men, as a rule, started their administrative careers in financial or tax-collection *prikazy*. Some were only nominally members of "estates" (*sosloviia*) other than *prikaznye liudi*, and yet some had undergone the period of training outside the *prikazy*.[19]

16. Demidova, "Prikaznye liudi," p. 346.

17. "*Vziat' v pod'iachie kto goden, iz kakikh chinov nibud', . . .*" AMG, 2: 481–82.

18. Bogoiavlenskii, "D'iaki," p. 223, found 55 such instances in the seventeenth century. Bogoiavlenskii provides no sources and only a handful of names, so that for the time being at least, one can neither check his figures nor argue differently. Yet, Bogoiavlenskii's list of merchants (*gosti*) is inexplicably short of at least a couple of names (A. Ivanov, M. Smyvalov), and his contention that the *dvoriane* accounted for 71 percent of those skipping prior service as *pod'iachie* needs to be modified; some, like Gerasim Dokhturov, were *moskovskie dvoriane* only because of their father's prior service as *pod'iachie* and *d'iaki* (that is, functionally, they were not really *dvoriane*). Some, such as Ivan and Konstantin Chepelev, who were bona fide *dvoriane* from the cavalry and served as *d'iaki* in the *Koniushennyi prikaz* (Stables Chancery), where it was more important to know about horses than to be an expert civil administrator. (That is, functionally, they were barely *d'iaki*.)

19. Among these we should include men such as A. A. Kurbatov taken into the service in 1699 from the serfs of P. B. Sheremet'ev, later *d'iak* (before 1706, TsGADA, Fond 210, Knigi moskovskogo stola, No. 176, fol. 235), and still later the vice-governor

Upon admission to service, the *prikaznye liudi* had to swear an oath of loyalty, obedience, honesty, and conscientious performance. Separate oaths were administered to different ranks.[20] Occasionally, besides the oath, the would-be *pod'iachie* had to find *pod'iachie* already in service to sponsor them and to sign a letter of guarantee of good behavior stipulating that they "shall work and attend to the tsar's business, . . . and shall not loaf or drink or engage in revelry or occupy ourselves with any other tomfoolery, nor shall we seek or accept a position in any other *prikaz*."[21]

Those admitted as *pod'iachie*-in-training were generally lads between the ages of ten and fifteen, and they spent the subsequent several years in various stages of training.[22] Each beginner was assigned "for learning" to a senior *pod'iachii*, who was responsible for the progress of his charges and made periodic reports on it. The concept of on-the-job training goes back to the sixteenth century, and can be documented as standard practice for the seventeenth. While it is true that the in-service training was necessitated by the lack of formal schools

---

of the Arkhangel'sk province; or L. E. Shokurin, who, in 1706, was made a *d'iak* from the servants ("*iz slug*") of the Savin Monastery (TsGADA, Fond 210, Knigi moskovskogo stola, No. 176, fol. 237).

20. PSZ I, 1649, Vol. 1, No. 114, pp. 311, 313–14. RIB, Vol. 9, pp. 518–20.

21. As in the case of four *pod'iachie* newly admitted to the Land Chancery in 1658, all four were transferees (Sokolova and fon Mekk, *Raskhodnye knigi*, p. 272). The letter of guarantee (*poruchnaia zapis'*) was standard practice for the *pristavy* (officers of the *prikaz*) and *storozha* (guards) in the *prikazy*, but it does not appear to have been standard for the *pod'iachie*. There is, however, further evidence that occasionally the *pod'iachie* were required to provide it. Thus, for example, in September 1682, all of the *pod'iachie* of the *Razboinyi prikaz* (Banditry Chancery) were required to produce *poruchnaia zapis'* (PSZ I, 1681, Vol. 2, No. 1043, p. 561).

22. The mean age at admission cannot be calculated in a manner that would withstand close scrutiny because of the lack of adequate records. The seventeenth-century Russians simply did not keep parish records or birth registers. Furthermore, the applications for admission never state the age of the applicant. But, by calculating the total years in service and adding on the likely age at the start, we can make an estimate which then we can compare with the few extant stated ages at the start (usually found in the petitions for retirement) and thus arrive at an acceptable guess. (For example, M. S. Koz'min, born 1690, became a *pod'iachii* in 1703 / RBS, Vol. Knappe-Kiukhel'beker, p. 62. T. Istomin, age 80 in 1664, served since the age of 15 / AMG, 3: 577.) The early-teens starting-age estimate is also supportable by the nature of the tasks performed by the beginners, by the number of years during which they are listed in the official lists by diminutives of the first names, by the fact that for an extended period of time they were not entitled to a salary and consequently could not support a family. Furthermore, no *pod'iachii*-in-training applied for grants toward marriage or housing, and in all instances of death of an apparently young *pod'iachii* it was the mother and not the wife applying for burial money.

[30]   *Borivoj Plavsic*

in Russia, it should not be viewed as indicative of backwardness, at least as far as administrative science is concerned. It was also practiced, and continued to be practiced, by Russia's West European counterparts, even in societies that had specialized formal schools.[23] Thus, even as the Petrine legislation provided for some new training facilities and modes of training, a specified number of slots were maintained in each administrative organization for on-the-job training.

The question to consider now is, What was the quality of the *prikaz* training and what social strata did it favor? Quality is, of course, always difficult to measure, and especially so in the absence of formal examinations. The demands placed upon the beginners were apparently considerable, for the dropout rate was very high, as attested by the ever-changing and disappearing names from the bottom of the official annual rosters. The *prikaznye liudi* in fact constituted the intellectual elite of Muscovy until the influx of non-Russians at the close of the seventeenth and the beginning of the eighteenth century. One cannot view as accidental the positions of the junior clerks Pamfil Belianinov and Nikita Zotov as teachers of, respectively, future tsars Fedor and Peter. If we examine any part of the written administrative legacy, be it from the intra-*prikaz* material or a contested civil case, we cannot but be impressed by the dispatch and competence with which even the most complex tasks were handled. Except in cases of deliberate foot-dragging, or in cases, such as Peter's request for a census in order to levy the new head tax, when the administrative machine was deliberately sabotaged by the entire serf-owning segment of society, all the evidence points to administrative efficiency.

The in-*prikaz* training clearly favored the entrants from the families of the *prikazyne liudi*. The admissions policy, the mode of training, and the relative social standing all support the above view, allowing for only one significant exception: those who could either acquire or supplement the necessary skills at home; that is, for the most part, the sons of clergy.[24]

The preceding statements regarding the efficiency of the adminis-

---

23. Cf. Wolfram Fischer and Peter Lundgreen, "The Recruitment and Training of Administrative and Technical Personnel," in Charles Tilly, ed., *The Formation of National States in Western Europe*, Princeton, 1975, pp. 516–19 *passim*.

24. The senior *pod'iachii* in charge of training would logically give preference to members of his family. On restrictive admission, see below, p. 000, and on social status, p. 000ff. Permanent last names, especially among the members of the lower strata of society, were still in the process of jelling throughout the seventeenth century; one can, therefore, identify men of clerical origin, and there are an inordinate number of them among the *prikaznye liudi*. Also noted in Bogoiavlenskii, "D'iaki," pp. 222–23.

trative machine and the size and complexity of its tasks clearly imply a rather high degree of specialization. No part of the *prikaz* document-producing process (*deloproizvodstvo*) skipped the successive stages of being composed—a rough draft (*chernovik*) was then edited and copied clean (*belovik*), with further copying depending on the nature of the matter—it is obvious that those at the bottom of the service ladder spent an inordinate amount of time on tasks requiring little or no specialized knowledge. The general operating procedure was uniform in all the *prikazy*, and consequently one was basically qualified to serve anywhere. Yet, if we examine the composition of the core staff of any one *prikaz* over a considerable period of time, we find significant constancy in its composition, by departments as well as by specific duties.[25] There is thus a definite pattern of specialization within the *prikaz* structure. About the personal specialization, however, we are forced to much more tentative conclusions.

There seem to have been two types of specialization: by the geographic area and by the kind of work. Those whose service in the *prikaz*, and in the field, related to western parts of Russia seem to have served the greater part of their careers in the same area, and the same can be said for those whose service was related to the east. In broad terms, the same is true of the type of work. It is no coincidence that those from a merchant background all started their careers in the *prikazy* dealing with fiscal matters and generally remained there. When, as in the case of Almaz Ivanov, they had experience in dealing with foreign merchants and knew foreign languages, they transferred to the Foreign Chancery, where these skills were needed.[26] Finally, we should note that the *prikaznye liudi* could and did shift their specialization, and that the two types of specialization are not necessarily mutually exclusive. Those who might be classified as specialists in the east (Siberia) were also specialists in trade. Thus the Chancery for Merchant Affairs was under the Siberian Chancery and specialized in fur-trade matters.

25. See Belokurov, *O Posol'skom prikaze*, *passim*, and Sokolova and fon Mekk, *Raskhodnye knigi*, *passim*. Belokurov (p. 14) expresses the opinion that even in the Foreign Chancery there was little specialization. Yet at the same time he admits that from the beginning of the seventeenth century some *pod'iachie* specialized in handling the treasury, and his short biographies show that several of the *d'iaki* were sent to negotiate with the Poles no less than eight times prior to and after attaining the *d'iak* rank.

26. Similarly, another merchant turned *d'iak*, Kuz'ma Borin, spent most of his administrative career in various fiscal *prikazy*, and in 1680 (while *d'iak*) owned some iron works; he was later to serve in the Silver Chancery, the Gold Chancery, and in 1700 when the Mining Chancery was established he was assigned to it. RBS, Vol. Betankur-Biakster, St. Petersburg, 1908, p. 225.

ACCOUNTABILITY

It has already been noted in the literature that service in a *prikaz* was a lifetime occupation and obligation.[27] One could be released from service for under-performance or failing to perform altogether. The annual payrosters are littered with the remarks of the supervisors "to be dismissed" (*otstavit'*), but this seems to have been a preserve either of the very young, that is, of the failing students, or of the very old or sick. Throughout this service, each of the *prikaznye liudi* was fully accountable for his own performance. A junior clerk in charge of cash kept a complete record of every penny received and disbursed and had to present periodically his books for inspection. Any shortage discovered was immediately recovered from him, or from his relatives.[28] Money was far from being the only item for which one was responsible. Perhaps even more important was the accountability of all *prikaznye liudi* for the state papers in their custody.[29] Each time a person took charge of a new office, at the center or in the provinces, a complete, detailed list of all documents and papers belonging to that post was made, and both the outgoing and incoming official, at whatever the level, had to verify it.

Although fully responsible for everything they did, or failed to do, the *prikaznye liudi* seem to have been accorded rather lenient treatment, given the standards of punishment in seventeenth-century Russia. This is hardly surprising, since not only were they judged by friends and even by members of their own family, but even more importantly, there was a perennial shortage of trained administrators.[30] The state

27. Demidova, "Prikaznye liudi," pp. 337–38.

28. PSZ I, 1680, Vol. 2, No. 802, p. 238 (on uniform accountability of all the *pod'iachie* in all the *prikazy*). A fine and most intricate example of official persistency over several years in recovering even small sums (just under 20 rubles) is the case of *pod'iachii*, later *d'iak*, Ivan Peskov, who was, in the mid-1640s, in charge of daily expenses of the Danish legation. (TsGADA, Fond 138, 1645 g., No. 5, fols. 89, 179–80.) Most of the *prikaznye liudi* died in office, and their widows or mothers were paid money for the burial, between one-half to full regular annual entitlement, but if there was a shortage for which the deceased was accountable, the required sum was deducted from the payment for the burial.

29. Even men of long and distinguished careers were not exempt from this rule, as witnessed by the investigation of the *d'iak* Efim R. Iur'ev in 1670, for taking home the state papers in his charge. (TsGADA, Fond 138, Op. 1, fol. 56 [1670 g., No. 6].) A *pod'achii* at least since 1637, and a *d'iak* in the Foreign Chancery since 1656, Iur'ev was a member of a number of successful embassies, and although the accessible record is not conclusive, it was apparently because of this transgression that he was removed from his post in the Foreign Chancery and reassigned to a less prestigious position.

30. In November of 1648, at the time of compilation of the new law code, the

simply could not afford to dispense with the services of competent *prikaznye liudi*, and in virtually all instances of demotion, exile, and other punishments—save, possibly, the confiscation of property—the sentences meted out were short-lived.[31]

ADVANCEMENT

Before proceeding with the discussion of advancement proper, we should point out here a very important fact overlooked by virtually all historians: Muscovy, unlike her Western European counterparts, did not know the phenomenon of venality of office. One could buy one's

---

lesser/provincial nobility (*gorodovye dvoriane i deti boiarskie*) presented a collective petition asking that the *d'iaki* and the *pod'iachie* once again be subjected to the jurisdiction of a single *prikaz*, arguing that as long as the *prikaznye liudi* were judged by the *prikazy* in which they served the petitioners could not hope for an impartial adjudication since "in these *prikazy* . . . [the disputes were examined by] the brothers, nephews, or children" of the very same men against whom the complaints were made. The petition was approved and the Petition Chancery resumed its jurisdiction over the *prikaznye liudi*. (TsGADA, Fond 210, Stolbtsy moskovskogo stola, No. 223, fols. 528, 530. Also in AMG, 2: 237–38, and P. P. Smirnov, *Posadskie liudi i ikh klassovaia bor'ba do serediny XVII veka*, Moscow and Leningrad, 1948, 2: 238, Note 1.) The law also required abstention/ nonparticipation of all officials in cases involving members of their family or their friends. PRP, Part 6, p. 77, Para. 3, *passim* (Law Code of 1649); PSZ I, 1681, No. 885, p. 346. To cite but a few instances of documented personnel shortage (*maloliudstvo*): TsGADA, Fond 210, Stolbtsy moskovskogo stola, No. 414, *chast'* 1, fol. 189 (1669–70); ibid., No. 375, fols. 502–506 (1661–62); TsGADA, Fond 138, No. 64, 1710–28 gg., fol. 97 (1720).

31. Even the junior *pod'iachie* (Peter Orekhov, Ivan Toropov, and Afanasii Sheshenin of the Foreign Chancery) fired in 1673 for an assortment of sins (laziness and different forms of irresponsible behavior) (TsGADA, Fond 138, 1672 g., No. 18, fol. 117), were all evidently reinstated in a very short time, to their exact previous positions and entitlements. (TsGADA, Fond 210, Knigi moskovskogo stola, No. 72, fol. 10 [1673–74], No. 73, fol. 14 [1674–75], No. 74, fol. 15 [1675–76], etc.)

Of the higher ranking *prikaznye liudi* we need only remember *dumnyi d'iak* Ivan T. K. Gramotin, whose activities during the Time of Troubles bordered on high treason and who in the 1620s went so far as to oppose no less a personality than the virtual ruler of Russia, father of the tsar, the Patriarch Filaret. Gramotin was duly exiled, but was reinstated soon after Filaret's death. (RIB, 9: 437–38; *Akty Istoricheskie* [hereafter AI], 3: 329, *passim*; Belokurov, *O Posol'skom prikaze*, pp. 107–10.) Gramotin presents, of course, an exception, for he could count not only on his great experience and ability, but also on the fact that he was related to the Romanovs through marriage. But there are examples of other *d'iaki* whose punishments were rescinded in a short time. In 1652 *d'iak* Griaznoi Akishev was fired (for taking bribes) and reinstated (AMG, 2:299). *D'iaki* Matvei F. L'vov, in 1664–65, and Andrei Shakhov, in 1674–75, were both demoted to *pod'iachie*, but neither demotion lasted. (Veselovskii, *D'iaki i pod'iachie*, pp. 307, 576.)

way neither into administrative service nor up the hierarchical ladder. Equally interesting is the fact that the professional administrative posts, that is, those filled by the *prikaznye liudi*, cannot in any way be construed as inheritable, despite the presence of many close relatives in individual *prikazy*.

In light of what was said above regarding the traditional view of Petrine reforms and the Table of Ranks, it is essential to consider in full the role of merit in the administrative service of the seventeenth century. Above, we noted that the admission to service often depended on family relationship to someone already in service; thus we must examine the possibility that nepotism was a basic principle of advancement within service. We should also consider at least two other possibilities: patronage and seniority.

A truly acceptable answer regarding nepotism can be arrived at only after all the family relationships are compared to all careers; as yet, we are not in a position to make this comparison. The question of patronage is even more complex, a veritable uncharted ocean.[32] Since all the above possibilities are clearly interlinked, merit, too, will have to wait for a fully supportable answer. Yet we do have some basis, at least, for a working hypothesis. Nepotism probably played a role in the training stage.[33] The experienced junior clerks would probably take more

32. The question of patronage is a puzzling one indeed. There are hardly any sources attesting directly to a patron-client relationship, and even in the few cases where there exists something in the way of evidence, as the following two examples show, one is hard put to draw any conclusion.

One of the most notorious of the false pretenders to the Muscovite throne of the seventeenth century, *pod'iachii* Timofei Ankudinov, was apparently a protege of the *d'iak* Ivan I. Patrekeev, and a friend of yet another *d'iak*, Ivan Peskov. Although Ankudinov was in due course drawn and quartered in Moscow, his two close personal friends did not suffer any ill effects, a striking outcome given the seriousness with which the Muscovite government viewed Ankudinov's activity. (Belokurov, *O Posol'skom prikaze*, p. 119; RBS, Vol. Aleksinskii-Bestuzhev-Riumin, pp. 152–54.)

Although a close collaborator and correspondent of Prince V. V. Golitsyn, throughout Golitsyn's tenure as the head of the Foreign Chancery, 1682–89, *dumnyi d'iak* E. I. Ukraintsev was completely unaffected by Golitsyn's fall from power. This was a remarkable development given the political situation of the day and the sweeping punishment and disgrace inflicted on Golitsyn's clan and supporters.

33. The lenient treatment accorded to the young transgressors offers some support to this argument. For example, the young *pod'iachii* of the Foreign Chancery Mikhail Belianinov was first included among those to be dismissed from service in 1673 (see above n. 31) and later instead given only a reprimand and a warning. It is more than likely that the young Mikhail was a relative of Panfil T. Belianinov, at the same time the senior *pod'iachii* of the Foreign Chancery and the tutor of the future Tsar Fedor. Alas, in his petition for admission to service, no date (TsGADA, Fond 138, 1672 g., No. 18, fol. 10), Mikhail omitted to claim a relationship.

seriously the task of teaching in the case of someone from the family. Seniority, taken to mean length in service, was of some significance with respect to job assignment, of somewhat greater significance in regard to salary, but does not appear to have been, as a rule, important in the promotion to the *d'iak* rank. The great majority of the *d'iaki* attained the rank at a relatively young age, bypassing other junior clerks of equal or higher relative hierarchical standing whose prior record of advancement was considerably slower. Merit thus appears to have been the basic vehicle of advancement.

The majority of applications for higher pay cite the ability to perform as well as those ahead of the applicant on the service ladder. Not only did these applications often result in a raise, but there seems to exist a definite positive correlation between the boldness of one's claim to merit (both competence and performance) and the subsequent career. A great number of the successful careers can be explained only in terms of merit. In fact, if we examine the promotion rate, past the training period (as expressed in the annual increment in regular salary), we can with certainty pick out those bound to achieve higher ranks.[34] Innate intelligence apparently played a part, but while it was necessary, it was not sufficient: to advance to the top, the *prikaznye liudi* had to be willing to undertake a multitude of challenging assignments. The more the assignments, the greater the degree of hardship and skill needed and acquired, the faster the advancement. Promotion to a *d'iak* rank was granted only in recognition of one's ability and service rendered to the state.

One of the finest scholars of the period, S. K. Bogoiavlenskii, has calculated that no less than 90 percent of those who attained the rank of *d'iak* in the course of the seventeenth century worked their way up from the junior clerks. Below we shall have occasion to disagree with Bogoiavlenskii's other figures, but here only a tentative modification will suffice: if anything, the percentage is understated, since prior service as a junior clerk was virtually the only way one could acquire

34. This observation is not, as it should be, based on sound statistical data; rather, it is based on the examination of a number of the careers of those who attained higher ranks (*d'iaki* and *dumnye d'iaki*), and on the partial data of the promotion rate of all the *pod'iachie* of the Foreign Chancery between 1645 and 1723. The latter calculation, which may well need to be revised, showed an advancement rate of the future higher echelon personnel 2.64 times greater for 1645–88 and 2.40 for 1689–1723, as compared to the advancement rate of those who remained in the *pod'iachii* rank for the rest of their careers. Further support of "merit argument" can be adduced by referring to the number of careers of members of the same immediate families in service at the same time in the same *prikaz* that show some younger siblings advancing at a faster rate than the older ones.

the necessary skill and, ipso facto, a prerequisite for an appointment as a *d'iak*.[35]

The best way to advance was to begin a career in one of the prestigious *prikazy*, such as Foreign, Land, or Interior and Military. Being near the tsar's person also helped. In the reign of Aleksei Mikhailovich, the great majority of the junior clerks of his own Secret Chancery (*Tainyi prikaz*), who were thus in daily contact with the tsar, achieved the rank of *d'iak*, and so did those assigned to the tsar's retinue in the field. But here what appears to be the royal favor could have been only a part of the reason behind success, since these junior clerks were originally selected for their above-average abilities.

INCOME: LEGAL AND ILLEGAL

The regular annual monetary entitlements—that is, the salary—were quite generous, and compared most favorably with the salaries of other state servitors. The *d'iak* salary was, as a rule, paid by the treasurers of the different tax collecting *prikazy* and not the *prikazy* in which one worked, as was the case with the junior clerks; thus it was not a part of the annual personnel budget of a *prikaz*. In a minority of cases, when a *d'iak* was either independently wealthy or was holding a particularly lucrative post, the salary was not payable either in part or in toto for a period of time. In the main, the *d'iak*'s annual salary ranged from 70 to 150 rubles, depending on the kind and importance of the posting, as well as on the level of the preceding entitlement. *D'iaki* were also entitled to payment in land (see below), and on special occasions received impressive cash bonuses.[36]

The salaries of the junior clerks ranged from 1 ruble or even .5 of a ruble, to about 50. For example, in 1669–70, the 626 junior clerks, representing almost all of those in Moscow then on the payroll, were receiving an average of 11.71 rubles. The corresponding figure for the 850 junior clerks in 1674–75 was 10.61 rubles.[37] It is important to

---

35. Bogoiavlenskii, "D'iaki," p. 220. The Time of Troubles seems to have brought forth a considerable number of *d'iaki* without prior record of service as *pod'iachie*. Owing to a variety of causes (fires, etc.), records for the early decades of the seventeenth century, as well as for the closing decades of the sixteenth, are very meager. It is possible that the percentage would be even higher if we had more complete data from this period and more complete information on all *pod'iachie*, especially the provincial and monastic, for the rest of the century.

36. Bogoiavlenskii, "D'iaki," pp. 234–36; Demidova, "Biurokratizatsiia," p. 220; Veselovskii, *D'iaki i pod'iachie, passim*; AMG 2: 38–39, *passim*, 3: 48, *passim*.

37. TsGADA, Fond 210, Knigi moskovskogo stola, No. 64, fol. 127, No. 73, fols.

remember here that these averages include a great number of the young, newest junior clerks, and that, consequently, the average for the middle- and senior-level junior clerks combined would be significantly higher, probably twice the above.

In addition to the regular salary, each junior clerk was entitled to, and received, approximately the same amount again in holiday pay. They also received, as a *matter of right*, additional payments for field service, within or without Russia, and grants in times of need: for marriage, for dowry, or for rebuilding houses destroyed by fire.[38] Not to be overlooked or omitted are also sizable payments in kind, that is, in grains and in salt, which in any one year, depending on the price fluctuation, could amount to yet another salary. After 1671–72 when the annual entitlement to a specific quantity of grains became payable in cash, a rather modern concept of "cost-of-living increase" was introduced: the cash payment was to be at the rate representing the mean price of grain on the Moscow open market between certain dates.[39] Given the wide fluctuation in the price of grain, this new means of payment argues rather strongly that the state took good care to assure adequate income for its administrators. Those who became too old to hold a regular job were still subject to assignments of a temporary nature, being in fact administrators-in-reserve, and were paid retirement pay.

Clearly, if we add up the combined legal earnings of the *prikaznye liudi* and compare it with the cost of living in the seventeenth century, we must judge the income of the entire group, with the exception of the newest junior clerks, to have been at least adequate, and, for the upper echelon, even ample.[40] The *prikaznye liudi* thus had no need to

---

131–43; S. M. Solov'ev, *Istoriia Rossii s drevneishikh vremen*, Moscow, 1962, 7: 309–11.

38. The exact relationship of regular and holiday pay varied from one *prikaz* to another, and also varied between the different strata of the *pod'iachie*. Those at the very bottom of the list, that is the *pod'iachie*-in-training, not entitled to the regular salary were entitled to holiday pay. Generally, those at the bottom, including the junior *pod'iachie* on the payroll, received more in holiday pay than in regular pay. One should not be misled by the fact that no money was ever paid automatically, and that the *prikaznye liudi* had to present a petition (*chelobitnaia*), individually or as a group, for each payment due them. These petitions were subsequently checked against the official records, necessary adjustments made (in case of a collective *chelobitnaia*, for example, those no longer serving in the *prikaz* were removed from the list, etc.), and payment authorized.

39. TsGADA, Fond 138, 1700 g., No. 59, fol. 2.

40. According to Kliuchevskii's compilation, the price of rye in the second half of the seventeenth century in the city of Moscow fluctuated from 0.12 to 1.30 rubles per *chetvert'*. (*Chetvert'* is approximately 2.10 hectoliters, a hectoliter in turn being

accept bribes to make a living, yet of bribes, needed or not, there is plentiful evidence. Some, probably slightly biased, sources indicate that certain types of private affairs, business and large-scale land administration, could be conducted with official sanction only through bribery.[41] Yet bribery was not the only source of illegal income; the *prikaznye liudi* also engaged in illegal trade and in milking the state treasury. Some of the highly enterprising administrators even succeeded in imposing their own private tax while on assignments in the provinces.[42] Many of the *prikaznye liudi* became truly rich. However, the fact that individual corruption was widespread does not necessarily mean that the administrative system as such was malfunctioning. The individuals basically tapped sources beyond the reach of the state. Many individuals engaging in large-scale illegal activities saw their estates confiscated, so that on balance the state treasury did not suffer great losses. It is the social cost of the corruption that should be investigated. Here, however, there is just not enough data even to speculate.

RECRUITMENT AND SOCIAL ORIGINS

It ought to follow from the above that the *prikaznye liudi* had a vested interest in limiting the admission to service to members of their own families. The same was true of the state, for, we must remember, Muscovy was a closed, strictly *soslovie-* (estate) based society. A decree of 7 December 1640, disseminated to all the *prikazy*, forbade the hiring of the sons of the clergy and of the middle and lower tax-paying strata

---

2.84 bushels. V. O. Kliuchevskii, "Russkii rubl' XVI–XVIIIv. v ego otnoshenii k nyneshnemu," pp. 107–83, in his *Opyty i issledovaniia. Pervyi sbornik statei*, Petrograd, 1918, p. 170.) A legal act from 1669 gives the following prices: for the best quality horse 8 rubles, for a three-year-old Russian mare 2.5 rubles, for a cow 2 rubles, for a bull 2 rubles, for a one-year-old pig 0.15 ruble. (PRP, Pt. 7, p. 422.)

41. See especially A. A. Novosel'skii, *Votchinnik i ego khoziaistvo v XVII veke*, Moscow and Leningrad, 1929, pp. 55ff., where it is clear that even a well-placed and well-connected (with the *prikaznye liudi*) person had to suffer his factors' paying bribes to the *pod'iachie* in order to conduct his affairs.

42. Probably the most imaginative and the most daring of these is the *d'iak* Mark Pozdeev from the first half of the seventeenth century. For his exploits, see *Dvortsovye razriady*, St. Petersburg, 1850, col. 535; AI, 3: 203, 210–17, 265; RBS, Vol. Plavil'shchikov —Primo, St. Petersburg, 1905, cols. 259–62. It is interesting to note here that although Pozdeev broke every rule in the book and in fact behaved as if he were an equal partner with the government in exploiting the Astrakhan' Province, his punishment too was short-lived, and he was soon back in a very important post.

of society, in effect limiting admission to only the sons of the *prikaznye liudi* and the different strata of the nobility. Similar, even if progressively less restrictive, decrees and their enforcement have been traced for the rest of the seventeenth century.[43]

There is considerable controversy regarding the social origins of the *prikaznye liudi*.[44] Some would have us believe that even the scions of princely families, admittedly from the impoverished branches, served at times as *d'iaki*.[45] The simple and documentable fact is that the preponderant majority of the *prikaznye liudi* came either from the *prikaz* milieu or from the clergy or other lower social strata. According to the official declarations (*skazki*) of 278 junior clerks of the Land Chancery made between 1706 and 1709, 30.9 percent were sons of the *prikaz* employees (25.5 percent of the junior clerks), 26.2 percent were sons of different types of clergy (to this we might add 1.8 percent sons of the monastic servants), 10 percent of the lower urban class (*posadskie liudi*). Only 6.8 percent came from the hereditary provincial nobility, and 7.6 percent from the nonhereditary provincial nobility.[46] Although these declarations are the earliest known to us of a sufficiently representative quantity, there is no reason to doubt that they are a valid representation of the entire preceding century, save possibly a slightly stronger presence of the sons of the *prikaz* personnel, and lesser proportion of the sons of the clergy, at different times.

Above we argued, along with Bogoiavlenskii, that at least 90 percent of the *d'iaki* had had prior service as junior clerks. Barring the existence of a promotion policy strongly favoring those of noble ori-

43. AI, 3: 108; RIB, 10: 234; PRP, Pt. 5, pp. 230, 358; Demidova, "Prikaznye liudi," pp. 349–51.

44. For a brief summary see Demidova, "Prikaznye liudi," pp. 333–34.

45. P. Ivanov's *Alfavitnyi ukazatel' familii i lits, upominaemikh v boiarskikh knigakh . . .* , Moscow, 1853, p. 230, lists among the princes Litvinov two *d'iaki* Bogdan and Timofei, ignoring the fact that both must have had prior service as *pod'iachie*, and the existence of other *pod'iachie* with the surname Litvinov. It is simply impossible to believe, given the standards of seventeenth century Muscovite consciousness of social standing, that any member of a princely family, however poor, would ever consent to serve as a *d'iak*, let alone a *pod'iachii*.

46. Percentages based on E. S. Zevakin's "Pod'iachie Pomestnogo prikaza nachala XVIIIv. (Po "skazkam" 1706–1709 gg.)," *Istoricheskie zapiski*, No. 11, 1941, pp. 280–81. Only 6.1% of the total failed to state their social origin. To the percentage of the hereditary nobility we must add one *zhilets* (0.3%), a title between provincial and Muscovite nobility (*gorodovye dvoriane* and *moskovskie dvoriane*) who is, in all likelihood, the only possible representative of the Muscovite nobility. We cannot unquestioningly accept Zevakin's classification of two sons (0.7%) of military "officers" as hereditary nobles, but it is a possibility; thus the 6.8% of the hereditary provincial nobility may need to be revised upward by 1%.

gin, this should mean that the above percentages relevant to the junior clerks of the Land Chancery are also representative of the social origin of the *d'iaki* group.[47] And so they are, for it is not until well into Peter's reign that we find a stated intent to favor the promotion of the nobility.[48] Until the post-Petrine period when the provisions of the Table of Ranks allowed in practice for the preferential advancement of

47. Bogoiavlenskii, in his "D'iaki," pp. 224–25, argues differently. He calculates that the majority of the seventeenth-century *d'iaki* were from the nobility (*"iz dvorian"*). To wit: 87% *circa* 1600, 79% in 1628, 66% in 1645, 53% in 1682, 64% in 1688, and somewhere between 60% and 64% in the reign of Peter I. (For Peter's reign only the percentage of appointments made is supplied. Other percentages as cited here are for all the *d'iaki* in the given year.) Neat and conclusive though it appears, this calculation calls for a closer scrutiny: (1) Bogoiavlenskii kept his sources to himself. Presumably he used the same file from which he published the *Prikaznye sud'i*, which for all its shortcomings is still a basic reference work. If so, it is possible that his calculation excludes the *d'iaki* who attained that rank but never served as *sud'i* in a *prikaz*. This could be a serious omission. (2) What criteria did he use for determining "nobility"? Apparently whether or not a given *d'iak* was recorded with a patronymic different from the last name. Given the even more questionable way in which he declared that such common last names of *pod'iachie* as Sekerin, Nekliudov, Krushchev, and Tiutchev belonged to the Muscovite nobility, simply because the last names also commonly appear in the lists of the Muscovite nobility, one cannot but wonder if he did not consult, in many cases where better evidence was lacking, the above-mentioned (n. 45) compilation of Ivanov which, despite its semiofficial character, is hardly trustworthy. The margin of error in this calculation could not possibly be less than 5% and possibly could be as high as 20–25%.

But Bogoiavlenskii's chief sin is in equating Muscovite nobility with the provincial nobility, including those who served *"po priboru,"* that is, the provincial nonhereditary gentry: there was a veritable gulf separating the two. The nobility serving *"po priboru"* was, in terms of rights and privileges, barely noble, and was economically likely to be in a position inferior to that of some of the more fortunate or more enterprising serfs. The Muscovite nobility were both socially and economically far better off, and any study worth its salt cannot fail to take cognizance of this fact. Why would a Muscovite noble subject himself to an economically and socially inferior position of a *pod'iachii*? Of course the answer is that he would not and that he did not. Bogoiavlenskii himself notes the disparity in social status between the *d'iaki* and the Muscovite nobility, even citing (ibid., p. 228) an example where the noble in question refused a direct appointment to the *d'iak* rank, until it was officially registered that he was accepting the appointment only on direct orders from the tsar and that his service as a *d'iak* would not demean his and his family's social standing.

Even if we allow that by "nobility" Bogoiavlenskii refers to the lower, provincial ranks, we cannot be satisfied, for this would mean an excessively high influx of the provincials into *prikazy* and would conflict with an apparently great father-son continuity in service among the *pod'iachie* and among the *pod'iachie* and *d'iaki*. (See below pp. 41–42.

48. PSZ, 1722, Vol. 6, No. 3,890, Pars. 13, 14 (1722 Table of Ranks, and elsewhere). But even this preferential treatment for the nobility required competence, lacking which, the commoners were to be appointed and if the position was sufficiently high, made noble.

the high-born, competence and hard work, not birth, were the chief criteria for advancement, as can be seen in examining the social origin of even a great many of the *dumnye d'iaki*.

SOCIAL STATUS AND MOBILITY

In social status the *d'iaki* ranked below the Muscovite nobility, but as the century progressed there are indications that the *d'iaki* were narrowing the gap. The *dumnye d'iaki*, of course, ranked higher, and there were instances where the scions of the well-established *duma* families were punished for insulting a *dumnyi d'iak*. The junior clerks ranked approximately with the lower provincial nobility. Given their social origin, then, for a good many of the *prikaznye liudi* there was no immediate social status incentive to seek service in the *prikazy*. But the incentive was there for everyone in the long run. The sons of clergy, of townsmen, of servants and peasants entered a more privileged estate. The sons of insignificant provincial nobles established themselves in Moscow. Furthermore, even in the estate-based society, money could influence one's social status. Despite the fact that the majority of the junior clerks never attained a higher rank themselves, it is safe to say that on a proportional basis the administrative service provided the fastest and safest way up the social ladder, superior even to the military. An application/petition by a *d'iak* to have his sons admitted to the Muscovite nobility was as good as granted. Thus, the provision for an automatic ennoblement in the Table of Ranks was no more than formalization of a long-standing practice, and inasmuch as it allowed for retroactive ennoblement of only one son, actually a step toward lesser social mobility. Until Peter's personal favorite, A. D. Menshikov, there is no example in the annals of Muscovite history to rival the spectacular career and rise of E. I. Ukraintsev, who started at the very bottom as a *pod'iachii*-in-training in the early 1660s and worked his way up to head the Foreign Chancery. In 1699 he was sent to negotiate with the Ottomans as "ambassador extraordinary, counselor to the *Duma*, and vicegerent of Kargopol."[49]

---

49. Belokurov, *O Posol'skom prikaze*, pp. 113–14, 123. Rather, there are other examples of similarly successful careers, but with the possible exception of A. L. Ordin-Nashchokin, all are from the administrative service.

FAMILIES IN SERVICE

Contemporaries of the *prikaznye liudi* and the modern students of Muscovy all agree that the *prikaznye liudi* came in "droves," that is, in large family groupings.[50] Even a glance at a list of the staff in any one year in a given *prikaz*, or at a list of all the *prikazy*, will reveal a great number of individuals with identical last names. This, of course, is not a proof that they were all related, but it is an indication. When we compile a list incorporating the patronymics, and correlate the respective years of active service and rank, we see that the opinions of the contemporaries are in fact correct. The *prikaznye liudi* did constitute one big conglomerate of families.

Although no administrative office was inheritable, the profession was. The only exception is the great majority of the sons of the *d'iaki* who did not follow in their fathers' footsteps and served as Muscovite nobles, a socially more prestigious service, and one could compile a very impressive list indeed of the careers of these sons. Family continuity in administrative service was great, and it becomes apparent when we consider not only the sons of *d'iaki* who were also *d'iaki*, but also *d'iaki* and junior clerks who were sons of junior clerks.[51] Finally, there is evidence, scattered but of sufficiently adequate representative quantity, that the *prikaznye liudi* had a strong preference for intra-group marriages, that is, unless they were able to—and a fair number of them did—marry either into the highest social strata or into real wealth.

ECONOMIC STATUS

Given the nature of their work and responsibilities, the *prikaznye lidui* were hardly able even to visit their landholdings—some never did— let alone see to the running of the estates; thus, it comes as no surprise,

50. See above n. 24; Demidova, "Prikaznye liudi," p. 345; S. B. Veselovskii, "Prikaznyi stroi upravleniia Moskovskogo gosudarstva," in M. B. Dovnar-Zapol'skii, ed., *Russkaia istoriia v ocherkakh i stat'iakh*, Kiev, 1912, 3: 185.

51. Bogoiavlenskii ("D'iaki," p. 225) calculates that for the entire seventeenth century only 26 *d'iaki* were the sons of *d'iaki*. In terms of family continuity in service this calculation is both inadequate and misleading. Here, at last, we were able to establish that the source of Bogoiavlenskii's count is his *Sud'i*. This means that he only counted those whom he lists as *sud'i*. There were considerably more *d'iaki* than there were *sud'i*, so that even father-*d'iak* / son-*d'iak* continuity would have to be greater.

especially if we take into account their income from the job as well, that *as a group* they were disinterested in landownership.[52] Based on the official depositions of virtually all the *prikaznye liudi* (of the junior clerks in 1665 and the *d'iaki* in 1684–85), the following observations may be made. The *d'iaki* and the junior clerks were entitled to considerably more land than they actually possessed.[53] Even some *dumnye d'iaki* owned no land although nominally entitled to sizable holdings. Much of the land that the *prikaznye liudi* did own was in the newly acquired areas, or areas being colonized, and either without peasants or not under cultivation, or both.[54] Even the land with peasants brought the owner negligible income. The ratio of escaped peasants from these lands seems to have been inordinately high. What good land they owned was either inherited, acquired through marriage, or purchased. The minority who purchased land did so more than once, mostly to invest unneeded capital and to back up their social aspirations, and only rarely to generate real income.

For the majority of the *prikaznye liudi*, then, landownership did not really reflect their relative economic status. As full-time and lifelong office workers, their true wealth is more likely to be expressed in the ownership of urban real estate, cash, and other liquid assets. The surviving documents, alas widely scattered and too few in number, do in fact attest to sizable, even huge, wealth accumulated during the administrative service. The relative socioeconomic presence of the *prikaznye liudi* in Muscovite society is best documented in tax-assessment rolls for the city of Moscow for 1716 and 1718–23. Even for the period

52. Iu. A. Tikhonov, *Pomeshchich'i krest'iane v Rossii, Feodal'naia renta v XVII–nachale XVIII v.*, Moscow, 1974, *passim*, presents some very strong evidence to the contrary, but the cases he discusses are few and are completely unrepresentative of the group. The same is true of Rozhdestvenskii's analysis of the *Boiarskaia kniga No. 12* (1646–47), which shows that some *d'iaki* possessed more land than even many members of the *boyar* and even princely families. (S. V. Rozhdestvenskii, *Sluzhiloe zemlevladenie v Moskovskom gosudarstve XVI veka*, St. Petersburg, 1897, pp. 227–31.) Nor should one be misled by the extensive landholdings of several *d'iaki* at the beginning of the eighteenth century. (*Materialy po istorii krest'ianskogo i pomestnicheskogo khoziaistva pervoi chetverti XVIIIv.*, Moscow, 1951, pp. 48–49, *passim*.)

53. Inexplicably, in light of the above cited statement (pp. 23–24). Demidova ("Prikaznye liudi," pp. 341–42) recognizes this fact and even notes that in 1666 of the 69 *d'iaki* no less than 27 (39%) had no land.

54. A similar situation prevailed among the 278 *pod'iachie* of the Land Chancery at the opening of the eighteenth century. See Zevakin, "Pod'iachie pomestnogo," p. 281. We ought to point out here that in 1665 the *pod'iachie* of the same *prikaz* possessed land well above the average for the other *prikazy*.

after the central chanceries with most of their staffs moved to St. Petersburg, our computation shows that one out of seven houses in the city belonged to the *prikaznye liudi*, and that compared to the rest of the population, including the high nobility and the large merchants, the *pod'iachie* fall just short of the mean tax assessment based on size of property owned, *d'iaki* considerably above it, and the *dumnye d'iaki* well above it.[55]

CONTINUITY

One of the best indications of the maturity of formal organizations and their staffs is staying power arising from their indispensability to the interests they serve, in our case the state. We may term this "permanence through professionalism." A test study made of some twenty-one *d'iaki* and *dumnye d'iaki* in the Military-Interior and Foreign Chanceries in the first decades of the seventeenth century shows that those already in service in the reign of Boris Godunov belonged to every faction during the Time of Troubles, and continued in service well into and beyond the reign of Mikhail Fedorovich. The continuity in the administrative careers and orderliness of promotions is most impressive if we consider that the period examined exceeds a quarter of a century that included famine, rebellion, civil war, foreign intervention, dynastic struggle, and several governments.[56] Undisturbed and unperturbed, the *prikaznye liudi* weathered the successive reigns and organizational groupings and regroupings as the century progressed.

Periodic reorganization and restructuring, usually only after the old order falls behind in performance, is in the nature of all complex formal organizations. It is also in their nature to resist change and innovation not accompanied by expansion. Throughout the seventeenth century and under Peter, the Muscovite professional administrators continued to proliferate at an ever increasing pace. This proliferation

55. Based on the fairly complete tax rolls for the entire city in *Perepisi moskovskikh dvorov XVIII stoletiia*, Moscow, 1896, pp. 1–248. We should make clear here that the above computation reflects properties assessed, and that since many *prikaznye liudi* owned more than one property, a computation of combined individual ownership would be considerably more favorable to the *prikaznye liudi*.

56. The only exception constituted the *dumnye d'iaki* who were changed with each accession to the throne, except the accession of Mikhail Fedorovich, who as a compromise candidate did not have the option of removing even those politically allied with previous regimes.

was accompanied by adequate and secure income, which kept pace with the inflation and continuous upgrading of the rank (*chin*).[57] Moreover, under Peter I, the *prikaznye liudi* saw their heretofore social superiors, the higher nobility, forced de jure and de facto into administrative service as professionals. Thus, even in the turbulence of the Petrine times, the *prikaznye liudi* went along with Peter's reordering of Russia, virtually the only social group not stalling.

It can be argued that in the long run the Table of Ranks and the accompanying legislation effectively closed the door to the very top for those who started at the very bottom, and that dazzling careers, such as those of E. Ukraintsev or F. Shaklovityi, were not to be possible. But that lies in the future. To the very end of Peter's reign there was little for the *prikaznye liudi* to worry about. A test study done of the personnel of the Foreign Chancery under Peter I shows, just as at the beginning of the seventeenth century, a remarkable continuity of service and orderliness of promotions. (A cursory examination of the staffs of other *kollegii* indicates that their staffs were developing along basically similar lines.) The only exception to the orderliness of promotions is a rapid advancement of professionals with new skills. But even these were either imported foreign professionals or the sons of the *prikaznye liudi*.

57. It was only in the later part of his reign that Peter halved the salaries, temporarily, of the staffs of some *prikazy/kollegii*.

CHAPTER THREE

THE ORIGINS OF THE NOBLE OFFICIAL: THE BOYAR ELITE, 1613–1689

Robert O. Crummey

The dominant social group throughout both Muscovite and Imperial Russian history has been the warrior-landowner, a group that eventually evolved into the pacific Russian nobility so familiar from the great novels of the nineteenth century. Crummey points out that the elite of the military servitor group began to be involved more and more in civil affairs in the seventeenth century. While this superior, enormously influential elite did not replace the professional clerks described by Plavsic, at the highest level some of these soldier landlords began to have careers that included prolonged periods of nonmilitary service, often in high office and at an early age. Thus, while membership in the Boyar Duma may correctly be called the capstone of many successful elite careers, it was not the end, as membership in many nineteenth-century councillary-political bodies was. Instead it was an exalted foundation upon which a socially and politically prestigious career could be continued to new heights.

At the highest level, as Crummey demonstrates, family connections and landholding were always important, but in the centralized Muscovite state where the tsar wielded enormous personal power, neither were ever the exclusive determinates of bureaucratic success. The obscure managed sometimes to rise in service, and even the wealthiest families depended on the sovereign for the maintenance of wealth and their position because the two were inseparable. Thus these immensely powerful elite families lived to some degree in an environment both rich and powerful, and insecure, a point reinforced by the findings of Meehan-Waters in her study of "noble bureaucrats" in Chapter Four. There was an element of capriciousness that unmistakably placed the individual's career in the hands of fate—or, at any rate, in the hands of factors he could not control or predict. The tsar, at this elite level, where offices were few and officeholders, their friends, and family were known to him, could determine within wide limits who should serve where and with what compensation. Such a determination could be based on personal friendship, political alignments at court, the power and wealth of one's family, and other factors having but little practical meaning for the task to be performed. Unlike the

*professional training and experience that became important components in the
more specialized careers described by Plavsic in Chapter Two, the components
of a successful elite career were often independent of the specific requirements of
a given position or job, and dependent instead upon the social and political
factors that the noble and his family could only partially control.*

*Russian official life was divided, in the seventeenth and eighteenth cen-
turies, into large and distinct career patterns and, correspondingly, into distinct
societies—the political elites and the chanceries. Selection into the political
elite was determined by genetic accident—which family one was born to and
whether one was male or female—and by the social and political experience of
the family and clan as much as of the individual. For civil officialdom, the
chancery clerks, selection clearly had its accidental dimension but, on the
whole, the career was more predictable in the sense that it was clear what
contribution the successful completion of certain training experiences and jobs
would make to an individual's advancement. In the case of the civil officialdom
we can speak of relatively regular and known norms for career development
(chinoproizvodstvo) just as the training of the d'iak introduced him to
standards of official procedure (deloproizvodstvo). In a sense, the boyar
elite constituted a political-bureaucracy, where politics and its accompanying
vagaries were much the more important element; the chancery clerks, on the
other hand, constituted a bureaucratized officialdom in which bureaucracy,
with its accompanying reliance upon training, specialization, regularity and
anonymity, was of greater importance. [THE EDITORS.]*

As a type, the noble official emerged in Russia in the seventeenth
century. In the sixteenth, the tsar's most prominent servitors were
clearly divided into two distinct groups—the warrior aristocracy
whose members spent almost all of their lives in the army, and the
bureaucratic officials who directed the operations of the emerging
chanceries (*prikazy*). Members of one group rarely, if ever, strayed
into the preserve of the other.[1] In the seventeenth century, however,

---

1. R. G. Skrynnikov in his recent *Ivan Groznyi*, Moscow, 1975, points out that some
court officials of the sixteenth century were in charge of nascent administrative departments (p. 192). His comment in no way contradicts the central argument of this paper.
First, if his assertion is correct, the number of such courtier administrators was very
small. Noble officials were numerous in the seventeenth century. Second, the courtier
administrators served at a time when the administrative chanceries were gradually
ceasing to be parts of the royal household management and becoming separate bureaucratic departments. By the early seventeenth century, that process was largely complete.
Indeed, in our period, some noble courtiers received posts in chanceries in which only
career administrators had previously served.

this neat pattern began to change. In increasing numbers, members of the warrior nobility crossed the line and occupied high positions in the rapidly growing network of chanceries. The careers of these seventeenth-century noble officials tell us a good deal about the ways in which Russia was governed in their time and the conditions in which they and their fellow nobles vied for power and wealth. As men who were both high nobles and high officials, moreover, they were the wave of the future. Their successors played a prominent role in the Russian administration into the twentieth century.

Before we examine the noble officials as such, we should see them in the context from which they emerged, the "power elite" of seventeenth-century Russia. Who made up this elite? The best answer seems to be the 427 members of the Boyar Duma, or royal council. In Muscovite Russia, the rulers very often rewarded their most distinguished servitors with one of the four Duma ranks—boyar, *okol'nichii*, *dumnyi dvorianin*, and *dumnyi d'iak*. Indeed, through most of the Muscovite period there were few outstanding generals, diplomats, or administrators who did not receive Duma rank at some stage of their careers. It was these men who had most power to shape the lives of their fellow citizens by making or implementing governmental policy.

To be sure, the assumption that the members of the Duma formed the "power elite" of Muscovite Russia needs some qualification, at least for the seventeenth century. Previous studies have shown, first of all, that in the last decades of the century, Duma rank lost much of its luster. In the 1690s, the Duma was swollen with undistinguished members while the ambitious and power-hungry clustered around the young Peter I. The Duma ceased to be significant either as an institution or as a collection of powerful officials by 1693 at the latest.[2] Secondly, if the power elite includes all those servitors who played a significant role in implementing policy, it contains many men who never received Duma rank in addition to those who did. In particular, social convention distorted the composition of the council: in the seventeenth century, chancery officials, traditionally excluded from the Duma's top two ranks, received less recognition than their power warranted. In spite of these qualifications, however, the membership of the Duma still seems to me the most illuminating focus of a study of power in seventeenth-century Russia.

A brief statistical profile is probably the best medium in which to portray the boyar elite. Before beginning, let us set down a few simple

---

2. Robert O. Crummey, "Peter and the Boiar Aristocracy, 1689–1700," *Canadian-American Slavic Studies* 8 (1974): 276–78.

rules that distinguish this study from its predecessors, notably Ia. E. Vodarskii's recent article.[3] First of all, our calculations include all Duma members, not only the boyars and *okol'nichie*, who usually came from distinguished families of long standing, but also the *dumnye dvoriane* and *dumnye d'iaki* of more humble origins. Secondly, in order to show change over the course of the seventeenth century, this essay will treat the century both as a whole and in seven subdivisions averaging about eleven years—1613–19, 1620–33, 1634–44, 1645–58, 1659–66, 1667–75, and 1676–89. Each subdivision begins and ends with a significant event in the lives of the members of the ruling elite—the election of Michael Romanov (1613), the return of Patriarch Filaret from captivity (1619), the death of Filaret and defeat in the war for Smolensk (1633), the accession of Alexis (1645), the fall of Patriarch Nikon (1658), the end of the war with Poland (1667), and the death of Alexis and the beginning of the long succession crisis that ended only with the emergence of the mature Peter I (1676). In this way, our calculations should prove a sensitive barometer of change over the course of the century. Finally, we will devote most of our attention to the ways in which the Duma served the crown.

The first obvious feature of the boyar elite is its growth during the century. The membership of the Boyar Duma increased from a low of 24 in 1630 to a high of 144 in 1686. Through most of the century, the number of members grew steadily. At three points, however, the size of the group jumped dramatically: it doubled between 1645 and 1652, the first years of the reign of Alexis, and registered sharp increases at the beginning of Fedor's reign in 1676 and Sophia's regency in 1682.[4]

---

3. Ia. E. Vodarskii, "Praviashchaia gruppa svetskikh feodalov v Rossii v XVIIv.," *Dvorianstvo i krepostnoi stroi Rossii XVI–XVIII vv*, Moscow, 1975, pp. 70–107. Vodarskii's tables present a great deal of useful information and his conclusions are eminently reasonable. Even so, his work might have been more revealing if he had taken a slightly different statistical tack. First, his decision to study only boyars and *okol'nichie* weighted his figures in favor of his conclusion that a limited number of aristocratic families dominated Muscovite political and social life in the seventeenth century. Had he included all Duma members in his calculations, his figures would have lent much greater weight to the same conclusion. Secondly, by treating the century as a single chronological unit, he ruled out most opportunities to study change within the course of the century. Yet, most historians agree that the seventeenth century was a period of rapid change in all spheres of national life. Thirdly, Vodarskii ducked the thorny question of the family or clan (*rod*). He simply ignored the possibility that men with a common surname might not belong to the same family in their own minds or those of their contemporaries. Finally, Vodarskii does not deal with the most important feature of the lives of seventeenth-century aristocrats—how they served the crown.

4. The membership of the Boyar Duma in the seventeenth century can be recon-

The changing size of the Duma reflects a dramatic change in the social origin of its members. Before we deal directly with this issue, however, we should discuss briefly the tricky question of the nature and size of the Muscovite clan (*rod*). Earlier studies including Vodarskii's and my own, treat all men who share a surname and a common genealogy as relatives. In some cases this procedure raises few objections. The Golitsyn family, for example, was as small as it was distinguished: the men who bore that name really were close relatives.[5] On the other hand, families like the Buturlins were large and sprawling: prominent representatives of the clan might well be very distant relatives.[6] How then is one to proceed? Can we justifiably treat all Buturlins as related in a meaningful sense?

A fully satisfactory answer must await the solution of a complex—and perhaps insoluble—question: What is a clan? To rephrase the same question, whom did a Muscovite noble think of as his kinsman? The most superficial perusal of the sources suggests that different circumstances brought forth different answers. When engaged in a precedence (*mestnichestvo*) dispute, a noble might well claim that all bearers of his name were superior to all kinsmen of his rival. On the other hand, when bequeathing his property, he would probably limit his generosity to his closest relatives.

Without a definitive answer to this vexing question, we must make tactical choices to distinguish between very close and very distant relatives. In this essay, members of the Duma will first be classified by membership in their general clan. Then we will make a special note of those who could claim a direct ancestor in Duma rank. Finally, we should note that married men enjoy the benefits and headaches of membership in two families. For this reason, we will also take note of any Duma member whose relative within three kinship links—either

---

structed from the following sources: Moscow. TsGADA, Fond 210 (Dokumenty Razriadnogo prikaza), Boiarskie knigi and Boiarskie spiski; *Dvortsovye razriady*, 4 vols., St. Petersburg, 1850–55 (hereafter DR); *Knigi razriadnye*, 2 vols., St. Petersburg, 1853–55 (hereafter KR); and a wide variety of sources that record the service assignments of seventeenth-century nobles.

The only published list of Duma members for the whole century is part of the so-called "Sheremetev list," *Drevniaia rossiiskaia vivliofika*, 20 vols., Moscow, 1788–91, 20: 86–131. For the years 1613–45, see Robert O. Crummey, "The Reconstitution of the Boiar Aristocracy, 1613–1645," *Forschungen zur osteuropäischen Geschichte* 18 (1973): 210–19 (hereafter "Reconstitution").

5. For the genealogy of the Golitsyns, see *Rodoslovnaia kniga kniazei i dvorian rossiiskikh*, 2 vols., Moscow, 1787, 1: 36–40 (hereafter RK).

6. For the genealogy of the Buturlins, see RK, 1: 338–46. See also "Reconstitution," p. 195, n. 30.

by blood or by marriage—was already in the Duma at the time of his appointment. These adjustments are simple, but should help us find the middle ground between too simple an approach that treats all Buturlins alike and excessive complexity that deals with each individual as a separate case.

Before turning to figures on the social origin of Duma members, we should review briefly the composition of the Muscovite nobility. At the pinnacle were two kinds of families. The princes traced their ancestry to the rulers of independent principalities of the appanage period. Over the centuries, some had fared better than others. The most successful had entered the service of the princes of Moscow, particularly in the late fifteenth and early sixteenth centuries.[7] There they worked alongside the old nontitled families whose members had served the rulers of Moscow beginning in the fourteenth century.[8] Lacking a title, the nonprincely families' claim to power and prestige rested on their loyal service to the crown from generation to generation. In the final analysis, however, their position was not significantly different from that of the princes, for a title meant very little without a record of distinguished service and the accompanying rewards.

Below the princely and nontitled boyar clans on the Muscovite service hierarchy came the Moscow gentry, the large group of men who served in the military entourage of the tsar and at his court. Under them, in turn, were the provincial gentry who made up the bulk of the cavalry units that, until the late seventeenth century, formed the core of the army. A clear line of demarcation separated the two groups. The Moscow gentry enjoyed the glamour of the capital and the practical advantages that flowed from proximity to powerful ministers and the tsar himself. Transfer from a provincial center to Moscow constituted a major promotion: demotion from Moscow to the provincial gentry was the worst kind of disgrace. In this study, we will consider as Moscow gentry any servitor whose father or uncle clearly served in Moscow.

Table 1 classifies Duma members into seven main categories by social origin—old princes, old nontitled families, new princes, Moscow gentry, provincial gentry, merchants and chancery officials.[9] In con-

7. See, for example, Gustave Alef, "The Crisis of the Muscovite Aristocracy: A Factor in the Growth of Monarchical Power," *Forschungen zur osteuropäischen Geschichte*, 15 (1970): 15–58, esp. pp. 53–56.

8. S. B. Veselovskii, *Issledovaniia po istorii klassa sluzhilykh zemlevladel'tsev*, Moscow, 1969, pp. 465–519.

9. The data for the tables come from a wide variety of sources. The most important sources on service are: DR; KR; S. K. Bogoiavlenskii, *Prikaznye sud'i XVII veka*,

trast to earlier studies, I define "old princes" as members of a princely clan that had one representative in the Duma at the rank of boyar or *okol'nichii* at least thirty years before their own appointment. Two considerations led me to adopt this sliding scale rather than any fixed chronological limit such as 1584. First of all, a fixed date would automatically skew my calculations in favor of greater social continuity at the beginning of the century and greater mobility at the end. Second, use of a fixed date like 1584 tends to suggest that the membership of the Duma before that date was stable. In practice, that was far from the case. Like any elite, the boyar group of the sixteenth century changed steadily and, at times, dramatically. To give one example, a few of the "distinguished old" families of our period first reached the Duma during the *oprichnina* (1565–72), Ivan IV's experiment in absolute rule and terror.[10] The choice of a thirty-year limit is arbitrary, yet defensible. Thirty years is significantly longer than one generation; a family which retained Duma rank that long had achieved a fairly firm hold at the summit of power. Moreover, even if we were to extend this period of time, the vast majority of those we have classified as "old" would still qualify.[11]

As Table 1 shows, families that served in the Duma in earlier times continued to play a dominant role in Russian political life. Over the course of the century, 46 percent of all Duma members came from aristocratic, that is, old princely and nontitled families. Descendants of

Moscow-Leningrad, 1946; S. B. Veselovskii, *D'iaki i pod'iachie XV–XVIIvv.*, Moscow, 1975; A. Barsukov, *Spiski gorodovykh voevod i drugikh lits voevodskago upravleniia moskovskago gosudarstva XVII stoletiia*, St. Petersburg, 1902; *Akty moskovskago gosudarstva*, 3 vols., St. Petersburg, 1890–1901 (hereafter AMG), and the *Boiarskie knigi* and *Boiarskie spiski*.

The most important genealogical works are: RK; G. A. Vlas'ev, *Potomstvo Riurika*, 2 vols. (Vol. 1 in 3 parts), St. Petersburg, Petrograd, 1906–18; A. B. Lobanov-Rostovskii, *Russkaia rodoslovnaia kniga*, 2 vols., St. Petersburg, 1895; P. V. Dolgorukov, *Rossiiskaia rodoslovnaia kniga*, 4 vols., St. Petersburg, 1854–57; V. V. Rummel', and V. V. Golubtsov, *Rodoslovnyi sbornik russkikh dvorianskikh familii*, 2 vols., St. Petersburg, 1886–87; L. M. Savelov, *Opyt rodoslovnago slovaria russkago drevniago dvorianstva. Rodoslovnye zapisi*, 3 vols., Moscow, 1906–9; N. F. Ikonnikov, *NdR, la Noblesse de Russie*, 25 vols., Paris, 1957–66 (hereafter NdR); A. V. Barsukov, *Rod Sheremetevykh*, 8 vols., St. Petersburg, 1881–1904. Because the percentages in the tables have been rounded off to even numbers, not all columns add up to 100%.

10. For example, the royal in-laws, the Sobakins and Cherkasskiis. The Godunovs, likewise in-laws, reached Duma rank soon after the end of the oprichnina. A. A. Zimin, "Sostav Boiarskoi dumy v XV–XVI vekakh," *Arkheograficheskii ezhegodnik za 1957 god*, Moscow, 1958, pp. 41–87, esp. pp. 72–79 (hereafter Zimin, "Sostav").

11. For the membership of the Duma up to 1584, see Zimin, "Sostav." For the years 1584–1613, we are still dependent on the "Sheremetev list," pp. 59–86.

TABLE III-1

Social Origin of Duma Members

		1613–19 N = 48	1620–33 N = 17	1634–44 N = 26	1645–58 N = 87	1659–66 N = 27	1667–75 N = 31	1676–89 N = 191	Total N = 427
Old princes	N =	17	5	6	29	9	4	35	105
	%	37	33	25	34	35	15	20	26
Old nontitles	N =	10	2	8	20	2	1	38	81
	%	22	13	33	24	8	4	22	20
Total aristocratic element	%	59	46	58	58	43	19	42	46
New princes	N =	8	4	3	8	2	2	12	39
	%	17	27	13	9	8	8	7	10
Moscow gentry	N =	7	1	4	21	10	8	72	123
	%	15	7	16	25	38	31	41	31
Provincial gentry	N =	1	3	2	4	2	6	10	28
	%	2	20	8	5	8	23	6	7
Merchants	N =	1	0	0	2	0	0	2	5
	%	2			2			1	1
Chancery officials	N =	2	0	1	1	1	5	6	16
	%	4		4	1	4	19	3	4
Other	N =	0	0	0	0	0	0	1	1
	%							1	0
Unknown	N =	2	2	2	2	1	5	15	29

SOURCE: See footnote 9.

the old aristocratic clans had even greater weight in the first half of the century. In the last years of Alexis's reign, their relative importance fell, but they staged a significant comeback in the years of succession crisis when they made up 42 percent of the new recruits to the Duma.

In the seventeenth century, the princely and boyar families met unprecedented competition from newcomers to the ruling group. In the early years of the century, the largest group of "new men" in the Duma was made up of princes whose families had no record of Duma service. As the century continued, however, the newcomers came in increasing numbers from the Moscow and provincial gentry. Of the two groups, far more representatives of the Moscow gentry succeeded in reaching the Duma. They constituted 31 percent of its membership for the whole century, and 41 percent of those promoted in 1676–89 came from its ranks. By comparison, few members came directly from the provincial gentry. To be sure, many of the twenty-nine men whose origins could not be identified rose either from the Moscow or provincial gentry. Still, if we were to add fifteen or twenty names to our lists of recruits from the provincial gentry, that group would still fall far short of the Moscow gentry as a source of Duma members.

Finally, our scattered sources indicate that the leading chancery officials of the day came from a variety of backgrounds. Three of five merchants listed in Table 1 served as experts on finance and taxation. Other *dumnye d'iaki* came from families with a long history of chancery service.[12] The social origins of some of their colleagues remain unknown.

Table 2 presents a narrower and more stringent test of social continuity among Duma members. As Table 1 has already suggested, descendants of former members reached the Duma in particularly great numbers under Michael Romanov. The reign of his successor, however, splits into two contrasting segments. Up to 1658, new recruits to the Duma followed the earlier pattern. Then, abruptly, the balance changed and new Duma members came overwhelmingly from families with no tradition of such honor. In the years 1659–75, 90 percent of the newcomers could not claim an ancestor with Duma service. Finally, in the years of interregnum, 1676–89, the old Duma clans improved their position; 24 percent of the new appointees had ancestors in the council. In sum, over the whole century, one quarter of the Duma's members came from a branch of their clan that had

12. N. I. Chistyi and A. S. and I. A. Kirillov. The others of urban origin were Kuz'ma Minin and Almaz Ivanov.

TABLE III-2

Was Duma Member a Direct Descendant
of a Man Who Was a Boyar or Okol'nichii
at Least Thirty Years Earlier?

		Yes	No	Total (N =)
1613–19	N =	19	29	48
	%	40	60	
1620–33	N =	5	12	17
	%	29	71	
1634–44	N =	10	16	26
	%	38	62	
1645–58	N =	31	56	87
	%	36	64	
1659–66	N =	4	23	27
	%	15	85	
1667–75	N =	2	29	31
	%	6	94	
1676–89	N =	46	145	191
	%	24	76	
Total	N =	117	310	427
	%	27	73	

SOURCE: See footnote 9.

already sent a representative to the top of the Muscovite system. These were the aristocrats of Muscovy.

Table 3 tests family connections in yet another way. At the time of their appointments, 43 percent of all Duma members had a relative within three kinship links who was already in the council (see Diagram 1).[13] Oddly enough, this figure remains almost constant

13. The diagram and the idea behind it come from Maurice Zeitlin and Richard Earl Ratcliff, "Research Methods for the Analysis of the Internal Structure of the Dominant Classes: The Case of Landlords and Capitalists in Chile," *Latin American Research Review* 10, No. 3 (1975): 5–62. The diagram is on page 27. I am grateful to my colleague Arnold J. Bauer for this reference.

TABLE III-3

Was a Relative within Three Kinship Links
Already in the Duma When Duma Member Appointed?

		Yes	No	Unknown	Total (N =)
1613–19	N =	22	26	0	48
	%	46	54		
1620–33	N =	5	12	0	17
	%	29	71		
1634–44	N =	10	16	0	26
	%	38	62		
1645–58	N =	37	48	2	87
	%	44	56		
1659–66	N =	12	15	0	27
	%	44	56		
1667–75	N =	12	17	2	31
	%	41	59		
1676–89	N =	82	104	5	191
	%	44	56		
Total	N =	180	238	9	427
	%	43	57		

SOURCE: See footnote 9.

throughout the seventeenth century. Apparently, family connections
are just as helpful in times of confusion and rapid change as in periods
of consolidation. Indeed, as the figures for the years 1620–33 suggest,
aristocrats seem to have less need of friends at court than parvenues.

To summarize, Tables 1 and 2 chart a dramatic change in the social
origin of Duma members in the reign of Alexis. Under his father,
Michael, well-established aristocratic clans dominated the royal council. Newcomers to Duma rank were comparatively rare and came most
often from previously unrepresented branches of the great princely
clans or from nontitled families whose members had long served the
tsars in positions just below Duma rank. Then, in Alexis's reign,
the balance changed. The old aristocratic clans provided less than
half of the Duma's new members. In their place appeared an increas-

DIAGRAM I

Kinship Links between Individual (Ego) and Selected Relatives

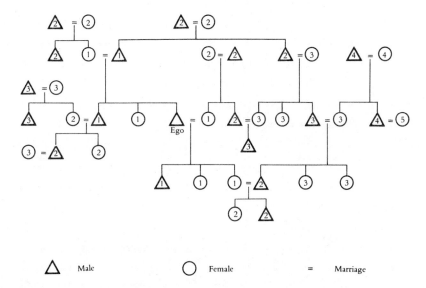

△ Male   ○ Female   = Marriage

ing number of social outsiders, including some from obscure provincial families. The trend to "democratize" the council's membership reached its height in the last years of Alexis's reign, 1667–75, then tapered off somewhat during the regency when the old families regained lost ground. Finally, Table 3 shows that family ties played, if anything, an even more important role in the success of parvenues than of their more favored competitors.

Landholding provided most of the income of the high nobles who made up the governing elite of seventeenth-century Russia. With the possible exception of some career bureaucrats, Duma members were landlords. Only an exceptional few engaged in any other economic ventures.[14]

14. The best study of one man's estates in the seventeenth century is: D. I. Petrikeev, *Krupnoe krepostnoe khoziaistvo XVIIv.*, Leningrad, 1967, on B. I. Morozov. Documents on Morozov's estates are published in *Akty khoziaistva boiarina B. I. Morozova*, 2 vols., Moscow-Leningrad, 1940–45. See also A. A. Novosel'skii, *Votchinnik i ego khoziaistvo v XVII veke*, Moscow-Leningrad, 1929. There are a number of shorter studies of seventeenth-century estates.

This statement refers to the high court nobility, not the chancery officials described in Plavsic's essay in this volume.

Our knowledge of the patterns of boyar landholding is very limited, since it rests primarily on a few summary lists of landholders for particular years. Those for 1613, 1638, 1647, 1653, 1678, and 1696 have been published. I have also used an incomplete unpublished list for 1670 fleshed out with landholding figures from *boiarskie spiski* (boyar lists) of adjacent years.[15] Until scholars complete systematic studies of the numerous land cadastres of the period, any conclusions about the prevailing patterns of landholding and their relation to political power will be tentative at best.

From the limited source material at our disposal, one thing is clear: the relationship between landed wealth and political power was complex. Tables 4 and 5 list the ten wealthiest individuals and families at various points in the century. The continuity from one list to the next is indeed remarkable. Families like the Sheremetevs, Cherkasskiis, Kurakins, and Odoevskiis remained in the top ten throughout the century. The Mstislavskiis and Morozovs disappeared from the list only when the male line died out.

Without question, wealth provided some of the advantages that helped members of these families remain in the Duma in generation after generation. At the same time, political power and favor could bring wealth. In the early years of Alexis's reign, for example, the

15. The summary lists of boyar landholding are to be found as follows:

1613—A. P. Barsukov, ed. "Dokladnaia vypiska 121 (1613) goda o votchinakh i pomest'iakh," *Chteniia v Imperatorskom Obshchestve istorii i drevnostei rossiiskikh pri Moskovskom Universitete*, 264 vols., Moscow, 1846–1918 (hereafter ChOIDR), 1895, 1: 1–24.

1638—A. I. Iakovlev, "Sluzhiloe zemlevladenie po dannym Prikaza sbora ratnykh liudei (1638 g.)," *Sergeiu Fedorovichu Platonovu. Ucheniki, druz'ia i pochitateli. Sbornik statei, posviashchennykh S. F. Platonovu*, St. Petersburg, 1911, pp. 450–53.

1647—S. V. Rozhdestvenskii, "Rospis' zemel'nykh vladenii moskovskago boiarstva 1647–8 goda," *Drevnosti. Trudy Arkheograficheskoi komissii Imp. Arkheologischeskago Obshchestva* 3 (1913): cols. 193–238.

1653—N. Nikol'skii, *Kirillo-Belozerskii Monastyr' i ego ustroistvo do vtoroi chetverti XVIIv.* Vol. 1, St. Petersburg, 1896, Appendix I, pp. xxvi–xxxiii.

1678—A. A. Novosel'skii, "Rospis' krest'ianskikh dvorov, nakhodivshikhsia vo vladenii vyshego dukhovenstva, monastyrei i dumnykh liudei po perepisnym knigam 1678 g.," *Istoricheskii Arkhiv* 4 (1949): 88–149.

1696—S. I. Elagin, *Istoriia russkago flota. Period azovskii. Prilozheniia*, Pt. I, St. Petersburg, 1864, 181–202.

The partial list for 1670 is TsGADA, Fond 210, Stolbtsy moskovskogo stola, No. 447, *Stolpik* 3 supplemented by figures in other *Stolbtsy moskovskogo stola* and *Boiarskie spiski* of the late 1660s and early 1670s in the same fond.

Only the 1696 list gives data on a significant number of lay servitors outside the Duma. It should be noted that I have used Iakovlev's 1638 figures as adjusted by Vodarskii.

Morozovs, already rich and distinguished, used their political influence to become the richest family of the realm. Even more startling are the classic success stories of the period. At various times in the century, I. T. Gramotin, L. S. Streshnev, I. D. Miloslavskii and L. K. Naryshkin rose from obscurity to prominence and wealth through talent, energy, ambition or good luck. The Streshnevs, Miloslavskiis, Naryshkins, and Lopukhins all got rich by marrying into the royal family. Political influence brought economic rewards, at least in their case.

In another sense, no family, however wealthy, could afford to rest on its laurels. The ancient custom of partible inheritance threatened every family with gradual impoverishment unless its members could keep replenishing the family fortune through state service. There were, to be sure, other possible brakes to prevent the slide toward poverty. At the present elementary state of our knowledge, however, there is little evidence that boyar families practiced some form of birth control or devised alternative inheritance arrangements. Apparently, even the richest families depended on state service for their continued prosperity.

The Muscovite government also encouraged its leading servitors by providing a wide variety of nonmonetary rewards. Very often, at the end of a successful mission, a general or diplomat received furs or a drinking cup as well as a raise in his formal salary and land allotment (*oklad*). Moreover, the elaborate rituals of the court provided many rewards. The court registers of the seventeenth century record innumerable occasions on which the tsar sent formal congratulations to commanders in the field or gave a reception in their honor once they returned to Moscow. A prominent place in court ceremonies, particularly royal weddings, was yet another form of recognition accorded the favored few.[16] In all these ways and more, the tsar and his advisers could keep leading servitors happy and in line.

Appointment to the Duma was usually the capstone of a career of service. Almost all its members completed an apprenticeship in the army, the administration, the court, or in a combination of several forms of service. How long did the apprenticeship last? To answer the question, I have estimated the ages of the Duma members at the time of their appointment. Since we know the birth dates of very few men of the seventeenth century, I assumed that each Duma member carried out his first recorded service assignment at the age of sixteen. In many

16. There are numerous examples in DR, RK, and AMG. See, for example, DR, 1: 329, 353, 3: 78–85, 880–81; AMG, 3: 169, 285.

TABLE III-4

Ten Wealthiest Individual Lay Landowners in Russia

	1613	1638	1647
1	F. I. Mstislavskii	I. N. Romanov	N. I. Romanov
2	D. T. Trubetskoi	F. I. Sheremetev	B. I. Morozov
3	F. I. Sheremetev	I. B. Cherkasskii	Ia. K. Cherkasskii
4	I. A. Vorotynskii	D. M. Pozharskii	F. I. Sheremetev
5	I. B. Cherkasskii	L. S. Streshnev	I. V. Morozov
6	V. P. Morozov	Iu. E. Suleshev	M. M. Saltykov
7	I. N. Romanov	D. M. Cherkasskii	N. I. Odoevskii
8	A. Iu. Sitskii	B. M. Lykov	G. I. Morozov
9	I. m. I. Odoevskii	I. T. Gramotin	L. S. Streshnev
10	D. M. Pozharskii	A. M. L'vov	V. I. Streshnev

SOURCE: See footnote 15.

cases, Muscovite traditions of service make our calculations easy. In the ceremonial life of the Russian court, for example, adolescents of the finest families very often performed certain roles, such as *rynda* or ceremonial bodyguard at formal receptions. When an individual's service record is sketchy, I have assumed that he was enrolled in service and given his own service estate and obligations at the usual age—fifteen.[17] In still other instances, it was necessary to reconcile the conflicting testimony of service and landholding records by educated guesses. Finally, it must be admitted that the careers of some men, particularly the chancery specialists, give no hint of their age when they reached Duma rank.

Despite these shortcomings, our calculations lead to a simple conclusion. The mean age of new appointees to the Duma remained nearly constant at forty-two throughout the century. In the years of

17. S. V. Rozhdestvenskii, *Sluzhiloe zemlevladenie v Moskovskom gosudarstve XVI veka*, St. Petersburg, 1897, pp. 297–98; V. O. Kliuchevskii, *Boiarskaia Duma drevnei Rusi*, Moscow, 1909, p. 392.

1653	1670	1678	1696
N. I. Romanov	M. Ia. Cherkasskii	I. A. Vorotynskii	M. Ia. Cherkasskii
B. I. Morozov	P. M. Saltykov	P. M. Saltykov	L. K. Naryshkin
Ia. K. Cherkasskii	Iu. A. Dolgorukii	Ia. N. Odoevskii	Ia. N. Odoevskii
I. D. Miloslavskii	Ia. N. Odoevskii	G. S. Kurakin	A. S. Shein
I. V. Morozov	A. S. Shein	P. V. Sheremetev	M. A. Cherkasskii
G. I. Morozov	R. M. Streshnev	I. B. Troekurov	F. D. Saltykov
N. I. Odoevskii	Iu. P. Trubetskoi	I. A. Golitsyn II	M. G. Romodanovskii
M. M. Saltykov	I. B. Miloslavskii	N. I. Odoevskii	I. B. Troekurov
L. S. Streshnev	M. S. Pushkin	I. B. Repnin	S. I. Saltykov
V. I. Streshnev	M. I. Morozov	F. F. Kurakin	A. I. Golitsyn

Patriarch Filaret's ascendancy, 1620–33, new members were slightly older—forty-six on the average. This figure provides further evidence that his government proceeded with extreme caution in making appointments to the council.[18] As the mean suggests, more than half of its members (53 percent) reached the Duma in early middle age, that is between thirty-five and forty-nine. The promotion of the very young was uncommon until the regency period, 1676–89, when 19 percent of the new appointees were under thirty. By the same token, few men reached the Duma after sixty. Only under Filaret was a significant proportion (24 percent) of the new recruits so old.

On the average, men entered the different Duma ranks at different ages. New boyars were, as a rule, younger than *okol'nichie* and new *dumnye dvoriane* were oldest of all. These figures are not surprising. They suggest that members of aristocratic families who entered the Duma as boyars could reach the top of the Muscovite hierarchy more quickly than those who had to work their way up the ladder of service

18. "Reconstitution," p. 197.

Robert O. Crummey

TABLE III-5

Ten Wealthiest Families in Russia

	1613ᵃ		1638		1647	
1	Mstislavskii	32,606	Romanov	3,473	Morozov	10,213
2	Trubetskoi	19,172	Cherkasskii	3,031	Romanov	7,012
3	Sheremetev	15,586	Sheremetev	2,417	Cherkasskii	5,173
4	Cherkasskii	9,975	Pozharskii	1,449	Streshnev	3,895
5	Vorotynskii	7,265	Streshnev	1,430	Sheremetev	3,446
6	Sitskii	6,800	Saltykov	1,013	Saltykov	2,736
7	Kurakin	6,410	Morozov	999	Odoevskii	1,728
8	Morozov	6,051	Lykov	829	Kurakin	1,297
9	Romanov	5,074	Golitsyn	819	Trubetskoi	1,104
10	Odoevskii	4,842	L'vov	738	Golitsyn	880

SOURCE: See footnote 15.

NOTE: For the sake of consistency, the figures include only the lands of family members who served in the Duma.

a. 1613 figures in *chetverti*, all others in peasant households.

without the aura of a great name or the support of a powerful clan.[19]

As we have shown, then, Duma members were usually men in the prime of life who had at least twenty years of experience in service.

Noble officials were a special group of servitors, men who held chancery office, yet performed other functions as well. Before we examine the different ways and circumstances in which they served, we should look at the service careers of the whole boyar elite of which they were members. To begin with, we will discuss their working lives before they received Duma rank.

Throughout the middle ages, the Russian nobility was a warrior caste. In the seventeenth century, most nobles remained military men.

19. The estimated average age at the time of appointment to the Duma was thirty-eight for boyars, forty-three for *okol'nichie*, and forty-five for *dumnye dvoriane*.

For a discussion of which families' members entered the Duma at the rank of boyar, see V. O. Kliuchevskii, *Boiarskaia Duma*, pp. 392–94. Kliuchevskii's main source was G. Kotoshikhin, *O Rossii v tsarstvovanie Alekseia Mikhailovicha*, St. Petersburg, 1906, p. 23.

1653		1670		1678		1696	
Morozov	11,636	Cherkasskii	6,730	Odoevskii	4,248	Cherkasskii	9,083
Romanov	7,689	Saltykov	2,606	Golitsyn	3,541	Naryshkin	8,049
Cherkasskii	6,790	Odoevskii	2,501	Saltykov	3,019	Saltykov	5,103
L'vov	3,172	Dolgorukii	2,259	Kurakin	2,828	Prozorovskii	3,833
Streshnev	3,116	Shein	1,100	Dolgorukii	2,733	Sheremetev	2,312
Saltykov	3,066	Khovanskii	934	Sheremetev	2,106	Odoevskii	2,185
Odoevskii	1,934	Miloslavskii	877	Troekurov	1,551	Shein	1,889
Kurakin	1,802	Streshnev	855	Romodanovskii	1,411	Lopukhin	1,835
Trubetskoi	1,490	Buturlin	808	Repnin	1,336	Golitsyn	1,518
Repnin	1,234	Trubetskoi	755	Streshnev	1,074	Miloslavskii	1,513

Table 6 illustrates the importance of military service in the early careers of future Duma members. Over the course of the century, over half served their apprenticeship exclusively in the army or the provincial administration which, in the seventeenth century, was basically an extension of the military. Another 21 percent were noble officials, serving in a combination of military and civilian capacities. Almost all men in this group were military servitors who also received posts in the chanceries. As we might expect, a background of military service was most common during the Time of Troubles, in the years around the war for Smolensk, and at the height of the Polish War. Even in times of peace, however, a majority of future Duma members spent at least part of their apprenticeship in military service.

Moreover, we should note, in a period of rapid change in military technology, almost all future Duma members served in the old-fashioned noble cavalry units. A handful—thirteen to be exact—rose from obscurity thanks to their service in units of other types. Of these, however, eight made their mark as commanders of the *strel'tsy*, the

TABLE III-6

Nature of Service before Promotion to the Duma

		1613–19 N = 48	1620–33 N = 17	1634–44 N = 26	1645–58 N = 87	1659–66 N = 27	1667–75 N = 31	1676–89 N = 191	Total N = 427
Military	N =	36	10	8	54	13	11	87	219
	%	75	59	31	62	48	35	46	51
Military & bureaucratic	N =	3	3	6	19	6	10	25	72
	%	6	18	23	22	22	32	13	17
Military & diplomatic	N =	2	1	3	3	2	0	6	17
	%	4	6	12	3	7		3	4
Bureaucratic	N =	3	2	4	2	2	2	14	29
	%	6	12	15	2	7	6	7	7
Diplomatic	N =	1	0	0	0	1	0	2	4
	%	2				4		1	1
Bureaucratic & diplomatic	N =	2	1	2	1	0	4	7	17
	%	4	6	8	1		13	4	4
Court official	N =	0	0	1	4	0	2	9	16
	%			4	5		6	5	4
None	N =	1	0	2	4	3	2	40	52
	%	2		8	5	11	6	21	12
Unknown	N =							1	1

SOURCE: See footnote 9.

supposedly obsolete infantry force founded in the sixteenth century. Only five rose to the Duma thanks to serving in new-style regiments. The technological wave of the future bore few seventeenth-century servitors to power.[20]

Taking the seventeenth century as a whole, the second most popular type of pre-Duma service was none at all. By that, I mean that 12 percent of all future council members served only in ceremonial functions at court. Their activities kept them close to the tsar and his favorites but gave them no preparation for useful service in later life.[21] We should note, however, that the use of young nobles exclusively as decorations at court functions was primarily an aberration of the late seventeenth century, particularly of the period of succession crisis. In those years, 21 percent of those who reached the Duma had apparently done nothing to justify their promotion.

Mere numbers understate the importance of chancery service in the lives of future Duma members. The pretensions and power of the central chanceries grew throughout the seventeenth century and drew the most powerful men of the time into administrative office.

Chancery officials bound for the Duma fall into two categories. First, there were the career officials. Seven percent of future council members served only in bureaucratic office and another 4 percent combined that activity with diplomacy. Those in the latter category were usually officials who carried on negotiations while simultaneously serving in a chancery other than the *Posol'skii prikaz* (Foreign Office). Even the combined figure of almost 11 percent seriously understates the importance of the chancery officials as a group. The discrepancy reminds us that the members of the Duma formed a social club as well as a governing elite.

Until the very end of the century, roughly the same number of outstanding career officials won promotion to the Duma in each decade. The reason is clear. Certain offices, particularly the directorships of the *Posol'skii* and *Razriadnyi* (Military Records) *prikazy*, automatically entailed membership in the royal council. Other officials like the head

20. The eight men who won advancement largely because they commanded *strel'tsy* were M. P. Kolupaev, A. N. Lopukhin, the two P. A. Lopukhins, A. S. Matveev, V. L. Pushechnikov, Ia. P. Solovtsov, and V. M. Tiapkin. The five who rose primarily through new style units were F. A. and F. T. Zykov, F. P. Naryshkin, A. A. Shepelev, and G. F. Tarbeev.

21. See N. N. Danilov's comments on V. V. Golitsyn's lack of practical experience in N. N. [Danilov], "V. V. Golicyn bis zum Staatsstreich vom Mai 1682," *Jahrbücher für Geschichte Osteuropas* 1 (1936): 10–11, 31.

of the *Pomestnyi prikaz* (Land Grant Chancery) frequently sat in the Duma as well.[22]

The second category of chancery directors was the noble officials, those who came from the warrior nobility and served in the army as well as the administration. Over the course of the century, 21 percent of all future Duma members carried out assignments in both spheres. The proportion of such men is particularly high in the middle decades of the century, especially in the years 1634–44 and 1667–75, periods of peace following major wars.

These noble officials displayed certain distinct characteristics. Almost all of them (97 percent) began their service in the army or at court. As a group, they came from somewhat less distinguished backgrounds than members of the Duma as a whole. As Table 7 shows, fewer of these noble officials came from the aristocratic group of old princely and nontitled families and proportionately more from the Moscow and provincial gentries. Indeed, it was Moscow nobles who made up the largest single contingent in the group.

When these noble officials reached the Duma, they normally (94 percent) entered at one of the top three ranks. On their way there, roughly 60 percent performed only one chancery function in a career spent mostly as a soldier or courtier: a quarter of them served in two *prikazy* and 15 percent in three or more. The offices that they held were significant, but not normally the most important in the Muscovite administrative system. To be sure, over half of them (64 percent) served as director of at least one chancery, but these were usually less important ones, while Duma members ran the most vital branches of the administration.

These officials served in the chanceries at different stages of their careers. About 40 percent moved back and forth between military and civil functions before reaching Duma rank; the other 60 percent served first in military, then in civil posts before their promotion. Most of the latter received only one posting to a chancery just before entering the Duma. A few, like G. S. Dokhturov, however, came from a noble background but spent the greater part of their careers in chancery service.[23]

While Duma members, these noble officials pursued widely differing careers. The great majority of them continued to serve, at least occasionally, in chanceries after they reached the Duma. Almost 35

22. See Bogoiavlenskii, *Sud'i*, pp. 119–31, 144–49.
23. Ibid., pp. 26, 34, 85, 91, 116, 119, 123–24, 130, 148, 166, 224; Barsukov, *Spiski*, p. 204; DR, 2: 681, 3:152; Supplement to Vol. 3, pp. 61, 128, 174, 247, 351, 380.

TABLE III-7

Social Origin of Men Performing
Both Military and Chancery Service
before Promotion to the Duma

			Social Origin of All Duma Members
Old Princes	N =	10	
	%	15	26
Old nontitled	N =	16	
	%	24	20
Total aristocratic element	%	39	46
New princes	N =	5	
	%	7	10
Moscow gentry	N =	25	
	%	37	31
Provincial gentry	N =	8	
	%	12	7
Merchants	N =	0	
	%		1
Chancery family	N =	4	
	%	6	4
Unknown	N =	4	
Total	N =	72	

SOURCE: See footnote 9.

percent served only in the chanceries and another 35 percent continued to combine military and civil functions. About 14 percent reverted to exclusively military service. Most of the remaining members of the group performed no service at all outside of formal court functions once they reached the Duma.

For a broader perspective on the relation between military and chancery service in the lives of the Muscovite elite, we should examine the activities of all Duma members. Table 8 shows, above all, that council members were much more likely to serve in the chanceries than men who had not yet reached that rank. The largest group of Duma members (36 percent) combined military and chancery service. Another 18 percent worked only in administrative offices. As the century passed, moreover, proportionately more men performed bureaucratic, and slightly fewer, mixed service. In contrast, over the century, roughly one-fifth of the Duma's members received only military assignments.

In the years of succession crisis, we can see one further change in the service patterns of Duma members. For most of the period, less than 10 percent performed no service at all outside the court, but, in the years after 1676, the proportion of idle Duma members rose to a staggering 31 percent. Some of these men, to be sure, had, in effect, retired after long and useful careers. Many, however, were the relatives or partisans of the ruling favorites and spent all of their time in attendance on the tsar. The palace in Moscow bore a vague resemblance to Versailles. In the Russian case, however, it is hard to see the advantage of turning nobles into courtiers in the worst sense of the word. There was no need to imprison Russian nobles in a gilded cage: for well over a century, their economic weaknesses and lack of alternative careers had bound them in service to the tsars.

As Table 8 shows, 250 Duma members or nearly 59 percent performed chancery service. Of these, 22 or roughly one in eleven were career administrative specialists who rarely, if ever, served outside the central chanceries. These men were the cream of the chancery officials described in Borivoj Plavsic's article. The remaining 228 were noble officials, men from the traditional military elite who nevertheless served in the chanceries. Of these in turn, 55 or about one-quarter served only in administrative office while Duma members. Most of the rest combined military and chancery service.

Two aspects of the noble officials' backgrounds deserve attention. First, pre-Duma careers of the noble officials as a group are remarkably similar to those of Duma members as a whole. As Table 9 shows, however, among the noble officials there were sharp divisions between those who, as Duma members, combined military and chancery service and those who served only in chanceries. The former were more likely to have served only in the army on their way to the Duma than either noble officials or council members in general. By way of contrast, the latter were more likely to have combined military and bureaucratic service or served only at court on their way to the top. Put briefly, exclusively military service most often led to mixed service, and mixed most often led to exclusively chancery functions.

TABLE III-8

Nature of Service while Duma Member

		1613–19 N = 48	1620–33 N = 17	1634–44 N = 26	1645–58 N = 87	1659–66 N = 27	1667–75 N = 31	1676–89 N = 191	Total N = 427
Military	N =	9	2	2	18	5	7	39	82
	%	19	12	8	21	19	23	20	19
Military & bureaucratic	N =	27	6	14	40	14	11	41	153
	%	56	35	54	46	52	35	21	36
Military & diplomatic	N =	0	0	0	4	0	1	4	9
	%				5		3	2	2
Bureaucratic	N =	6	2	4	12	4	7	42	77
	%	13	12	15	14	15	23	22	18
Diplomatic	N =	1	0	0	1	1	0	1	4
	%	2			1	4		1	1
Bureaucratic & diplomatic	N =	0	6	3	5	1	3	2	20
	%		35	12	6	4	10	1	5
Court official	N =	0	0	1	0	0	1	2	4
	%			4			3	1	1
None	N =	5	1	2	7	2	1	60	78
	%	10	6	8	8	7	3	31	18

SOURCE: See footnote 9.

Robert O. Crummey

TABLE III-9

Noble Officials' Pre-Duma Service

		Men Serving in Army & Chancery while in Duma N = 154	Men Serving in Chancery Only while in Duma N = 54	Total of Both Groups N = 208	Entire Duma Membership
Military	N =	93	19	112	
	%	60	35	54	51
Military & bureaucratic	N =	24	21	45	
	%	16	39	22	17
Military & diplomatic	N =	7	2	9	
	%	5	4	3	4
Bureaucratic	N =	8	2	10	
	%	5	4	5	7
Bureaucratic & diplomatic	N =	3	0	3	
	%	2		1	4
Diplomatic	N =	2	1	3	
	%	1	2	1	1
Court	N =	2	4	6	
	%	1	7	3	4
None	N =	15	5	20	
	%	10	9	10	12

SOURCE: See footnote 9.

Secondly, the social origin and standing of the noble officials also distinguished them from Duma members as a whole. Taken as a group, the noble officials were more likely to come from aristocratic backgrounds than Duma members, as Table 10 illustrates. About 52 percent of the noble officials were aristocrats in comparison with 46 percent of all Duma members. The most startling contrast appears when we compare the origins of noble officials who mixed army and chancery service with those who performed only bureaucratic functions while in the Duma. The latter were, as a group, far less aristocratic (34 percent) than the Duma members taken together; more than half of them had risen from the Moscow gentry. By contrast, 59 percent of the noble officials who performed mixed service came from aristocratic families.

The careers of our noble officials most frequently took one of four paths. Many began service with an apprenticeship in the army alone. Once in the Duma, however, they combined military and chancery

TABLE III-10

Social Origin of Noble Officials in the Duma

		Men Serving in Army & Chancery N = 154	Men Serving in Chancery Only N = 54	Total of Both Groups N = 208	Entire Duma Membership
Old princes	N =	54	9	63	
	%	36	18	31	26
Old nontitled	N =	34	8	42	
	%	23	16	21	20
Total aristocratic element	%	59	34	52	46
New princes	N =	22	2	24	
	%	15	4	12	10
Moscow gentry	N =	35	26	61	
	%	23	51	31	31
Provincial gentry	N =	5	3	8	
	%	3	6	4	7
Chancery officials	N =	0	3	3	
	%		6	2	4
Other	%				2
Unknown	N =	4	3	7	

SOURCE: See footnote 9.

service. Prince Iu. A. Dolgorukii is a case in point. A distinguished lineage and marriage to a member of the powerful Morozov family undoubtedly helped him to reach boyar rank at an unusually early age, about thirty. Before his promotion, he served only at court and in the army guarding the southern frontier. In more than three decades in the Duma, Dolgorukii served in many capacities. At one time or another, he directed ten different chanceries, including several of considerable importance. For several years in the 1650s, he was head of the *Pushkarskii prikaz* (Artillery Chancery) which organized the artillery and, beginning in 1663, he directed the Kazan' Office that administered the conquered lands of the former Khanate. In the years between, from 1658 to 1660, he twice commanded the Russian army on the Lithuanian front and served a stint on the southern frontier as well. At the beginning of the 1660s, moreover, he conducted negotiations with ambassadors from Sweden. At the height of his career, then, he was a jack-of-all-trades. Yet, chancery service remained an important part of his public life and, in one sense, caused his death. As head of the *Streletskii prikaz* (Musketeers' Chancery), he was lynched by the mutinous Moscow garrison under his command.[24]

In the second pattern, a noble official combined military and chancery service in all stages of his career. V. S. Volynskii needed roughly ten years more than Dolgorukii to reach the Duma. Along the way he served as governor of the military outpost on the Terek River just north of the Caucasus. On the eve of his promotion to the Duma, he served in the *Razboinyi prikaz* (Brigandage Chancery), the office charged with stamping out brigandage. He continued to carry on a wide variety of functions during his twenty-five years in the Duma. He served on the Polish front and did another stint in the south as governor of Astrakhan'. Some of his most important assignments were diplomatic: he headed the Russian delegation that negotiated the Treaty of Kardis with Sweden and he later discussed the prospects for a full peace treaty with Poland. In addition to his other commitments, he served in important chancery positions. He headed the *Chelobitnyi prikaz* (Petitions Chancery) in the early 1660s, returned to *Razboinyi prikaz* in the late 1660s and 1670s and, at the end of his career, directed the *Posol'skii prikaz* and served in the Great Treasury as well.[25]

The third path led from exclusively military to exclusively chancery service. Prince P. F. Volkonskii spent most of his career at court and in a succession of military commands and provincial posts of secondary importance. In his brief time in the Duma, however, he served outside the court in only one capacity—as head of the Petitions Chancery.[26]

In the last pattern, the Duma member in question served only in the chanceries after a career in both the central administration and the army. G. B. Nashchokin reached Duma rank near the end of a long and interesting life. At the end of the 1640s, between court and military functions, he served a brief stint in the Vladimir Judicial Chancery. Later, after service in the Polish Wars, he returned to chancery service in the *Kholopii prikaz* (Bondage Chancery). Then, in 1662, he went to

24. Bogoiavlenskii, *Sud'i*, pp. 44–45, 64–65, 136–37, 167, 195, 196, 201, 202: DR, 2: 368, 3: 3, 45, 941; Supp. to Vol. 3, pp. 132, 192, 223; AMG, 2: 612–16; 3: 119, 163–71: *Dopolneniia k Aktam Istoricheskim, sobrannym i izdannym Arkheograficheskoiu Komissieiu*, 12 vols., St. Petersburg, 1846–75, 10: 23–25 (hereafter DAI).

25. Bogoiavlenskii, *Sud'i*, pp. 28, 130, 141–43, 195–96, 220; DR, Supp. to Vol. 3, pp. 231, 286; AMG 2:620, 3: 525–26; *Akty Istoricheskie, sobrannye i izdannye Arkheograficheskoiu Komissieiu*, 5 vols., St. Petersburg, 1841–42, 4: 184, 292; *Pamiatniki diplomaticheskikh snoshenii drevnei Rossii s derzhavami inostrannymi. . .* , 10 vols., St. Petersburg, 1851–71, 6: 1048–49, 1123–24 (hereafter PDS).

26. Bogoiavlenskii, *Sud'i*, p. 219; DR, 2: 392, 588, 602, 625, 661.

Denmark as Russian ambassador and, on his return, took over the direction of the *Iamskoi prikaz* (Post Chancery). After his promotion to the rank of *dumnyi dvorianin*, he worked exclusively in this last capacity.[27]

The description of these four careers leads to several general observations. First of all, each man moved back and forth between military and chancery service. Indeed, the main difference between the careers of Dolgorukii, Volynskii, and Nashchokin lies in the time at which each received Duma rank. More distinguished social origins and better family connections brought the two former men into the Duma far earlier in their careers than Nashchokin, who worked his way up from the lower ranks of the court nobility.

Secondly, the surviving evidence gives few indications that any of these men had special talent or training for chancery service. Contemporaries apparently thought of Dolgorukii primarily as a military man.[28] His strength in this area may account for his postings to the Artillery and Musketeers (*Streletskii*) Chanceries and perhaps even his work in the Kazan' Office. It is impossible, however, to explain his other offices and those of Volynskii, Volkonskii, and Nashchokin on functional grounds. For all we know, the administration would have worked just as well if they had served in entirely different capacities.

Thirdly, these careers suggest that, toward the end of their working lives, noble officials tended to serve mainly in the chanceries. A job in the comparative comfort of Moscow was fitting pasture for an old war horse.

Noble officials' chancery service took a wide variety of forms. In this paper, we can only examine a few of the most common. The most imposing figures of the seventeenth-century administration were the royal favorites who occupied a position like that of prime minister. As I have pointed out elsewhere, men like B. I. Morozov built their power on a foundation of several chancery offices carefully chosen to provide income, control over military forces, and regular access to the tsar's person.[29] Later in the century, favorites like A. S. Matveev and V. V. Golitsyn made the directorship of the Foreign Office the central support of their position.[30] In so doing, they broke the tradition that

27. Bogoiavlenskii, *Sud'i*, pp. 173, 206–7, 225; DR, 3:210, 417, 427; Supp. to Vol. 3, p. 313.

28. See, for example, Meyerberg's comment in his "Puteshestvie v Moskoviiu . . . ," ChOIDR, 1873, 3:73–74.

29. "Reconstitution," p. 205.

30. On Matveev, Bogoiavlenskii, *Sud'i*, pp. 15–16, 130, 195; DR, Supp. to Vol. 3, p. 1411; DAI, 6: 101; A. I. Zaozerskii, *Tsarskaia votchina XVII v.*, Moscow, 1937, pp.

the *Posol'skii* and *Razriadnyi prikazy* remain the exclusive province of career administrators and be closed to noble officials.

On a less exalted plane, some men served only in chanceries like the Gold and Silver Offices and the Tsaritsa's Workshop, which provided for the court. This was true, for example, of favorites like I. M. Iazykov.[31] Such men occupied a position very similar to those who performed only ceremonial functions at court.

A number of noble officials, like Volkonskii, served for many years in only one chancery. F. K. Elizarov put in twenty years in the *Pomestnyi prikaz*, his only office.[32] N. M. Boborykin worked only in the *Bol'shoi prikhod* (Great Income) and a subsidiary.[33] At the other extreme there were those who served only briefly in one chancery. Such men were particularly likely to receive their assignment in the judicial chanceries, the Petitions Chancery, the offices supplying the court, or in what Bogoiavlenskii calls the *Sysknye prikazy* (investigative chanceries).

Finally, many noble officials held several offices at different times. Nashchokin's career is a good example. The pattern was extremely common: to refer only to the letter *A* on the list of Duma members, I. V. Alfer'ev held two very brief chancery appointments and G. M. Anichkov, a more substantial figure, served consecutively in the Great Court Chancery, the Court Judicial Chancery, and the *Novaia Chet'*, a revenue collecting agency.[34]

As a distinct type of servitor, the noble official emerged in the seventeenth century. As we have observed, more than half of the members of the Boyar Duma who were not specialists in bureaucratic techniques held chancery office at some time in their careers. Given their lack of special training, it is likely that, in most cases, their subordinates in the chancery did the routine work. Yet the fact remains that these prominent men moved into top positions in the central administration. The most important question is why. In particular, why did the change take place in the seventeenth century?

It is not hard to imagine why chancery service appealed to the most prominent Russian nobles. As I have suggested elsewhere, administrative office gave the holder income in the form of fees and bribes, com-

---

285–86. On Golitsyn, see Bogoiavlenskii, *Sud'i*, pp. 58–59, 130–31, 137–38; DR, 4: 357; PDS, 6:1030; N. N. Danilov, "Vasilii Vasil'evic Golicyn (1682–1714)," *Jahrbücher für Geschichte Osteuropas* 2 (1937): 556.

31. Bogoiavlenskii, *Sud'i*, pp. 53, 98, 215.

32. Ibid., pp. 122–23.

33. Ibid., pp. 34–35, 44.

34. Ibid., pp. 20, 43, 91, 178, 184.

mand of a body of scribes or soldiers, and opportunities for building networks of clients. For men of a traditional military caste, moreover, serving in an office in Moscow near the court was far more comfortable and offered better prospects for advancement than the obvious alternative, life in the army in the field.

What the noble officials had to contribute to the governing of Russia is a more complex issue. First of all, the nature of seventeenth-century politics almost certainly contributed to the emergence of the noble official. For much of the century, the tsars were young or incompetent, and favorites or groups of advisers ruled in their names. Such politicians had a free hand to do whatever was necessary to make themselves wealthier or more powerful. Understandably, they made themselves heads of important chanceries. Administrative office also served as a reward which they could give kinsmen or potential supporters. In that sense, the practice of awarding chancery office to court nobles helped give coherence to a political system that needed it badly.

More significantly, although noble officials had no special training in bureaucratic techniques, they had a distinct contribution to make. In Brenda Meehan-Waters's phrase, their specialty was leadership. In the seventeenth century, the Russian administration system grew very rapidly. The number both of officials and of chanceries increased sharply. In this situation, the tsars' government needed many new administrators. As is well known, Muscovite Russia's urban population was too small and poorly developed to fill the need. The government had no choice but to turn to the nobility. The most valuable recruits were those who entered the chanceries young, learned the routine of work on the job, and stayed for life. But even the noble officials who lacked such training could make a contribution. They were accustomed to positions of command. Moreover, they gave the chancery milieu a higher social tone and, in their persons, connected it with the Boyar Duma, the court, and the rest of the nobility, still the mainstay of the army.

The best proof of noble officials' usefulness is the attitude of Peter the Great, a ruler whose power and strength of character allowed him to treat the nobility as he liked. Peter looked to the nobles to lead the administration as well as the army. He encouraged many of its most prominent representatives to serve both in the field and in the chancery. By continuing seventeenth-century practices in a new institutional and cultural setting, Peter guaranteed that the noble official had come to stay for another two centuries.

CHAPTER FOUR

SOCIAL AND CAREER CHARACTERISTICS OF THE ADMINISTRATIVE ELITE, 1689–1761

Brenda Meehan-Waters

The territorial expansion of the Russian Empire continued throughout the eighteenth century, putting new demands on the state apparatus and expanding career opportunities for state servants. Peter the Great was primarily concerned with the mobilization of the state's resources for war, and because of this he not only introduced new technology and many aspects of Western social life but he also eliminated the traditional boundaries that had tended to separate civil and military careers. The landlord-warriors were made full-time officials, including the elite group that Meehan-Waters studies. For them a civil post might be a welcome respite from military service, but it was also the fulfillment of an essential task for the state. Still, at the sub-elite and chancery levels (such as those discussed earlier by Plavsic) the civil career remained clearly separate from the military one.

Peter the Great was also responsible for the first serious attempts to train elite officials for high-level state service. These efforts did not have a lasting impact on the civil side, but the elite schools for military officers established by Peter's immediate successors were to give great prestige and cohesion—and to confer career advantages—for those privileged few who could gain admittance to them. Peter also introduced a uniform system of ranking higher- and middle-level servants of the state through his famous Table of Ranks. In establishing a systematic and interchangeable hierarchy of civil, army, naval, and court ranks, Peter introduced Russian elite officialdom to one of the pillars of bureaucratic organization—uniform ranking and definition of career development, chinoproizvodstvo. While the steps that must be taken to achieve advancement had been relatively clear for the lower ranks in the seventeenth and eighteenth centuries, elite advancement and office procurement were—and would continue to be—subject to noninstitutional influences well beyond the control of the administration. These influences included factors with which we are now familiar: family and clan connections, and even the whim of the already powerful, including the tsar himself. Still, the principle of chinoproizvodstvo, or uniform career development, was now the law, even for the most exalted officials of the civil and military hierarchies. As time passed, *the procedure for progression through the ranks would be refined, clarifying and stabilizing the "rules" for success as a civil official even at the elite level of government. Meehan-Waters makes it abundantly clear that at first the impact of this system of* chinoproizvodstvo *was limited. Orlovsky, in Chapter Ten will show, moreover, that well into the nineteenth century, the law was circumvented, or bent. Still, with time and with the growth of the administrative apparatus, regularity and predictability became the rule rather than the exception for official careers, as Bennett (Chapter Seven) and others show. Among other consequences, the rules of* chinoproizvodstvo *would limit the arbitrariness of choice about who would serve and what his compensation would be; in addition it would limit the impact of other selection factors for the elite, including, especially, the genetic, the political, and the social. With the introduction of* chinoproizvodstvo *to the official elite, Russian politics was beginning to be bureaucratized.* [THE EDITORS.]

State-building is an act of aggression. It combines the conquest of new territories with the conquest of new spheres of governmental responsibility. Geographically, it expands boundaries and secures borders; administratively, it commits the government to promote actively the general good through an increased regulation of the social, economic, and political lives of its citizens. The creation of a modern state requires the assertion of sovereignty abroad and of preemptive rights at home.

In both these senses, Peter the Great (1689–1725) accelerated the development of the Russian state. Under his leadership, Russia emerged as a major military and political power in Europe. Faced with Russia's victory over Sweden, conquest of the Baltic territory, and serious inroads into Turkish domain, European monarchs begrudgingly began to recognize the Muscovite tsar's claim to the title of emperor of Russia. Domestically, Peter shaped the imperial state through the definition of new ends of government and the creation of new forms for achieving these ends.

Committed and competent personnel were essential in the process of state-building as they would be in the later stabilization and maintenance of the autocracy. The pivotal Petrine decree shaping the structure of the Imperial bureaucracy was the Table of Ranks of 1722, which created a parallel set of hierarchical offices for military, civil and court service, ranging from the fourteenth rank, the lowest, to the first rank at the apex. All officials, regardless of lineage, were to work their way up through the ranks. Commissioned officers in the military (ranks fourteen and above) were recognized as noblemen, as were sons born after their fathers' attainment of the necessary rank. All officials holding offices in one of the top eight ranks, whether military, civil, or court, became hereditary nobles.[1]

This essay focuses on the top echelon of state personnel, those officials holding the highest four military and civil ranks within the structure of the Table of Ranks. It begins with a list of the so-called *generalitet* (the 179 officials in the top four military and civil ranks) in the year 1730. The list is lean, giving in most cases only the name of the official and his service title (*chin*) in January of 1730.[2] Sometimes the office (*dolzhnost'*) of the official is indicated; occasionally the year of birth and/or death is noted. The paucity of information on the social and career backgrounds of the officials makes it a far cry from the rich personnel records (*formuliarnye spiski*) of the late eighteenth and nineteenth centuries. Nevertheless, by supplementing this list with genealogies, family archives, and official government records of service, the social characteristics and individual service careers of the elite have been reconstructed in surprising detail.[3]

1. PSZ I, Vol. 6, No. 3,890.

2. The list of the *generalitet* was edited by M. Longinov, "Russkii Generalitet v nachale 1730 goda," in P. I. Bartenev, ed., *Osmnadtsatyi vek. Istoricheskii sbornik*, Moscow, 1869, 3: 161–77.

3. This essay is part of a work in progress entitled *Autocracy and Aristocracy: The Russian Service Elite, 1689–1761* (New Brunswick: Rutgers University Press, forthcoming). The major sources for this study include: TsGADA, Fonds 286 (Gerol'dmeisterskaia kontora), 1,239 (Saltykov), 1,263 (Golitsyn), 1,272 (Naryshkin), 1,278 (Stroganov), 1,280 (Sukhotin), 1,289 (Shcherbatov), 1,290 (Iusupov), 1,365 (Buturlin), 1,373 (Dolgorukii), 1,386 (Saltykov), 2,105 (Meshcherskii); Gosudarstvennaia biblioteka im. V. I. Lenina. Rukopisnyi otdel, Fond 255 (Rumiantsev); Gosudarstvennyi istoricheskii muzei. Otdel pis'mennykh istochnikov (GIM), Fonds 25 (Apraksin), 170 (Urusov), 274 (Veliaminov); Leningradskoe otdelenie instituta istorii akademii nauk, SSSR (LOII), Fonds 115 (Naumov), 141 (Cherkasskii), 234 (Shuvalov), 238 (Likhachev collection), 259 (Olsuf'ev); Gosudarstvennaia publichnaia biblioteka im. M. E. Saltykova-Shchedrina. Rukopisnyi otdel (GPB), Fond 457 (Makarov); Tsentral'nyi gosudarstvennyi voenno-istoricheskii arkhiv SSSR (TsGVIA), Fonds 54 (Voennaia kollegiia), 105 (Buturlin); *Alfavitnyi ukazatel' familii i lits, upominaemykh v boiarskikh knigakh, khraniashchikhsia v 1-m otdelenii Moskovskogo arkhiva Ministerstva iustitsii s oboznacheniem sluzhebnoi deiatel'nosti kazhdogo litsa i godov sostoianiia v zanimaemykh dolzhnostiakh*, Moscow, 1853; Erik Amburger, *Geschichte der Behördenorganisation Russlands von Peter dem Grossen bis 1917*, Leiden, 1966; I. Andreevskii, *O namestnikakh, voevodakh i gubernatorakh*, St. Petersburg, 1864; A. Barsukov, *Spiski gorodovykh voevod i drugikh lits voevodskago upravleniia moskovskago gosudarstva XVII stoletiia*, St. Petersburg, 1902; V. N. Berkh, *Spiski boiaram, okol'nichim i dumnym dvorianam s 1468 g. do unichtozheniia ikh chinov*, St. Petersburg, 1833; S. K. Bogoiavlenskii, *Prikaznye sud'i XVII veka*, Moscow, 1946; *Dvortsovye razriady*, 4 vols., St. Petersburg, 1850–55; *Razriadnaia kniga, 1475–1598 gg.*, Moscow, 1966; *Razriadnaia kniga, 1550–1605 gg.*, Moscow, 1975; *Razriadnaia kniga, 1559–1605*

Although the list is restricted to the names and service titles of officials in the year 1730, the period under study roughly spans the years between 1689 and 1761, from the reign of Peter I to the eve of Catherine II. The oldest official in the 1730 *generalitet* was born in 1658; the youngest in 1708. There are at least two generations within this elite, a phenomenon illustrated by the fact that six officials in the 1730 *generalitet* had sons also included in that group. Four officials listed in the 1730 roll were actually in retirement, while others continued to serve actively into the 1770s. In order to take advantage of this time dimension, I have divided the elite into four age cohorts in order to study serially service-pattern changes over time.

All the officials studied spent at least part of their service careers under the restless rule of Peter the Great. Most of them held responsible positions, and many of them achieved prominence, during his reign. They were the agents of Petrine transformation even as they themselves were transformed. They fought wars that expanded the borders of Russia, and they negotiated treaties that legitimated the victories of the battlefield and the Russian ruler's aspiration to an imperial title. They subdued the new territories and administered the

---

gg., Moscow, 1974; *Razriadnye knigi, 1598–1638 gg.*, Moscow, 1974; I. E. Zabelin, "Dopolneniia k dvortsovym, razriadam," in *Chteniia v imperatorskom obshchestve istorii i drevnostei Rossiiskikh pri Moskovskom universitete*. Vols. 1 and 3 (1882), and 2 and 4 (1883). The most important genealogies are: A. Bobrinskii, *Dvorianskie rody vnesennye v obshchii gerbovnik vserossiskoi imperii*, 2 vols., St. Petersburg, 1890; P. V. Dolgorukov, *Rossiiskaia rodoslovnaia kniga*, 4 vols., St. Petersburg, 1854–57; R. I. Ermerin, *Annuaire de la noblesse de Russie*, 2 vols., St. Petersburg, 1892; A. B. Lobanov-Rostovskii, *Russkie rodoslovnye knigi*, 2 vols., St. Petersburg, 1895; N. I. Novikov, *Rodoslovnaia kniga kniazei i dvorian rossiiskikh i vyezhikh*, 2 vols., Moscow, 1878; V. V. Rummel, *Rodoslovnyi sbornik russkikh dvorianskikh familii*, 2 vols., St. Petersburg, 1886–87; P. N. Petrov, *Istoriia rodov russkogo dvorianstva*, Vol. 1, St. Petersburg, 1886; L. M. Savelov, *Opyt rodoslovnago slovaria russkago drevniago dvorianstva. Rodoslovnye zapiski*, 3 vols., Moscow, 1906–9; and G. A. Vlas'ev, *Potomstvo Riurika* 2 vols. (Vol. 1 in 3 parts), St. Petersburg, Petrograd, 1906–18. The following articles were also of particular use: Robert O. Crummey, "The Reconstitution of the Boiar Aristocracy, 1613–1645," *Forschungen zur osteuropäischen Geschichte*, 18 (1973): 187–220; and Ia. E. Vodarskii, "Praviashchaia gruppa svetskikh feodalov v Rossii v XVIIv.," in N. I. Pavlenko, ed., *Dvorianstvo i krepostnoi stroi Rossii XVI–XVIIIvv.*, Moscow, 1975, pp. 70–107. Important biographical information is found in: F. Bantysh-Kamenskii, *Biografii rossiiskikh Generalissimusov i General Fel'dmarshalov*, 2 vols., St. Petersburg, 1840; same author's *Slovar' dostopamiatnykh liudei russkoi zemli*, 5 vols., Moscow, 1836; *Entsiklopedicheskii slovar'*, 41 vols. in 82, St. Petersburg, 1891–1904; and *Russkii biograficheskii slovar'*, 25 vols., St. Petersburg, 1896–1918. The data on the *generalitet* drawn from these sources have been coded and computer analyzed; the computer program follows the "Statistical Package for the Social Sciences," explained in N. Nie, *SPSS: Statistical Package for the Social Sciences*, 2nd. ed., New York, 1975.

old, expanding everywhere the burdens of taxation, conscription, and service. They hunted down those who fled the growing power of the state; and they spied upon each other. They jealously sought the privileges and titles of the new order, and they learned to measure their success in terms of ranks earned.

By 1730, all of them had achieved ranks that were the equivalent in the late Petrine service system to the rank of general, hence the collective sobriquet of *generalitet*. Their service titles in that year were distributed as shown in Table 1.[4]

These officials had worked their way to the apex of the Petrine service hierarchy, and occupied the most important offices in the government. They form a collective success story, prompting the curious historian to discover the roots of their success. Our analysis deals with such factors as social origins, kinship ties, serf-ownership, and education in order first to discern the social characteristics of the Russian elite, and second to explore the impact of these characteristics on success in the rank system and on the attainment of key administrative offices.

SOCIAL ORIGINS

The degree to which the expanding state structure of Petrine Russia created opportunities for social mobility for those of lower origin recently has become a subject of intensive investigation. In his exhaustive study of the impact of the Petrine Table of Ranks on the civil bureaucracy, the late Soviet historian S. M. Troitskii found the social composition of the bureaucracy at mid-eighteenth century to take the pyramidal lines shown in Table 2.[5]

Taken as a whole, only 22 percent of the 5,379 officials studied were of noble origin (*sluzhilye liudi po otechestvu*). However, it should be noted that over half of the group studied were *kantseliaristy* (clerks) (Category IV), i.e. chancellery bureaucrats whose positions placed them below the Table of Ranks. If one were to limit the analysis to those holding positions within the Table of Ranks (Troitskii's first three categories), the ratio of officials of noble origin to those of non-noble origin is virtually equal (1,022:1,029). At the elite level, 88 percent of higher civil officials were of noble origin. Although Troitskii

---

4. M. Longinov, "Russkii Generalitet v nachale 1730 goda," pp. 161–71.

5. S. M. Troitskii, *Russkii absoliutizm i dvorianstvo v XVIII v. Formirovanie biurokratii*, Moscow, 1974, p. 215.

TABLE IV-1

Distribution of Service Titles among the *Generalitet*, 1730

Rank	Service Title *(Chin)*	Number	%
I	field marshal (*Fel'dmarshal*)	5	3
II	general (full) (*general-anshef*)	8	4
III	lieutenant-general (*general-leitenant*)	25	14
IV	major-general (*general-maior*)	63	35
I	chancellor (*kantsler*)	1	1
II	actual privy councillor (*deistvitel'nyi tainyi sovetnik*)	8	4
III	privy councillor (*tainyi sovetnik*)	18	10
IV	actual state councillor (*deistvitel'nyi statskii sovetnik*)	37	21
II	admiral	2	1
III	vice-admiral (*vits-admiral*)	3	2
IV	rear-admiral (*kontr-admiral*)	2	1
	None [a]	7	4
	Total	179	100

SOURCE: See note 4.

a. Had held *generalitet* rank but stripped of rank before 1730.

Brenda Meehan-Waters

TABLE IV-2

Social Origin of Central and Provincial Officials

Category	Total Number Studied	Of Noble Origin		Of Nonnoble Origin	
		N =	%	N =	%
I (Ranks 1–5)	145	127	88	18	12
II (Ranks 6–8)	562	432	77	130	23
III (Ranks 9–14)	1,344	463	34	881	66
IV (Offices below Table of Ranks)	3,328	138	4	3,190	96
Total	5,379	1,160	22	4,219	78

SOURCE: See note 5.

gave information on the social groups composing the non-noble elements of the officials he studied, he did not give a breakdown of the groups encompassed under his general rubric, "of noble origin."

The 1730 elite group enables us to study in detail the origins of top officials in both military and civil ranks. My procedure is that throughout this study the social origin of a Russian official is determined by the known service position of his father. Where this is unknown, the official's origins are listed as unknown, even though his family name might be included among *sluzhilye liudi po otechestvu* in the Muscovite service records of the seventeenth century. This cautious norm for determining social origins thus underestimates the number of officials whose fathers were nobles.[6]

6. The category of unknown means either that the father is unknown or that the service position of the father is unknown. For detailed information on the beginning and highest service positions of the fathers and grandfathers of the Russians in the *generalitet*, see B. Meehan-Waters, "The Muscovite Noble Origins of the Russians in the Generalitet of 1730," *Cahiers du Monde Russe et Soviétique*, 12 (1970): 42–75. However,

The Muscovite nobility (*sluzhilye liudi po otechestvu*) was a hetero-geneous group, based on service and functioning within a distinct hierarchy of ranks or *chiny* similar to the Petrine Table of Ranks. There were three sets of these hierarchies: the duma ranks, the Moscow ranks, and the provincial ranks.[7] In categorizing the social origins of the Russians in the 1730 elite, I have used roughly comparable terms: boyar elite, Moscow gentry, and provincial gentry. An official is con-sidered part of the boyar elite if his father (or grandfather) sat in the powerful Boyar Duma in the seventeenth century, before the acces-sion of Peter I in 1689. (Such officials are the descendants of the boyar elite analyzed by Robert Crummey; their relative weight in the 1730 group, and the extent of their control of key institutions is a good index of the extent to which the elite of Moscow continued to domi-nate top positions in the Petrine system.) Those officials whose fathers held the ranks of *stol'nik* or *stripachii* are labelled Moscow gentry; together with the boyar elite, they formed the upper service class of the Muscovite state in contrast with the less prestigious and more populous provincial gentry.[8]

The social origins of the 1730 elite cluster are shown in Table 3. Although foreigners comprise 30 percent of the top officials, their role in Russian political life was circumscribed. Over 40 percent of the foreigners had a known expertise (whether technical, military, or legal) compared with less than 30 percent of the Russians. The pri-mary role of a foreigner—be he a civil or military expert—was to instruct Russians in needed skills. Heinrich von Fick, an expert on jurisprudence and on the Swedish collegial system, had the formidable task of restructuring the central government departments into a col-legial system appropriate to Russia's needs. The bylaws that Fick helped to draft for the new colleges clearly placed non-Russians in a subservient position. Foreigners were prohibited from serving as president of a college.[9] By a decree of 19 March 1719, foreigners

---

some of the data in this article is in need of revision as a result of further archival and genealogical research. For example, at the time of writing the *Cahiers* article, I was unable to identify the fathers of forty-two of the Russians in the *generalitet*; this number has been reduced to twenty-nine.

7. N. P. Pavlov-Silvanskii, *Gosudarevy sluzhilye liudi*, St. Petersburg, 1909. For an extended discussion of the definition of Muscovite nobility, see my review of Troitskii's *Russkii absoliutizm* in *Kritika: A Review of Current Soviet Books on Russian History*, 12, No. 1 (1976): 26–41.

8. Richard Hellie, *Enserfment and Military Change in Muscovy*, Chicago, 1971, pp. 22–24.

9. PSZ I, Vol. 5, Nos. 3,133 and 3,202.

TABLE IV-3

Social Origin of the 1730 Elite

	N =	%
Russians		
Muscovite nobility		
Boyar elite	47	26
Moscow gentry	38	22
Nonnobles	11	6
Unknown	29	16
Total	125	70
Foreigners		
Born in Russia	3	2
Other	51	28
Total	54	30

SOURCE: See note 3.

serving in the College of State Revenues (*Kamer-kollegiia*) and the College of State Expenses (*Shtats-kontora*) could not be privy to detailed reports on the state budget. As foreigners, the vice-presidents of the colleges had to be chosen by the Senate, and were required to take a special oath of loyalty. In August of that year, all foreigners serving in the colleges fell under these rules. Their required oath pledged "life-long service, equal to a native and true slave and subject."[10]

EDUCATION, SOCIALIZATION, AND THE GUARDS

The imperial state expected a lifetime of service from its officials, whether native or foreign. For Russians compulsory service began early. In order to prepare Russians for effective service to that state, in

10. D. Polenov, "O prisiage inozemtsev, prinatnykh v russkuiu sluzhbu pri Petre Velikom," *Russkii arkhiv* (1862), No. 2: 1,734.

1714 Peter I made education (mathematics, geometry, and grammar) mandatory for young nobles between the ages of ten and fifteen.[11] Though most of the officials in the 1730 elite group were born too early to be affected by the decree of 1714, many of them had nevertheless been trained and educated at Peter's insistence before then. Thirty-one of the Russians in the elite group had studied abroad, while two had matriculated in Russian higher educational institutions, making a total of 26 percent of the Russians in the 1730 elite group who had formal education.

Many Russians in the elite group, particularly young aristocrats, began service at court. Several of them were companions of the young Tsar Peter and soon found themselves enrolled in the *Poteshnye*, the cadet regiments of Peter's youth.

Technically co-tsar with his half-brother Ivan from 1682, Peter left the reins of government to his older half-sister, Sophia, who acted as regent until 1689, while he devoted himself to organizing his "play regiments" in the suburbs of Moscow. Young men from the court and the neighboring area were carefully recruited to fill the ranks of the *Poteshnye*; in this way he ensured total loyalty. Officered by militarily proficient foreigners, the training and the military exercises soon became deadly serious, with real ammunition and real casualties. Peter's play mirrored his future imperial designs.

From haphazard beginnings in 1683, these regiments developed into the crack military units known as the Preobrazhenskii and Semenovskii Guards Regiments, which Peter I personally led into battle. The emperor relied heavily on his guards officers, entrusting them with important diplomatic, political, and administrative tasks. They symbolized the qualities of leadership he most admired; they were Westernized, they were militarily proficient, they were predominantly noble, and they were loyal to the new order.

The guards regiments formed an essential component in training the new leadership of Russia: one-third of the Russians in the 1730 elite group began service in the guards, and 41 percent were enrolled in a guards regiment at some point in their career.[12]

11. PSZ I, Vol. 5, No. 2,778.

12. The guards membership of the *generalitet* was derived from: I. V. Annenkov, *Istoriia leibgvardii konnago polka, 1731–1848*, St. Petersburg, 1849; A. Chicherin, *Istoriia leibgvardii preobrazhenskogo polka, 1683–1883*, 4 vols., St. Petersburg, 1883; P. Dirin, *Istorii leibgvardii semenovskogo polka, 1683–1883*, 2 vols., St. Petersburg, 1883; S. Panchulidzev, *Sbornik biografii kavalergardov, 1724–1889*, 4 vols., St. Petersburg, 1901; the archive of the Izmailovskii Guards Regiment in the Archive of Russian and East European History and Culture, Columbia University.

With Russian institutions of secular education in their infancy, the guards assumed an educational role during Peter's reign. At his insistence young nobles were educated through study abroad or through service in the guards, or a judicious mixture of the two. An ukase of 1714 forbade noblemen who had not served in the guards from becoming officers.[13]

Since service was compulsory for the nobility, and since the guards regiments were training ground for all officers and the surest path to promotion, nobles vied for places in these regiments despite the necessity to pass through the ranks. As it was impossible to enroll all young noblemen in two regiments, the question therefore arose of which nobles to accept: an ukase of 1721 specified that guards soldiers should be taken from "distinguished nobles" (*znatnoe shliakhetstvo*), but there remained the problem of defining *znatnoe*. In 1724, the War College asked the emperor whether "distinguished nobles" should be understood to include those nobles with one hundred peasant households and over, or those of a certain class in the Table of Ranks. To this inquiry, Peter I cryptically replied: *Znatnoe dvorianstvo po godnosti* ("distinguished nobles according to fitness").[14]

After the death of Peter the Great, under the pressure of the nobility to ensure a privileged educational path to officer status, the Corps of Cadets was established in 1731. The educational function of the guards declined, although they remained important in court politics and aristocratic self-definition. This development is anticipated in the changes in educational patterns of the elite when analyzed by age cohorts (Table 4).

The guards were important not only in training the military elite of Russia, but also in molding its top government administrators. Sixteen percent of the 1730 elite group associated with the guards became presidents of colleges, other than the Admiralty and War Colleges, 27 percent of them helped formulate central state policy, 45 percent of them became senators, and 84 percent of them had a mixed service career, which included the holding of both civil and military offices.

SERF-OWNERSHIP

The economic status of the Russian elite—the sources of its wealth and the roots of its weakness—is a complex subject that I have dealt

13. PSZ I, Vol. 5, No. 2,775; repeated in "Voinskii ustav," No. 3,006.
14. PSZ I, Vol. 7, No. 4,589. For an analysis of the social composition of the Petrine

TABLE IV-4

Education and Guards Association of Russians in the Elite,
by Cohort (percentage)

Cohort		Formal Education[a]	Began Service in Guards	Guards Association[b]
I	Born before 1670 (N = 22)	25	25	57
II	Born 1670–79 (N = 25)	20	35	50
III	Born 1680–89 (N = 28)	24	38	48
IV	Born after 1690 (N = 25)	47	26	47

SOURCE: See note 3.

a. Studied abroad or in a Russian educational institution.
b. Enrolled in one of the guards regiments, but did not necessarily begin service in the guards.

with elsewhere.[15] However, it is central to the purposes of this study to determine if there is a correlation between serf-ownership and the attainment of high office or rank. The Muscovite tradition had been to grant settled estates (*pomest'e*) to the nobility in exchange for service. Beginning in 1714, however, Peter I attempted to place state service on a new financial footing by substituting the granting of estates with yearly salaries.[16] From this point on, there was no necessary correlation between service to the state and estate holding.

In theory, the possibility arose that Russian officialdom could be divided into those officials descended from the Muscovite nobility who inherited estates, and those who did not. In reality the situation

---

officer corps, see M. D. Rabinovich, "Sotsial'noe proiskhozhdenie i imushchestvennoe polozhenie ofitserov reguliarnoi russkoi armii v kontse severnoi voiny," in N. I. Pavlenko, ed., *Rossiia v periode reform Petra I*, Moscow, 1973, pp. 133–71.

15. "Sources of Wealth of the Russian Elite from Peter I to Catherine II," paper presented at the Cornell University Conference on Russian Officialdom, 9–10 May 1975.

16. S. M. Troitskii, *Russkii absoliutizm i dvorianstvo v XVIIIv.*, pp. 253–54.

was not so static, since nobles who had not inherited estates could purchase them or acquire them through a profitable marriage alliance. And yet it is important to study the government's policy in granting estates after 1714 to see if any pattern appears. Did the crown attempt to grant estates to those who held high rank but few estates, or did it base its awards solely on favor and merit, regardless of previous wealth? Was the ruling elite synonomous with the serf-owning aristocracy, and what role did the government play in this development?

Of the 179 officials in the 1730 elite, 56 are definitely known to have inherited estates. (This is an underestimation of actual inheritance rates due to the paucity of records.) Fifty-seven officials received estates from the crown at some time during their careers. This number included 18 officials who had already inherited an estate, and 39 who had not. This means that 32 percent of those who inherited an estate were also granted an estate, while only 24 percent of those who did not inherit an estate were granted one. The government clearly did not use the practice of granting estates as a means of rewarding those who had no estates to the neglect of those of inherited wealth.

The total number of officials in the *generalitet* known to have owned serfs is 111 (62 percent). Included are the ten largest serf-holders in Russia as well as landowners of modest estates. The mean number of male serfs owned was 5,471 (N = 74). The range by social origin is shown in Table 5. Serf-holding correlates with certain high offices such as senators, governors, and presidents of the ministerial colleges; however, it is not statistically significant as a predictor of speed of promotion through the Petrine ranks system.

KINSHIP AND MARRIAGE TIES

The kinship and marriage ties of the Russian elite show that 54 percent of the wives of the men of the *generalitet* came from *generalitet* families, while 58 percent of their sons and daughters chose partners from these same families.[17] Almost two-thirds of the 1730 elite were related by blood or marriage to someone else in the *generalitet*; 76 percent of the Russians had such ties.

17. Meehan-Waters, "The Russian Aristocracy and the Reforms of Peter the Great," *Canadian-American Slavic Studies*, 8 (1974): 294–97.

TABLE IV-5

Mean Number of Male Serfs by Social Origin

Boyar elite	8,415	N = 34
Moscow gentry	3,830	N = 21
Other Russians (and unknown)	2,955	N = 12
Foreigners	3,668	N = 7

SOURCE: See note 3.

CAREER PATTERNS OF THE RUSSIAN ELITE

Although almost two-thirds of the *generalitet* held military service titles in 1730, it would be misleading to conclude that they all occupied a military office. There was a substantial discrepancy, as we shall observe later, between service title and office. But the very fact that all of the titles were judged in relationship to their military equivalents indicates the dominance of the military model in Petrine Russia. Peter's personal mania for all things martial, the unprecedented successes of the new army, and the importance of the military in the expansion of the state, gave the armed forces in Russia an unparalleled prestige. Boyars and princes coveted the rank of general, and military uniforms permanently replaced the gold-threaded robes of Muscovy. It was a mandarin's nightmare, and a field marshal's dreamland.

Throughout this period, the distinction between military service and civil service became blurred, and the majority of elite officials held both military and civil offices during their careers (68 percent of the *generalitet*). The full-time career civil servant found himself in the minority (27 percent of the *generalitet*) but even more rare was the exclusively military servitor (5 percent of the *generalitet*) (Table 6).

Table 7 contrasts the percentage of those with entirely military careers, of those with entirely civil careers, and of those with mixed careers who (1) had formal education, (2) were associated with a guards regiment, or (3) were Russians.

Lifetime civil servants were three times as likely to have a formal education as a full-time military officer. Enrollment in a guards regiment formed the crucial training ground for the latter—all of whom were associated with a guards regiment. One out of every four offi-

TABLE IV-6

Specialization of the Elite

Career	%	Number[a]
Entirely civil	27	36
Entirely military	5	7
Mixed	68	91
Total	100	134

SOURCE: See note 3.

a. Excludes officials for whom there is insufficient career data.

TABLE IV-7

Social Characteristics by Career Types (percentage)

	Entirely Military	Entirely Civil	Mixed
Formal education	14	45	25
Guards association	100	. . .	52
Social origin			
Boyar elite	43	31	33
Moscow gentry	27	22	23
Other and unknown Russians	27	28	21

SOURCE: See note 3.

cials with a mixed career had some formal education, and slightly over half of them were associated with the guards. With the exception of the relatively higher proportion of descendants of Muscovite aristocracy who spent an entire service career in the military, social origins do not seem to make a significant difference in the type of career (military, civil, or mixed) of an elite official.

In order to determine whether the ratio of elite officials with entirely civil careers increases over time (and thus whether there is a pattern of increasing specialization), we have analyzed the career types of the elite group by age cohort (Table 8). The data suggest a pattern of decreasing specialization for the first three age cohorts, with a sudden increase in the fourth cohort of officials with entirely civil careers, and officials with entirely military careers, and a corresponding decrease in the proportion of elite officials with mixed careers. Thus the youngest officials in the 1730 group—the ones most likely to have active careers spanning into the 1750s and 1760s—were more likely to have specialized service careers than their predecessors. My hypothesis holds that their careers reflect the measures taken after Peter I's death to limit intervention by the military in the civil administration and to sharpen jurisdictional boundaries between the civil and military spheres.

The very low number of officials with entirely military professions, and the high number of officials with mixed careers indicates that the eventual emergence of the bureaucracy as a specialized stratum of society must be the result not only of the professionalization of the civil bureaucracy as a group, but also of the professionalization of the military as a group. The high number of mixed careers does not mean simply that middle-aged officers "retired" into civil positions. During this period, militarily trained men switched with surprising frequency from military offices to civil offices and back to military service again. Of those officials with a mixed military-civil career type, 76 percent (69/91) switched back from a civil to a military office at least once. A detailed study of the careers of the elite indicates that for many officials these switches occurred throughout their careers.

By no means all officials began their long climb up the Table of Ranks through a military office. Table 9 indicates the type of first office held by a member of the *generalitet*.

There were many factors affecting the speed with which an official worked his way up through the Table of Ranks. One that is of central import to determining the changing social characteristics of Russian officialdom is the influence of social origins. We approach this problem by first analyzing differences in the mean age at appointment to a given rank for officials of differing social origins, and second by analyzing differences in the mean number of years spent in a rank.

Table 10 indicates the mean age at appointment to selected military and civil ranks by social origins.

It is noticeable that in all ranks the mean age of officials of foreign and of boyar elite origins are below the mean age for the sample group as a whole. Among Russians, in each rank, descendants of the boyar

Brenda Meehan-Waters

TABLE IV-8

Career Types by Birth Cohorts (percentage)

Cohort[a]	Entirely Civil	Entirely Military	Mixed
I (born before1670)	29	6	65
II (born 1670–79)	22	0	78
III (born 1680–89)	16	0	84
IV (born after 1690)	35	9	56

SOURCE: See note 3.

a. N = 134.

TABLE IV-9

First Office of Elite Official

Type of Office	Number	%
Military	83	46
Civil	55	31
Court office	19	11
Diplomatic	7	4
Other	15	8
Total	179	100

SOURCE: See note 3.

elite were appointed to a rank at an earlier age than descendants of the Moscow gentry, and in all but the rank of lieutenant general the latter were appointed earlier than other Russians.

As anticipated, the average number of years that an elite official spent in each rank was also influenced by his social origins, though the extent of the influence varied from rank to rank. Thus 14 percent of the variance in the mean number of years held as lieutenant general is explained by social origins, 26 percent of the variance as full general,

TABLE IV-10

Mean Age at Appointment to a Rank by Social Origin

Military Rank	Mean Age	Civil Rank	Mean Age
General		Actual privy councilor	
(entire group, N = 27)	53.4	(entire group, N = 21)	55
Boyar elite	51.1	Boyar elite	54
Moscow gentry	59	Moscow gentry	56.2
Other Russians	60	Other Russians	66
Foreigners	52.8	Foreigners	39
Lieutenant general		Privy councilor	
(entire group, N = 41)	49.3	(entire group, N = 26)	45.9
Boyar elite	48.3	Boyar elite	43.9
Moscow gentry	57.3	Moscow gentry	45
Other Russians	53.8	Other Russians	51.1
Foreigners	39.7	Foreigners	41
Major general		Actual state councilor	
(entire group, N = 44)	44.6	(entire group, N = 26)	41.9
Boyar elite	43.9	Boyar elite	37.7
Moscow gentry	49	Moscow gentry	38.7
Other Russians	52	Other Russians	47.9
Foreigners	37.9	Foreigners	46

SOURCE: See note 3.

36 percent in the ranks of privy councilor, and 52 percent for an actual state councilor.

For the purpose of further exploring those factors associated with success in the imperial system of ranks, we have computed the mean number of years it would take an official to work his way up from the sixth military rank (colonel, *polkovnik*) to the second (general, *general anshef*). The group studied includes officials who held civil offices during some of the transition from colonel to general. Following the "Statistical Package for the Social Sciences" we asked the computer to perform an analysis of variance in order to determine the relative weight of kinship, serf-ownership, education, and social origins on the speed with which an official passed through these ranks. Kinship, serf-ownership, and education proved statistically insignificant as correlates of rates of promotion. Social origin was the only statistically significant variable (t of 2.063, statistically significant at 1.8333).

Table 11 contains the differences in mean number of years spent in the selected ranks for each of these variables. One should approach this last analysis with caution because of the small number of officials studied (eleven). However, it should be remembered that the very paucity of the group is due first to the fact that a very limited number of officials ever reached the second rank—in 1730 there were only eight officials in Russia fitting that category; secondly, complete information on the year of the official's appointment to each rank, and on his kinship ties, social origins, education, and serf-ownership does not always exist.

One of the most striking insights from this data is that high rank came after long years of service, the average official spending almost twenty years in his rise from the sixth rank to the second. Equally noteworthy is the fact that the Russians spent almost six years more than the foreigners in their climb to the top. The obvious reason is that foreigners had a greater military expertise than Russians, and the relative speed of their rise through the ranks indicates that the Table of Ranks created a service system responsive to competency and achievement.

All of the data we have studied indicates that foreigners and descendants of the boyar elite were appointed at an earlier age to a rank, and passed through a rank, ahead of other Russians. Unlike the foreigners, descendants of the boyar elite not only operated successfully within the rank system, but also had a disproportionate control of top administrative offices. Their continuity testifies to the privileged position of birth when combined with successful adaptation to the modernizing mores of Petrine reform. The "old dogs" survived by learning "new tricks."

PROFILES OF TOP GOVERNMENT ADMINISTRATORS

Now we will look at such top government offices as the presidents of colleges, and the senators and governors, to see how their career patterns and social characteristics differ from those of the *generalitet* as a group.

The general pattern we have observed of officials switching back and forth from military to civil service was equally true of the presidents of colleges—the eighteenth-century equivalent of the heads of ministries. We study the career patterns of presidents of colleges in some depth to learn about the social and career characteristics of the higher civil service in the first half of the eighteenth century. For this

TABLE IV-11

Mean Number of Years from
Polkovnik to *General Anshef*

Variable	Years
For entire group (N = 11)	19.8
Kinship ties	
For those with	20
For those without	18
Serf-ownership	
For those with serfs	18.8
For those without serfs	20.7
Formal education	
For those with	21
For those without	17.8
Social origins	
Russians	22.5
Foreigners	16.6

SOURCE: See note 3.

reason, we exclude from consideration the presidents of the military colleges—the Admiralty and War Colleges. On this basis, twenty officials in the 1730 group held the office of president of a college at least once in their careers.

The typical president of a college began service in the military, with 30 percent starting in the guards, 20 percent in the army and 7 percent in the navy. As illustrations: Prince D. M. Golitsyn began service as a courtier but was later sent to Italy to study navigation and was appointed a captain in the guards upon his return;[18] Prince A. G. Dolgorukii began as an apprentice to his father, the Russian ambassador to Warsaw, just as the young Count Musin-Pushkin was initiated into state service as an apprentice in Holland.[19] Only two presidents of colleges held service first in the civil service: A. V. Makarov, who started as a junior clerk (*pod'iachii*) and was the son of a junior clerk;

18. *Entsiklopedicheskii slovar'*, 17: 48.
19. *Russkii biograficheskii slovar'*, 6: 500; *Entsiklopedicheskii slovar'*, 39:223.

and Shafirov, who worked as a translator in the Chancellery of Foreign Affairs (*Posol'skii prikaz*) and was the son of a translator.[20]

One of every three presidents of a college studied abroad, making this a more educated group than the *generalitet* as a whole. It was also a more aristocratic group, with half of the members stemming from the boyar elite and another 20 percent from the Moscow gentry. Only one foreigner became president of a college, the Moscow-born Iakov Vilimovich Brius (James Daniel Bruce), son of a Scottish colonel in the new regiments of foreign formation in Muscovy.[21] Finally, the economic base of presidents was above the norm. The mean number of serfs owned by presidents of colleges was 10,215, almost twice as many as the average member of the *generalitet*.

An analysis of the kinship ties of presidents indicates a social network of considerable extent as befitting their backgrounds and their achievements in the new Russia. For the sake of precision, we limit our study of kinship relations to the first and second degree. (A first-degree relationship—kin by blood—indicates that a president of a college is the brother, father, son, uncle, or first cousin of another president. A second-degree relationship—kin by marriage—means that one president of a college is married to the daughter or the sister of another president, or has a sister or daughter who is married to another president.) Twenty-nine percent of the presidents of colleges had both a first-degree and a second-degree relationship to another president, 10 percent had only a first-degree relationship, and 5 percent had only a second-degree relationship. In sum, 43 percent of the presidents of the colleges had a first- or second-degree relationship to at least one other president in the 1730 elite group.

The service titles (*chin*) and ranks held by presidents of colleges differed considerably. In theory, the Table of Ranks stipulated that every office (*dolzhnost'*) had a parallel service title (*chin*) to be carried by the official holding that office. According to this logic, the president of a college (except for the president of the "First Three Colleges"—

20. GPB, Fond 457 (Makarov), uncatalogued collection. On Shafirov, see A. Tereshchenko, *Opyt obozreniia zhizni sanovnikov, upravliashikh inostrannymi delami v Rossii,* 3 vols., St. Petersburg, 1837, 3: 199–205; and *Russkii biograficheskii slovar',* 12: 553–66. I agree with Longinov's categorization of Shafirov as a Russian rather than a foreigner: he was the son of a baptized Jew from Polish territory that became part of Muscovy in the middle of the seventeenth century; Shafirov married a Russian and his children made excellent marriages with aristocratic families.

21. Bobrinskii, *Dvorianskie rody vnesennye v obshchii gerbovnik,* 1: 331. Although James Daniel Bruce was born in Moscow, I have categorized him as a foreigner because he did not convert to Orthodoxy and was perceived by contemporaries as a member of the foreign community.

War, Admiralty, and Foreign Affairs—who held higher ranked titles) should hold the fourth-rank civil title of actual state councilor, to correspond with the fourth-rank civil office of college president. Helju Bennett has recently pointed out the discrepancy between service title and office at a later period.[22] An analysis of the service titles of presidents of colleges from the 1730 elite group indicates that the divergence existed virtually from the beginning of the new service system.

If we exclude the presidents of the First Three Colleges, as well as those who headed a college before the institution of the Table of Ranks, we have a total of seventeen presidents. However, since five of these top officials headed two different colleges in their service careers, we obtain twenty-two service titles to check for correspondence with the service regulations established by the Table of Ranks.

Not surprisingly, practice departs from theory. Six presidents of colleges held military service titles while holding the office of president: two held the *chin* of general (rank II), three were major generals (rank III), and one was a rear admiral (rank IV). Six presidents of colleges held the prescribed service title of actual state councilor (rank IV), while eight presidents held the higher civil *chin* of privy councilor (rank III) and one held the fifth *chin* of state councilor. The direction of the departure from the rules was in favor of the elite officials, with ten of them holding higher service titles than they were entitled to by virtue of their office.

The irregularities included not only inflation of title but also the use by five officials of military service titles while holding civil office. The government railed against the practice of appropriating military titles for civil work, and yet encouraged it by clearly valuing military service over civil. The bind for civil office holders is sharply illustrated by two contradictory laws of 13 November 1731. First, the government insisted that all military servitors should enjoy precedent over their counterparts in civil service, and then forbade men in the court and civil service from calling themselves by military titles.[23] This was a hard pill for former generals to swallow; that they refused to do so is indicated by the government's necessity to repeat in both 1736 and 1793 the prohibition against using military *chin* for civil offices.[24]

---

22. Helju Bennett, "The Evolution of the Meanings of *Chin*: An Introduction to the Russian Institution of Rank Ordering and Niche Assignment from the Time of Peter the Great's Table of Ranks to the Bolshevik Revolution," *California Slavic Studies*, 10 (1977): 1–43.

23. PSZ I, Vol. 8, Nos. 5,877 and 5,878.

24. Ibid., Vol. 9, No. 7,021; Vol. 23, No. 17,159.

Several presidents had been military leaders before heading a college, and two of them returned to field command after serving in these cabinetlike top civil administrative units. The presidency remained an appointive office; its occupants came from the same elite group of officials as governors and senators. Thus there was virtually no institutional identification associated with becoming president of a college. Elite officials played administrative leapfrog, hopping from military command to presidency of a college, to governorship of a province, to the Senate, perhaps back to the presidency of another college, and so on throughout their busy and demanding service careers. No president of a college spent his whole career working in the collegial system—the colleges themselves were too new, having replaced the chancellery (*prikaz*) system in 1717. Chancellor Gavril Ivanovich Golovkin showed the greatest professional stability: specializing in foreign affairs at an early age, he headed the *Posol'skii prikaz* from 1706 to 1717, and became president of its successor institution, the College of Foreign Affairs, on its founding. He served in that office until his death in 1734.[25] A combination of royal connections, diplomatic skill, and a liking for the post accounts for his unusual accomplishment.

Despite the hierarchical structure of the collegial system, few officials worked their way up the ladder of promotion within a given college. The *cursus honorum* seldom took the route from college councilor to vice-president to the presidency. Vice-presidents were often foreigners or Russians of lower social origins with special expertise. Only one president of a college had been vice-president before assuming the top job. Aleksei Zybin (patronymic unknown, father's office unknown, social origins unknown, dates of birth and death unknown) began service in the navy and developed into an expert mining engineer. In 1724 he was appointed vice-president of the Mining College, and became de facto head of the college in 1726, upon the death of the president. He was not formally appointed president, however, until two years later.[26]

Although the heads of the military colleges have been excluded from our sample of presidents of colleges, it should be noted that the general taboo against foreigners and Russians of nonnoble origins heading a college applied to these institutions as well. Despite the almost total domination of the naval elite by foreigners, the presidency of the admiralty was generally reserved for a native son. Admiral

25. A. V. Tereshchenko, *Opyt obozreniia zhizni sanovnikov upravliavshikh inostrannymi delami*, 2: 1–35.

26. D. A. Korsakov, *Votsarenie imperatritsy Anny Ioannovny*, Kazan, 1880, p. 208.

Sivers (Sievers), who was well liked as long as he was vice-president of the admiralty, overstepped his bounds when he attempted to become president. Aware of the customary exclusion of foreigners from heading colleges, Vice-President Sivers nevertheless sat in the president's chair when the office fell empty after Admiral Apraksin's death. But from that moment on, Sivers began to sign his name in Russian rather than Latin script. He exercised the prerogative of involvement in court intrigues, and was dismissed in 1732.[27] The outstanding military leader of Empress Anna Ivanovna's reign, Field Marshal Minikh (von Münnich) ran the War College from 1732 to 1741. For this, and other acts of hubris, he was sent to Siberia in 1741.[28]

Eighteenth-century Russia also had an idea of the proper type of person to be governor of one of its provinces. In 1708, Peter I divided Russia into eight provinces headed by governors. With the exception of the talented but low-born Menshikov, Peter hand-picked his first governors from the top nobility, including his relatives F. M. and P. M. Apraksin, boyar T. N. Streshnev, the Princes M. P. Gagarin, D. M. Golitsyn, and P. A. Golitsyn, and P. S. Saltykov.[29] His regents reflected his own regality. In 1712, Kurbatov was appointed vice-governor of Arkhangelsk, even though he had the duties and powers of governor. Solov'ev has suggested that the reason for this was that Peter did not want the son of a nonnoble to be on the same footing with a Prince Golitsyn.[30] Got'e has also perceptively noted that the de facto governor of a province could carry the title of either governor or vice-governor, depending on his status.[31]

The thirty-seven officials in the elite group who were governors at least once in their career were closely related to other governors, in a pattern similar to presidents of colleges. Forty-six percent of them had both a first-degree relationship and a second-degree relationship to another governor, with an additional 3 percent having just a first-degree relationship, bringing the total with either a first- or second-degree relationship to 49 percent. The mean number of serfs held by

27. *Russkii biograficheskii slovar'*, 18: 405.
28. "Ekstrakt iz doprosov byvshago fel'dmarshala grafa Minikha," *Russkii arkhiv* (1864), No. 6: 506–33. For Münnich's own explanation of his fall, see *Zapiski fel'd-marshala grafa Minikha*, St. Petersburg, 1874, pp. 79–85.
29. S. M. Solov'ev, *Istoriia Rossii s drevneishikh vremen*, 15 vols., Moscow, 1962–66, 8: 351.
30. Ibid., p. 459.
31. Iu. V. Got'e, *Istoriia oblastnogo upravleniia v Rossii ot Petra I do Ekateriny II*, 2 vols., Moscow, 1913–41, 1: 208.

governors as a group was 10,169, slightly less than the mean number held by presidents, but still impressive by any standard.

The office of governor was not included in the Table of Ranks, and thus norms were not established for whether a governor should hold a military or a civil service title, or for what rank the office should carry. The career patterns of the 1730 elite indicate, however, that the majority of governors held military titles during their tenure as governor (Table 12). The diversity of service titles reflects the fluidity of the service system. *Chin* was partially determined by the responsibilities of a governor in a given province. As a rule, border territories and recently conquered provinces were headed by military governors. (It was here that the occasional foreigner was found as a governor.) The interior provinces and Siberia were usually under the direction of officials knowledgeable in civil administration and finance who carried civil-service titles. But even here exceptions abounded. Graf P. I. Musin-Pushkin was actual state councilor while governor of Smolensk in 1730; from 1735 to 1740 Graf Aleksander Borisovich Buturlin held that post while enjoying the title of major general.[32] The same Musin-Pushkin once again held the fourth civil *chin*, actual state councilor, while administering Kazan;[33] his predecessor, V. N. Zotov, was a major general.[34]

The variety of offices held before becoming governor, and of service titles held while serving as governor, was matched by a rich diversity of posts held after that office. Despite the stereotyped image of a governor as an old soldier put out to pasture in the provinces, many governors held important positions in the central administration following their time as governor. For eighteen of the thirty-seven officials who held the post of governor, being a governor was their last known office. But for the remaining nineteen officials, other appointments followed. Eight of them subsequently became presidents of a college or head of chancellery, five became members of such top central governing institutions as the Supreme Privy Council or the Kabinet, three received diplomatic and/or court appointments, two became councilors to the War College, and one resumed military command.

As in the case of presidents of colleges, the diversity of service titles of governors suggests that rank and title did not flow from the office

32. PSZ I, Vol. 10, No. 7,557; TsGVIA, Fond 105 (Buturlin), op. 201, d. 2, "Imennye ukazy Imperatritsy Anny Ioannovny."

33. Longinov, "Russkii Generalitet v nachale 1730 goda," p. 170; *Entsiklopedicheskii slovar'*, 39: 223.

34. *Russkii biograficheskii slovar'*, 7:473.

TABLE IV-12

Service Titles of Governors

Rank	Military Service Title	No.	Rank	Civil Service Title	No.
II	general	1	II	actual privy councilor	3
III	lieutenant general	10	III	privy councilor	3
IV	major general	10	IV	actual state councilor	3
V	brigadier	1		service title unknown	6
VII	guards captain	1			

SOURCE: See note 3.

but rather from the official. The person was as important as the post in determining the relationship between *chin* and *dolzhnost'*. A Russian official of this period more commonly worked his way up a clearly defined hierarchy of service titles than of offices. The institutions of government changed constantly, and jurisdictional problems prevailed. Although the Table of Ranks suggests divisions of tasks and responsibilities, boundaries remained weak not only between the military and the civil, but also between the army and the navy, and the central and provincial administration. With loose lines of demarcation, the movement within the parallel hierarchies of civil, court, and military offices was as frequently horizontal as vertical. Finally, certain key offices, such as the Senate, remained outside of (and above) the hierarchical structure of the Table of Ranks.

During the early years of his reign, Peter I scarcely distinguished between himself and his government. His government was where he was, as itinerant as the campaign-obsessed tsar. It was not until 1711, on the eve of leaving for the Pruth campaign, that Peter decided to establish a central institution, the Senate, to run the government in his absence. As the tsar explained in his edict, "We have appointed a Governing Senate to whose edicts all will be obedient as if it were we ourselves, under threat of severe punishment and death."[35] Like the tsar, the Senate was to act as one—its vote was to be unanimous. It

35. Quoted in L. J. Oliva, *Russia in the Era of Peter the Great,* Englewood Cliffs, 1969, p. 83.

was a heady thing to be a Petrine senator; they were appointed with care. Even after the establishment of the Table of Ranks, the Senate remained outside the structure of hierarchical offices. Peter wished the Senate always to remain an appointive office, and did not want to give the illusion that an official could work his way up through the ranks to this illustrious post. Hence it was not a graded office, and had no specified *chin* attached to it.[36]

The actual power of the Senate fluctuated in the first half of the eighteenth century, going into decline during the reigns of Peter II and Anna Ivanovna and regaining its import under Empress Elizabeth, but it always remained a prestigious appointment and a forum for central state policy. As intended, senators were the most aristocratic of all elite office-types. Of the fifty-three officials in the 1730 elite group who held the office of senator at least once in their service careers, 55 percent came from the boyar elite and another 26 percent from the Moscow gentry. Only four foreigners were appointed to the Senate. The high percentage of aristocratic senators and low number of foreigners does not, as might be argued, reflect a possible aristocratic bias in the 1730 group, the top officials at the end of the reign of Peter II. Seven of the senators studied had been appointed by Peter I, ten by Catherine I, only six by Peter II, twenty-one by Anna Ivanovna, five by Anna Leopoldovna, three by Elizabeth, and one by Catherine II. They thus reflect the general bias of that culture as well as the social characteristics of senators as a group throughout the first half of the eighteenth century.

The most interrelated of all top officials, 70 percent of the senators had both a first- and a second-degree relationship to another senator. An additional 4 percent had only a first-degree relationship, while another 2 percent had only a second-degree tie. In sum, three out of every four senators each had a close relative in at least one other senator. While the kinship ties of senators was higher than that of either presidents of colleges or governors, their mean number of serfs—9,884—was lower, though still well above the norm for the *generalitet* as a group. The educational qualifications of senators paralleled those of presidents of colleges. Sixteen senators studied abroad and two in Russian higher educational institutions; thus one-third of the senators had a formal education.

Russian officials were appointed to the Senate in the prime of their life; it was not an honorary appointment given as compensation for

36. PSZ i, Vol. 5, No. 3,978.

their dotage. Half of the senators were appointed for the first time before the age of forty-nine.

Senators were chosen from among top officials in the military, civil and court structures. Forty-two percent of the senators had exclusively civil careers, compared with 27 percent of the *generalitet* as a whole. For a brief period, presidents of colleges were ex officio senators; this practice was discontinued owing to the heavy workloads associated with both offices. But the social and career characteristics that led an official to be chosen as president of a college were also likely to make him a prime candidate for the Senate or the governorship of a province. Elite statesmen circulated among the top positions in government, leaving few openings for those who came from a lower promotional pool.

Seven officials in the elite group held the three prestigious offices of senator, or governor, and of president of a college during their service careers. These outstanding statesmen numbered six offspring of the boyar elite—Graf A. B. Buturlin, Prince A. G. Dolgorukii, Prince D. M. Golitsyn, Graf P. I. Musin-Pushkin, A. L. Pleshcheev, and Prince Iu. Iu. Trubetskoi—and one of the Moscow gentry—V. I. Novosiltsev. There were no foreigners in their midst and no low-born Russians. Thus, at the apex of government, distinguished lineage was an important, though perhaps unconscious, prerequisite for the job. Yet the very success of these noble bureaucrats testifies also to a lifetime of distinguished service, achievement, and their ability to adapt to the standards of the "New Russia."

IMPACT OF THE TABLE OF RANKS
ON THE RUSSIAN NOBILITY

Distinguished birth and family connections assisted nobles both in securing high offices and in climbing through the ranks, but the essential point is that no matter how aristocratic or how favored a Russian noble was, he had to pass through the service ranks. The government obligated him to serve the state as long as he was fit to do so and set the conditions for that service. The *Voinskii ustav* of 1716 formalized the chain of command and the hierarchy of ranks for the military;[37] in 1722 the Table of Ranks established a similarly rigid ladder of civil and court ranks, based on the military model. Both the obligation to serve,

37. Ibid., No. 3,006.

and the obligation to work one's way up through an established hierarchy of ranks, was accepted by the 1730 elite group. Virtually no one skipped a rank after the promulgation of the Table of Ranks.

The career patterns of the elite group reveal a double truth: nobles dominated the bureaucratic structure, and the bureaucratic structure dominated the nobles.[38] The process of state-building demanded a fully mobilized society and a lifetime commitment to government service. At least half of the elite officials died in office. Others went into nominal retirement, only to find their leadership talents called upon again and again by a demanding and personnel-shy government. The military archives are filled with the letters of tired and ailing officers pleading to be allowed to retire, or barring that, to take a leave of absence in order to visit their families and their estates. The government's routine response was a request for a medical examination or other proof of ill health.[39]

After studying the lifetime service careers of the 1730 elite, I believe these officials can aptly be called noble bureaucrats, because of their peculiar combination of ascriptive and achieved characteristics, and their necessity to exercise these talents within a structured and mandatory service system.

These noble bureaucrats were all nobles within the Petrine definition of nobility as achieved through high rank earned in government service. Most of the Russians were nobles twice over, having earned this status through rank and inherited it through birth.

The Table of Ranks did not directly affect the legal status of old noble families. What it provided was a specified set of rules by which foreigners and nonnobles could become equal to hereditary nobles, through distinguished service. The Table of Ranks was a means for the giving of nobility to those who had none via the achievement of rank; and the giving of rank to those who already had nobility.

The Petrine service system bureaucratized nobles in a variety of ways. A noble's status in society became irrevocably linked to the rank he earned in service. All official queues—whether at court, at church, or noble balls—were assembled according to rank; honorific forms of address followed a similar, rigid protocol. Rank imposed

38. For a perceptive treatment of the psychological impact of the service system on the nobility, see Marc Raeff, *Origins of the Russian Intelligentsia: The Eighteenth-Century Nobility*, New York, 1966. See also Michael Confino, "A propos de la noblesse russe au XVIIIᵉ siècle," *Annales. Economies-Sociétés-Civilisations*, 22 (1967): 1163–1205.

39. TsGVIA, Fond 105 (Buturlin), op. 201, d. 14 (Reports of the *Moskovskaia meditsinskaia kontora* to General Buturlin. 1743).

a structure upon government service, and formalized the relations between subordinates and superiors.

Elite officials had to combine ascriptive qualities such as noble birth and family connections with achieved characteristics such as education, training, and expertise. First preference would be given to the old nobility, provided they acquired new skills and new fashions. The guards regiments initiated the nobles into the new service system and familiarized them with the latest that modern science, i.e. military technology, had to offer. It was nobles who were sent abroad to study; elite institutions were established at home to ensure that the privileged elite became an educated elite.

Elite nobles were bureaucrats in the sense that they were career servitors, lifetime government servants. Less than one-third of them spent their entire careers in civil service, but they were all professional state servitors at a time when the state had not clearly delineated military and civil boundaries.

They were professionals again in the sense that they were state servitors first and landowners second. Although the 1730 elite group included in its ranks the largest serf-holders in Russia, their prime energies went to the state, with all but a handful viewing their estates as simply a source of income. Prince Dolgorukii indicated in a service profile (*skazka*) in 1755 that he did not know the number of serfs he owned, since he had been immersed in government service for so long.[40]

Finally, at the elite level, officials were professional administrators. They specialized in positions of command, whether on the battlefield or in the top organs of government. They led armies, headed colleges, governed provinces and sat in state councils. Their expertise was leadership, and their qualifications were distinguished birth and distinguished service.

40. TsGADA, Fond 286 (Gerol'dmeisterskaia kontora), kniga 439, fol. 222.

The author would like to thank the University of Rochester for its generous provision of computer time and, in particular, Mark Friedrich of the History Department for his invaluable help in programming. The author is also indebted to Professor Marc Raeff for his acute comments on an earlier version of this chapter.

CHAPTER FIVE

EIGHTEENTH-CENTURY NOBILIARY CAREER PATTERNS AND PROVINCIAL GOVERNMENT

Robert D. Givens

O*fficialdom, as we have already seen, was not monolithic in Russia, but was rather divided into several structures or even societies. In the capitals, Moscow and then St. Petersburg, there was concentrated a body of administrative specialists whom we could call bureaucrats par excellence because of the narrowness and exclusiveness of their training and career experience, and because their somewhat elevated social status was entirely the product of their professional roles. Also concentrated in the capitals, but extending out from them and maintaining close contact with them, were the elite officials, the heads of administrations, the governors, and those marked by birth, wealth, their peers, and their superiors for early success. Givens introduces us here to yet another structure of Russian officialdom and its corresponding society, that of the provincial nobility. Clearly the stepchild of the administrative family, this group is distinguished from the chancery clerk-specialists by birth, land- and serf-holdings, and the fact that the early portions of their careers were often in the military. The provincial nobility were also distinguished from the elite administrators by birth (since all families were not socially elite just as all offices were not politically elite) and by those components of career experience that resulted in failure, or mere survival, instead of great success.*

Prior to the "reforms" of Catherine the Great, provincial government was as close to nonexistent as the political and fiscal survival of the empire would tolerate. Local landlords were usually absent, away on military assignment, and, as Givens shows, the few "professional" civil officials of the mid-eighteenth century were given little status or support. Catherine's effort to bolster local government by encouraging nobles, freed from obligatory service, to enter local affairs was only modestly successful, and the paramount importance and prestige of central, and particularly military, service survived at least down to the end of the eighteenth century. According to Givens, most provincial officials had at least ten years of military service prior to assuming local civil office. Assumption of these new duties presumably required skills other than those necessary to military service. Yet, unlike the capitals, there existed in the provinces only the barest excuse for a body of professionally trained clerks who could assume the functions for which the nobles were unprepared. In spite of this, no effort was made to train, or retrain, the nobles themselves. Evidently military experience and noble status were considered sufficient qualification.

As Pintner shows (Chapter Nine), the subordinate and impoverished status of provincial service continued on into the nineteenth century. Still, with time and the extension of increasingly uniform standards, this situation will begin to change—not so much so that provincial service, even today, is seen as equal to service with great ministries in the capitals, but in the sense that provincial service gradually becomes a common part of the career experience leading to important positions in the central government. As Orlovsky (Chapter Ten) indicates, this is already true of some careers in the second half of the nineteenth century. Sternheimer (Chapter Twelve) and Daniels (Chapter Thirteen) further underscore the important role that provincial service comes to play for the aggressive and energetic official in the more highly bureaucratized officialdom of the twentieth century. [THE EDITORS.]

Few students of Russia's past would question the predominant impact of state service on the lives of those who claimed membership in the noble estate. Indeed, this duty has frequently become a barometer of general social change, so much so that its persistent diminution during the eighteenth century has been taken as an index of the country's growing Westernization.[1] It would clearly be difficult to exaggerate the effect of an obligation that dogged the individual *dvorianin* from the time of his primary education, continuing throughout his career, and often ending with his death or debility. If this formal obligation was ended by statute in 1762, its impact on Russian society clearly did not vanish with a stroke of the tsar's pen. One important factor in evaluating the aftermath of this experience is the question of initiative. Did the noblemen have no choice other than to submit more or less automatically to a congeries of decrees emanating from St. Petersburg? Observers have frequently answered in the affirmative, an approach epitomized by Koshelev's description of the nobility as the

---

1. Richard Pipes has recently defended the traditional view that the service obligation ended because of nobiliary pressure on a weakened monarchy. The result, in his opinion, was the formation of a "privileged and leisured class" (*Russia under the Old Regime*, New York, 1974, p. 133 n.).

dough from which the state baked its officials (*chinovniki*).[2] However widely accepted this view, it remains a generalization that does not allow us to determine whether choice influenced a nobleman's career at all, or the possible variations it produced. By examining the records of a number of servitors we will not only be able to derive a more accurate notion of the background of the typical nobleman-official, but will also utilize the results to interpret the workings of Russia's provincial administration.

As is well known, the most prestigious posts in Russia were in the armed forces. The entire transformation presided over by Peter I virtually marched to a military tempo as the tsar-reformer specified new obligations that various strata of the population owed the state. By and large these demands fell into two categories: participation in, and support of, the army and fleet. Just as war became a perpetual activity of the Russian state during Peter's reign, so did military service expand into a permanent duty for the noblemen. To an extent it was easy for the nobles to appreciate how crucial the armed forces were to the country's security and new international position. The esteem that the profession of arms enjoyed in Russia, moreover, differed little from that of other European societies during this period.[3]

But the needs of the state that Russia's rulers sought to define in the eighteenth century did not end with the development of an officer corps that had mastered contemporary techniques of warfare. As Peter himself was well aware, absolutist rule required continual information about the realm.[4] This, of course, necessitated a qualified corps of civilian administrators. In order to attract capable personnel the tsar realized he must make civilian posts desirable. Although the status of civilian positions included in the Table of Ranks did not rival that of ranks held by military officers, they did offer material incentive in the form of salaries and promotions for diligent performance.[5] These benefits were instituted in order to encourage members of the *dvorianstvo* to become civilian officials.

Still, the statutes of the Petrine state often meant less in practice than their imposing language would suggest. Judging by the decrees themselves, there were a number of noblemen who ignored repeated sum-

---

2. P. Miliukov, *Ocherki po istorii russkoi kultury*, Moscow, 1918, 1: 237.

3. "Society became sharply divided into those who were trained for officers and those who could not claim commissioned rank; and 'honor,' implying the right to fight duels, was restricted to members of the officer-class" (L. Namier, *England in the Age of the American Revolution*, New York, 1961, p. 7).

4. S. Troitskii, *Russkii absoliutizm i dvorianstvo v XVIIIv.*, Moscow, 1974, p. 56.

5. Ibid., pp. 104–6.

monses that they and their sons report for service. The threats of punishment that loomed ever more menacing in these commands appear to have had little impact on absenteeism (*netstvo*).[6] In the case of civilian service the nobles did not defy the state as openly, but failed nonetheless to comply with the wishes of the central government.

To be sure, practice had shown that nonmilitary officials were held in low repute. During the first half of the century special detachments (*ekzekutsii* and *syshchiki*) were continually sent to provincial Russia to ensure that numerous taxes were collected, to curb banditry, or simply to check on the performance of existing personnel. In general, these military units behaved quite brutally toward their civilian colleagues, even those who belonged to the nobility.[7] A further reminder of the low position they occupied in the state's priorities came when the salaries of many provincial administrators were cut or eliminated outright after the reform of 1727. By encouraging what essentially was a reversion to the former practice of "feeding" on the region they managed through taking (or demanding) bribes, this alteration surely did not endear the servitors to the local residents.[8] Further, those civilian officials who expected assiduous performance would bring about their advancement in the officialdom must have been disillusioned by the number of promotions that went to favorites, scions of prominent families, or men who had distinguished themselves in the military.[9] Perhaps such factors explain why many civilian servitors used military titles to which they had no valid claim. The practice was widespread enough to require a special edict prohibiting it.[10]

The above factors obviously did not affect each individual in the same way, but there is no question that as a group the noblemen preferred service in the armed forces. Peter I saw the matter quite differently, and sought to have nobles fill the more important civilian posts. A decree of 1724 expressly prohibited the appointment in most

6. An edict of 1722 admitted that previous measures had failed to secure compliance, and went on to threaten all who did not heed the summons of the state in the future with proscription (PSZ i, Vol. 6, No. 3,874). For the comments of a contemporary see I. Pososhkov, *Kniga o skudnosti i bogatstve*, ed. B. Kafengauz, Moscow, 1951, pp. 93ff.

7. The *ekzekutsii* were sent to collect taxes and arrears, the *syshchiki* to eradicate banditry. Both frequently clashed with the regular administrators (Iu. Got'e, *Istoriia oblastnogo upravleniia v Rossii ot Petra I do Ekateriny II*, 2 vols. Moscow, 1913, 1941, 1: 86–89, 107–9.

8. The legislation reduced the outlay for wages to the pre-1700 level, and permitted minor officials "to satisfy themselves from affairs" (PSZ i, Vol. 7, Nos. 5,039, 5,126, 20 March, 22 July 1727). See also Iu. Got'e, *Istoriia oblastnogo*, 1: 31–33.

9. S. Troitskii, *Russkii absoliutizm*, pp. 129–30.

10. PSZ i, Vol. 8, No. 5,878, 13 November 1731.

cases of nonnobles as secretaries, the officials responsible for the bulk of the regime's paperwork.[11] However, the expectations Peter may have had that noblemen would fill secretarial posts went unfulfilled. Faced with an acute shortage of office workers, the state was forced to recruit members of nonprivileged social strata. Commoners also entered the lower administrative echelons in the provinces, where their appointments often escaped detection.[12] Although commoners were formally barred from filling secretarial posts until 1762, many of these positions were held by the descendants of office workers (*prikaznye liudi*) prior to that time.[13]

The nobles' desire to avoid administrative duties thus collided with the regime's efforts to preserve the social composition of the officialdom. Even the so-called junker program that sought to train adolescents for civilian posts met with slight success. According to a 1737 decree, nobles from fifteen to seventeen could be assigned to the civil service, subject to the approval of the Senate.[14] To ensure that the cadets could maintain themselves "honestly," living on their own means and their salary, a property qualification was instituted. Only young nobles whose families held at least 100 serfs could be posted to the Senate; those with at least 25 could be placed only with the colleges or chancelleries. This restriction may also have been designed to counteract the contemporary view that such duties were merely a haven for noblemen whose families could not afford to equip them for service in a regiment.[15]

Despite the attempt to pick the most capable personnel for civil service, the government soon discovered that its criteria were unsuitable. A 1740 law complained that not only did the "base and mediocre" (*podlyi i posredstvennyi*) cadets lack any desire to study civil procedures, but the sons of prestigious nobles were also not applying themselves. All apparently wished to begin their careers in the military.[16] During

---

11. PSZ I, Vol. 7, No. 4,449, 31 January 1724.

12. A. Romanovich-Slavatinskii, *Dvorianstvo v Rossii ot nachala XVIII do otmeny krepostnogo prava*, Kiev, 1912, p. 227. A decree of 3 May 1742 prohibited provincial governors from hiring or dismissing secretaries without the Senate's approval (PSZ I, Vol. 11, No. 8,550).

13. The prohibition was ended by PSZ I, Vol. 12, No. 11,510. Troitskii has shown the considerable extent to which *prikaznye liudi* held lower echelon administrative posts in 1755 (p. 215).

14. PSZ I, Vol. 10, No. 7,201, 6 March.

15. N. Belozerskaia, "Odin iz predkov Pushkina (materialy dlia kharakteristiki nravov russkogo obshchestva XVIIIv.)," *Istoricheskii vestnik* 76 (1889): 437. See also N. Tolubeev, *Zapiski N. Tolubeeva (1780–1809)*, St. Petersburg, 1899, p. 61.

16. PSZ I, Vol. 11, No. 8,043, 24 March.

the reign of Elizabeth, schools were established in St. Petersburg and Moscow to train civil servants. Young noblemen attended on a part-time basis, while not working at the bureaus to which they had been appointed. Neither of these educational institutions appears to have enjoyed much success, and we are told that the students were frequently absent. What lessons they did attend were quickly forgotten.[17]

The attitudes toward civilian duties that had developed among the noblemen when service was compulsory continued to be a factor in Russian life following the termination of this requirement. Peter III, in his very edict that released members of the *dvorianstvo* from the obligation which had been in effect throughout the century, noted with satisfaction a change in the nobles' conduct. While the early decades of the century had been marked by evasion, claimed the statute, the state could now rely upon the nobility to volunteer for service. Responding to the demands of the tsars could be likened to matriculation in a difficult course, and the noblemen were thought ready for commencement. Nonetheless, the state left itself the option of returning to former practice, and requiring service once again if the supply of nobiliary manpower dropped below the requisite level.[18] Judging from the experiences of the decades that followed this decree of 1762, its authors appear to have been justified in their expectations. Both the military and the civilian arms of the Russian state had sufficient personnel—at least in the middle and upper grades. However, staffing the expanded governmental apparatus of the final third of the century was not the sole function assigned to the noblemen.

Not only did Catherine II's provincial reform of 1775 bring about a thorough reorganization of Russia's internal management, but it also offered the nobles an opportunity to select those who would fill certain positions in the locality.[19] The main purpose of the decree was to make the administration more efficient, largely by improving communication between the provinces and the capital. In creating a nucleus for nobiliary organization at the smallest administrative subdivision—the district (*uezd*)—the empress and her advisors sought to enlist the resident nobles in their reforming efforts. Presumably the administrators and judges the noblemen were to select would be able subordinates of centralized absolutism. Since the whole process whereby the

17. A. Presniakov, "Pravitel'stvuiushchii senat v tsarstvovanii Elizavety Petrovny i Petra Feodorovicha," *Istoriia pravitel'stvuiushchego senata za dvesti let, 1711–1911*, 5 vols., St. Petersburg, 1911, 2: 184–85.

18. PSZ I, Vol. 15, No. 11,444, 18 February 1762.

19. PSZ I, Vol. 20, No. 14,392, 7 November 1775.

noblemen gathered in each government (*guberniia*) to cast their ballots was closely supervised by appointed officials of the monarchy, such as the governor, the new arrangement must have been reminiscent of compulsory state service. Still, a concerted effort was made in the early years of the reform to encourage the nobles to attend the convocations and to publicize their proceedings in the official newspapers appearing in St. Petersburg and Moscow.[20] If the government had required attendance, moreover, the entire rationale of elective service would have been lost, and it would have been obvious that the assemblies were merely a rubber stamp in the tight grip of the monarch. Catherine's approach, therefore, did not involve heightened control over the new institutions, and she even relaxed the supervision of her agents over the *dvorianstvo* after the initial convocations.[21]

Since the officials they were to elect shared responsibility for local affairs with appointees of the central government, the nobles clearly did not gain an autonomous sphere of activity in provincial Russia. The governor, representing the long arm of St. Petersburg, supervised all who held the new positions after their election. Nonetheless, nobles who served as district police captains (*kapitan ispravnik*) and members of the lower local court (*nizhnii zemskii sud*) directed the police in each district, while a nobleman presided as judge of the district court (*uezdnyi sud*). In addition to these posts, noblemen chose members of certain appellate courts, agencies of public welfare, and the so-called conscience court (*sovestnyi sud*) that heard equity cases. The total number of offices filled by the nobles came to about one-third of the seventy-five permanent positions that were established in each government by the new system.[22] None of these posts can be termed inconsequential, and it is arguable that some might have enabled the nobles to develop footholds of local power. One essential ingredient was lacking, however—any real interest in elective office. Even in the first flush of enthusiasm following the enactment of the reform, few

20. The assemblies received considerable mention in both the *Sanktpeterburgskie vedomosti* and the *Moskovskie vedomosti* during the years following the inception of the reform.

21. Prior to the second assembly of the Tver' nobility in 1778, Catherine spelled out the role of the governor-general in a letter to Jacob Sievers, one of her most trusted lieutenants. Henceforth, the nobility was not to be subject to the close direction that had marked its first meetings. Rather than preside in person, the governor-general would send written instructions to the assembled nobles (LOII, Fond 36, d. 401, fols. 175–76). For the eventual statute see PSZ I, Vol. 20, No. 14,816, 25 November 1778.

22. N. Eroshkin, *Ocherki istorii gosudarstvennykh uchrezhdenii dorevoliutsionnoi Rossii*, Moscow, 1960, p. 165.

assemblies attracted more than a third of the total nobles living in a given government; the numbers who turned out for later triennial meetings declined steadily.[23] Significantly, this drop is not restricted to just a few governments, but can be demonstrated wherever we have data for successive assemblies (Table 1).

Because the nobles' tepid response to the elections can be observed from their very inception, it is probable that we are witnessing the result of long-standing attitudes. Furthermore, given the common background of compulsory service, it would be reasonable to assume that certain aspects of this experience made the nobles resist participating in the assemblies. Prior to 1775 the mid-level officials whose duties most resembled later forms of elective service were the commandants (*voevody*) and their assistants (*voevodskie tovarishchi*). Until they were phased out following the 1775 reform, these positions were a widespread form of civilian service in provincial Russia. Responsible for a number of judicial and administrative functions, these officers were accorded a relatively high rank and salary. As a rule provincial officials were paid less than their counterparts in either Moscow or St. Petersburg,[24] but a provincial commandant still held the sixth rank in the official hierarchy in 1763, earning 600 rubles annually.[25]

Although nonnobles were appointed as commandants or assistants, it was more usual for noblemen to be named—both at the provincial and district levels.[26] What was the ordinary service background of men who held this appointment? Drawing on official records, it is possible to answer this question for the period on the eve of the provincial reform—1773. The following data are drawn from the register of

23. The property qualification imposed by some of the governors-general does not seem great enough to explain the poor turnout. Sievers, for example, allowed only those nobles owning at least twenty serfs to vote for marshal; the qualification was reduced to ten when the nobles chose the remaining officials (*Sanktpeterburgskie vedomosti*, No. 11, 5 February 1776). These limitations, of course, did not restrict attendance at the assemblies themselves, although they may have dissuaded poorer nobles from coming.

24. S. Troitskii, *Russkii absoliutizm*, p. 257.

25. Both the assistant commandant at the provincial level and the district commandant held the eighth rank and earned 375 rubles per year; the district assistant commandant earned 250 rubles per year (PSZ I, Vol. 44, Pt. 2, *Kniga shtatov, otdeleniia* III–IV, 69). A rough basis of comparison may be afforded by the fact that in the early 1760s a senior professor at the Academy of Arts earned 700 rubles a year, a senior doctor in Moscow up to 1,000, and the chief assistant to a provincial governor from 600 to 750 (*Kniga shtatov, otdeleniia* III–IV, 57–80).

26. Before the 1775 reform, the largest administrative unit in the Russian Empire, the government (*guberniia*), was divided into provinces (*provintsii*), which in turn were divided into districts (*uezdy*). For details, see V. Kabuzan, *Narodonaselenie Rossii v XVIII–pervoi polovine XIXv.*, Moscow, 1963, pp. 180ff.

TABLE V-1

Nobles (Adult Males) Attending Assemblies, 1776–1783

| | Assembly | | |
Government	1st	2nd	3rd
Tver'	562 (1776)	418 (1779)	
Smolensk		400 (1778)	
Novgorod	722 (1776)	399 (1780)	
Kaluga	478 (1777)	348 (1779)	
Pskov	654 (1777)	400 (1781)	
Iaroslavl'	705 (1777)	402 (1780)	301 (1783)
Vladimir	520 (1777)	372 (1780)	
Kostroma	400 (1778)	200 (1781)	
Orel	379 (1779)		
Voronezh	283 (1780)		
Tambov	400 (1779)		
Nizhnii Novgorod	203 (1779)		
St. Petersburg	108 (1780)		
Kursk	389 (1779)		
Simbirsk	350 (1780)		
Chernigov	360 (1782)		
Moscow	400 (1782)		

SOURCE: *Spisok dvorianstva tverskogo namestnichestva byvshemu pri pervom ego sobranii v Tveri*, Ianvar' 1776, St. Petersburg, 1776; *Spisok dvorianstva novgorodskogo namestnichestva*, St. Petersburg, 1776; *Sankt-peterburgskie vedomosti*, 1777–81; TsGADA, Gosarkhiv, razriad 16, d. 636, 729, 777, 931, 951, 1,012; S. Larionov, *Opisanie kurskogo namestnichestva*, Moscow, 1786; *Stoletie viatskoi gubernii, 1780–1880*, Viatka, 1882; S. Liubetskii, *Otgoloski stariny*, Moscow, 1867.

civilian officials that was compiled annually for the Senate by the Master of Heraldry and the Academy of Sciences.[27] Included are 365 commandants and their assistants (those serving in the Baltic regions are omitted). Although this includes only so-called civilians, its military character is quite apparent: only 58 of the officials were in the civilian arm of the state service throughout their careers, spending no time at all in the military. For the remaining 307, state service began with a term in Russia's armed forces. Of this number there is specific evidence that 289, or 79 percent of the total, transferred from the military to civilian service. The remaining 18 probably followed the same pattern, but this is not noted in our source. Although there is no specific mention as to whether these men were born into the ranks of the *dvorianstvo*, it would be a safe assumption that a sizable majority belonged to the hereditary nobility.

Returning to those who left the military, it is possible to determine when they terminated this phase of their careers and entered civilian service (Table 2.) It is evident that a high percentage of the provincial administrators made this shift after at least a decade and a half in the military. For nearly 60 percent, life as a civilian official began after a minimum of twenty-one years in some branch of the Russian armed forces.

Another way of examining the service background of those who were provincial administrators in 1773 is to determine the number of years these men spent as civilians. Table 3 is based on the amount of time that elapsed after an individual left the military until the compilation of this roster. Over half of this group were in their first decade of civilian service, while over 90 percent had been considered civilians for fifteen years or less. Although the duties of a commandant and his assistant originally had emphasized manning outposts of the empire, by the eighteenth century the responsibilities had come to be those of

27. Before the abolition of compulsory service for the nobility all data on governmental personnel were kept by the Master of Heraldry. It was this agency that in 1754–56 conducted the very detailed survey of civilian officials that has become the source for Professor Troitskii's investigations. Subsequent rosters in the eighteenth century were not as detailed but were kept current: a decree of 1764 required all agencies to inform the Senate twice a year of both the number of servitors and their career history (PSZ I, Vol. 16, No. 12,030, 30 January). This information first was verified by the Master of Heraldry, then sent to the Academy of Sciences, which drew up the final register, known as an *Adres Kalendar'* (S. Troitskii, *Russkii absoliutizm*, pp. 162–63). Although its form varied, this publication continued to appear every year, virtually until the end of the eighteenth century. For the publication history, see *Svodnyi katalog russkoi knigi grazhdanskoi pechati XVIII veka, 1725–1800*, 4 vols., Moscow, 1963–66, 3: 157.

TABLE V-2

Length of Military Service of Provincial Commandants and
Assistant Commandants before Taking Civilian Posts (N = 285)

Years	0–5	6–10	11–15	16–20	21–25	26–30	Over 30
Number of Commandants	1	9	42	70	59	68	36
%	0.4	3	14.7	24.6	20.7	23.9	12.6

SOURCE: *Spisok nakhodiashchimsia v grazhdanskoi sluzhbe vo vsekh prisutstvennykh mestakh s pokazaniem kazhdogo vstupleniia v sluzhbu i v nastoiashchii chin na 1773 god*, St. Petersburg, 1773.

NOTE: Median = 22.6 years.

TABLE V-3

Civilian Service of Former Military Personnel Serving as
Commandants and Assistant Commandants in 1773 (N = 289)

Years	0–5	6–10	11–15	16–20	21–25	26–30
Number of Commandants	86	91	84	22	5	1
%	29.8	31.5	29.0	7.6	1.7	0.3

SOURCE: See Table 2.

NOTE: Median = 8.8 years.

a fiscal and administrative agent of the crown. Even if such responsibilities cannot be described as complex, the vast majority of men who held these posts do not seem to have been well prepared, either in terms of their training or experience. It is not surprising that former officers who had little knowledge of the conduct of state business made poor officials. Local residents often complained about the commandants, referring to them as "wolves," and their penchant for graft was indicated by the popular saying:

> The horse loves oats
> The soil manure
> And the commandant the bearing [of payment].[28]

This sizable contingent shows the extent to which the typical career of a noble who served as a civil official in eighteenth-century provincial Russia emphasized military duties. When we remember that the average noble youth entered active service in his late teens, it is clear that the average commandant or assistant commandant was a man about forty who had probably spent half of his life in the armed forces (see Table 4). This contention is borne out by examining the ages of another group of commandants and their assistants who were based in Moscow government in 1775, two years later than the group we have been considering.

If we regard these men as occupying the middle level of Russian administration, their ages are somewhat older than the average for similar administrators in other parts of Europe.[29] A more significant factor in their outlook was provided by their military background. During the period he spent in either the army or navy, the Russian nobleman was certainly subject to the many rigors of military life. War probably heightened privations that were the norm in peacetime and provided experiences fresh in the memories of the men who had fought in the Seven Years' War or the Turkish conflict. While the commandant who assumed his post after this type of service was usually not enfeebled, he had ample reason to regard his new duties as a respite from past efforts. This office was seen more as a sinecure than a challenge; his performance, consequently, was not notable for its assiduity. Indeed, were further efforts likely to bring him additional rewards at the closing stages of his career?

Servitors familiar with eighteenth-century practice could easily equate a provincial berth with a pension. A decree enacted in 1716 had provided that officers unfit for further service were to be transferred to garrison duty or to civilian posts in the provinces. Although some were paid a definite salary, the state does not appear to have made ex-

---

28. *"Loshad' liubit oves, zemlia navoz, a voevoda privoz"* (M. Mikhel'son, *Russkaia mysl' i rech'*, St. Petersburg, 1912, p. 399).

29. J. Armstrong estimates that promotion to the middle grades usually came when the average administrator was between his late twenties and middle thirties (*The European Administrative Elite*, Princeton, 1973, p. 239). Of course, much depends on what is meant by a "middle-level" administrator, but the commandants (and especially their assistants) had little to do with formulating policy, and largely carried out general directives of St. Petersburg.

Robert D. Givens

TABLE V-4

Ages of Provincial Administrators

	Commandants		Assistant Commandants	
Age	*Number*	*%*	*Number*	*%*
30–39	7	25	10	42
40–49	13	46	9	37
50–59	6	22	5	21
60–69	2	7		
Total	28	100	24	100

SOURCE: TsGADA, Fond 400, d. 4.

tensive financial provisions, and the burden of supporting ex-officers fell on the monasteries.[30] Faced with this alternative, it is not surprising that former servitors regularly requested to be posted to the provinces. Petitions were addressed frequently to the Senate by noblemen who found their incomes inadequate after they left the military, occasionally speaking of genuine poverty. A retired colonel, Peter Semikov, petitioned in 1764 to gain appointment as a civilian official. Drawing attention to his prior career, Semikov claimed he had served for thirty years without reproach, yet at present received but sixty rubles annually.[31] Among the requests submitted the following year was that of a certain Iz'edinov, who had been in the army for twenty-six years. Lacking an estate, he could not continue without a livelihood, and asked to be appointed to "civic affairs."[32]

Because there was no systematic arrangement for pensions during much of the eighteenth century, noblemen serving as officers were uncertain as to the precise amount they would receive upon retirement. Catherine II did make an attempt in 1764 to prescribe certain requirements that would qualify an individual for a pension. Extended

30. L. Sazonov, "Pensii," *Voennaia entsiklopediia*, ed. K. Velichko, V. Novitskii et al. 18 vols., Petrograd, 1911–15, 17: 238.

31. *Senatskii arkhiv*, 15 vols., St. Petersburg, 1888–1913, 14: 395.

32. Ibid., 15: 906.

service was necessary: only after a term of thirty-five years, commencing no earlier than the servitor's fifteenth birthday, could he retire at half pay. Any official who was found guilty of a criminal offense forfeited this benefit. To finance pensions the state established a fund of 25,000 rubles, but the sum proved to be inadequate, and the following year saw tighter restrictions placed on those who might retire from service.[33] Even after this change, the evidence indicates that the system did not function smoothly: complaints about inequities continued to be sent to the Senate. Moreover, a pension was still regarded as a form of monarchical benevolence, rather than an impersonal reward. Surely it was far easier to be recommended for a grant by influential friends than to endure the vicissitudes of service for over three decades.

If a nobleman who entered the military in his teens did not want to continue to serve until age fifty, he could still take leave but received no compensation. In peacetime there was usually a surfeit of officers, and the government showed no reluctance in allowing them to quit the armed forces. Salaries that did not have to be paid represented a distinct saving for the treasury.[34] In addition to seeking an end to the discipline of military life, officers may have been prompted to retire in order to gain a promotion of one rank. This advancement, instituted by the 1762 statute that released the nobles from service, pertained if the officer had held his present grade a minimum of three years.[35] Those promoted in this manner, however, were ineligible for pensions.[36] It was apparently easy to abuse this provision. Writing of the army in 1782, a general mentioned with disfavor "unworthy and lazy officers" who retired and subsequently reentered the military with a higher rank. In the process they held higher grades than their colleagues who had remained on duty.[37] The same advancement, interestingly enough, applied when the officer transferred to civilian service, even if some years had elapsed since his departure from the military. In this case the grade accorded corresponded to a servitor's final military rank.[38] With such inducements it is little wonder that those who quit the armed forces often wanted to become civilian

---

33. PSZ i, Vol. 16, No. 12,175, 7 June 1764.

34. I. Dologorukov, *Zapiski kniazia I. M. Dolgorukova 1764–1800*, Petrograd, 1916, p. 41. The period referred to is the 1780s.

35. PSZ i, No. 11,444, art. 2.

36. S. Troitskii, *Russkii absoliutizm*, p. 148.

37. S. Rzhevskii, "O russkoi armii vo vtoruiu polovinu ekaterininskogo tsarstvovaniia," *Russkii arkhiv*, No. 3 (1879): 358.

38. PSZ i, No. 11,444, art. 8.

officials. On occasion the servitor himself did not even have to request a transfer. Those officers who were judged incompetent even by the lax standards of the late-eighteenth-century Russian army were at times dropped from its active list and subsequently became candidates for provincial service.[39]

The career patterns summarized above show why younger or more ambitious members of the *dvorianstvo* hardly aspired to a civilian post in provincial Russia. In pursuing the military career so esteemed by the nobles, an individual could clearly not remain in one place. Although it is difficult to indicate where a nobleman would serve in the course of a typical career, he usually held a series of assignments throughout the Russian Empire. A servitor may have been unable to predict the specific posts that led to the rewards of a high rank, but one thing was certain: important officials in Imperial Russia did not often begin their climb to success in a provincial chancery.

In order to complete our description of Russian provincial servitors, let us consider the men who remained in the civil service throughout their careers. One such group of officials served in the provinces as secretaries (*sekretari*)—in either a government or provincial bureau. A secretary had little formal responsibility for administrative or judicial decisions but clearly had some say about the daily operation of the office to which he was assigned. Besides drafting official documents, the secretaries were charged with recording judicial proceedings. Since the *sekretar'* had to bring any statutes that related to a particular case to the attention of his superiors,[40] he likely had a fair knowledge of the uncodified laws. Whatever their abilities, the secretaries were not accorded a prestigious rank. Those serving at the provincial level held the thirteenth grade, while district secretaries were accorded grade fourteen, the lowest in the Table of Ranks. The long hours these officials were required to spend at their desks scarcely made the post an attractive one.[41] Although the annual salaries these officials received—225 rubles at the provincial and 200 rubles at the district level[42]—did not mean impoverishment, there was little likeli-

---

39. F. Vigel', *Zapiski*, 2 vols., Moscow, 1891, 1: 31–32. Vigel' also mentions that older nobles were recruited for the post of counselor (*sovetnik*) in the provinces.

40. A. Lykoshin, "Sekretar," *Entsiklopedicheskii slovar'*, ed. F. Brokgaus and I. Efron, 41 vols., St. Petersburg, 1890–1904, 29: 320.

41. PSZ I, Vol. 11, No. 8,140, 19 June 1740, required secretaries to be at their desks after dinner and prescribed fines if they failed to obey. The long hours are also mentioned by V. Srezhnevskii, "Prikaznye liudi v nizhegorodskom namestnichestve," *Deistviia nizhegorodskoi gubernskoi uchenoi arkhivnoi komissii*, 5: 44.

42. PSZ I, Vol. 44, Pt. 2, *Kniga shtatov, otdeleniia* III–IV, 69.

hood a secretary could better his lot in the course of his career. Quite in contrast to their superiors, these men knew only one form of state service: of 286 secretaries in Moscow government in 1773 only *one* had ever been in the military. Moreover, the period these men had spent in the civilian branch certainly made them career servitors (Table 5). On the basis of their experience these secretaries seem far better equipped to conduct the daily business of Russia's administration than were their superiors, the commandants. Still, despite their service background, they could not claim a commensurate rank or hope to ascend the official hierarchy. The mediocre grades these men held after decades as civil servants showed how little the government valued their abilities.

If the above practices were prevalent in local administration on the eve of the 1775 reform, how did they fare during the remainder of Catherine's reign? Is there any reason to believe that those who staffed the provincial offices in subsequent decades differed from the officials we have examined? Since the posts of commandant and assistant commandant were done away with after 1775, there is no roster exactly like that used above for the later period. However, an analogous list of certain officials does provide the same information about their backgrounds.

Among the more important appointive offices created by the reform of 1775 were those of director of the economy and chairman of the judicial chamber. The director of the economy was second in command of all fiscal matters within the government; the two chairmen of the judicial chambers (one in charge of civil cases, the other criminal) supervised the courts. Like the previous commandant, these officials were appointed, in this case by the governor-general. Both posts conferred a relatively high rank in the Russian civil service—the judicial chairmen were accorded the fifth grade, the directors of the economy the sixth.

Tables 6 through 9 describe the careers of officials who either were in charge of the court system or economic affairs in each government in 1788. Included are thirty-eight directors of the economy and sixty-seven chairmen of the judicial chambers. The two groups are drawn from the entire Russian Empire, excluding two Baltic governments. As a whole, this contingent had a background quite similar to that of the commandants and assistants we have already examined; they were predominantly hereditary nobles who had begun serving the Russian state in its armed forces (Table 6). Although the position of director of the economy was sometimes held by a civilian, the vast majority did hail from the military. For those staffing the courts the pattern of

TABLE V-5

Civilian Service of Provincial Secretaries in 1773 (N = 226)

Years	0–5	6–10	11–15	16–20	21–25	26–30	Over 30
Number of Secretaries	28	10	13	36	31	49	59
%	12.4	4.4	5.7	15.9	13.7	21.7	26.1

SOURCE: See Table 2.

NOTE: Median = 24.7 years.

TABLE V-6

Service Background and Social Origin of Provincial Officials in 1788

Officials	Original Form of Service		Social Origin	
	Military	*Civilian*	*Noble*	*Nonnoble*
Directors of Economy				
N =	30	8	22	9
%	79	21	71	29
Chairmen of Judicial Chambers				
N =	57	10	45	7
%	85	15	87	13

SOURCE: "Spisok nakhodiashchimsia v guberniiakh predsedateliam palat i direktoram ekonomii, Aprel', 1788," Hermitage Collection, GPB.

a military background is similar to that already noted. The data indicate that men who were not born into the nobility were apparently not barred from attaining important rank in provincial Russia, but advancement to the upper echelons seems a clear exception to the rule.[43]

43. Troitskii has provided the most detailed analysis of this phenomenon during the 1750s (*Russkii absoliutizm*, ch. 4).

If the bulk of these officials were originally military personnel, at what stage did they shift to civilian status (Table 7)? Even if those who held the post of director did transfer at a slightly earlier stage in their military careers, 75 percent still spent at least a decade in the armed forces before turning to civilian service. The judicial personnel as a rule left later in their careers; nearly 70 percent had been in the military for at least fifteen years prior to the start of their civilian duties. It should be noted that the former officer did not always begin the new phase of his career immediately upon leaving the armed forces, but sometimes lived for several years as a private citizen. Adding this intermediate period would make our sample of officials serving in 1788 somewhat older than would be indicated simply by the length of time they held their positions. A reasonable estimate of their average age would be between thirty-five and forty-five.

A further effect of the hiatus that occurred in the careers of several of these officials was a reduction in the total amount of experience they had in the civilian branch of the Russian administration. Their lack of familiarity with official procedure was another trait they shared with those who quit the military in the 1760s and subsequently entered the civil service. Indeed, the median years of civilian service are virtually the same for the two groups (Table 8). Like the servitors we have previously examined, a significant number of the officials who supervised economic or judicial aspects of provincial government were relative novices. Over 70 percent of the directors of the economy and over 60 percent of the judicial chairmen had seen but a decade elapse since beginning their civilian careers. For the most part these men had been relatively high ranking officers in the military. Although they continued to enjoy the perquisites of a prestigious rank when they worked in the state administration, there is ample reason to question whether their abilities were commensurate. The talents that contributed to an individual's success in the military were surely of little use in dealing with economic or legal matters. Because provincial administrators were accorded greater responsibility after 1775, their jobs demanded more specialized knowledge and it became even more difficult for those who had known only military life to perform adequately. Still, such factors do not appear to have prevented a continuation of the same sequence we have described above. Posted to rural areas of the country late in their careers, the administrators probably looked upon the duties they performed as sinecures.

Considering the background of the judges chosen by local noble residents, it is not surprising that they paid little attention to legal niceties. Men whose training and experience had emphasized the arts

TABLE V-7

Length of Military Service before Transfer

Directors of Economy (N = 24)[a]						
Years	0–5	6–10	11–15	16–20	21–25	26–30	Over 30

Years	0–5	6–10	11–15	16–20	21–25	26–30	Over 30
Number of directors	2	4	7	4	5	1	1
%	8	17	29	17	21	4	4

Chairmen of Judicial Chambers (N = 54)[b]							
Years	0–5	6–10	11–15	16–20	21–25	26–30	Over 30
Number of Chairmen	1	6	10	21	11	4	1
%	2	11	19	39	20	7	2

SOURCE: See Table 6.

a. Median = 14.8 years.
b. Median = 18 years.

of warfare could hardly be expected to be at home with legal procedure. To make matters worse, the tedious pace of litigation did not encourage nobles to seek redress in the courts, and they at times settled their quarrels in a most arbitrary and even brutal manner.[44] Distance also contributed to these attitudes, so that the laws were probably disregarded most often in outlying regions of the empire where supervision tended to be lax. In 1780 Governor-General R. Vorontsov reported that he found the courts in Vladimir, Penza, and Tambov to be "in tolerable order." He still considered it necessary to urge the judicial personnel to study the new institutions and not to deal with matters outside their jurisdiction. In all likelihood the Tambov courts did not deserve even Vorontsov's mild words of praise, for he went on to report that it was very difficult to find people eager to staff them:

44. S. Bogoslovskii, "Byt i nravy russkogo dvorianstva v pervoi polovine XVIII veka," *Nauchnoe slovo* 6 (1904): 34.

TABLE V-8

Length of Civilian Service of Former Military Personnel in 1788

*Directors of Economy (*N = 31*)*[a]						
Years	0–5	6–10	11–15	16–20	21–25	
Number of Directors	8	14	4	4	1	
%	26	45	13	13	3	

*Chairmen of Judicial Chambers (*N = 43*)*[b]							
Years	0–5	6–10	11–15	16–20	21–25	26–30	31–35
Number of Chairmen	11	16	11	1	2	1	1
%	26	37	26	2	5	2	2

SOURCE: See Table 6.

a. Median = 8.2 years.
b. Median = 8.8 years.

"A large part of the local nobility is not practiced in anything other than slander, and there are those who do not comply with any law whatsoever. The state peasants are excessively oppressed and provoked by them. Their cases take up much of my time, and are quite deplorable."[45]

Since no permanent justices presided over the elective courts, these bodies had scant opportunity to become experienced in trying cases. Although some incumbent judges were retained after 1775, the evidence shows no widespread pattern of reelection. Given the course of a typical career, it was unlikely that a nobleman who had once been elected to the district or conscience court would continue his judicial duties. According to the above data the former officers who held this post did not often advance to one of the appointive chambers in the government. Of the sixty-seven chairmen whom we considered

45. Report 7 June 1780, TsGADA, *Gosarkhiv, razriad* 16, d. 636, fol. 44.

earlier, only seven had previously sat on the nobiliary elective courts. It seems that if the judges chosen by the *dvorianstvo* ever revealed any legal talent, their abilities were not utilized by the crown.

These negative features of provincial government during the final decades of the eighteenth century were an outgrowth of the nobles' response to the assemblies. Rather than participate in the elections or become candidates for the new offices, they continued to climb the traditional ladder to success in Russia. Because service in the locality had been the final stage in the careers of many servitors, it undoubtedly held little attraction for younger noblemen. The low rank conferred on the secretaries likewise deterred the ambitious from becoming permanent provincial officials. As can be seen from the records of the directors of the economy and the chairmen of the judicial chambers, appointive posts followed the same pattern. Over a decade after the reform of 1775, the bulk of those holding these significant positions in the localities were retired military personnel. Moreover, the practice of choosing officers who had been pensioned off to hold the elective posts apparently became so common that an imperial decree was required to assure noblemen that they would not forfeit their pensions by serving in this capacity.[46]

This persistent social backdrop to Russian local government surely had an adverse effect on the new institutions. By permitting elected officers of the *dvorianstvo* to hold positions at the local level the crown sought to improve the overall quality of Russian internal administration. Given the long-standing pattern of state service, however, few noblemen were apt to become eager partners in such an endeavor. Rather than lend their energy to improving the local administration, younger nobles much preferred a military career. The following remarks of N. Tolubeev, who was compelled to enter the civil service owing to his difficult financial straits, well illustrates the prevalent attitude at the end of the eighteenth century: "I exerted little enthusiasm when serving in the criminal chamber and whatever I did was like [the work of] present day peasants on *corvée* [*barshchina*]. This was particularly the case when I saw two sons of our neighbor who had been appointed to some regiment in [their] uniforms—with lace on their red collars. I lamented for a long time that I could not follow them and could not even be transferred to the regiment."[47] Reversing the sequence we have described, Tolubeev eventually secured a post in the military.

46. PSZ i, Vol. 21, No. 15,140, 24 March 1781.
47. N. Tolubeev, *Zapiski*, p. 34.

One final aspect of elective service that contributed to its unpopularity among the noblemen was the relatively low rank it conferred. Only four officials the nobles elected were accorded even the seventh rank in the imperial service (Table 9). The modest ranks that came with elective service meant less pay for those who held them. As the government was well aware, salaries became more important as an incentive for nobiliary service after 1762, and it was necessary to heighten incentive by raising the pay scale.[48] Pay usually depended on one's specific job, so that a servitor's position in the hierarchy did not always indicate his income. The chairmen of the judicial chambers, for example, received 840 rubles annually, while the director of the economy (who held a lower rank) received 1,000. At the most the officials elected by the nobility were paid 360 rubles per year (the salary of one holding the seventh rank).

Surely the above considerations were related to the attitude of the Kursk nobility, whose behavior was described in a 1788 report to Prince Viazemskii, the procurator-general.[49] The procurator of this government informed his superior that nobles elected by their colleagues seldom completed their terms of office, requesting instead to be relieved. Although these officeholders based their appeals on cases of supposedly incurable illness, the local procurator found such maladies "difficult to believe." Behind these dubious claims lay the undeniable fact that it was "contrary to the nobles' wish to continue the service with which they were charged." Their reluctance disrupted the flow of official business. To ensure that the elective officers would not constantly fluctuate, the local procurator made a recommendation often heard in Russia when quasi-autonomous institutions failed to live up to expectations—tighter state control. In the future, nobles who sought to resign elective offices owing to ill health should have to present their requests to the local marshal of the nobility and then submit to a medical examination. The procurator was really admitting that elective duties had become a new form of compulsory service for the noblemen, one so unpalatable that those who were selected entered fraudulent claims to escape it.

In evaluating developments within an autocracy it is logical to place considerable emphasis on the effect of governmental policy. Monarchical intention, however, comprised but one aspect of the social evo-

---

48. S. Troitskii, *Russkii absoliutizm*, p. 265.

49. P. Stromilov to Viazemskii, 23 June 1788, TsGADA, Fond. 248, d. 6,560, Chap. 2, fols. 81–85.

TABLE V-9

Officials Elected by the Nobles of
Each Government with Service Rank

Official	*Rank*
Government level	
1 marshal	. . .
10 assessors (*zasedateli*)	
of upper local court	VII
2 assessors of conscience court	VII
District level	
1 marshal	VII
1 district court judge	VII
2 assessors	IX
Lower local court (police)	
1 police captain	IX
2 assessors	X

SOURCE: V. Grigor'ev, *Reforma mestnogo uprav-leniia pri Ekaterine II*, St. Petersburg, 1910, p. 239.

lution we have been examining. Within the narrow limits of choice accorded them the Russian nobles sought the most advantageous duties, shunning those that were neither prestigious nor remunerative. During the long period when state service was required of all adult members of the *dvorianstvo* their options were indeed circumscribed, yet the noblemen demonstrated their preferences clearly. Whatever the needs of the state for competent officials, the nobles evinced little desire to accept civilian posts, seeking instead the glamour and rewards of a military career.

Nobiliary preferences attained particular significance in the one region where members of this estate had an opportunity to gain some autonomy—the provinces. By following the normal pattern of service, however, the nobleman filled a post in rural Russia toward the close of his career. Not only did this pattern make the provincial administration less suitable for younger noblemen, but the status of career civil servants also lessened its attractions. One merely had to consider the usual career of the secretaries to appreciate how little the regime valued men who had spent decades at a provincial desk. While the 1775 reform altered many features of Russia's internal government, it did little to affect the established service patterns. Just as the commandants and their assistants had received their appointments following at least a decade in the armed forces, so were the administrators of the late 1780s also ex-officers. Although the elective duties that followed the new legislation increased the participation of the noblemen in local affairs, appointments in the countryside were still thought suitable only for veterans who deserved to be put out to pasture. The men who served under such conditions had little incentive to perform diligently but marked time in posts that were akin to retirement. As long as the nobles hewed to the well-trodden path of state service it was unlikely they would be concerned about the operation of Russia's provincial government.

CHAPTER SIX

THE EMERGENCE OF A MILITARY-ADMINISTRATIVE ELITE IN THE DON COSSACK LAND, 1708–1836

Bruce W. Menning

The focus of Menning's discussion is the origin of a very special kind of local officialdom. What we encounter here is an illustration of the way the rapidly expanding Russian Empire made use of the local institutions and elites in frontier areas as the empire's influence spread. Where use could be made of them—as was the case with the Cossacks—or when they were so powerful as to require extraordinary energy to destroy—also the case with the Cossacks—they were not displaced as William the Conqueror displaced the Saxon elites, but absorbed and transformed. What is striking is the rapid and very nearly complete transformation of the freebooter Cossack captain into Russian gentryman. Once the central government of the tsars became the prime source of favor and wealth, the process that Menning describes seems to be self-generating. The central government gained more-reliable servitors and the Cossack elite a more comfortable and secure life for themselves and their descendants. As in the case of the Russian nobility, the Cossack elite was "organized" by the Table of Ranks—success in service, measured by rank, ennobled them and in many cases enabled them to achieve the status of landlord as well. Surely here we see an extreme illustration of the possible impact of bureaucratization on social and even economic relations. Even in their relatively disorganized and impaired form of the early nineteenth century, the bureaucratic principles of uniform organization, ranking, and career development effected a remarkable social transformation.

In the previous chapter Givens pointed out the limited qualifications of noble provincial officials and the poor quality of local administration. The fact that the regime abetted the extension of the same system in the Don suggests that even if it was not adequate for all the needs of the central government, not capable of ensuring an enlightened, impartial officialdom, nevertheless, no other alternative existed. Still, one must observe that, given the times and the intractable nature of the problem of controlling the Cossack borderlands, the remarkable transformation finally effected in Cossack society suggests this administrative solution was adequate. A combination of thoroughly unen-

lightened self-interest with externally imposed administrative structures, statuses, and objectives was the minimum necessary solution to the problem of Cossack integration into the empire. [THE EDITORS.]

A survey of Don Cossack history from the era of Peter the Great through the first decade of Nicholas I's reign reveals what appeared to have been a nearly unbroken series of successes for the forces of Imperial Russian expansion and centralization against traditional Cossack autonomy and separatism. By following a dual policy of subordination and perpetuation,[1] Peter and his successors were gradually able to transform the highly volatile Don Cossack Host (*Donskoe voisko*) into an obedient and pliant instrument designed to meet the military needs of the Imperial Russian state. Nowhere were the effects of this transformation more evident than in the realm of local government, where landmarks along the way to subjugation included administrative subordination of the host to the Imperial Military College (1721), tsarist appointment of the Don Cossack ataman or chieftain (1723), the institution of a Host Civilian Government (1775), and the implementation of a major local governmental reform, the Statute on the Administration of the Don Cossack Host (1836).[2]

Less obvious, though perhaps more important than various legislative acts coupled with institutional change, was the gradual emergence under imperial tutelage of a local governing elite.[3] During the eighteenth century, one of the more important aspects of imperial policy had aimed at stimulating the transformation of local notables, the Don Cossack elders (*starshiny*), into a privileged class of Don nobility. Through influence, judicious appointments, and administrative fiat, various sovereigns, most notably Peter I, Catherine II, and Paul I, gradually turned the process of social differentiation that had spawned the elders to the advantage of the state. In accomplishing this goal, St. Petersburg fostered the emergence of the elders, assumed control

1. The words "subordination and perpetuation" were deliberately chosen by the writer to reflect the dual aspect of Imperial Russian policy in the Don: to subjugate the Cossacks while simultaneously retaining or perpetuating their traditional military organization.

2. A brief summary of the appropriate legislation appears in Erik Amburger, *Geschichte der Behördenorganisation Russlands von Peter dem Grossen bis 1917*, Leiden, 1966, p. 342; the legislation itself appears in PSZ I, Vol. 6, No. 3,750, Vol. 10, No. 7,525, Vol. 20, No. 14,252, and PSZ II, Vol. 10, No. 8,163.

3. Throughout this chapter, the term "elite" is used in a purely descriptive fashion, without any normative connotations.

of their selection, and by bowing to their seemingly limited interests and aspirations, transformed them into collaborators of imperial rule in the Land of the Don Cossack Host (*Zemlia voiska Donskogo*). The new elite's compliance with imperial policy was purchased with material awards and blandishments: the elders received money, honors, offices, ranks, and significantly, access to the status of Russian nobility. By the end of the eighteenth century, the central government had created out of the elders and their heirs a local nobility whose members owed their positions and their loyalties to St. Petersburg and not to their fellow Cossacks. With little or no need to oppose the Russian hegemony, the new Cossack nobles formed a reliable source of local administrators and military officers.[4]

The objective of this study is to present a descriptive analysis of the process, people, and problems associated with the emergence of the Don Cossack nobility. The subject matter seems especially appropriate to a volume on Russian officialdom in that the Cossack nobles, none of whom were exempt from state service, collectively constituted a corps of local officials who served as principal intermediaries between the imperial government and the Cossack rank and file. In their twin capacities as military officers and civil administrators, these officials were of pivotal importance both in transmitting and transforming the imperial will. Their persistent ability to remain powerful and prominent may be explained only by referring to a complex set of factors, including the identity of the persons concerned, the historical and institutional context in which they operated, and the measures and methods they used to achieve and retain their positions.

An additional aspect of this study involves an attempt to analyze the consequences of the Cossack nobility's rise to fame and fortune. Such an analysis seeks to avoid a recurring weakness of research on elites: failure to devote sufficient attention to the broader social and political implications associated with their appearance. Traditionally, scholars have been eager to amass a wealth of information characterizing various elites, but they have been less willing to speculate about how those characteristics affect elite behavior.[5] The Cossack case seems to invite such speculation, if only because the area and people involved were sufficiently limited to exclude a host of complicating factors, which often bedevil the work of scholars studying larger groups. Then, too,

4. The best historical survey of the Cossack nobility's rise to power is A. P. Pronshtein, *Zemlia Donskaia v XVIII veke*, Rostov-na-Donu, 1961, pp. 146–66 and 176–83.

5. See, for example, Robert D. Putnam, *The Comparative Study of Political Elites*, Englewood Cliffs, 1976, pp. ix–x.

the relevant literature on Cossack history—primary and secondary, Imperial Russian and Soviet—touches the consequences engendered by the rise of the nobility so often and at such great length that it is virtually impossible to discuss Don Cossack noble officials without reference to the larger social and political issues created by their existence.[6] Over a period of time, because of their collective behavior, they paradoxically came to represent Imperial Russia's greatest asset and greatest liability in the Land of the Don Host. How the Cossack nobles emerged as both heroes and villains in a larger imperial drama remains a crucial chapter in the history of the Don Cossacks.

The Don Cossack Host was originally formed of various types of refugees, fugitives, and freebooters, most of whom migrated to the Don steppe to escape or avoid the social and political ills of sixteenth-century Muscovite Russia. Once in the steppe, these immigrants combined with various other people of uncertain ethnic origin to form a single host or *voisko*. As settlers in the "wild steppe," the Cossacks formed an independent polity whose members enjoyed a high degree of freedom, because they owed allegiance to no master and were beyond the reach of any law. Sharing the hardships, hazards, and rewards of a dangerous frontier existence helped to foster among the Cossacks not only a feeling of solidarity and egalitarian camaraderie, but also a tradition of rudimentary democracy. All important decisions within the host were made democratically by an informal popular assembly (*krug*, or circle) of adult male Cossacks. The executive power of the *krug* was an elected ataman, or chieftain. Only in time of war did the ataman exercise dictatorial power, and even then his fellow Cossacks could hold him accountable for his actions and decisions. This pattern of government was repeated on a lower level in every *stanitsa*, or settlement, where an elected ataman managed governmental affairs for a local assembly, which met only periodically or in the event of emergency.[7]

6. A sampling would include "Pis'ma Aleksandra Ivanovicha (vposledstvii kniazia) Chernysheva Arseniiu (vposledstvii grafu) Zakrevskomu, 1820–1822 gg.," *Sbornik Imperatorskogo russkogo istoricheskogo obshchestva*, 148 vols., St. Petersburg, 1867–1916, 78: 451–54 (this collection is hereinafter cited as SIRIO); V. Martynov, *Donskoe dvorianstvo i zaselenie ikh zemel' krest'ianami (istoricheskii ocherk)*, St. Petersburg, 1891, *passim*; P. P. Sakharov, "Beloe rabstvo na Donu; k piatidesiatoi godovshchine osvobozhdeniia donskikh krest'ian," *Donskaia tserkovnaia starina* 3 (1911): 138–87; and M. M. Postnikova-Loseva, "Iz istorii sotsial'no-ekonomicheskikh otnoshenii na Donu v XVIIIv.," *Istoricheskie zapiski* 60 (1957): 248–69.

7. The origins and early history of the Don Cossack Host are discussed at length by

In addition to the legendary heritage of freedom and democracy, life on the frontier bred in the early Cossacks perhaps the most enduring and contrasting characteristic of their society, a tradition of military service. With no natural boundaries to stem the tide of hostile invasion, every Cossack learned to maintain his own horse, equipment, and arms in a state of constant readiness to repel foreign incursion. To the dismay of their traditional Tatar and Turkish enemies, the Cossacks quickly proved themselves adept students in the hard school of steppe warfare. Mounted on tough little steppe ponies and equipped with sabers, lances, and primitive firearms, the Don warriors soon mastered the age-old techniques of nomadic combat—ride hard, strike unexpectedly, and retire rapidly. In innumerable hard-fought skirmishes on the frontier, the Cossacks forged the beginnings of a military way of life that was to extend into the twentieth century.[8]

In contrast, Cossack autonomy and the concomitant sovereignty of the host's democratic institutions failed to stand the test of time. Throughout the second half of the seventeenth century, the Cossacks, who had previously considered themselves only occasional military allies of the tsar, witnessed a dramatic decline in the host's political fortunes. In part, this decline stemmed from developments of an internal nature, including renewed immigration, factionalism, an uneven distribution of wealth and influence, and a gradual erosion of egalitarian practices, all of which combined to exert a steadily corrosive effect on Cossack democracy and society. When these same factors helped spark two serious anti-tsarist uprisings among the Cossacks within thirty-seven years, the host, divided against itself, first lost ground and then capitulated to growing tsarist political and military power in the south steppe. After the suppression of Razin's rebellion in 1670–71, Moscow struck a serious blow against Cossack autonomy by depriving the host of its right to harbor fugitives and to conduct an independent foreign policy. Moreover, every Cossack was forced to swear an oath of loyalty to the Muscovite tsar. In the wake of Bulavin's revolt of 1707–8, Peter the Great began implementing

A. P. Pronshtein, "K istorii vozniknoveniia kazach'ikh poselenii i obrazovaniia sosloviia kazakov na Donu," in V. A. Aleksandrov, M. T. Beliavskii, et al., eds., *Novoe o proshlom nashei strany*, Moscow, 1957, pp. 158–73; and S. G. Svatikov, *Rossiia i Don*, Vienna, 1924, pp. 11–16, and 33–41.

8. On the early military history of the Cossacks, see, D. A. Skalon, ed., *Stoletie Voennogo Ministerstva*, 48 pts. in 13 vols., St. Petersburg, 1902–14, Vol. 11, Pt. 3, pp. 59–61; and V. D. Sukhorukov, *Istoricheskoe opisanie Zemli voiska Donskogo*, Novocherkassk, 1903, pp. 73ff.

those measures that were to culminate in the complete subjugation of the Don Host during the remainder of the eighteenth century. As this process unfolded, surviving democratic institutions among the Cossacks either declined in importance, were eliminated, or were subsumed into a system of local administration that brought the Cossacks firmly under Imperial Russian hegemony.[9]

Once the Land of the Don Host became a province of the Russian Empire, the Cossacks came to occupy a unique status as a privileged military class within imperial society. Because the host's martial strength offered a valuable asset both in defending against southern enemies and in providing a useful screen to cover the colonization of the southeastern frontier, St. Petersburg made special efforts to preserve and even improve the system of Cossack military service. In encouraging the Cossacks to maintain their traditional military organization, imperial sovereigns from the time of Peter the Great granted them a series of rights and privileges designed to perpetuate the Cossack system as it had evolved from the sixteenth century. These rights and privileges—including chiefly the affirmation of the Cossacks' status as free men, the Cossack right to common ownership of all land within the territory of the Don Host, exemption from taxation and other fiscal burdens, and the right to sole use of all Don water and land resources—were essentially the same advantages that Cossacks had enjoyed from the first days of the founding of their settlements. Now, however, within a larger imperial context, these rights and privileges set the Cossacks apart as a special segment of the population. At the same time, these rights and privileges were also to afford the eighteenth-century Cossack nobility an opportunity to enrich themselves at the expense of the host's military preparedness.[10]

The ancestors of the late-eighteenth- and early-nineteenth-century Don nobility were the *starshiny* or elders who had come to dominate Cossack political and social life by the end of the seventeenth century. The designation *starshina* first seems to have appeared in the 1640s, when it was applied to any Cossack who held an important military

9. There are numerous accounts of relations between the Don Cossacks and Moscow during the seventeenth century. One of the best and most recent is S. G. Pushkarev, "Donskoe kazachestvo i Moskovskoe gosudarstvo v XVII veke," *Zapiski russkoi akademicheskoi gruppy v S. Sh. A.* 2 (1968): 5–28.

10. "Prava i privilegii voiska Donskogo, Rossiiskimi gosudariami darovannye," *Donskie voiskovye vedomosti*, No. 43 (29 October 1863): 245–47; and V. D. Sukhorukov, *Statisticheskoe opisanie Zemli Donskikh kazakov, sostavlennoe v 1822–32 godakh*, Novocherkassk, 1891, pp. 111–17.

command or political position.[11] In accordance with the customs of Cossack democracy, upon completion of his duties or term in office, an elder lost his title and reverted to the status of common Cossack. However, during the second half of the seventeenth century, a small group of notable people (*znatnye liudi*) began to retain the title of elder without regard to the actual holding of office. They constituted a limited number of Cossacks who wielded disproportionate power and influence by virtue of military or political experience, personal wealth, and family connections. As these elders emerged to occupy a prominent position in Cossack society, their title began to imply not only military and political power but also social position. By the 1680s, the Cossacks themselves began to observe that they, too, had their boyars and *voevody*.[12]

The appearance of what the Cossacks (and Russians in general) called "notable people" was in large part a function of an important trend that witnessed the increasing concentration of power in a diminishing number of hands. The origins of this trend lay partially with the ephemeral nature of the host's democratic institutions and partially with the tendency of a few individuals, whether by personal magnetism, military leadership, or various other attributes and achievements, to remain in important positions for lengthy periods of time. Added to this potentially dangerous combination was the corrosive influence of Muscovite absolutism which, in pursuing the age-old dictum "divide and conquer," saw the emerging elders as its natural allies in the struggle to extend tsarist power to the south steppe. The rank-and-file Cossacks might resist the flow of events—as they did in 1670–71 and again in 1707–8—but time and power seemed inexorably to favor Moscow (or St. Petersburg) and the elders.

The office of Don Cossack Host ataman offered what was perhaps the classic example of the above forces at work. Since the Cossacks imposed no limitation upon the number of times an individual might hold significant positions within the host government, no one seems to have expressed serious alarm or surprise when a few Cossacks of exceptional stature were returned repeatedly to elective office. For example, A. P. Pronshtein, a leading historian of the Don Cossacks, has noted that between 1637 and 1661, only seven different men occupied the position of Don Host ataman, a post ordinarily subject to

---

11. A. Leonov, "Voiskovoi krug," *Donskie voiskovye vedomosti*, Nos. 26 and 27 (10 July 1862): 157; Martynov, *Donskoe dvorianstvo*, p. 4; and Mikhail Kharuzin, *Svedeniia o kazatskikh obshchinakh na Donu: Materialy dlia obychnogo prava*, Moscow, 1885, pp. xxii–xxiv.

12. Pronshtein, *Zemlia Donskaia v XVIII veke*, p. 148.

annual election. One of the seven, Naum Vasil'ev, served a total of thirteen years after being elected ataman on at least five known occasions.[13] This tendency became even more pronounced during the second half of the seventeenth century, when two extraordinary leaders, Kornilii Iakovlev and Frol Minaev, came to exercise a near monopoly over the office of the ataman. Frol Minaev alone, the progenitor of the prominent Frolov family of Don Cossacks, was elected ataman some twenty times between 1680 and 1699.[14] Repeated tenure in office enabled Frol Minaev and similar leaders to cultivate what often amounted to a personal relationship with Moscow, to appoint sons, relatives, and friends to important political, military, and diplomatic posts, and to enjoy personal benefit from a variety of sources ranging from unequal distribution of the annual tsarist subsidy to the financing at a handsome return of covert raiding operations against merchants plying trade routes crisscrossing the Black Sea or nearby basin of the Caspian.[15]

Still another aspect of the growing tendency to concentrate power in close proximity to the ataman was the gradual emergence of a council of elders (*sovet starshin*). At first, this body was merely an informal aggregation of former atamans and other influential leaders whom the Cossacks named to advise the host ataman on matters of importance arising when the *krug* was not in session. Since the *krug* met at most only several times per year or in the event of emergency, the council of elders eventually came to exercise considerable influence over the direction of Cossack affairs. The elders did not possess veto power over the decisions of the ataman, but no chief executive could long afford to disregard the weight of their collective opinion.[16] At the same time, when the ataman and the elders acted in concert with sufficient determination, they sometimes succeeded in commanding obedience even from the normally unruly *krug*. In 1683, for example, a Muscovite official supervising the shipment of the annual tsarist subsidy to the Don reported that the ataman and his elders so dominated the *krug* that none of the rank and file dared openly challenge their proposals on the distribution of the subsidy.[17]

More important to the ataman than the council of elders, which might include members only vaguely associated with the chief ex-

13. Ibid., p. 146.

14. M. Sebriakov, "Donskoi Ataman Frol Minaev," *Kazachii sbornik*, Novocherkassk, 1887, p. 38.

15. Svatikov, *Rossiia i Don*, pp. 119–20.

16. S. G. Svatikov, "Donskoi Voiskovoi Krug," *Donskaia letopis'* 1 (1923): 193–94.

17. Pronshtein, *Zemlia Donskaia v XVIII veke*, p. 147.

ecutive, was a steadily growing network of elite affiliations based primarily on patronage.[18] While the ataman lacked the power outright to control elections to other high-ranking positions, such as the two host *esauly* (the ataman's chief deputies), he exercised wide discretion over the appointment of a series of secondary officials. Such appointments usually encompassed important field commands, membership in diplomatic missions, and a variety of other liaison assignments. Obviously, retaining one of these positions was contingent upon a display of loyalty to the ataman, in return for which the incumbent enjoyed a certain amount of prominence among his fellow Cossacks, and even more important, the possibility of obtaining direct access to the sovereign or his deputies.

Two separate but related institutions, the winter (*zimovaia*) *stanitsa* and the "light" (*legkaia*) *stanitsa*, demonstrated the increasing importance of patronage. The first was an official delegation of a *stanitsa* ataman and 100 Cossacks appointed annually by the host ataman to spend the winter in Moscow, then return to the Don during the following spring as an escort for the annual subsidy. In contrast, the light *stanitsa* was a much smaller delegation (one ataman and five to ten Cossacks) of varying membership dispatched to Moscow for the accomplishment of specific missions, such as receiving decrees of importance to the Cossacks or escorting official prisoners to the tsarist capital for interrogation.[19] In the era before Razin's rebellion, each of these two types of delegations also fulfilled an important diplomatic function. However, even after the Don Host became a territory of the Russian Empire and diplomatic formalities were no longer necessary, these institutions retained significance as means of cultivating relations between the imperial throne and the Cossacks. Indeed, the Cossacks themselves were quite content to maintain the tradition and even expand the limits of participation, with the result that the imperial government was eventually forced to promulgate an elaborate series of regulations on the protocol governing the dispatch of official missions.[20] Cossack enthusiasm stemmed primarily from the benefits conferred by participation, including likelihood of an audience with the sovereign and guarantee of substantial financial reward. By the

18. The structure of the following argument profits greatly from Putnam, *The Comparative Study of Political Elites*, pp. 57–63.

19. M. M. Postnikova-Loseva, "Iz istorii Donskogo kazachestva XVIII v. (Formirovanie dvorianskogo klassa na Donu v XVIII v.)," Candidate dissertation, Moscow State University, 1944, p. 47.

20. A. A. Lishin, comp., *Akty otnosiashchiesia k istorii voiska Donskogo*, 3 vols in 4, Novocherkassk, 1894, 2, Pt. 2, p. 48.

second or third decade of the eighteenth century, an elder serving as ataman (often the host ataman himself) of the winter *stanitsa* might expect to receive as much as 500 rubles in gold and various other gifts such as expensive gold drinking vessels, sabers, decorations, and portraits of the sovereign encrusted with precious gems. In 1725, the Military College expended more than 5,000 rubles to purchase gifts for that year's annual winter *stanitsa*, while the five light *stanitsy* required an additional disbursement of nearly 2,000 rubles. Little wonder that St. Petersburg soon found it necessary to publish strict rules limiting the frequency and number of participants in each of the delegations! For an elder returning to the Don, one of the greatest symbols of prestige was to drink wine from a gift vessel before his fellow Cossacks assembled in the *maidan*, the traditional meeting place for the *krug* in the square in front of the Cherkassk cathedral.[21]

The efficacy of this act bore testimony both to the growing weight of tsarist intervention in Cossack affairs and to the importance of the elders as surrogates of Muscovite power. Until the reign of Peter the Great, conventional political wisdom suggested that the tsarist government, lacking the ability to maintain a permanent armed presence in the south steppe, refrain from flaunting its newly won ascendency among the Cossacks. Therefore, except for extracting an oath of loyalty—accompanied by the famous kissing of the crucifix—and imposing a limited number of restrictions upon Cossack conduct, tsarist authorities studiously avoided direct confrontation with the Cossacks.[22] It was easier to rely upon the host ataman and the Cossack elders to serve as collaborators of Muscovite rule by encouraging them to maintain a precarious order in local government, to raise the requisite number of cavalrymen upon demand, and to implement tsarist decrees among the often recalcitrant rank and file. Elders who assumed a serious role in local politics soon found themselves caught in a hazardous balancing act in which they faced the all but impossible task of reconciling the growing needs of Moscow with the near-anarchic demands of Cossack freebooters who wanted more freedom, not more control.[23] Those who succeeded in mastering this balancing act received a measure of fame, official recognition, emoluments, and gifts of various kinds. Those who failed, including such elders as Efrem Petrov, founder of the famous Don Cossack Efremov family, lost their heads in retributions which accompanied the next popular uprising among the Don Cossacks.

21. Postnikova-Loseva, diss., pp. 49–50.
22. Pronshtein, *Zemlia Donskaia v XVIII veke*, pp. 147–48.
23. Svatikov, *Rossiia i Don*, pp. 117–18.

Kondratii Bulavin's antitsarist revolt of 1707–8 convincingly demonstrated that elder rule alone was not sufficient to ensure a quiet Don. Accordingly, Peter the Great undertook an energetic program of vengeance coupled with the imposition of important institutional changes within the Cossack Host. In 1709, after slaughtering thousands of Cossacks and depriving the host of more than half a million acres of land, Peter enjoined a quiescent *krug* to select his personal nominee, Petr Emel'ianovich Ramazanov, host ataman for life. Following Ramazanov's death in 1715, the Cossacks learned that the election of each new host ataman was subject to tsarist approval. Finally, in 1723, the tsar simply appointed Andrei Lopatin to fill the vacancy created by the death of the last elected ataman, Vasilii Frolov. This turn of events, together with the host's administrative subordination to the Military College in 1721, hastened the *krug* on its eighteenth-century journey into political oblivion.[24]

As the locus of power shifted from the *krug*, a new institution, the Chancery of Elders, rose to reflect the concentration of authority in an ever-narrowing circle of Cossacks. After the Don Host became part of the Russian Empire, a considerable amount of correspondence began to flow from the imperial capital to the seat of Cossack government in Cherkassk. To aid the ataman in expediting the handling of this correspondence, a chancery gradually emerged as part of the ataman's personal coterie of supporters and advisers. In the tradition of the Council of Elders, this chancery at first was a purely informal organization intended to facilitate the flow of pressing administrative business. Members of the chancery were elders who, in the course of assisting the ataman, gradually began to take an active part in the day-to-day decision of legal and administrative questions related to host government. Records indicate that the Chancery of Elders had begun to function in the 1720s; two decades later, it was an acknowledged organ of local government, in some ways a successor to the *krug* in areas of competence not subsumed into the imperial government as part of the tsarist policy of centralization. Accordingly, the chancery, always under the leadership of an appointed ataman, became a repository of many of the *krug*'s former prerogatives, including wide judicial and administrative powers, both civilian and military.[25]

Another agency reflecting the growing capacity of the elders to dominate local affairs was the *sysknoe nachal'stvo*, an organ of local government unique to the Don. This institution first appeared in re-

24. Svatikov, "Donskoi voiskovoi krug," p. 196.
25. Pronshtein, *Zemlia Donskaia v XVIII veke*, pp. 232–33.

sponse to a short-term need and then gradually evolved to bridge the gap between host government in Cherkassk (and its successor, Novocherkassk) and the more than one hundred *stanitsy* in the countryside. The origins of the *sysknoe nachal'stvo* lay in the second quarter of the eighteenth century with the occasional appointment of special elders (*narochnye starshiny*) whose mission it was to search for, apprehend, and return to their masters fugitive serfs migrating to the Don in quest of freedom. At first, these elders operated on a case-by-case basis, but gradually their existence became permanent. The whole of the Don Host Land was divided into districts, the number varying from four to eleven during the eighteenth century, and each district was placed under the jurisdiction of an appointed "elder on search." These districts came to be known as *nachal'stva* (commands) and their chief officials as *sysknie nachal'niki* or *sysknie starshiny* (search leaders or search elders). With the assistance of several junior officers, the elders on search patrolled the steppes with small detachments of Cossacks on internal military service. The elders' primary task remained the apprehension of fugitives, but over a period of time these officials came to wield considerable civil and military power. By 1802, when the host government fixed the number of search districts at seven, the search elders' functions had come to resemble those of district police officials in most Russian provinces. In addition, the search elders assisted the host ataman in such purely military matters as the raising and dispatch of Cossack regiments for active service. The search elders constituted the chief civil and military link between the host government and the *stanitsy*, and even without the attributes of civil office, the possession of elder rank alone made them a force to be reckoned with in the determination of local affairs.[26]

Thus, various changes accompanying the Don Host's assimilation into the Russian Empire either directly or indirectly paved the way for a further consolidation of power in an ataman-centered constellation of elders. With the destruction or atrophy of the Host's democratic institutions and with tsarist policy clearly committed to a course of governing the Cossacks through personal representatives, the Don entered an era characterized by some historians as dynastic rule.[27] Between 1716 and 1772, the ascendency of two Don Cossack elder

26. Lishin, *Akty*, Vol. 2, Pt. 1, p. 353; Pronshtein, *Zemlia Donskaia v XVIII veke*, pp. 249–51; I. P. Popov, comp., *Materialy k istorii Dona*, Novocherkassk, 1900, pp. 8, 11–15; and *Tsentral'nyi gosudarstvennyi voenno-istoricheskii arkhiv SSR*, Fond 330 (*Kazachii otdel Glavnogo shtaba*), op. 2, d. 35, *chast'* 11, fols. 267–79; this Archive is hereinafter cited as TsGVIA.

27. L. M. Savelov, *Donskoe dvorianstvo*, 2 vols., Moscow, 1905, 1914, 1: 7–8.

families in particular, the Frolovs and the Efremovs, rendered this claim difficult to refute. In the absence of any local barriers to the attainment of what came close to absolute authority, the scions of these two families successively attempted to administer the Don as their private fiefdom. Long tenure in power enabled them and an assortment of accomplices to influence the election of minor officials, take control of the distribution of tsarist subsidies, and regulate the appointment of friends, relatives, and henchmen to prestigious military and administrative positions. Simultaneously, the attainment of elder rank, the most important key to social (and military) advancement and subsequent imperial recognition, came to depend largely— but not solely—upon finding favor with a small ruling oligarchy of Cossack families. Once entrenched, they were nearly impossible to dislodge.[28]

The first of these families, the Frolovs, served as an important element of continuity between the seventeenth- and eighteenth-century Cossack elders. Though they were never destined to attain the power and wealth of the Efremovs, the Frolovs seemed typical of several important families that rose to prominence during and after the reign of Peter the Great. After the death of Ataman Ramazanov in 1715, Peter refused to approve of the *krug*'s nomination of a replacement, Maksim Kumshatskii, thereby opening the way for the successive elections—with tsarist approval, of course—of Maksim Frolov (d. 1716) and Vasilii Frolov, the latter serving from 1717 until 1723 as the last elected ataman.[29]

The Frolov family's next generation, the third, revealed something of the growing network of kinship relations that was to dominate the local Cossack elite for the next century. Ataman Frolov's son, Ivan Vasil'evich Frolov, achieved elder rank in 1729, after which he assumed command of Cossack forces successively in Persia and on the Tsaritsyn fortress line. In 1738, as a mark of special recognition for meritorious service, Empress Anna Ivanovna awarded him the rank of brigadier in the Imperial Russian Army. His sister, Akulina Vasil'evna, married Roman Emel'ianovich Ramazanov, brother of the Cossack who had held office as host ataman in the period immediately following Bulavin's rebellion. Ivan Ivanovich Frolov, the son of Frol Minaev's third son, served as appointed ataman of the Don Host between 1734 and 1738. His wife was Evfimiia Andreevna Lopatina,

---

28. Ibid., pp. 8–9.

29. L. M. Savelov, "Sem'ia Frolovykh na Donu," *Trudy XVI arkheologicheskogo s"ezda v Chernigove v 1908 g.*, 3 vols., Moscow, 1909, 3: 364–65.

daughter of the elder who had held office from 1723 to 1734 as the first appointed ataman. Ivan Ivanovich's sister, Anna Ivanovna Frolova, married Brigadier Ivan Matveevich Krasnoshchekov, one of the outstanding Cossack military figures of the entire era.[30] Not surprisingly, some Cossacks openly voiced concern over the possibility that the Frolovs might establish hereditary right to leadership of the Don Host.[31]

Those who expressed alarm probably overstated the case, for the strength of kinship ties, while considerable, was far from absolute. Nor did the presence of such ties necessarily always account for the governing and social activities of the Don elders. Despite the significance of family as an ascriptive factor in the definition of the Cossack elite, the actual holding of important office still depended largely upon the ability to achieve. Even more important, family ties were not proof against the kinds of internal dissension generated by factors ranging from honest differences of opinion to such basic emotions as greed, fear, hatred, and jealousy. In part, what terminated the Frolov ascendency in 1738 was a petition brought against Ataman Ivan Ivanovich Frolov by two other Cossack elders, Danila Efremov and Brigadier Ivan Krasnoshchekov, and transmitted to the imperial government through Field Marshal P. P. Lacy. In the petition, Krasnoshchekov, the ataman's brother-in-law, contended that Frolov had seriously affronted various elders (especially the Efremovs) and that a continuation of his administration would render living in the Don very difficult for both the Efremovs and the Krasnoshchekovs.[32] That same year, the Military College, which had never been very pleased with Frolov's handling of border disturbances connected with the Nogai Tatars, removed the ataman, promoted him to brigadier, and then replaced him with the elder Danila Efremov. Simultaneously, the empress also elevated Efremov to brigadier status, since for reasons of prestige and authority the new ataman had to possess rank equivalent to the most senior officers under his command.[33]

As the Frolov experience indicated, the pronounced drift to single-family rule did not necessarily preclude the rise of other individuals and families during the same period. One family and its adherents could not possibly eclipse all other contenders, if only because some

30. Savelov, *Donskoe dvorianstvo*, 2: 12–14.

31. Pronshtein, *Zemlia Donskaia v XVIII veke*, p. 147.

32. S. M. Solov'ev, *Istorii Rossii s drevneishikh vremen*, 3rd ed., 30 vols. in 7 bks., St. Petersburg, 1911, Vol. 20, Bk. 4, col. 1,380.

33. I. A. Andreev, *Materialy dlia istorii voiska Donskogo*, Novocherkassk, 1886, pp. 33–34.

of those contenders were contemporaries claiming the same kind of leadership credentials. In addition, other Cossacks of a more lowly background often served within various field commands of the Imperial Russian Army, and the Don ataman simply lacked the power to control all the circumstances under which potential rivals brought themselves to the attention of influential persons. Indeed, during the eighteenth and early nineteenth centuries, some possibility always existed for the injection of fresh blood into the Don elite, especially through what became a time-honored route for the Cossacks: conspicuous military service, as exemplified by the Denisov, Sebriakov, Ilovaiskii, and Platov families.[34]

The primary organs of local government, especially the Host Chancery, were all but useless as instruments for resolving most differences within the Don elite. Unlike the old *krug*, there was little room for factionalism within either the chancery or the growing corps of host functionaries. The logical result was that dissidents, outsiders, and those who had fallen from favor often took their cases to higher authorities, and it was not unusual for the Military College and the Ruling Senate to witness members of notable Cossack families conduct savage verbal attacks upon one another. When carried to extreme, such dissonance threatened the internal stability of the entire Don Host.[35]

The Efremovs, successors to the Frolovs, epitomized the phenomenon of one-family rule with all its strengths and weaknesses. Danila Efremov and Stepan Efremov, father and son, occupied the office of host ataman in succession from 1738 to 1772. Particularly during the tenure of Stepan Danilovich Efremov, both the Military College and the Ruling Senate in St. Petersburg were deluged with charges of misconduct of all kinds, brought by rank-and-file Cossacks. Stepan Danilovich enjoyed the favor of Catherine the Great because he had supported her accession to the throne, but accusations of treacherous dealings with the Nogai Tatars eventually brought about his downfall and arrest.[36]

34. A. P. Chebotarev, ed., "Zapiski Donskogo Atamana Denisova, 1763–1841," *Russkaia starina* 10 (1874): 20. Much of this discussion is based on the painstaking genealogical research of L. M. Savelov as presented in his *Donskie dvorianskie rody*, Moscow, 1902, 1: 28–36, 81–100; and in his *Neskol'ko rodoslovii (Otdel'nyi ottisk iz Dvorianskogo Adres-Kalendaria za 1899 god)*, n.d., pp. 13–14; Savelov's contributions to the development of Russian genealogical studies are summarized by A. I. Aksenov, "Ocherk istorii genealogii v Rossii," in B. A. Rybakov, V. L. Ianin et al., eds., *Istoriia i genealogiia*, Moscow, 1977, pp. 75–79.

35. See, for example, Solov'ev, *Istoriia Rossii s drevneishikh vremen*, Vol. 23, Bk. 5, col. 769.

36. Postnikova-Loseva, diss., pp. 61, 101, 263–64; Andronik Savel'ev, comp., *Tre-*

Unlike some of the former free Cossack hosts, the Don Cossacks emerged relatively unscathed from the campaign of wholesale retribution visited upon the borderlands in the aftermath of Pugachev's *jacquerie*. The Iaik Host, which had provided much of the initial impetus behind the pretender's movement, was completely reorganized and renamed the Ural Host. Because the loyalty of the Zaporozhians had long remained suspect, Catherine simply disbanded the Sech' and ordered its inhabitants dispersed.[37] Even if the Don was the homeland of Pugachev, and even if the rank and file in scattered areas had occasionally waivered in their support of the empress, the Land of the Don Host was not to share the fate of Iaik and Zaporozhian Cossacks.[38] Catherine herself had helped insure the Don's allegiance both by stationing troops in potentially troublesome *stanitsy* and by adopting conciliatory policies during the confusing period following Stepan Efremov's arrest. More important, at critical junctures the Don Cossack elders had aided their own cause and that of their fellow Cossacks with important displays of loyalty. With little prodding from St. Petersburg, it was the elders who burned Pugachev's house and they who renamed his home *stanitsa* Potemkinskaia (formerly Zimoveiskaia). It was they who had vied with one another in the face of some difficulty to lead detachments of loyal Cossacks against the rebels. Finally, it was one of them, A. I. Ilovaiskii, who mercilessly drove his Cossacks as part of a successful last-ditch effort to capture Pugachev deep in the wastes of the trans-Volga steppe.[39]

Local successes aside, the shock of Pugachev and the Efremov affair, which came to be celebrated in the Don for its seamier aspects, including a divorce of doubtful legality and Stepan's predilection for Kalmyk girls, underscored the need for serious alterations in local government. True, the Don Cossacks and their elders had survived an

khsotletie voiska Donskogo, 1570–1870 g.: Ocherki iz istorii donskikh kazakov, St. Petersburg, 1870, pp. 85–89; A. Karasev, "Ataman Stepan Danilovich Efremov (1753–1772 g.g.)," Istoricheskii vestnik 89 (1902): 876–77; "Materialy dlia istorii voiska Donskogo: O voiskovom Atamane Stepane Efremove," Trudy oblastnogo voiska Donskogo Statisticheskogo Komiteta, 2 vols., Novocherkassk, 1867, 1874, 2: 48–49; this collection is hereinafter cited as TOVDSK.

37. V. A. Golobutskii, Chernomorskoe kazachestvo, Kiev, 1956, pp. 108–10.

38. Svatikov, "Donskoi Voiskovoi Krug," pp. 203–4.

39. A. P. Pronshtein, ed., Don i nizhnee Povolzh'e v period krest'ianskoi voiny 1773–1775 godov, Rostov-na-Donu, 1961, pp. 9–11; Savel'ev, Trekhsotletie voiska Donskogo, pp. 92–93; N. F. Dubrovin, 3 vols., Pugachev i ego soobshchniki, St. Petersburg, 1884, 2: 245–46; and Mikhail Seniutkin, Dontsy: Istoricheskie ocherki voennykh deistvii, biografii starshin proshlogo veka, zametki iz sovremennogo byta i vzgliad na istoriiu voiska Donskogo, 2 pts., Moscow, 1866, Pt. 1, p. 50.

important test of their loyalty, but now the task was to distinguish between the useful and the potentially harmful and to discard the latter without doing irreparable damage to the military whole and without creating undue apprehension among the Cossacks. In the ensuing reforms, this was exactly the course that Catherine and her favorite, G. A. Potemkin, attempted to pursue by balancing changes in administrative form with adjustments in the nature of Cossack officialdom.

It had been especially fitting for the elders to rename Pugachev's birthplace after Potemkin, for he, more than any other imperial functionary, would leave his stamp on Don Cossack government during the last quarter of the eighteenth century. By virtue of his positions as governor-general of New Russia, vice-president of the Military College, and commander-in-chief of all light cavalry and irregular hosts, Potemkin exercised a threefold supervisory authority over the conduct of Cossack affairs. In 1775, with the embers of Pugachev's house scarcely grown cold and with Efremov only recently tucked away safely in exile, Potemkin undertook a series of changes to forestall any recurrence of the host's earlier governing ills. First, he separated Cossack governing affairs into their two distinct elements, military and civilian. The host ataman, as commander of the Don Cossacks, retained his traditional authority in the military sphere. Next, Potemkin created a new institution, the Host Civilian Government (*Voiskovoe grazhdanskoe pravitel'stvo*) to replace the Chancery of Elders within the realm of civilian affairs. The new Host Civilian Government functioned under the chairmanship of the ataman, but to prevent a reversion to Efremov-like practices, Potemkin laid down new regulations governing the composition and operation of local administration. The Host Civilian Government consisted of seven members: the ataman, two permanent judges appointed by the empress, and four assessors elected by the host elders. The new organization functioned collegially, with all decisions the products of majority vote. Through the ataman and the two permanent judges, St. Petersburg retained the initiative in local affairs, and through the four elected assessors, the Don Host elders were assured some voice in provincial administration. Finally, Potemkin directed that in cases in which host law conflicted with imperial law, the latter was to have precedence.[40]

To assure the Host Civilian Government a reasonable chance of

---

40. PSZ I, Vol. 20, Nos. 14,251 and 14,252; Pronshtein, *Zemlia Donskaia v XVIII veke*, pp. 240–43; and Marc Raeff, "The Style of Russia's Imperial Policy and Prince G. A. Potemkin," in Gerald N. Grob, ed., *Statesmen and Statecraft of the Modern West: Essays in Honor of Dwight E. Lee and H. Donaldson Jordan*, Barre, Mass., 1967, pp. 8–9.

success, Potemkin devoted special attention to the problem of personnel, and he appointed A. I. Ilovaiskii, a man of proven loyalty and high local standing, as ataman.[41] To enhance the new ataman's standing among his fellow elders, the empress herself signed a promotion order advancing Ilovaiskii to the rank of army colonel. Meanwhile the elders elected four of their own number to assume positions as assessors within the Host Civilian Government.[42]

To complement separate changes in structure and personnel, Potemkin next turned to the Cossack elders as a group, those officers who collectively over the long run would retain custodianship of local military and civil administration. As early as 1767, Ivan Ianov had proposed that Cossack elders receive status equivalent to the Russian nobility.[43] Potemkin now recommended to the empress that she comply with this request, and on 15 February 1775, Catherine II accorded all Don Cossack elders the status of staff officers within the Imperial Russian Army. Their title, *voiskovoi starshina*, remained the same, but after 1775 Cossacks bearing that designation were recognized as regular officers subordinate to the army rank of second major and senior to captain. In accordance with the Table of Ranks promulgated in 1722 by Peter the Great, possession of staff-officer rank automatically conferred hereditary nobility upon the holder. Catherine's legislation thus amounted to a tremendous vote of confidence in the Don elders, even though she placed them in a somewhat anomalous position within the conventional military hierarchy—as irregular regimental commanders, the elders were senior to regular company commanders but junior to battalion executive officers.[44]

Historians have ascribed varying degrees of importance to Catherine's legislation elevating the Cossack elders uniformly to noble status. Prerevolutionary observers frequently regarded 1775 as a crucial turning point in the evolution of local society. Soviet historians, ever anxious to discern the wellsprings of class discontent, have viewed the ennoblement of the elders as license to pillage the rank and file. In the

41. TsGVIA, Fond. 52 (*Potemkina-Tavricheskogo G. A.*), op. 194, d. 93, *chast'* 1, fols. 38, and N. F. Dubrovin, ed., *Bumagi Kniazia Grigoriia Aleksandrovicha Potemkina-Tavricheskogo*, Vols. 6, 7, 8 of *Sbornik voenno-istoricheskikh materialov*, 16 vols., St. Petersburg, 1893–99, 6: 11–12.

42. M. S. Frenkin, "Donskoe kazachestvo v poslednei chetverti XVIIIv. (Period voiskovogo grazdanskogo pravitel'stva 1775–1796 gg.)," Candidate dissertation, Moscow State University, 1939, p. 88.

43. "Proekt zakonov o pravakh voisk kazach'ikh podpisannyi chlenami komissii o gosudarstvennykh rodakh," SIRIO, 36: 240–41.

44. PSZ I, Vol. 20, No. 14, 251.

West, Marc Raeff, more intent perhaps on writing about Potemkin than the Cossacks, treats the creation of noble elders as a capstone to Cossack policy rather than as a chapter in a continuing story.[45] While none of these interpretations is wholly inaccurate, none of them fully assesses the impact of Catherine's action within the full context of developing Cossack policy and practice.

In reality, there was nothing novel about the appearance of a hereditary elite within the Land of the Don Cossack Host, even outside the family of the ataman. In the quest to maintain supremacy and pass it to their heirs, Cossack notables had long encouraged the custom of seeking officer rank not only for their supporters, but also for their offspring and relatives. The Cossacks accomplished this objective in two ways. By far the more common was to introduce the scions of well-known families to active military service at a very early age, often under the tutelage of a sympathetic uncle or parent. It became customary for elders and other officers, and sometimes even for common Cossacks, to take their sons on campaign at the age of ten and in some cases even earlier. Unlike their contemporaries within the Russian nobility, who did not actually serve with their units until mid- or late adolescence, Cossack candidates for elder rank shared in the hazards of campaign. Andrian Karpovich Denisov, later ataman of the Don Cossacks, began his active service at age twelve, while Mikhail Sidorovich Sebriakov began his at age nine. Service at an early age brought these and other boys to the attention of both Cossack and non-Cossack field commanders, and under the right set of circumstances, increased the aspirants' opportunities for early promotion to officer rank.[46]

A second method of securing elder status was simply to petition for the promotion of boys and young men to elder rank, either on the merits of their fathers' service or on the promise of illustrious future service. In 1738, for example, the fourteen-year-old Vasilii Akimovich Mashlykin received elder title and command of the regiment that his deceased father had led into mortal conflict with the Turks at Perekop. In 1764, Il'ia Denisov's brother, Stepan Petrovich, and his two sons, Grigorii Il'ich and Mikhail Il'ich, all received elder rank in recognition of Il'ia's distinguished service during the Seven Years' War. Similarly, in 1773, Il'ia successfully petitioned the empress to grant his youngest son, Avksentii, elder rank for his father's "service and labors."[47]

---

45. V. B. Bronevskii, *Istoriia Donskogo voiska, opisanie Donskoi zemli*, 4 vols., St. Petersburg, 1834, 2: 156–57; Pronshtein, *Zemlia Donskaia v XVIII veke*, pp. 176–82; and Raeff, "The Style of Russia's Imperial Policy and Prince G. A. Potemkin," pp. 9–10.

46. Savelov, *Donskoe dvorianstvo*, 1: 11.

47. Postnikova-Loseva, diss., p. 55.

Thanks to such promotions and the practice of entering service at an early age, the possession of elder rank had a strongly hereditary quality to it before Catherine ever actively intervened in local affairs to endow the elders with the status of hereditary nobility. In 1777, the Host Civilian Government submitted a service list of elders to the Military College revealing that the Cossacks counted in their midst ninety-six elders on active service. Of this number, sixty-two, or nearly two-thirds, were designated as having come from "elder families," that is, from elder parentage. Of the remainder, thirty possessed a rank-and-file background, while the remaining four came one each from a clerical family, the Polish nobility, the Chechens, and the family of a Prussian surgeon.[48]

In a similar vein, there was nothing novel about the occasional Cossack possession of regular officer rank. As early as 1738, Empress Anna Ivanovna had elevated three officers, Danila Efremov, Ivan Ivanovich Frolov, and Ivan Matveevich Krasnoshchekov, to the rank of brigadier. In the period before 1775, at least two other elders, Fedor Ivanovich Krasnoshchekov (1755) and Sidor Nikiforovich Sebriakov (1759) had followed in their footsteps. Moreover, in 1763, the same Krasnoshchekov had attained the rank of major general, an honor accorded up to that time only to Danila Efremov. In addition to these prominent examples, a scattering of other Cossacks had received army rank before the advent of Potemkin, usually in acknowledgement of distinguished military service.[49]

What was new about the legislation of 1775 was the way that it uniformly distributed noble title among the Cossack elders. The elder active service list for 1777 showed only twenty-five elders of ninety-six holding regular army rank: three colonels, five lieutenant colonels, and seventeen first majors. The majority of these officers traced their dates of rank only to 1774 and 1775, when it appeared that Catherine and Potemkin had begun granting such promotions as a special reward for service either in the First Turkish War or in the Pugachev insurrection.[50] Rather than continue this practice of raising elders selectively to the nobility, Catherine and Potemkin now decided to grant noble title uniformly to all the elders. This would tend both to broaden the base of imperial support among the elders and to reduce the amount of jealousy and bickering among individuals of unequal

---

48. TsGVIA, Fond 52, op. 194, d. 147, fols. 246–82.

49. Andreev, *Materialy dlia istorii voiska Donskogo*, p. 36; and Savelov, *Neskol'ko rodoslovii*, pp. 13–14.

50. TsGVIA, Fond 52, op. 194, d. 147, fols. 246–82 *passim*.

status. At the same time, the government retained the option of selectively granting regular rank in exceptional circumstances. The result was a continuation of the two-tier rank system, but an avoidance of discrimination between noble and nonnoble elders.

Other notable aspects of the 1775 legislation included the degree of control and system that it imposed on the promotion process, at least at the upper reaches of the hierarchy. Already in 1754, Empress Elizabeth Petrovna had forbidden promotion to elder rank without the approval of the Military College.[51] However, the Military College seems only to have exercised sporadic control over the promotion process, and in any case, the Efremovs tended to dominate local political life. With the arrival of Potemkin on the governing scene in 1774, there was little doubt that the entire promotion process would come under far closer scrutiny, if only because Potemkin's military and administrative activities kept him in close physical proximity to the Cossacks. In 1775, the elder Semen Turoverov routinely petitioned the Military College for permission to retire, requesting at the same time that his elder rank be passed to his son, Fedor. The Military College at first acceded to the request, then hurriedly withdrew Fedor's elder rank when Potemkin discovered that the younger Turoverov was only seven years old.[52] After 1775, the Host Civilian Government regularly submitted lists of serving and retired elders to the Military College. These lists included not only the names, but also the ages, dates of rank, dates of entry on initial active service, dates of subsequent service, rewards received, and the results of any judicial proceedings against the elders.[53] In exchange for freer access to the ranks of Russian nobility, the Cossack elite was subjected to a greater degree of scrutiny and control. This development in turn corresponded with St. Petersburg's growing emphasis on centralization and subjugation.

One major drawback in legislation equating Cossack elders with the Russian nobility was the failure to make any provision for the lower rungs on the Cossack rank ladder. Ironically, it was Catherine's son, Tsar Paul, who hated Potemkin and nearly everything his mother's favorite stood for, who rectified this discrepancy and thus carried Potemkin's plans to their logical conclusion. In 1798, as "a mark of recognition" for "the zeal and service" of the Don Host, Paul

51. Lishin, *Akty*, Vol. 2, Pt. 2, pp. 776–77; and Savel'ev, *Trekhsotletie voiska Donskogo*, p. 73.

52. Seniutkin, *Dontsy*, Pt. 2, pp. 10–11.

53. Ibid., some archival examples are TsGVIA, Fond 52, op. 194, d. 147, fols. 134–36, and Fond 13 (*Kazach'ia ekspeditsiia pri kantseliarii Voennoi kollegii*), op. 1, d. 144, *chast'* 1, fols. 157–60.

decreed that all Cossack officers be recognized as members of the nobility. The Cossack rank of elder was equivalent to army major, *esaul* to captain (*rotmistr*), *sotnik* to lieutenant (*poruchik*), and *khorunzhii* (Cossack ensign) to cornet. During the following year, 1799, Paul further decreed that Cossack officers on campaign at a distance greater than sixty-six miles from their homeland receive stipends from St. Petersburg equivalent to allowances awarded officers of the Imperial Russian Army.[54]

The laws of 1775 and 1798 established the broad framework within which members of the Don Cossack elite were integrated into the ranks of the Russian nobility. Table 1, based on materials gathered from several sources, indicates the size of the Cossack officer contingent at several levels before, during, and after legislation governing the advance to noble status.[55] The figures shown represent a reasonably accurate statistical summary of the Don Host's growth expressed in terms of military manpower for the interval between 1770 and 1842. The years chosen constitute random instances for which comparable information was available. Complete and accurate figures for the eighteenth century were difficult to obtain because of deliberate local attempts to conceal statistics from St. Petersburg and because of shoddy bookkeeping and reporting practices. Ataman Stepan Efremov was notorious for submitting inaccurate summaries designed to hide instances of local corruption and mismanagement.[56] In addition, the Don Host government seems to have made no effort to retain information on the number of junior officers within the host before Paul's legislation of 1798. Figures for the eighteenth century occasionally vary with similar figures used by A. P. Pronshtein in his *Zemlia Donskaia v XVIII veke*, because Table 1 includes both active-service and retired segments of the Cossack population.[57] For the nineteenth century, most cases of absolute increases in numbers can be attributed either to population growth or to stricter enforcement of regulations requiring mandatory registration for military service. Finally, the rela-

---

54. PSZ i, Vol. 25, No. 18,673; PSZ i, Vol. 25, No. 19,135.

55. This table is a compilation of widely scattered data from the following sources: 1770— TsGVIA, Fond 20 (*Voinskaia ekspeditsiia Voennoi kollegii*), op. 1/147, d. 11, fol. 8; 1775—TsGVIA, Fond 52 op. 194, d. 93, fols. 200–203; 1797—TsGVIA, Fond 41 (*Saltykova, N. I.*), op. 2/200, d. 626, fols. 111–12; 1819—TsGVIA, Fond 230 (*Orlova, A. P.*), op. 1, d. 24, fol. 3; and 1842—*O voennom upravlenii voiska Donskogo 1842 g.*, n.d. [p. 5].

56. See, for example, the incident described in Dubrovin, *Pugachev i ego soobshchniki*, 1: 112–13.

57. Pronshtein, *Zemlia Donskaia v XVIII veke*, p. 180.

TABLE VI-1

Number of Serving and Retired Officers and Cossacks in the Don Host, 1770–1842 (number of total retired in parentheses)[55]

	1770[a]	1775	1797	1819	1842
Brigadiers, general officers			10 (1)	28 (15)	35 (18)
Elders, staff officers	61	108 (27)	243 (24)	440 (252)	425 (292)
Junior (*ober*) officers				2,202 (908)	2,200 (965)
Rank-and-file, *uriadniki* (Cossack sergeants)	25,547	25,000[b]	33,059 (6,350)	70,810 (20,599)	134,742 (28,603)

Source: See note 55.

a. The Don Host reported only irregularly before 1775 on officers and Cossacks in a retired status.
b. An estimate.

tive stability in the size of the Don officer corps after 1819 was largely a function of St. Petersburg's ability to impose a ceiling on the number of Cossack regiments and therefore also on the number of Cossacks needed to provide officer cadres for those regiments.[58]

Significantly, what these figures fail to convey to the historian is a sense of the distribution of political and military power among the members of the Don elite. The legislation of 1775 and 1798 produced in the Don a nobility whose members accounted for perhaps 4 percent of the local population in the beginning of the nineteenth century. Beyond precluding a return to one-family rule, neither Potemkin nor Paul had much immediate effect on the upper reaches of the local elite, that is, on those high-ranking officers in whose hands almost invariably lay the most powerful offices of the Cossack host. Potemkin and Paul seem to have had their greatest impact in decreasing friction among families and individuals, in clarifying rules of conduct, and in institutionalizing the process through which local notables became Russian nobles. Otherwise, neither the military administrator nor the autocrat did much to alter an emerging pattern of oligarchical family rule already present in an incipient form during the Efremov years. Subsequently, members of those families which had risen to prominence either because of or in spite of the Efremovs became the chief beneficiaries of imperial governing policies in the Don.

This meant that there came to exist within the Don nobility a core of perhaps only a dozen families whose members constituted the real Cossack governing elite. Following the fall of the Efremovs, representatives of these families—Platov, Grekov, Kuteinikov, Ilovaiskii, Kurnakov, Denisov, Popov, Martynov, Mashlykin, Andriianov, Kirsanov, Karpov, Pozdeev, Krasnoshchekov, Krasnov, and a few others —became firmly entrenched in the host's leading administrative and military posts, where they exerted decisive influence on the course of local affairs. Now called the Cossack *chinovniki*, the nobles from these families were the "upper crust" of Don Cossack society. In contrast with lower-ranking officers less removed from their rank-and-file backgrounds, the *chinovniki* were usually either the elders or the descendants of elders who, throughout the last third of the eighteenth century, had actively advanced the cause of securing for themselves noble status. Frequently united by common interests, backgrounds, and aspirations, these local leaders existed as a kind of closed society within a closed society. They were very often related either by

---

58. Svatikov, *Rossiia i Don*, pp. 269–70; see especially PSZ i, Vol. 10, No. 8,163, Pt. 2, arts. 453, 467, and 473–77.

kinship or marriage, and they frequently saw themselves as the protectors and advocates of their own small ruling group. In turn, the *chinovniki* were the men upon whom St. Petersburg relied heavily to provide the Don Host with stable and reliable leadership. Thus, although there were several thousand nobles within the Cossack Host, only several hundred—the members of older and well-established families—formed the backbone of the Cossack elite.[59]

The persistence with which these families were able to retain power was perhaps best demonstrated by their representatives' ability to hold office as successive atamans in the era between 1797 and 1836. Don atamans for this period included respectively Vasilii Petrovich Orlov (1797–1801), Matvei Ivanovich Platov (1801–18), Andrian Karpovich Denisov (1818–21), Aleksei Vasil'evich Ilovaiskii (1821–27) and Dmitrii Efimovich Kuteinikov (1827–36). All of these officers shared various attributes which by now even the casual observer would have come to expect of a Don ataman: entry on active service at an early age, minimal literacy, and a distinguished service career. Interestingly enough, all of them possessed some previous administrative experience before assuming office as host ataman.[60] Above all, they were officers who came from the illustrious ranks of the Don aristocracy. Indeed, this was the one qualification which distinguished them from dozens of potential competitors for power. Success tended to breed still more success, and the Don elite were no exception to the rule.

After having literally fought and inveigled their way into the ranks of the Russian nobility, the next logical step for the Cossack *chinovniki* was to acquire corporate status through the organization of a regional noble assembly. However, unlike the nobility in the majority of Russian provinces, the collective existence of the Don nobles as a special class never received official sanction. Selected Cossack officers had become nobles not by virtue of birth, but by way of the "back door," through service and the attainment of army rank. As early as 1760, the Don elders had ascribed to their own group the title "host society"

59. "Atamanstvo Denisova i komitet 1819 goda," *Donskaia gazeta* (24 June 1873), p. 98, and Antoine Louis de Romano, *Coup d'oeil philosophique sur le pays occupe par les Cosaques du Don*, 2 vols., Milan, 1807, 2: 186–87.

60. Biographical data on these officers is found in the following sources: *Istoriia leib-gvardii kazach'iago Ego Velichestva polka (sostavlena ofitserami polka)*, St. Petersburg, 1876, pp. 40–41; Savelov, *Donskie dvorianskie rody*, pp. 10–13, 73–74, 121–22; A. Kirillov, "Voiskovoi ataman voiska Donskogo graf Matvei Ivanovich Platov i ego administrativnaia deiatel'nost'," *Sbornik oblastnogo voiska Donskogo Statisticheskogo Komiteta*, 13 vols., Novocherkassk, 1901–15, 9: 8–20; Skalon, ed., *Stoletie Voennogo Ministerstva*, Vol. 11, Pt. 3, pp. 596–98, and Seniutkin, *Dontsy*, Pt. 2, pp. 32–36.

(*voiskovoe obshchestvo*) to differentiate themselves from the Cossack rank and file, but St. Petersburg never approved this collective designation for the elders. Shortly after the beginning of the nineteenth century, M. I. Platov had encouraged the Cossack nobles to elect district and host deputies; however, these elections failed to evoke any kind of legal recognition. Later, in 1816, Platov pressed the imperial government for permission to allow the Don nobles to elect marshals of the nobility on the provincial pattern, but the Ruling Senate answered that no precedent existed to create a special class of Cossack nobles with corporate legal status.[61]

Much of the reluctance to award the *chinovniki* the final fruits of victory—a collective legal identity—sprang from a number of doubts that had risen concerning the exact position of the Cossack nobility. As early as 1801, Prince A. I. Gorchakov, scion of a famous Russian family and personal representative of Tsar Alexander I, had conducted an inspection tour of the Don Host Land. Upon returning to St. Petersburg, Prince Gorchakov reported to the Ruling Senate that emerging inequalities in the Cossack system of land tenure were threatening the entire structure of Cossack military service and thereby undermining the interests of the Imperial Russian state. Gorchakov's report was a landmark in Cossack history, not because it initiated any immediate action, but because it prompted a series of high-level discussions acknowledging for the first time that Don Cossack society was on the verge of breakdown. The delicate balance between right and obligation that had guided the evolution of the Cossack military class during much of the eighteenth century suddenly revealed great instability. To make matters worse, disaster had struck primarily in the area of landholding, the very cornerstone of the whole system by which the Cossacks rendered their valuable military service to the tsarist state.[62]

Many high-ranking administrators who debated Gorchakov's report within the Ruling Senate either found fault with the Cossacks themselves or were almost overzealous in their efforts to blame local administration for the imbalances that had appeared to menace Cossack society. Other observers, including Prince Gorchakov, correctly perceived a direct cause-and-effect relationship between the presence of a newly created Cossack nobility and the appearance of land prob-

61. Svatikov, *Rossiia i Don*, pp. 247–48, 264.
62. Gorchakov's report and the subsequent debate are found in Skalon, ed., *Stoletie Voennogo Ministerstva*, Vol. 11, Pt. 4, pp. 39–47.

lems. However, none recognized that the growing crisis, in which the Cossack nobility indeed played a crucial role, was the logical outcome of prior Imperial Russian policy.

The rise to power and prestige was accompanied by a basic change in attitude on the part of the new Cossack nobility. For members of many prominent Cossack families in the beginning of the eighteenth century, the driving force behind aspiration to elder rank had been the attainment of fame and glory, especially through conspicuous and heroic military service. By the end of the eighteenth century, however, glorious military service had become not an end in itself, but only the means to an end—the acquisition of noble status with all its privileges and material benefits. Upon completion of whatever service was necessary to reach and rise in noble rank, the Cossack dreamed less of combat and conquest than of retiring to a quiet, sedentary life on a modest estate carved out of some portion of the Don steppe. Frequently, not even the most ambitious and militarily oriented Cossack officer could withstand the almost magnetic attraction of the gentleman farmer's indolent life. One of the most famous Cossack leaders of the era, A. K. Denisov, spoke often of retirement, and after temporarily leaving active service in 1788, he wrote, "I am going home and will learn to plow and live by my labors."[63]

As members of the Cossack military and administrative elite turned their thoughts increasingly to the acquisition of the attributes of landed gentry, they directed their efforts at attaining the land necessary to sustain their ambitions. A few fortunate officers, including M. I. Platov and Fedor Denisov, received imperial grants to large tracts of land located outside the boundaries of the Don Host. The majority of the Cossack elders and their noble heirs received no such grants and therefore had to satisfy themselves with whatever land they could obtain within the boundaries of the Cossack Host. Over the span of four or five decades—from the last quarter of the eighteenth century through the first quarter of the nineteenth century—the activity of the Cossack officers ignited a land stampede in which they appropriated to their personal use widely varying amounts of land. When the dust of this stampede settled, statistics gathered by survey teams in 1821–22 revealed that the Don nobility, constituting less than 4 percent of the Cossack population, controlled approximately 27 percent of all arable land within the Don Territory.[64]

---

63. Quoted in Pronshtein, *Zemlia Donskaia v XVIII veke*, p. 175; see also, Peter Simon Pallas, *Travels through the Southern Provinces of the Russian Empire in the Years 1793 and 1794*, 2 vols., London, 1802–3, 1: 469.

64. The Don nobility appropriated approximately ten million of the thirty-eight

During the same years that saw the rise of the Cossack nobility and the mass alienation of host land, the question of serfdom first assumed major importance in the Don. A stable working force was the sine qua non of the noble drive to achieve the status of landed gentry. In the absence of an alternative, non-Cossack immigrants of Ukrainian and sometimes Russian origins provided the bulk of this working force. From the beginning of the eighteenth century, when the shortage of manpower had first prompted the Cossacks to limit admission to their society, an unceasing flow of immigrants had created a separate group of non-Cossack peasants who constituted a valuable reserve of agricultural labor. Because the majority of these peasants were fugitives, their exact legal status was always uncertain, but they were not regarded as serfs, at least not until 1796. By that time, most of them, in a series of developments unique to the Don, had fallen under the control of the Cossack nobles, who made the peasants instrumental in the quest for a larger share of Cossack land.[65]

During the first two decades of the nineteenth century, the social changes that had led to the introduction of serfdom, together with the alienation of vast reserves of Cossack land, contributed significantly to the emergence of serious problems within Don Cossack military society. These problems, of which land shortages and the appearance of bitter animosities were the most important, helped lead the Cossack Host to a state of impending breakdown.

From the point of view of the imperial government, which had come to rely increasingly on the services of Cossack cavalry, Don land problems threatened the most serious consequences. While all Cossack rights and privileges were intended to ensure the continuing welfare of the Don Host, since the time when grain growing and stock raising had become the chief elements within the Cossack economy, collective use of the land constituted the key source of wealth and prosperity among the Cossacks. With the amount of land in general use declining

---

million acres of land within the boundaries of the Don Host. See Sukhorukov, *Statisticheskoe opisanie Zemli Donskikh kazakov, sostavlennoe v 1822–32 godakh*, p. 116; and V. A. Zolotov, "Don i Priazov'ia v period krizisa feodal'no-krepostnicheskoi sistemy i razvitiia kapitalisticheskikh otnoshenii," in E. I. Demishina, V. A. Zolotov et al., eds., *Istoriia Dona s drevneishikh vremen do Velikoi Oktiabr'skoi sotsialisticheskoi revoliutsii*, Rostov-na-Donu, 1965, p. 195.

65. In 1796, there were 58,492 serfs working the holdings of various Don Cossack officers. By 1816, this number had risen to 78,991. For the appropriate legislation, see PSZ I, Vol. 24, No. 17,638. The best accounts of the serf problem among the Don Cossacks include A. A. Karasev, "Donskie krest'iane," and V. N. Vetchinkin, "Ocherk pozemel'nogo vladenniia na Donu v sviazi s razvitiem mezhevaniia," in TOVDSK, 1: 72–118, and 2: 1–93.

rapidly—thanks to the activities of the Cossack nobility—and with the Cossack population growing, there appeared an acute shortage of land in many areas of the Don. Indeed, information gathered during extensive surveys in 1821–22 revealed that in many *stanitsy*, the allotment of land available to each Cossack family had fallen to ten or twelve acres. This was approximately one-third to one-fifth of the amount considered necessary to provide the minimum material needs of the average Cossack military man and his dependents.[66]

As a direct result of land shortages, many Cossacks found themselves unable to meet the material requirements of outfitting themselves for military duty. Because the Don Host government often concealed information regarding the number of destitute Cossacks, exact statistics on the failure of Cossacks to meet their obligations are not always available. However, judging from reports submitted to the host from various settlements, nearly every *stanitsa* possessed Cossacks who no longer had the means to enter military service. In many cases, to help these Cossacks, *stanitsa* assemblies dipped into their own meager treasuries to supply funds for the purchase of horses and equipment. Typical was a report of Alekseevskaia *stanitsa*, in which the ataman wrote, "Cossacks Grigorii Samokhvalov, Dmitrii Stepanov, and Grigorii Samonov, who, because of poverty, were not able to buy horses, have purchased them at the expense of the *stanitsa*."[67] During 1812, when 50,000 Cossacks were mobilized to aid in the defeat of Napoleon, the scene in Alekseevskaia *stanitsa* was repeated many times throughout the Don Land.[68] After the wars of 1812–15, the practice of subsidizing poverty-stricken Cossacks continued. During 1818, for example, the Don Host government and various *stanitsy* disbursed a total of 41,584 rubles to help outfit Cossacks for campaign. Because individual disbursements averaged fifty rubles or less, the above figure indicates that 800 or more Cossacks received aid to serve in only a single year.[69] Neither the *stanitsy* nor the host possessed the resources to continue their mass subsidization for Cossack military service.

Allied with the problem of food shortages and creeping poverty

66. "Bumagi A. I. Chernysheva po delam Donskogo komiteta 1821–1824 gg.," SIRIO, 121: 394.

67. *Gosudarstvennyi Arkhiv Rostovskoi Oblasti*, Fond. 338 (*Stanichnye pravleniia*), op. 2, d. 94, fol. 113; this archive is hereinafter cited as GARO.

68. GARO, Fond 338, op. 3, d. 267, fol. 1; GARO, Fond 338, op. 3, d. 267, fols. 3–5; and I. S——v, "Doreformennaia stanichnaia obshchina," *Donskie oblastnye vedomosti*, No. 68 (24 March 1902): 2.

69. GARO, Fond 341 (*Voiskovaia kantseliariia voiska Donskogo*), op. 3, d. 141, fol. 1,240.

was a rising tide of animosity between the Cossacks and their officers. Although the two groups never clashed openly, signs of hostility were readily evident, especially in the relationship between the Cossacks and their officers' serfs. Because the Cossacks feared their noble superiors, resentment against the officers usually assumed the form of attacks against the closest tangible representatives of noble depredations —the serfs. In *stanitsy* in which Cossacks and serfs often had to coexist on the same land, there were many fist fights, a few murders, and a number of instances in which Cossack mobs attacked groups of serfs. For the rank and file, these manifestations of violence provided an outlet for frustrations accumulated over the years as they had helplessly watched the disappearance of ever-increasing amounts of land.[70]

For the serfs, hostilities added to a feeling of dissatisfaction associated with their position as a substantial non-Cossack minority within the Don population. Most serfs were of Ukrainian origin, and the majority of these had fled impending serfdom in their homeland to lead a freer life among the Cossacks. When these fugitives arrived in the Don to reside on officer holdings, they fully expected eventual acceptance into Cossack society. Instead, they were reduced to the status of serfs, a development creating among them a smoldering resentment that found expression in unrest and rebellion. As early as 1812, serfs in two separate officer settlements, Voskresenovka and Kalitvensk, rose against their masters and were quelled only by the dispatch of Cossack cavalry squadrons from Novocherkassk. In 1818, during a brief visit of Tsar Alexander I to Novocherkassk, a group of serfs attempted to present him with a petition citing what they felt was their intolerable position. However, their efforts only earned them beatings and other recriminations. Finally, in 1820, four major serf settlements, including primarily the villages of Major General Martynov, rose against their owners in an open rebellion, the pacification of which required six Cossack and regular cavalry regiments.[71]

Even before the peasant uprising of 1820 attracted wide attention to

70. Vetchinkin, "Ocherk pozemel'nogo vladeniia na Donu v sviazi s razvitiem mezhevaniia," pp. 36–37; GARO, Fond 338, op. 2, d. 1,252, fols. 6–9; Karasev, "Donskie krest'iane," pp. 82–83; and I. I. Ignatovich, *Krest'ianskoe dvizhenie na Donu v 1820*, Moscow, 1937, pp. 43–45.

71. Skalon, ed., *Stoletie Voennogo Ministerstva*, Vol. 11, Pt. 1, p. 166; GARO, Fond 304 (*Oblastnoe dvorianskoe sobranie*), op. 1, d. 666, fols. 2–3; GARO, Fond 410 (*Oblastnoi voiska Donskogo predvoditel' dvorianstva*), op. 1, d. 24, fols. 1–2; and L. M. Frantseva, "Uchastie Donskikh kazakov v otechestvennoi voine 1812 goda," Candidate dissertation, Rostov-on-Don State University, 1949, p. 47.

problems in the Don, the tsar and other high-ranking imperial functionaries had concluded that land shortages and both Cossack and serf
difficulties owed their origins to the excesses of the Cossack nobility.[72]
For this reason, Alexander I and the Ruling Senate had failed to
acquiesce with Ataman Platov's 1816 request to grant the Cossack
nobles corporate status. Moreover, in 1819, one year after Platov's
death, the emperor willingly accepted a proposal of the new ataman,
A. K. Denisov, to convene a special committee whose task it would be
to consider a complete codification of Cossack law.

Unknowingly, by requesting a convocation of a committee to study
Cossack law, Denisov had set in motion a chain of events that was to
culminate in a thorough reform of Cossack government and landholding practices. Through previous correspondence with Ataman
Platov and through the reports of various ministries and departments
of the Ruling Senate, the tsar had come to believe that many aspects of
Don administration badly needed review and adjustment. With Cossack military successes during the recent Napoleonic campaigns in
mind, the tsar had grown increasingly apprehensive over the effects
that land shortages were having on the valuable system of Cossack
military service. Therefore, in 1819, the emperor authorized Denisov
to convoke the committee in Novocherkassk as earlier proposed. The
only alteration to the ataman's recommendation was the emperor's
request that his own personal representative, the non-Cossack General
A. I. Chernyshev, be added to the personnel of the committee that
soon became known as the Committee of 1819.[73]

Under Chernyshev's driving guidance and with the emperor's permission, the Committee of 1819 gradually extended its jurisdiction to
include undertaking an extensive examination of local administration
and landholding patterns. This study, conducted with the aid of survey
teams between 1819 and 1821, tended to confirm Prince Gorchakov's
earlier conclusion: the Don nobility bore primary responsibility for
the severe dislocations that had emerged to threaten the future of the
Cossack Host.[74] The very group whose existence the imperial authorities had so carefully and patiently cultivated now appeared to

72. SIRIO, "Pis'ma Aleksandra Ivanovicha (vposledstvii Kniazia) Chernysheva Arseniiu Andreevichu (vposledstvii grafu) Zakrevskomu, 1820–1822 gg.," pp. 451–52;
TsGIA, Fond 651 (*Vasil'chikovy, Kniaz'ia*), op. 1, d. 200, fol. 3, and Fond 1409 (*Sobstvennoi E.I.V. Kantseliarii*), op. 1, d. 2,477, fols. 17–18.

73. A review of the work conducted by the Committee of 1819 appears in Svatikov,
Rossiia i Don, pp. 277–85.

74. Many of the reports and materials gathered in connection with the Committee's
work were published in N. F. Dubrovin, ed., *Sbornik istoricheskikh materialov izvleche-*

have become a major liability in the Land of the Don Cossack Host. To alleviate the worst aspects of disruption and turmoil associated with the appearance of the Don nobility would require major reform legislation. Accordingly, General Chernyshev and the Committee of 1819 began work on a comprehensive plan for reorganizing Don government, institutionalizing the Cossack military system, and regulating land use within the boundaries of the Don Host. This work was eventually incorporated in the publication of the Statute on the Administration of the Don Cossack Host (1836).[75]

For members of the Don elite, the Statute of 1836 and the politics of reform leading to it marked the passing of an era. The political and military needs of the eighteenth century had required a breed of local giants, leaders of larger-than-life stature who possessed the qualities necessary to communicate the imperial will to the often unruly rank and file. The elders and their aristocratic descendants operated at a time when the imperial presence remained distant and when local institutions were undergoing fundamental changes. Indeed, the emerging Cossack elite participated actively in the redefinition and transformation of those institutions to the extent that its members bore a large share of the responsibility for making the host what it was by the reign of Alexander I. However, once the host had demonstrated its worth and reliability, governing emphasis fell increasingly less on subordination than on perpetuation. If the old elite stood in the way of realizing the Cossacks' full military potential, then the elite too would have to change. Just as Potemkin had reduced the elders' power to alter or defy orders, now Chernyshev would have to reduce the elite's capacity to harm the host. Throughout the 1820s and 1830s, Chernyshev hewed away at the powerful position of the old aristocracy through a combination of closer supervision, restrictive legislation, and direct intervention in local appointments. Subsequently, new civil and military administrators might or might not come from the ranks of the old elite. Those who did basked in the reflected glory of an illustrious ancestry, but thanks to Chernyshev's changes, they no longer possessed the capacity seriously either to threaten the host's existence or to challenge the sovereign's will.

---

nnykh iz *Arkhiva Sobstvennoi Ego Imperatorskogo Velichestva Kantseliarii*, 15 vols., St. Petersburg, 1876–1915, Vols. 8 and 9; for an indictment of the Don nobility, see especially, 8: 360–63, 460–63, and 476–82.

75. PSZ I, Vol. 36, No. 27,819; the Statute officially went into effect on 1 January 1836, but had been officially published on 26 May 1835; it appears in PSZ II, Vol. 10, No. 8,163.

CHAPTER SEVEN

CHINY, ORDENA, AND OFFICIALDOM

Helju Aulik Bennett

The Table of Ranks has been mentioned in several of the preceding chapters, as it inevitably must, since it provided the overall formal structure in which the official, civil or military, worked. Bennett examines the total system in which the official lived as a social environment created by the parallel hierarchies of rank titles (chiny) and a ranked hierarchy of actual jobs or offices (dolzhnosti), and by the evolution of an additional, complex system of ceremonial awards (ordena), which added a degree of highly formalized flexibility to the simple numerical hierarchy of Peter's Table.

The interaction and overlapping of the two systems and its effect on the professional and the personal life of the official is vividly illustrated by Bennett. For all its apparent similarity to the "GS" ratings of the American civil service, or to a set of military ranks, the Russian system was quite different in its pervasiveness and its effect on society. Chinoproizvodstvo was not simply promotion, but a process that determined one's status in society as a whole. Deloproizvodstvo was not simply the conduct of affairs, but the conduct of affairs according to the rules of a highly structured system, where the rules not only governed promotion but the award of decorations for "exceptional merit" and, in turn, those awards entailed a whole range of legally defined rights and duties.

In a formal sense, the highest ranking bureaucrat was the foreign minister, who was normally the only civil official to hold rank number one; but we may well consider the tsar himself to have been the "official number one." He was formally free to appoint anyone he wished to any post, but the rules of chinoproizvodstvo, in fact, limited the group from which he could choose. The system of ceremonial awards was one way of overriding the rules, but it too, in turn, became so formalized that it added only a limited degree of freedom to the sovereign's discretion. Only a handful of "outsiders" could be added to those who "were seen" by the tsar, and they were always to be outnumbered by the many who acquired their awards through routine channels in effect, if not in form, by chinoproizvodstvo. [THE EDITORS.]

A study of imperial officialdom requires not only a description of the legal statuses, the types of wealth and incomes, the social and educational characteristics of the men who comprised it, but also an examination of the institutions that influenced their lives and work. The most important of these institutions in prerevolutionary times were *chiny* and *ordena*, the rules of rank ordering and the ceremonial awards system. These two institutions had to be taken into account at nearly every step of an official's career. The rules of *chin* provided the vocabulary by which an official was identified in documents, and implicitly rated the institutions and classified the offices in which he moved. *Chiny* further defined formal qualifications for promotion, working relationships, and benefits, thereby establishing the legal standard according to which an official's status was determined. The institution of *ordena* provided yearly incomes and social privileges, some duplicating those given by high *chiny*, a modicum of security for family and others that had independent value. Certainly, with medals, ribbons, jewels, making visible the attainment of preferences in service, *ordena* enhanced an official's status. The more important function of *ordena*, however, was the access to the emperor that they provided, hence the awarding process constituted a crucial method of screening men for roles in politics; those not awarded *ordena* benefits were more likely to do the routine secretarial and administrative work in government.

A study of *chiny* and *ordena* is a prerequisite for understanding various complex issues of Russian social history; here, however, the discussion of these institutions will be limited to how they affected civil officialdom. Wider questions, such as the role *chiny* played in changing the social composition of officialdom, how *ordena* affected elite recruitment, how both institutions provided a means by which administrative chiefs exercised their authority, or how they helped to influence the categories in which officials thought, will be dealt with speculatively, as problems needing further investigation.

Chiny derived from Peter the Great's Table of Ranks and constituted in the first instance a rating system applied to institutions.[1] Classifying all state functions, military, civilian, and ceremonial on a fourteen-level scale, it was both uniquely comprehensive and in a sense simple. A series of offices rated equally comprised each level or *klass* of as-

---

1. The first section of this paper is a restatement and expansion of information also found in my "Evolution of the Meanings of *Chin*: An Introduction to the Russian Institution of Rank Ordering and Niche Assignment from the Time of Peter the Great's Table of Ranks to the Bolshevik Revolution," *California Slavic Studies*, 10 (1977): 1–43.

cending importance on an office pyramid, and the determination of their placement was based not on function, but loosely, or approximately, on the frequency of dealings with the autocrat in the line of duty that the holders of these offices had. In its most abstract sense, the Table of Ranks established a scale for measuring distance from the emperor, consequently defining the relative status of each institution and its officials, and the power and privileges of the men who served in them as a function of distance from, or the frequency of access to him. The autocrat, at the apex of this structure, was empowered to change its arrangements whenever warranted. He could reclassify offices and even institutions by simply moving their component parts up and down on the rating scale, or he could abolish an institution's connection with the state by removing it from the chart.[2]

Since most but not all government offices were rated, there was a difference in power between institutions that had a rating scale worked out for them and those that did not. The ratings were usually assigned by an authorization order or *shtat*; thus, institutions with ratings were designated *shtatnye*, while those without were *ne-shtatnye*. The *shtat* from which information was taken for a master sheet or *rospis'*[3] rated institutions by providing for a specific number of classified offices (*klassnye dolzhnosty*) at each level within an institution. Unclassified offices, those not rated or listed in the authorization forms, also existed, but only service in classified offices counted as "actual state service" and entitled one to rights and benefits guaranteed for officials in law. Others doing unclassified service eventually secured rights, but this usually followed specific legal changes or personal favors and tended to take a long time.[4]

The number of classified institutions in the country and the number

2. Evidence for changes in ranking structures of institutions can be found in various ways. For instance, provisions are made for preferring *chinovniki* whose positions have been abolished for new posts. *Svod zakonov rossiiskoi imperii*: Vol. 3, *Ustav o sluzhbe grazhdanskoi*, St. Petersburg, 1857, article 363. The *Ustav o sluzhbe* (Statute on Service) is Volume 3 in all editions of the *Svod zakonov* (Digest of the Laws), the basic imperial legal code, but the *Ustav o sluzhbe* was reissued more frequently than the entire *Svod*. Hereafter citations are made to the *Ustav o sluzhbe* followed by the edition year.

3. An example of a master list is "Obshchee raspisanie klassnykh dolzhnostei v imperii," St. Petersburg, 1900. Variant forms are included in *Ustav o sluzhbe*, 1842, 1857, and 1897.

4. H. A. McFarlin, "The Extension of the Imperial Russian Civil Service to the Lowest Office Workers: The Creation of Chancery Clerkship, 1827–1833," *Russian History*, 1 (1974): 1–17. This article contains a discussion of a major reform that extended civil-service rights to previously unclassified categories. *Ustav o sluzhbe*, 1842, art. 532, however, still talks of *bez-shtatnye mesta* and *sverkhshtatnye chinovniki*.

of classified offices in any given institution tended to rise over the years. Many social institutions that came into existence after Peter's reforms were outside the classified-office scheme, but were eventually integrated, at least indirectly, into it. These included the nobility's institutions, various educational establishments, and local government offices, etc.[5] This process of classifying activities arising from various social needs accounts in part for the expansion in numbers of imperial officials noted by Soviet and Western scholars.

There was a connection between *chin* ratings given to offices and the laws governing social class (*sosloviia*) rights. The laws regulating social differences provided that only some strata enjoyed the prerogative to serve in classified offices. Nobility, personal nobility, and hereditary honorary citizenship are designations of groups that had either unlimited or abridged rights to serve during the eighteenth and nineteenth centuries. The "right to serve" then was comparable in some sense to the right to private property, in that both were limited to "privileged" classes. Throughout the imperial period, the right to service was gradually extended to a greater number of social classes, sometimes by direct autocratic grant, but more often in indirect ways, as for instance, through educational institutions, or service in "unclassified" or chancery service. It was this process that not only altered the status of groups which were considered privileged, but also substantially changed the social composition of those classes from which the government could routinely recruit its officials (without having to appeal to laws of exception or use of personal influence).

Another fundamental requirement established by the Table of Ranks law was that all officials who had a place or office in the classified

5. PSZ i, 1762, Vol. 1, No. 11,454, p. 924. *Ustav o sluzhbe*, 1845, arts. 57–132, states rights of graduates to enter service at assigned levels. "O priniatii v sluzhby po razlichniiu prav predostavliamykh raznymi uchebnymi zavedeniami," in L. M. Rogovin's edition of the *Ustav o sluzhbe* (1896 edition), St. Petersburg, 1915, p. 198, art. 466 (hereafter Rogovin), contains an example of a law which provides that Imperial Alexander Lyceum officials when transferring to service would be promoted two ranks higher than the rating of the offices they left. Whenever possible, I use Rogovin's edition of the last officially published Civil Service Code. It has several advantages for those who wish to survey changes in civil-service practices. For instance, Rogovin incorporates alterations made in the code as a result of the 1905 Revolution and gives one an opportunity to weigh the relative permanence of any one section of the code by giving dates and numbers of specific legislation that introduced changes. See also PSZ iii, 1899, Vol. 9, No. 6,169, p. 249, appendix "Raspisanie dolzhnostei neperemennykh chlenov i sekretarei gubernskikh prisutstvii, predsedatelei, sekretarei, perevodchikov, uezdnykh s"iezdov, zemskikh nachal'nikov, uezdnikh chlenov, okruzhnago suda i gorodskikh sudei."

office scheme were themselves to be rated or given *chiny*. In service records, a distinction was made between the office a person held and his *chin*. The first was listed under a column labelled *dolzhnost'*, sometimes *klass*, and the second under *chin*.[6] The difference between them could be better understood if we used another word for translating rank given to persons (calling it a grade for instance, a practice I've adopted elsewhere), but established usage as well as standards of consistency adopted for this volume forbid this. Nevertheless, we must bear in mind that rank given to persons was different from the rating of office, and having rank did not per se mean that the person who possessed it occupied an office at all or exercised authority. Yet all persons serving in classified offices possessed *chiny* or were working toward attaining them. The rank given to persons was determined by a combination of factors; a person's educational background (the type of school he graduated from and the grades he earned for academic performance influenced entrance level *chin* rights, for instance), the time spent in service, the quality of connections or favor, etc. Real talents and skills also contributed to earning rank. Though a person's rank was separate from the rating of the office he held, in law the total number of ranks a person could earn ostensibly reflected the total number of levels in the office-rating scale. In practice, ranks one, eleven, and thirteen were seldom awarded, hence the total number of ranks that an official could earn was actually eleven. But the climbing of the larger office hierarchy depended upon possession of and the level of *chin*; and the number of the *chin* a person possessed gave an observer approximate information about an official's success in climbing the pyramid of rated offices. From an official's rank one could determine the distance he had already climbed, the number of levels he still had to go, and comparing both to an official's age, one could see if an official was a success or a failure in service.

The most important part about *chin* to a working official was that a rank fixed or tethered an official to a level in the pyramid of offices by limiting the number of offices he could legally hold. The rules worked out in Nicholas I's reign required that one could be appointed to work in all offices rated the same as the rank an official had, and one step

6. The difference between the rating of institutions and the ranking of persons can be seen not only from the language of the various laws but from the fact that separate lists were composed for each type of rating. For example, *Spisok grazhdanskim chinam pervikh shesti klassov po starshinstvu*, St. Petersburg, 1851, and "Obshchee raspisanie," cited in note 3, are different kinds of documents. The one deals with classified offices and the other with ranked men. See Rogovin, art. 271, for example, for the way language was used to differentiate between these two ideas.

higher and two lower. Discrepancies tolerated between an official's rank and office rating varied in different reigns, but throughout the imperial period the government's policy was to prefer men whose appointments could be made in terms of established rules. Whenever exceptions became necessary, the government tried to write regulations, which amounted to providing for new laws to cover the necessary exceptions rather than throwing the limiting law out. In any case, the limiting laws established in Nicholas I's reign before 1855 were still in effect in Nicholas II's reign in 1900.[7] According to law, promotion in *chin* was based on assessment of performance judged in two ways. A rank could be earned for seniority, or for merit. The *chin* earned for seniority indicated that its recipient had spent a minimum number of years required for a rank in an office, and hence it was routinely given at intervals prescribed in the civil-service laws. On the other hand, *chiny* earned for merit were based on exceptional service performed while on the job and allowed for a faster rate of promotion than allowed for in seniority rules.

Though office and rank were earned by a process following separate rules, the two processes were interdependent in that acquiring an advantage in one had to take place in sequence or after gaining advancement in the other. A typical career probably proceeded like a game of hopscotch. For example, a person with "*chin* rights" found a place in the classified office scheme within the range allowed by, or predictable from, his *chin*. He then served the requisite number of years to earn a rank that corresponded to the office rating in which he was already serving. His rank at this point had the effect of ratifying his right to the office he already held. Putting in more time entitled the office-holder to a higher rank, which was usually given to him before he changed his service post. At this stage the rank acquired was a permission to compete from a position of strength for a higher-rated office whenever a vacancy occurred. If an official found a better-rated office, he could be appointed without legal difficulties. If on the other hand he was not able to find an office, or if he did not have skills to qualify him for changing jobs, or if he did not know the right people who could help him in securing the better post, his promotions in rank, though continuing for a time, would inevitably stop. Usually, however, by this method of alternating time spent in office and gain-

7. Rogovin, art. 271; *Ministerstvo finansov 1802–1902*, 4 vols. in 2, St. Petersburg, 1902, 2: 22–23, 24. The law of 20 Dec. 1894 released certain categories of workers in the ministry of finance from *chin* seniority requirements, and permitted persons with higher education and special training to be hired for some offices even if they had no rank at all.

ing better ranks and then higher-rated offices an official could proceed from ranks fourteen through five and be appointed to offices allowable for those ranks. At this point the climbing of the "ladder to success" stopped because many offices that were rated above four, and all ranks of four or better required imperial confirmation and support from persons whom the emperor knew. Higher ranking also required enjoying "access to the emperor," a separate "right" not enjoyed by most officials. This fact had far-reaching implications for officials who wished to attain higher office, a topic to which we shall return shortly.

Perhaps the most famous literary example of a lower official, and of a limited career, is that of Akakii Akakievich, a "permanent" or eternal *nadvornyi sovetnik* (court councilor), a man of the relatively high rank of seven who occupied a lowly copyist's office, one whom no amount of prodding by a kindly superior could encourage to master a more complex task that would presumably have qualified him for a post worthy of his rank.[8] In real life, however, we find persons whose ranks were lower than the rating of the offices they were appointed to. They were considered to be "above their rank," and their appointment was thought to be irregular and was usually made with some difficulty if at all.

Ranks in Russia affected pay, but less so than would be expected from experience with ranking systems found elsewhere. Lower officials were paid according to scales, differing not only according to the region of service and rank earned, but also according to allowances at the command of superiors. Sometimes the superior received a lump sum for paying for services performed by lower officials, and it was up to him to apportion it. Higher officials were paid according to the office held, or by special arrangement.[9] In any case, especially after the promulgation of the general civil service laws in the 1830s, ranks entitled officials to membership in a "service group" for which benefits and vacation time, travel pay, housing allowances, and pension

---

8. N. V. Gogol, "The Overcoat," in *Diary of a Madman and Other Stories*, trans. Ronald Wilks, New York, 1972, pp. 71–109. Both Joyce Toomre and David P. Bennett pointed out that Akakii Akakievich's lack of promotion was the result of his own character and values and not the result of overt discrimination.

9. P. A. Zaionchkovskii, *Pravitel'stvennyi apparat samoderzhavnoi rossii v XIXv.*, Moscow, 1978, pp. 77–90. This recently published Soviet work discusses in some detail the differences in salary and living conditions of various types and ranks of officials, local and central. It makes particular note of (p. 75) the awarding of "*arendy*," i.e. gifts of income to be derived from land grants, which supplemented many high-officials' incomes.

rights, survivor benefits, and the kinds of uniforms that could be worn were worked out in detailed regulations.[10]

Ranks also had social significance that was predictable from the number of a rank, and the title associated with it. The title "chancellor" given to officials of first rank, though seldom attained, was a sign of having reached the top of the pyramid above which no civil official could rise. "Actual state councillor," the title given to possessors of fourth rank, and "collegial assessor" and "collegial registrar," titles given respectively to persons of the eighth and fourteenth rank, designated watersheds in official success and in attainment of civil rights. Rank fourteen, for instance, signaled the beginning of an official's service career, and the date of its award was often taken as a basis for calculating seniority in classified offices and eligibility for awards, celebrating jubilees, and so on.[11] The rank of four (before 1843 rank eight, and 1843–53 rank five) was especially important for half-nobles or the *raznochintsy*, the partially privileged classes permitted to enter government service who could, by accumulating promotions, earn the full complement of nobility's rights and thus in effect enter a new juridical category. As can be imagined, attaining rank in service as a means for improving civil rights, owning rural property and serfs, freedom from corporal punishment, etc. (the rights belonging to nobles before 1861) made attaining rank in service an object of fierce competition among those half-nobles who served, and it affected their attitude to promotion.[12]

Another complex set of "rights" that inhered in *chiny* consisted of specifying degrees of politeness due each official from his fellows: in effect regulating manners. Each official could be addressed, according to his rank designation, by an honorary sobriquet that reflected his attainment in climbing the office pyramid, or rank earned. *Vashe vysokoprevoskhoditel'stvo*, a title by which a very highly ranked person was addressed, usually translated as "your excellency," meant much

10. *Ustav o sluzhbe*, 1842, art. 240. "Ustav o pensiiakh i edinovremennykh posobiiakh, raspisane okladov dlia opredeleniia pensii grazhdanskim chinovnikam po ikh dolzhnostiam." This is a statement of the pension statute of 6 December 1827 incorporated in the *Ustav*. Various exceptions and additions were made for *ne-shtatnyie* officials: see arts. 5, 8, 15, 54. The law that limited awarding of *chiny* for "excellence" dated from November 1835, Rogovin, art. 271. According to the same source, it was upheld as late as 9 July 1892.

11. Rogovin, art. 543; addendum to art. 167. Also *Ustav o sluzhbe*, 1842, art. 935, appendix: pp. 390–495, arts. 936, 950.

12. Helju Aulik Bennett, "The *Chin* System and the *Raznochintsy* in the Government of Alexander III," Ph.D. dissertation, University of California, Berkeley, 1971.

more. It not only took a longer time to say than other titles, but also implicitly conveyed the meaning "you who are set above, or higher than, and have a right to go in front of others." It clearly showed a difference in status from those addressed *vashe blagorodie*, a considerably shorter and less efflorescent title usually translated as "your honor" that was used for lower officials. This title actually implied noble birth (well-born). The language emphasizing differences in status was marvellously responsive to Russian authors exploiting it to describe all kinds of human foibles, failings, and vanities, and conveying pictures of the idiocy of the official world.[13] Gogol's *Inspector General*, for instance, is a play about the officialdom of a small town, which turns out in force to meet Khlestakov, an itinerant nobody, who has been mistaken for a high official on an inspection mission. They bribe him and curry favor with him, but it is Khlestakov himself who constantly alters the titles of rank, and offices in which he ostensibly works (sometimes several times in one scene), and this aspect of his language is what reinforces the feeling of flightiness and headlong rush associated with the play and with Khlestakov's character.

In addition to titles, the ranks four and higher were special in that they gave a "right to court" where extensive and explicit rules governing standing places, order of movement, and order of speaking regulated all human conduct and interaction. The most highly organized of these occasions were the grand processionals when Their Imperial Majesties moved from palace apartments to church and back. The lists assigning standing places were published ahead of time and were the result of laborious weighing and comparing of prerogatives of highly ranked civil officials with highly ranked court officers, His Imperial Majesty's suite members, military personnel, foreign ambassadors, the recipients of imperial orders, and so forth.[14] The right to stand next to the imperial guards, and so to be "seen" first and last by the imperial couple leaving and returning to the palace, seems to have been especially coveted by many courtiers as well as civil officials.

13. Fyodor Dostoevsky, "Bobok," in *The Gambler, Bobok, A Nasty Story*, trans. Jessie Coulson, New York, 1966, pp. 163–81. In this story a man overhears the dead in their graves continuing their status disputes. A. P. Chekhov, "Anna on the Neck," in *The Portable Chekhov*, ed. Avraham Yarmolinski, New York, 1947, pp. 268–85.

14. An example of one such list available in the Library of Congress is *Vysochaishe utverzhdennyi poriadok torzhestvennago vykhoda v zimnem dvortse 26go Noiabria 1897 goda, v den, ordenskago prazdnika Sv. velikomuchenika i pobedonostsa Georgiia*, St. Petersburg, 1897; Rogovin, art. 527. It explains what the rights of state secretary were in relationship to those of the *kamerjunkers*. As it turns out, the precedence right depended upon the rating of a *kamerjunker*'s office as well as the vintage of his *chin*, when compared to the same attributes of the state secretary.

Discussing the social prerogatives implicit in high rank and "court rights" brings us naturally to the other institution that affected officialdom, the *ordena*. The imperial ceremonial awards, of which the *ordena* were a part, were extensive and various. In the largest sense they were comprised not only of *chiny* given at will, but awards of titles of gentleman of the bedchamber, page of the bedchamber, secretary to His Imperial Majesty, titles of military entourage and senatorships, gifts of land, monies, swords, portraits, embroidered kaftans, and imperial expressions of gratitude and good will.[15] The most complex and at the same time systematically organized part of the ceremonial awards were the *ordena*. In time they were integrated with the *chin* rules and played a particularly important part in elite recruitment and social change among high officialdom.

Physically, the Russian *ordena*, like other European decorations were jewels of honor made of gold, silver, or less valuable alloys, either enameled or decorated with polychrome designs, precious stones, crowns, swords, oak leaves, and more.[16] Each was to be worn with a prescribed color of ribbon, either across the shoulder, on the neck, or in a buttonhole, according to its "degree." The placement of one medal was affected not only by the quantity and quality of other medals worn with it, but also by the uniform worn and the occasion attended.[17] The most elaborate order, the St. Andrew decoration, was a pendant in the shape of a double-headed eagle. Some variants of it contained a cross at its center showing a miniature painting of the saint crucified. When awarded with a collar, the medal was worn on a chain of small golden-rimmed eagles. The workmanship of the jewelry was painstaking and sometimes compared well with what can be found in the Fabergé goods produced in imperial factories at the end of the empire. The combining of simplicity in composition with intricate em-

---

15. A good summary of the various awards, their European and Russian origins, etc., can be found in E. Karnovich, "Sluzhebnye dolzhnostnye i soslovnye znaki otlichii v rossii," *Istoricheskii vestnik*, 22 (1885): 235–57, 263–581. That Peter I knew about European orders can be concluded from the fact that he commissioned a special translation of a Swedish book on European orders. Adriaan Schoonebeck, *Istoriia o ordiinakh ili chinakh voinskikh nache zhe kavalersikh obderzhashchaia ustavleniia povedeniia i praktiku printsipal'nykh deistv i velikomagisterskikh so oruzhiem i ikh figurami*, Moscow, 1710.

16. Robert Werlich, *Russian Orders, Decorations, and Medals*, Washington, D.C., 1968, contains color illustrations of many Russian orders, (St. Andrew on pp. 1–3).

17. N. N. Panov, *Istoricheskii ocherk rossiiskikh ordenov i sbornik osnovnykh ordenskikh statutov*, 2nd ed., St. Petersburg, 1892, appendix 6, pp. 71–100, contains rules published in 1889 for wearing orders and medals.

bellishment gave some orders intrinsic value as works of art. This was recognized by the Soviet commissions who preserved some medals while melting down quantities of all other kinds of Russian treasure, as well as by the collectors in the West who have treasured Russian orders.[18]

The imperial *ordena*, unlike European orders that grew up over a long period of time beginning with the crusades, were created piecemeal during the eighteenth century, with Peter the Great himself founding the "Order of St. Andrew the First Called by Christ to Follow Him." Later monarchs introduced a variety of orders, many of which were only infrequently awarded. The true founder of the institution, however, was Paul I; in addition to adopting and initiating many new orders, he promulgated in 1797 a decree that organized most medals already in use into a hierarchy of orders and combined them all as "degrees" into a unified chapter, or *kapitul*, as the institution was called. The St. Andrew order, which was to remain the most prestigious order throughout the imperial period, was designated the first or senior order in this hierarchy. Alexander I and Nicholas I changed the hierarchy somewhat by integrating the St. George and St. Catherine orders (created by Catherine the Great but left out by Paul; the first was to become an important military order, and the second was reserved for the grand duchesses and selected women of Russia); and by assimilating the Polish orders of St. Stanislaus and the White Eagle; founding what amounted to new degrees of established orders (the St. Vladimir, and St. Anna) and several quasi-orders or medals of honor mainly for long-term soldiers and state servants in recognition of "long-term and impeccable service in civilian and military spheres."[19]

During the remainder of the nineteenth century no major new orders (though there were many medals worn like orders) were created. Change in the system of awards derived instead from alterations in the administration, benefits, prerogatives and eligibility requirements for orders, and from defining more precisely their relationship to other state institutions, most particularly to the *chin* system.

Presiding over the institution of orders was the emperor. Its actual

18. Paul Hieronymussen, *Orders and Decorations of Europe in Color*, New York, 1967, pls., pp. 314–19; M. J. Larson [psued.], *An Expert in the Service of the Soviet*, London, 1929, trans. Angelo S. Rappoport, talks of standards used for preservation when melting down old silver, etc.

19. P. von Vinkler, *Ocherki istorii ordenov i znakov otlichiia Rossii*, St. Petersburg, 1899, pp. 12–14. Describes order structure before Paul's reforms. Panov, *Istoricheskii ocherk*, pp. 1–91; contains a short history and statutes of orders after Paul's reign, pp. 183–277.

administrator, however, was the chancellor of the orders, who after the order reforms of 1842 was also the minister of the Imperial Court and a senior cavalier in the brotherhood of St. Andrew chapter of the orders. It was his duty to see that the prerogatives and rights of recipients were safeguarded and that the rules and procedures established for dispensing orders were followed.[20] These rules were not only spelled out in separate *orden* statutes but were integrated into the fundamental laws of the empire, in the Statute of the Imperial Family, the Statutes of the Ministries, the Civil Service Codes, the tax laws, etc., all of which were first published during Nicholas I's reign in a separate code.

According to the statutes, all orders were awarded on the emperor's authority and for qualities and services "known to him" personally. In practice, it was only the awards of the senior orders, like the St. Andrew and St. Alexander Nevsky, and the first degrees of the lesser orders, that were made upon his initiative or even signed by him. Awards of lower degrees of the St. Anna, St. Vladimir, and the St. George (each of which had four degrees or more, depending on how jewels added to each were counted) were awarded for the most part through routine procedure for deeds spelled out in regulations. Candidates were recommended by witnesses to a deserving act, their names were forwarded by an appropriate administration, screened by a committee at central orders administration at the Ministry of Court, and then forwarded on an approved list to the emperor's chancery for signature. When the *orden* recipient was informed of his election and the patent and pin were transmitted to him during formal ceremonies, he became a cavalier, or order-brother, and could display the order as dictated, decorate his stationery, his samovar, and his "personal things" with the emblem, and enjoy the social and symbolic benefits the order entitled him to.

The benefits the awards gave were various, depending in some measure upon the service rights enjoyed by the receiver, the order received, and its degree. Like *chiny*, most orders until the 1840s gave social mobility to nonnobles, a fact that enabled a nonprivileged person to attain "right to office," and other benefits. More relevant for the men who were officials, most of whom could be presumed to be nobles or to have "service rights" by virtue of education, were the

---

20. *Svod zakonov* 1, 1843, orden statutes: arts. 174, 178; Panov, *Istoricheskii ocherk*, p. 287, arts. 49–50. All information about benefits of orders, obligations, social etiquette prescribed, etc., is drawn either from order statutes, histories of orders, or biographies of officials.

other benefits. When first founded, most orders were awarded with generous sums of money, and family fortunes were made for generations to come. Once the awards were institutionalized, however, the state treasury provided for a set capital sum for each order-chapter and, as a result, the grants diminished and were limited to a specified number of members whose names were inscribed in a special list. The "commanders," as these pensioners were called, enjoyed what amounted to a guaranteed income for life, a portion of which was dispensed yearly. A new candidate became a beneficiary only when an "opening" appeared in the list, as when someone was dropped from the list, usually because of a death in the group or when additional "places" were funded from the treasury. Eligibility for inscription, or place in waiting for it, was determined by seniority counted from the date a particular degree of order had been received. It was possible for a person to lose his "place" in waiting when he got a higher award of the same order. Eligibility for impeccable or long-term-service medals (*znak ot'lichiia besporochnoi sluzhby*) was counted from the date of receipt of the lowest or "first classified rank," i.e. the fourteenth.

Another benefit implicit in orders arose from education opportunities and financial aid given to families. Children of deceased or poor holders of *ordena* were considered to have preferential admission rights to institutions supported by funds or "under the protection of" the imperial family or those of the orders themselves. For instance, sons and grandsons of highly decorated members were admitted, if need be, to subsidized places in the imperial lyceum, while daughters of impecunious members were entitled to an education in the institutions for young ladies protected by the reigning empress, and upon marriage or graduation were given a lump-sum payment. Pension payments to officials due from the state were continued for a time to widows after the death of an official who had an *orden*.

Officials themselves received benefits in climbing the *chin* ladder.[21] For instance, some lower awards granted "additional years of seniority," which meant that one year's work in the classified offices was

---

21. *Svod zakonov* 1, 1842. *Uchrezhdeniia gosudarstvennye: Book 6, Uchrezhdenie ordenov i drugikh znakov otlichiia*: arts. 298, 303, 305, p. 283; arts. 202, 226, 229, 230, 232, 233, p. 569; Panov, *Istoricheskii ocherk*, p. 174. *Vysochaishe uchrezhdennaia kommissiia dlia peresmotra ustava o sluzhbe grazhdanskoi v gosudarstvennyi Sovet (4 Iiulia 1901 goda)*, St. Petersburg, 1901. This is a folio-sized book summarizing findings and recommendations of a commission that attempted to reform civil-service rules. In the main, it finished by integrating the *chin* and *orden* institutions. See, for instance, the large chart appended to end of the volume titled *nagradnaia skala*, which integrated all orders and medals with steps in the *chin* hierarchy.

counted for two or more, if one received the right type of award. This speedier accumulation of seniority in fact conferred eligibility for a higher office upon a recipient at a younger than usual age.

Social benefits conferred by high orders, the Andrew, Nevsky, Vladimir (similar benefits were conferred by the George, which was a battle decoration) to give them their colloquial names, and even the first degrees of less prestigious orders, were implicit in the "right of access to court" dispensed with them. This "right" constituted a legal permission to move in the same sphere as the autocrat who in Russia was the source of all law. Access to him as a birth-right was limited by fundamental laws and ceremonial tradition and was enjoyed freely only by imperial family members, descendants of illustrious families —those to whom Peter the Great had reserved "free access" to himself in the Table of Ranks law[22] and temporarily by the officials of the court and *sanovniki*, "called" to their posts by the emperor personally. Thus gaining this "exclusive" right by award conferred great distinction on whomever was selected. Its possession was valued by officials not only for reasons of prestige, but for the various kinds of service advantages that followed from gaining it.

Orden awards imposed social obligations, which paradoxically in their very performance became or were the means of gaining further advantages. One such obligation was the requirement to appear at yearly feast days of the orders, days during which new cavaliers were officially admitted to the order. Absence was fined. Another obligation —participation in court functions when their order was listed in the court calendar[23]—was considered an especially tedious burden by many older cavaliers. The most ephemeral obligation stated in order laws was that all cavaliers lead an exemplary and chivalrous life, to be

22. Basil Dmytryshyn, *Imperial Russia: A Source Book, 1700–1917*, 2nd ed., Hinsdale, Ill., 1974, pp. 17–19, contains a translation of portions of The Table of Ranks Statute of 24 January 1722.

23. *Pridvornyi kalendar' na 1879 god*, St. Petersburg, 1879, pp. 341, 366, 368, 536, 511. This is one in a series of small books that were published yearly until 1917 listing the regular festivals, who was to attend, in what kind of uniforms. The books invariably include a *polozhenie o vykhodakh pri vysochaishem dvore* and *vkhod za kavalergardov* lists. Extension of "rights to court" to new social categories can be found in the short history "Pridvornye chiny i pridvornoe vedomstvo," *Entsiklopedicheskii Slovar'*, ed. F. A. Brokgauz and I. A. Efron, St. Petersburg, 1894, 25: 154–58; William Prall, ed., *The Court of Alexander III: Letters of Mrs. Lothorp, Wife of the Late Honorable George van den Lothorp, Former Minister Plenipotentiary and Envoy Extraordinary to Russia*, Philadelphia, 1910, pp. 3, 35–36, 57, 60–61, 63, 67–69. These letters home show that the prescriptions for precedence order and the wearing of decorations were punctiliously followed in practice.

obedient to the laws of God, loyal to the monarch, and helpful to their fellow man. This was given specific meaning, however, by the fact that *orden* corporations subsidized a network of charitable, educational, and eleemosynary institutions in behalf of which candidates were to expend their efforts.[24] Among them were hospitals for the poor, shelters for widows, orphans, and retired officials, various chapels and churches at the capitals, and hospices at places of pilgrimage.

All members of orders were expected to contribute either energy or money for maintaining these services. The novices paid installation fees and pensioners had deductions made from their awards for "costs" and charitable purposes. (Only recipients of medals earned for long-term service, and those persons awarded decorations with precious stones by the emperor's own hand, were exempt.) The grand dukes who received senior orders at birth[25] and well-born monied aristocrats extended these activities to the social realm by sponsoring bazaars, balls, benefits, and so on. These were important occasions of the social season, providing opportunities for old aristocrats and the newly wealthy to compete for honor by displays of generosity. The poorer order brothers, unable to compete with gifts of money, were expected to volunteer, whenever called upon for help, in managing this sizable establishment. The benefit that order members gained in being admitted was membership in "high society," or ever closer integration with people, who as K. P. Pobedonostsev said, "lived on mountaintops."[26]

Because of concurrent leadership found in high-society charities and state institutions, and administrative ties between high state offices and order chapters, men in high society were easily recruited to other tasks. The Empress Mary Institutions, for instance, the supervisory

24. *Orden* statutes for 1842, *Svod zakonov* 1, arts. 243–44 (hereafter *Orden* statutes 1842) provide for supervision of hospitals, etc. The size of the charitable establishment can be gauged from other documents. See for instance "Sobstvennaia Ego Imperatorskago Velichestva kantselariia," *Entsiklopedicheskii Slovar'*, St. Petersburg, 1900, 30a: pp. 653–57, for a partial listing of institutions "protected" by members of the imperial family.

25. *Svod zakonov* 1, 1842, *Osnovnye gosudarstvennye zakony*, "Uchreszhdenie o imperatorskoi familii," art. 113. Provides for awarding highest orders of the empire to all of the grand dukes upon christening and for other preferences and privileges. Prince V. P. Meshcherskii, *Dnevnik za 1889 god, Noiabr' i dekabr' za 1890 god . . .* , St. Petersburg, n.d., pp. 136, 137, reports about Sheremetev giving the opera *Boris Godunov* as a benefit for the St. George Society. It was sold out at the high price of 10 rubles a seat.

26. Konstantin P. Pobedonostsev, *Reflections of a Russian Statesman*, ed. Murray Polner, Ann Arbor, 1965, p. 235. He also makes ironic comments about the "society" that gives to charity by dissipation.

body to which many charities reported when recommending their members for awards, was actually a department of His Majesty's Own Chancery with direct access to the emperor and through him to a series of other institutions.[27] The parent administration of the orders for most of the nineteenth century, the Court Ministry, was itself one of the highest ranking ministries in the state and also managed the imperial household and court. As a result, it had great influence in the staffing of the palace establishment. The most prestigious members of the various orders, the grand dukes who served as protectors and contributors to select charities, were the emperor's relatives and powerful because of this family tie, but they also exercised influence because they traditionally commanded, or held appointments in the guards, navy, or other sections of the military establishment. Since any of these functionaries could help an official secure a good post, recommend for a promotion, or "request" an award, their influence could be brought to bear upon making a career. All men in high society, however peripherally included, became men "with connections and influence." Minor favors, as for instance a recommendation that resulted in the receipt of an award in low degree, gave disproportionate advantage to the official who received it.[28] For example, even a lowly award allowed for subtracting a specified amount of time from the obligatory waiting period established for requesting *chiny* "for excellence," i.e. *chiny* given out of turn. This meant that higher *chiny* could be requested for decorated officials more frequently and as a result those officials were more easily appointed to a greater range and number of rated offices.[29]

Membership in high society was also important, because it was the first step in attaining entrance to a special group the Russian officialdom was particularly in awe of, the group colloquially named the

27. V. N. Stroev, *Stoletie sobstevennoi ego Imperatorskogo velichestva kantseliarii*, St. Petersburg, 1917, pp. 239, 244, contains partial lists of institutions under protection of imperial family members.

28. *Al'manakh soveremennykh russkikh gosudarstvennykh deiatelei*, ed. Konstantin A. Skal'kovskii, St. Petersburg, 1897; and *Nekrologi chlenov gosudarstvennogo soveta 1869–1890*, St. Petersburg, 1870–99, contain biographies of a great number of Russian officials that show how valuable service in the court-connected establishments was for making a "career" in service.

29. Dmitrii I. Abrikossow, *Reflections of a Russian Diplomat*, ed. George Alexander Lensen, Seattle, 1964, p. 85, makes comments about differences between protected and unprotected officials. V. N. Lamzdorf, *Dnevnik 1891–1892*, ed. F. A. Rotshtein, Moscow, 1934. For angry denunciation by a career official of patron's interference in course of promotions, entries for 2, 4, 1892, pp. 341, 342, 345. Lamzdorf, *Dnevnik, 1886–1890*, Moscow, 1926, p. 26.

znatnyi. The *znatnyi* were by definition, persons known to the emperor, in actuality those persons enjoying either a "right" of access to the emperor, or a "right to court" with opportunity to make use of it. The *znatnyi* were important because in Russian society in which the emperor was personally responsible for a wide range of government tasks, among them executing law, making law, making current policy, appointing a series of high and medium level officials only rudimentary institutions had developed that supported him in performing his duties. For instance, the institution available to him to help in gathering data about appointable officials who could be given ambassadorships, made chancery chiefs or members of collegial bodies, or appointed to the numerous offices rated at level three or better (and sometimes as low as four), selections he was responsible for making,[30] was a section of a chancery which was often moved in the nineteenth century between various administrations, which gathered personnel records for high officials. In practice, information that the emperor actually relied upon in making appointments derived mainly from the circle of *znatnyi*, and as often as not, it was communicated orally during informal sessions. Since the laws and traditions that limited the "right of access" to the emperor as a special right were enforced by the men around the emperor, they not only controlled access, but had the power to choose who would be admitted, from among those who did not possess this right, to the emperor's presence. The *znatnyi* as a result were in a crucial position to control information, to provide the emperor with alternatives to choose from when exercising his theoretically unrestrained and unlimited powers. The membership of the *znatnyi* as a result constituted the most influential, and most often resorted to, candidates for high office.

The final and most important benefit that orders conferred was that they had not only the power to add to the *znatnyi* group, but could be used at times for introducing men outside the *znatnyi* group, and sometimes those who did not enjoy the insider's good will or favor to the "sight and sound" of the emperor.[31] The reason why the *ordena* could serve as a means for introducing outsiders to the circle derived

30. *Svod zakonov rossiiskoi imperii (neofitsial'noe izdanie)*, 16 vols., ed. A. F. Volkov and Iu. G. Filipov, St. Petersburg, 1904, 1: 91 defines which offices and officials are imperial appointments. The emperor's authority is extended in some instances below office level four; Rogovin, art. 168; arts. 169–70, 174 indicates proper appointment procedure; *Svod zakonov*, 1842, ministerial statutes, book 4, arts. 237, 238, and 246 about ministerial authority over subordinates and "access rights" to the emperor.

31. *Orden* statutes, 1842; *Svod zakonov*, 1904, 1: 5 extends power of granting nobility by award. St. Vladimir first degrees gave hereditary nobility. All degrees of St. George

from the fact that *orden* laws since their inception specified that *ordena* were to be given at the emperor's discretion, and that awards could be "requested" by others besides chiefs of state offices and ministers, by men in court, grand dukes, and by institutions specifically given a "right to recommend" for awards: among them the Red Cross, the Imperial Academy of Sciences, and others. The awards could be requested for "anyone" among a variety of specified social groups, which included merchants, priests, and men of various lower social categories, even ex-poll-taxable ones, if they had obtained an education, or distinguished themselves by conspicuous public service in designated fields, or attained at least a minimum *chin* in civil service. The result of giving *ordena* to men outside the *znatnyi* circle had various consequences, depending on the seniority of the award given and the social group to which the recipient belonged before receiving the award. If the award (of high degree, i.e., one granting its recipient "access to court") was given to persons already enjoying a "right" to attend court either by virtue of a title or by birth, the award reinforced the dominance of "established classes" because it merely gave those who possessed "access" the occasion and opportunity to make more frequent use of it. When the award was given to persons who did not have prior "access rights" to the emperor's circle by other means (as in fact awards often were during periods of reform activity when high officials recruited expert help in drafting legislation or investigating local conditions from nonnoble classes and rewarded them with awards), then the awards had the result of "democratizing" the membership of the *znatnyi* group by giving outsiders entrance to this special circle. The general result of awarding high orders was to admit all their possessors to an arena of politics by granting a routine means of becoming involved in a social group where decisions were discussed and where the emperor's choices were at least subject to some scrutiny and minimum criticism.[32]

I suspect that most men who vied for orders did not hope to attain influence in lawmaking or participation in decision making carried on in "higher spheres." They probably vied for orders because of the

---

medal gave the same benefits. *Ustav o sluzhbe*, 1842, arts. 1,088, 1,089, 1,104–19, refers to regulations that increasingly narrow award giving criteria. There is a law that no longer permits requesting awards for oneself.

32. D. L. Ransel, *The Politics of Catherinian Russia, the Panin Party*, New Haven, 1975, pp. 23, 30, 36–61, 105, 109, 164, 232, 233, 236, 247, shows how awards were instruments for building family and party influence in government. This is not his conclusion, but his frequent references to awards warrant it.

more modest social benefits in the awards, which gave them advantages and honor in their own group. For instance, a man who attained some success in government because of high *chiny*, high office, or because he gained access to court through the good offices of a patron, might wish for an award because it gave him independent access to higher spheres and hence independence from the whim of any one patron. Another might strive for orders because of the access they gave to a grand stage for himself and his family, for social interaction. Chapter houses, grand ducal residences, and imperial palaces served as gathering places and social clubs during festivals and hence provided a setting for members which otherwise only the very wealthy could afford, or provide for themselves. Orders might also be desirable because by prescribing uniforms and choreographing manners, their rules helped to mitigate the rigorous requirements of etiquette and proper dress, nuances in which, when not formally dictated, were difficult to master for newcomers. Lapses, however, invited ridicule in less formal or controlled social settings.

Though it seems that poorer social groups among officialdom had more to gain from orders than established officials, the memoirs and other personal records available show that even men of great wealth, privilege, and cosmopolitan manners, already enjoying access to court by birth or titles, vied for them. This can be explained by the fact that high awards (unlike *chiny*, given mainly for time served, and court titles, often suspected of being awarded for reasons of nepotism) enjoyed wide social regard and were considered a recognition of personal excellence; if recently awarded, they were signs of current imperial favor. All possessors, however, regardless of social origin, enjoyed security of membership in "higher spheres." A cavalier, since he was duty bound to appear at court as prescribed by law, could not be excluded, as could persons who enjoyed access by court titles requiring in addition specific invitations.

Since honor was a legally defined right, it was inviolable, like rights to noble status, to private property, and rights to *chin*, and could not be confiscated or lost without due process of law. Even if a judgment was made requiring its loss by a court, the judgment itself required imperial confirmation. Especially important for older families was the fact that whenever an order-decorated official lost an office or fell into disfavor, he continued to appear at court.[33] The continued access to

<hr/>

33. *Orden* statutes for 1842, arts. 243, 244; Richard Graf von Pfeil, *Neun Jahre in Russischen Diensten unter Kaiser Alexander III*, Leipzig, 1907, p. 135. The author describes the festivities for the St. George order in the mid 1880s and incidentally shows

the emperor in effect guaranteed some influence in policy making and some leverage in directing the course of government even after service posts were lost to better-trained men, and one's economic condition began to deteriorate.

The descriptions of *chiny* and *ordena* given above have been supported in the main by references to laws and institutional histories. The fact, however, that *chiny* and *ordena* were integral parts of Russian life can be seen by perusing Russian literature and memoirs, many of which illuminate life among officialdom. If artists must be presumed to use a language whose meaning is understood by readers, the fact that Russian authors made frequent use of titles of *chin*, references to order colors and designs, allusions to clothing prescribed in civil-service regulations, constitutes proof that prescriptions dictated by law were sufficiently followed by society so that references to them could serve a literary purpose. The varied ways in which these institutions guided career paths and influenced official sensibilities can best be assessed by referring to materials left by officials themselves. Only a few of the many that could be described can be referred to here.

A. V. Nikitenko, a censor and teacher in institutions affiliated with the war ministry and the charitable establishments under special protection of the reigning empresses, was an official who rose from lower estates during Nicholas I's reign.[34] He left a diary, which begins in the 1820s and ends in the 1870s, thus covering the reign of Nicholas I and a good portion of the reign of Alexander II. His frequent references to *chiny* and *ordena* show us not only the pervasiveness of the institutions but the various effects they had on his own and his fellow officials' careers. For instance, he mentions his disappointment when a recommendation for an Anna II degree, a relatively low order requested for a fellow official, was not forwarded to higher authorities because the superior was apparently afraid to use the good will he enjoyed by drawing on it for the benefit of a lowly subordinate. When Nikitenko himself received a St. Stanislaus II degree several years later he reports that a delegation of his colleagues who had usually ignored him and

---

how dismissed ministers and others in disfavor participated in these functions; E. M. Feoktistov, *Vospominaniia za kulisami politiki i literatury*, Leningrad, 1929, pp. 112, 173, 181. Lamzdorf, *Dnevnik, 1891–1892*, 17 April, 19 November, 4 December 1891, and 1 May 1892, pp. 96, 199, 201, 212, 332.

34. A. V. Nikitenko, *Dnevnik v trekh tomakh*, 3 vols., 1826–57, Vol. 1, Moscow, 1855, pp. 45, 56, 171, 172, 242–43, 282, 458; Helen Salz Jacobson, trans. and abridger, *The Diary of a Russian Censor Aleksander Nikitenko*, Amherst, 1975, pp. 13, 51, 189, 257, 266, 332, 357, 365.

his work came to congratulate him and to thank him for bringing imperial attention upon the institution they all worked in. His appointment to more important offices and his rise in society, which gave him greater opportunities to report on manners and mores, were all related in some measure to attaining higher ranks and better decorations, which opened more doors. The relationship between his rise in service and his expanded social universe is recorded in a code that can be understood if we note the uniforms he reports seeing at various receptions and festivals, the colors of decorations he refers to, and we recall which of them were associated with what level of orders in the hierarchy established by Paul. When he eventually reports attending festivals where guests were resplendent in "diamonds" and "blue sashes" we can be sure that he has been admitted to a social group where possessors of the most prestigious order, the St. Andrew medal, and of decorations granted with diamonds only at the emperor's personal behest, were much in prominence.

Both D. A. Milutin, the minister of war in Alexander II's reign, usually a factual and humorless man devoted mainly to business, and P. A. Valuev, the minister of interior,[35] who usually sounded like a world-weary courtier, frequently refer to *chiny* and *ordena* received, denied, stolen, and so forth, showing that even the most important ministers of widely differing temperaments were deeply interested in the social dramas played out in terms of ceremonial awards.

The continued influence of *chiny* and *ordena* to the very last days of the empire in the reign of Nicholas II can be seen from the memoirs of Count S. Iu. Witte and the letters of the last empress.[36] Witte is known in history books for the role he played in preparing the manifesto that conceded the founding of the Duma in 1905, and for his industrialization programs. Hence he is seen as a forward-looking, modern official, yet his memoirs are replete with gossipy references not only to *chiny* but to the old chivalric institution of orders. Count Witte tells us of his social disabilities before he was awarded high *chiny* and high orders,

35. D. A. Miliutin, *Dnevnik D. A. Miliutina*, Moscow, 1947, Vol. 1 (1873–75), pp. 107, 118, 122, 125, 130, 131, 132, 153, 167, 175, 177, 225, 226; Vol. 2 (1876–77), pp. 110, 115; P. A. Valuev, *Dnevnik P. A. Valueva, Ministra Vnutrennykh del*, Moscow, 1961, Vol. 1 (1861–64), pp. 55, 138, 139, 200, 264; Valuev, *Dnevnik 1877–1884*, ed. V. Ia. Iakovlev-Bogucharskii, Petrograd, 1919, pp. 10, 12, 129, 130, 133, 134. Valuev indicates that a lapse of time was expected before higher awards were given. He mentions, however, that he received a St. Andrew "only three years" after receiving a St. Vladimir.

36. S. Iu. Vitte, *Vospominaniia, 1849–1894*, Moscow, 1950, 1: 17, 213, 332–33, 359. Alexandra Fedorovna, *Letters of the Tsaritsa to the Tsar 1914–1916*, Stanford, 1973. Letter of 5 June 1916, No. 298, p. 363.

and the reaction of others when he received foreign decorations. He volunteers a great deal of information about the difficulties his brother had in receiving a medal he had won for conspicuous valor on the battlefield. The empress on her own account seems puzzled by the regulations that toward the end of the empire increasingly enveloped the giving of orders and *chin* awards. In a letter to the emperor she wonders how it is possible to limit awards for heroism. She had just met a young officer who had earned all the awards proper to his rank and, despite further heroic deeds, he could receive no more.

Considering the evidence derived from varied types of historical materials, from laws, institutional histories, memoirs, and literature, we can conclude that *chiny* and orders were a pervasive and deeply ingrained institution affecting many aspects of a Russian official's life. Though considered to be separate institutions by the contemporaries, the *chiny* and *ordena* were in practice different facets of a comprehensive structure of obligatory rating and rewarding, of an institution that can be labeled a niche-assignment system. The *chin* system, however, had a more direct bearing on organizing an official's work and upon his economic status, while the *orden* institution influenced his social opportunities, or at least that portion of it which brought him into contact with high society and his superiors. The ranking system clearly needed to be taken into account whenever an official considered making a profession of the government, especially so if he derived from less privileged status groups, or aimed at improving the juridical category he belonged to in the Russian social hierarchy. Also, in that they guaranteed access to a social sphere where politics, while not legal, had to be tolerated, the orders had special relevance to those who were interested in acquiring social influence or roles in politics. The orders and the etiquette prescribed by their ceremonies affected an individual's aesthetic and historical consciousness. Though difficult to document, these aspects can be reconstructed from manifest behavior and directly quoted statements of individuals.

Orders had been introduced in Russia by monarchs, named in honor of princes and saints whose deeds were widely known from national legends, and whose names were familiar to the Russian population. The orders had been awarded to many favored by fortune and sometimes to important statesmen. Any recipient who entered a brotherhood at however low a degree had good reason to feel himself a member of a special circle, an heir to a long historical tradition. The order festivals celebrated yearly reminded him of his attained status and dramatized special days in his life. Even officials who did not belong to an order were involved in this drama. They waited eagerly for the "days of benefice" to find if they had been included among the new recruits. The ceremonials and awards days punctuated the social season, and their recurrence gave a rhyme and structure to an official's year as the mere passing of summer and winter did not. Insofar as predictability of events is at the source of human ability to deal with one's environment, social and natural, and the basis for a sense of safety, we can imagine how this anticipated coming and recurrence of significant days gave a sense of orderliness and even security to an official's life. A paradoxical consequence of focusing upon recurrence marked by ceremony, however, was that whenever the festivals were disarranged or cancelled, or when observances were scrimped upon, as they necessarily were during times of social change and stress, the very absence of usual activities and traditional ways of structuring time tended to increase anxiety among officials.[37] Given our vantage point in another time, which allows us to view the lives of many individuals as completed stories, we can see how officials' ideas and actions, for instance, their attitude to authority, the details of their work, and finally the difficulties they encountered in attempting to make changes, also were derived from or aggravated by the existence of these institutions.

The orders as well as *chiny* were extensions of the institution of, and the principles of, autocracy. They served as a highly effective means by which one man could make his "will" felt among various social classes, social institutions, and individuals whom he personally never encountered. Merely by altering either the "rights" of a class vis-à-vis *chin* scale, or an institution's ratings in its charter, or benefits a person could expect by working for a rank or when transferring from one institution to another, the autocrat could alter their "position" in the network of relationships that enveloped many Russian institutions, relationships which were visible to all because they were quantifiable. The emperor could raise an institution's attractiveness to an employee by giving it higher than usual "*chin* rights" or enhanced opportunity, to be "recommended" for orders. The emperor could, by giving an order or rank, or by holding hope out for either, punish an official, reward a loyal one, or bring a recalcitrant opponent around to his views.[38]

37. Lamzdorf, *Dnevnik, 1891–1892*, entries for 3, 7, 26, 29 November 1891, pp. 194, 198, 208, 210, show reactions of various people to absence of ceremonies.

38. Two recent works about the great reform period, which show incidentally the difficulties that highly rated ministers had in gaining consent of their colleagues for any kind of change: Daniel Field, *The End of Serfdom: Nobility and Bureaucracy in Russia: 1855–1861*, Cambridge, Mass., 1976, pp. 95, 113–14, 137, 142, also shows how decora-

The fact that all orders derived in law from the emperor's authority and were in practice given out under his seal, and in ceremonies where he was present, testified to (as all awards did) his largesse and "splendor." Since the awards gained had the effect of making life easier, more interesting, more comfortable and "free" in a restraint-ridden society, they effectively demonstrated the emperor's power. Their very existence was a means of making the emperor's presence palpable, and they constituted a major way of making real and believable the very assumptions upon which the political culture and autocratic state rested (premises that seem preposterous to persons in a culture founded upon a presumption of equality, bargaining, and contract) that he was personally the source of benefits and advantages, as well as of formal law: assumptions that were axiomatic not only among officialdom but also among many other groups in Russian society.

The chieftains or administrative superiors, the *nachal'niki*, who supervised the officialdom's work exercised enormous power and were important by virtue of the same institutions. They were men placed in high posts usually no more than one or two steps below the emperor in the rating scale, and could by that fact alone be considered "men on high" or *verkhovniki*. For as long as they kept their footing in their high perch, they were important also because they shared in the emperor's power to initiate change, a fact that made the Russian *nachal'niki* a rather different breed of men than the administrative chiefs or supervisors they are usually compared with. They were, as their name in Russian indicates, empowered to "begin" or initiate changes, while others were denied this "right," or had to petition for it, or to exercise it only when explicitly commissioned to do so. The authority the chieftains of this kind exercised over the public derived in no small measure from their power to enforce the prescribed role differences allocated to various social groups by the ranking rules themselves.

The *nachal'nik*'s importance for lower officialdom derived not only from his association with those on high, but from the concrete obligations he had in overseeing a lower official's daily work and especially in gaining recognition and rewards for it in the coin of *chiny* and *ordena*. He could support or not a request for a promotion, he could forward or not a recommendation for an award. What he authorized

---

tions were used to bring opponents of government policies around to supporting its actions; and S. Frederick Starr, *Decentralization and Self-Government in Russia, 1830–1870*, Princeton, 1972, pp. 26–28, 31, 176.

to be written down in an official's record, the comments he made about his subordinates, had consequences. For instance, a simple reprimand given verbally by a superior could be embarrassing but did not necessarily have a long-term effect on a lower official's life. A written reprimand, however, became a *poroch*, a peccatum, almost literally a stain that blotted out an interval of accumulated time, a *srok* (a total time unit legally prescribed) that an official needed in order to qualify for certain medals or higher *chiny*. Since the decision about what to write down, when to write down, and if to write down was a matter of discretion and sometimes of whim, this minimal power gave a chieftain considerable influence over the progress of subordinates in Russian office hierarchy. Officials who did not receive a superior's recommendation might be able men, but they were not generally considered "best qualified." Their appointments, if they were resorted to at all, required more paperwork, better justification, unusual procedures, tasks that tended to make the appointments more difficult to complete; those officials themselves became second choices in the selection process, and like second choices everywhere, were less often appointed, less visible and less likely to have opportunities to demonstrate what they could accomplish. The generally subservient attitude to authority seen among Russian officialdom; the hand kissing, the self-effacement, the cowering rush to do a superior's will regardless how trivial, characteristics of officialdom that offended the independent, puzzled the foreigner, and were systematically practiced by cynical careerists, derived from the existence of these institutions rather than from a Russian's innately low moral fiber.[39]

The existence of the *chin* and order rules, which subordinated lower officials to their superiors, were the source of the power that lower officials in turn enjoyed over all others who dealt with them from the vantage point of "society." The lower official enjoyed power vis-à-vis "society" because he was in charge of the actual work of dispensing documents that any individual needed to deal with the system of assigned rights. All information certificates, affidavits, testimonials

39. Hans-Joachim Torke, "Das russische Beamtentum in der ersten Hälfte des 19. Jahrhunderts," in *Forschungen Zur Osteuropäischen Geschichte*, Osteuropa Institut an der Freien Universität Berlin, Berlin, 1967, 13: 309, includes a letter of an experienced official advising a younger one to be subservient and ingratiating; Bernard Pares, *Russia between Reform and Revolution: Fundamentals of Russian History and Character*, 1907; reprinted New York: 1962, pp. 159–60; Marquis de Custine, *Journals of the Marquis de Custine: Journey for Our Time*, ed. and trans. Phyllis Penn Kohler, New York, 1951, p. 71 refers to the high costs of the system of subservience; Abrikossow, *Reflections*, pp. 71, 86 about a small Gogolian clerk who hoped to rise by a chance visit of the emperor.

to "rights" possessed, awards earned, and certificates to time accumulated needed to be written down, copied, handed out, notarized, vouched for, stored, transmitted from office to office, and fees and oftentimes bribes were collected for "processing" them all. Deciding who had what rights constituted the essence of *chinoproizvodstvo*, while processing papers about rights enjoyed was *deloproizvodstvo*, and both activities in turn were the source of much work in many offices. The power and opportunity for "lower instances" to delay decisions on any one occasion by insisting on right forms, or by misplacing or delaying the sending of documents[40] could be used to show either how important or how conscientious an official was. In the end, however, the *formal'nost'*, a Russian word often translated by a misleading cognate "formalism," did not rise out of intentional malfeasance, or from the scribbler's blood flowing in a *chinovnik*'s veins, but from the nature of the system itself. The very existence of a hierarchy of ranking and rating, the practice of rewarding, with the various requirements that many fine distinctions be made between "rights" and "privileges," and the consequent need to petition and permit and the concomitant work validating many routine human activities required much processing and paperwork.[41] And as in any recurrent process this work itself gave rise to a need to define the proper ways to go about it, i.e., to have recipes for action.

The great difficulty of accomplishing things, the lack of flexibility or slowness, rose in important ways from the *chin* and *orden* system prescribing specific ways in which initiative could be taken. It rose also from the fact that all men who work in terms of a system necessarily assimilate its rules at a preverbal level, which consequently made them in some sense inaccessible to rational discourse and hence to the possibility of change. Regardless of political persuasion, a profound

40. L. A. Tikhomirov, *Vospominaniia Leva Tikhomirova*, Moscow, 1927, "Dnevnik," 1889 for 2 May, 2, 24, 30 June; 22 July, 13 Sept., 26 Oct., 30 Nov., pp. 352, 355, 357, 358, 368, 370, 371, shows extensive problems with certificates, and a *chinovnik*'s arrogance.

41. Rogovin, art. 138, refers to documents published by the Second Section of H. M. Chancery on 12 December 1874 which attempted to settle the problems connected with revising institution's classification lists; *Spisok vysshikh chinov tsentral'nykh ustanovlenii ministerstva vnutrennikh del*, St. Petersburg, 1916: *Spisok chinov ministerstva imperatorskogo dvora 1914 god*, St. Petersburg, 1914; *Ustav o sluzhbe*, 3, in *Svod zakonov*, 1842; 1,092, appendix to pars. 503 and further, provides a sample of the correct forms of *spiski* required for awards. "Forma spiska o nagradakh' grazhdanskikh chinovnikov" required name, *chin*, office, level of office, what degrees of orders received, what *razriad* assigned to by pension statutes of 1834. Interesting new additions to be found in these *spiski* is the requirement that "time served" in last office, when given last *chin*, and when last received an award are to be indicated.

psychological characteristic of most officials whose written work I have seen seems to be the way they shared assumptions about how things should be done and what constituted "order."[42] Indeed, men who were against the government, who left it for science and "public life," tended to think in terms of the niche-assignment traditions (a word I've used for the sum total of rules-ordering of rights and rewards). Mendeleev, for instance, an official better known as the man who invented the periodic table classifying chemical elements, seems to have done so from an ability to deal with widely divergent elements that had been incompletely organized in his day, from an expectation that principles could be found by which even undescribed elements might be organized. Mendeleev found these principles to order the elements and brought a simplicity to the chaotic picture of the chemical world, giving his peers a way to speak about it in a simple language. Pobedonostsev, a contemporary who shared Mendeleev's assumptions about the necessity of order in the world, however, had no sympathy for the social elements he saw contending for a place in the existing hierarchy rating and opposed all attempts to find a new synthesis, because he considered the claims of new social groups to be per se a symptom of "loss of values" and their increasing vehemence a sign of impending collapse.

Given the pervasiveness of the institutions of order and *chiny* and the psychological assumptions that would be natural for persons to adopt who lived within the system, it is easy to see why modernization of Russian officialdom and society could only proceed at a snail's pace. For the Russian officialdom to become a modern officialdom it needed not only to train its men in new skills, to allow new social groups a role in its tasks, but above all, it needed to give up a comprehensive, highly complex, socially and economically serviceable set of rules, or legal fictions, which integrated many facets of the official's life into an "organic" whole. It might be expected that a willingness to abolish these institutions would be found only among an isolated few among Russian officialdom. As can be seen from the support the state secretary to His Majesty, A. A. Polovtosv, gave to a project to abolish the *chin* system, these men existed. That he realized how difficult it was can be seen from the letter he wrote to Alexander III in which he

---

42. Horst Bieneck, *Bakunin: An Invention*, trans. Ralph R. Read, London, 1977, p. 89, indicates that Bakunin designed a decoration for Marx. "The Relations between the Properties of Elements and Their Atomic Weights," in *Moments of Discovery*, Vol. 2, *The Development of Modern Science*, New York, 1958, pp. 819–37.

stated: "Of course, there will be a time when it will be difficult for a historian to explain the meaning of *chin*. But for now it is impossible not to take account of the fact of the existence of this institution which has endured for a century and a half and rooted itself in a Russian's ways of doing things and in his ambition."[43]

43. A. A. Polovtsov, *Dnevnik gosudarstvennogo sekretaria A. A. Polovtsova*, 2 vols., Moscow, 1966, Vol. 1 (1883–86), 17 Dec. 1886, p. 467.

CHAPTER EIGHT

THE EVOLUTION OF CIVIL OFFICIALDOM, 1755–1855

Walter M. Pintner

P*intner identifies strong elements of both social and economic continuity in the composition of Russian officialdom from 1750 to 1860. However, he shows that this should not obscure very important changes in the nature of service and the kind of officials it produced. As in previous centuries, nobles predominated in high positions and commoners in low. The prevalence of large landholders in elite positions declined only moderately over the century. But, as the civil service grew greatly in size, the nature of the official career was transformed. In particular, as the number of offices and officeholders expanded the importance of uniform career development (chinoproizvodstvo) and uniform structure and procedure (deloproizvodstvo) also increased—perhaps for no other reason than to secure what it was thought would be uniform, central control over an already sprawling administration. At any rate, two of the most important additions to Peter the Great's uniform rank system are imposed upon officialdom during the period studied by Pintner, this era of rapid growth. In 1802 Emperor Alexander I created the uniform ministerial structure, which was to dominate the division of bureaucratic functions in Russia until the end of the empire and, in a real sense, up to the present time. Second, a subtler but equally important change was effected, as Pintner shows, by the introduction of what amounted to a formal-education requirement for anyone who aspired to high- or even middle-level office. Career preparation now came to be within the jurisdiction of the civil bureaucracy itself, since the formal educational institutions were controlled largely through the bureaucracy. The unity of military and civil service, which had served the landholding elite so well in the eighteenth century, had thus ended and the career civil official emerged as a clearly recognizable type above the lowest level.* [THE EDITORS.]

Russian historians, both those within Russia before and after the revolution, and those beyond its borders, have traditionally tended to see the history of that country in terms of a tripartite division: tsar, nobility, and peasants. They have bemoaned the lack of a "third estate," or as an early nineteenth-century minister of finance put it, "We lack an educated prosperous middle class—needed for a thousand uses."[1]

Each of these three elements has been examined with care by historians. The powers of the sovereign, the status of the nobility, the enserfment and emancipation of the peasantry, have been the subjects of many studies, as have the interrelations of the three groups. The noble's obligation to serve the tsar and the peasant's enserfment for the benefit of both the landlord and the central political authority has been the focus of careful work.

However, it is only very recently that historians have begun to examine the men who operated the Russian state as a social group. Of course it is true that the activity of senior officials has been the stuff of political history, and it must be. No sovereign can act alone. The Menshikovs, Panins, Czartoryskis, and Speranskiis who enjoyed the favor of the ruler at one time or another certainly made their mark. Leading statesmen and favorites, however, come and go, but someone must always be there to give advice, to take orders and pass them on to an ever-widening circle of officials who, at some point, may or may not actually try to do what was originally intended. Who these people were, how they were trained, what kind of careers they normally had, where their loyalties can be presumed to have lain, that is the social history of officialdom.

For a very long time indeed this group has constituted a separate occupational group, perhaps a hidden "third estate" within Russian society. Historians have not totally ignored officialdom, but they have usually seen it in terms of something else—service or part of the life and political role of the landowning nobility, service as a way for the humble man, usually described as a priest's son, to rise in status and become a noble, or civil service seen as a residual category, a way of life that was rejected by some groups, by the nobility in the later eighteenth century or by the intelligentsia in the nineteenth.

Recent research, however, enables us to develop a reasonably detailed picture of Russian civil officialdom. The earlier chapters in this volume have demonstrated that the civil service was by no means a creation of Peter I. He did create the basic structure that governed its operation down to the revolution of 1917, the famous rank (*Chin*) system of 1722. It was, as Bennett demonstrates, a measure designed to better motivate and better organize the service that had been tradi-

---

1. Egor Frantsevich Kankrin, *Im Ural und Altai: Briefwechsel zwischen Alexander von Humboldt und Graf Georg von Kankrin aus den Jahren 1827–1832*, Leipzig, 1869, p. 39.

tionally rendered by the upper levels of Russian society to the tsar. That it had the effect of allowing a certain number of lower-class individuals to at least get their start on the ladder of success was an accidental circumstance reflecting the need to fill openings at a given time, and not part of the intention of the legislation. Indeed numerous decrees testify to the fact that such was not the intention. Whether or not the Table of Ranks did create a new social reality, opening careers to talent, regardless of the purpose of the law, is a matter that will be considered shortly.

The aim of this discussion is broader than that. It is necessary to examine the evolution of officialdom from the relatively minor occupational specialty of a few individuals to an important and recognized, if not popular, element of society. It was a process that involved two major developments: (1) simple increase in total numbers, and (2) a much more complex process of differentiation from other groups (particularly the nobility) through increased specialization in function.

Satisfactory data on the total number of officials is unavailable. It is clear, however, that there was a very large increase in size between 1755 and 1855. For the mid-eighteenth century (1755) Troitskii estimates, on very solid grounds, a total of about 10,500, including those below the fourteenth rank, in all agencies, central and provincial. Of those 10,500, only 2,051 held rank fourteen or higher. A decade later the *shtaty*, or the authorizations for staff of Catherine II, called for a total of 16,504. For the early nineteenth century, more approximate estimates by Torke suggest a total of 38,000 around 1800. Official figures for 1856 are 113,990, of whom 82,325 (72 percent) held rank fourteen and up, a much greater proportion than the 20 percent in the mid-eighteenth century.[2] Using the rough estimates of total population that are available, these figures suggest a decline in population per official from around 2,000 in 1755, to 1,400 in 1763, about 1,000 in the early nineteenth century, and around 500 by the 1850s. The absolute values of these estimates may well be off by several hundreds but the trend is unmistakably, and sharply, downward.[3]

2. S. M. Troitskii, *Russkii absoliutizm i dvorianstvo v XVIIIv., Formirovanie biurokratii*, Moscow, 1974, pp. 176–77. Troitskii suggests a maximum undercount of 10 percent, which would bring the total to 12,000. The *shtaty* are in PSZ I, 1763, Vol. 44, Pt. 2, supplement to statute No. 11,991. For the early nineteenth-century estimates, see Hans-Joachim Torke, "Das russische Beamtentum in der ersten hälfte des 19. Jahrhunderts," *Forschungen zur osteuropäischen Geschichte*, 13 (1973): 136. For 1856, P. A. Zaionchkovskii, "Vysshaia biurokratiia nakanune krymskoi voiny," *Istoriia SSSR*, No. 4, (1974) p. 155. For 1847 and 1857, see P. A. Zaionchkovskii, *Pravitel'stvennyi apparat samoderzhavnoi Rossii v XIXv.*, Moscow, 1978, pp. 67–68.

3. Population estimates are from V. M. Kabuzan, *Narodonaselenie Rossii v XVIII–*

Changes in the per capita figures imply an increased impact of officialdom on society at large. The ordinary citizen was more likely to come into contact with an official, for better or worse, in 1855 than in 1755. The government was trying to do more things and, although it frequently failed to achieve its ends, more people inevitably came to be involved.

For the nature of officialdom itself, "official society," the per capita figures are less important than the changes in absolute size. Officials at any point in the hundred-year period undoubtedly perceived their tasks as overwhelming in relation to the resources available to them. That officialdom as a whole was having a greater impact on society than in the past would have been very difficult to recognize. On the other hand, the change from a group of 2,000-odd officials with rank, to 75,000 a century later must have transformed the nature of relationships among officials. It represents the shift from a group in which, if you did not actually know everyone, at least you could know about everyone. With an anonymous mass of 75,000 the impersonal ruler or "objective standards" of some sort must have played a greatly increased role in establishing the relationship of officials to each other and the nature of their careers. Only if Russian officialdom had become divided into essentially autonomous subdivisions could this result have been avoided. There is ample evidence that such was not the case in the central agencies. Provincial service may well have retained many "traditional" characteristics precisely because it was subdivided by province and, except at the highest level, officials were likely to spend their entire career in a single locality.

Many of the more specific developments to be examined undoubtedly reflect the adjustments made necessary by the growth in the total size of officialdom. The characteristics that will be discussed are: (1) social origins—where did the official's father fit into the legal structure of Russian estates (*sosloviia*)? (2) the economic status of the official and his immediate family as measured by serf-ownership; (3) career pattern, that is, how did a career normally begin and progress throughout a man's life? and finally, (4) the education or training an official received, or did not receive, prior to entering service. No one of these elements is, alone, particularly meaningful. The most numerous and important group among officials was those legally defined as noble,

---

pervoi polovine XIXv. (po materialam revizii), Moscow, 1963, pp. 164–65. For numbers of officials, see Troitskii and Torke cited above, and also the discussion in S. Frederick Starr, *Decentralization and Self-Government in Russia, 1830–1870*, Princeton, 1972, pp. 48–49.

but to say an official is a noble or a noble's son, for example, tells little about his social relationship to civil officialdom. One must ask, Is he from a landed family? Has he served in the military, or possibly in an elite regiment in Petersburg or the provinces? Has he had any higher education? Only by putting all these things together can one meaningfully categorize the members of the civil service.

The Russian nobility, of course, was a relatively large and diverse group. Some families traced their origins back to independent princes of the appanage period; others proudly claimed a history of service to the grand prince of Moscow for many centuries. Most, however, were descended from the *pomeshchiki*, the service gentry, of more recent years. In the course of the late seventeenth century and particularly during Peter's reign, the overall nature of state service was transformed from one in which the nobility itself formed the mass of unruly cavalry forces—supplying their horses and supplies—to a system in which the nobility formed the officer corps and civil officialdom that directed and supported a much larger force of peasants conscripted and transformed into infantrymen.

The Table of Ranks, as already suggested, was designed to provide nonmonetary rewards for service by creating a tidy hierarchy of service and increasingly greater prestige with each higher rank. However, even though it was not designed to democratize service, the possibility exists that it did tend to do that, because hereditary nobility could be earned by reaching the requisite rank. The 90 percent of the population who were peasants were effectively excluded from state service by the realities of Russian life: their isolation, total lack of education, and their position as de facto chattel slaves. That they were also excluded from service by law in 1727 simply confirms the assertion that social mobility was not a purpose the Table of Ranks was designed to serve.

Who then did serve the state as civil officials in the mid-eighteenth century? Using very detailed data compiled by Troitskii, we can provide a reasonably accurate answer—*Someone whose father had also served the state.* At the upper ranks about 90 percent were sons of nobles and the nobility was by law at that time a class of servitors. If we take all officials with rank fourteen or higher, about half are sons of nobles and 20 percent were the sons of *prikaz* workers, the lower ranking clerks of the civil establishment. Eight percent were foreigners and the rest were drawn from the lower levels of the town population—tradesmen, craftsmen, and so forth. The sons of priests, the historian's favorite source of educated manpower, are almost entirely lacking (Tables 1 and 2). The importance of coming from a family with a background

TABLE VIII-1

Social Origin of Central-Agency Officials, 1755

Rank Level[a]	Noble	Personal Noble	Prikaz	Ecclesiastical	Merchant	Lower	Foreign[b]	N =
Top								
N	64	0	1	3	2	1	2	73
%	88	0	1	4	3	1	3	
Upper middle								
N	125	7	16	0	1	14	17	180
%	69	4	9	0	0.6	8	9	
Lower								
N	225	42	142	28	2	154	55	648
%	35	6	22	4	0.3	24	8	
Total								
N	414	49	159	31	5	169	74	901
%	46	5	18	3	0.5	19	8	

SOURCE: S. M. Troitskii, *Russkii absoliutizm i dvorianstvo v XVIII v., formirovanie biurokratii*, pp. 213–15. Troitskii's data is based on an exhaustive study of a remarkably complete census of officialdom carried out in 1754–56. For officials holding rank 14 or above, 95 percent of central agencies and 85–90 percent of provincial agencies were covered. On the basis of generally convincing data, Troitskii was able to assign a probable social origin to all of the officials included. For other major variables such as landholding or type of career the number of cases with no data is very small, rarely reaching 10 percent and usually much less. Troitskii's material comes as close to a "saturation-sample," that is, the total population in question (except for the officials below the fourteenth rank in the Central Agencies), as any historian is ever likely to get for a large group.

a. "Top," "Upper middle," and "Lower" refer to ranks 1–5, 6–8, and 9–14, respectively, in the Table of Ranks, in this and all subsequent tables.
b. Does not include Non-Russian subjects of the empire, largely German and Polish.

of service is even more strikingly demonstrated by the 3,328 clerks below the lowest rank who were working in the provinces, 76 percent of whom were the sons of men who had done the same thing. The rest were largely urban lower class in origin. Certainly, as of 1755, there is no evidence that the Table of Ranks was diluting noble preponderance in the civil administration but, nevertheless, laws were enacted in subsequent years to restrict the entry of nonnobles and make their promotion more difficult. It would appear, however, that there were enough commoners, at least at the lower levels and a few at the top, to be worrisome to the nobility.[4]

The latter eighteenth century has been called the "century of the nobility," and the early nineteenth century, particularly the reign of Nicholas I, the era of bureaucratic predominance. Yet if one looks at

4. See, for example, PSZ I, 1765, Vol. 17, No. 12,464; Vol. 19, 1777, No. 13,596 and No. 13,760; Vol. 25, 1798, No. 18,755.

TABLE VIII-2

Social Origin of Provincial Officials, 1755

Rank Level	Noble	Personal Noble	Prikaz	Ecclesiastical	Merchant	Lower	Foreign	N =
Top								
N =	35	0	0	0	0	1	1	37
%	94	0	0	0	0	3	3	
Upper middle								
N =	259	0	1	4	1	51	1	317
%	82	0	0.3	1	0.3	16	0.3	
Lower								
N =	143	3	44	5	10	135	53	393
%	36	1	11	1	3	34	14	
Below *chin*[a]								
N =	138	21	2,354	234	28	549	4	3,328
%	4	1	71	7	1	16	0.1	
Total								
N =	575	24	2,399	243	39	736	59	4,075
%	14	1	59	6	1	18	1	
Total (excluding below *chin*)								
N =	437	3	45	9	11	187	55	747
%	59	1	6	1	1	25	7	

SOURCE: Troitskii, *Russkii absoliutizm*, pp. 213–15.

a. "Below *chin*" means an office job that did not entitle the holder to at least the lowest, fourteenth rank. There were a number of such positions and they came to be identified in a named hierarchy of four levels.

the social origin of civil servants over the hundred years from the 1750s to the 1850s one finds very modest change. The higher ranks are largely filled by men whose fathers were nobles—but a quarter to a third are of nonnoble origin. At lower levels the proportions are reversed. On the surface at least we are confronted with a situation of remarkable stability (Tables 1–6).[5]

In order to decide whether or not this picture of stability is actually

5. Zaionchkovskii in *Pravitel'stvennyi apparat*, pp. 26–29, gives a breakdown of mid-nineteenth-century officials of lower and upper-middle ranks drawn from data on men accused of illegal activity on duty. The proportion of nobles is much lower than in our Tables 5 and 6, where the data are based on the complete personnel records of entire agencies. Zaionchkovskii's data also include a substantial number of *raznochintsy*, a category almost never used in the personnel records. Officials accused of misdeeds were less well educated than the overall agency staffs. See Zaionchkovskii, *Pravitel'stvennyi apparat*, p. 33, and our Chapter 9, Table 2, below.

TABLE VIII-3

Social Origin of Central-Agency Officials, Early Nineteenth Century

Rank Level	Noble	Junior Officer	Civil Service	Ecclesiastical	Merchant	Lower	Foreign	Non-Russian	N =
Top									
N =	35	5	0	6	3	4	5	0	58
%	60	9	0	10	5	7	9	0	
Upper middle									
N =	147	29	8	12	10	20	17	5	248
%	59	12	3	5	4	8	7	2	
Lower									
N =	262	233	80	78	63	151	31	4	902
%	29	26	9	9	7	17	3	0.4	
Total									
N =	444	267	88	96	76	175	53	9	1,220[a]
%	37	22	7	8	6	14	4	1	

SOURCE: Data from service records in the Central State Historical Archive in Leningrad (TsGIA). Data was gathered by the author from nearly 8,000 individual service records (*formuliarnie spiski*) in Collection (*fond*) No. 1,349. According to law, each government agency was supposed to submit a complete set of service records of all of its employees with rank (*chin*) each year to the Heraldry Office. A relatively small proportion, but still substantial amount, of this enormous mass of paper has survived. Almost none of the material had ever been used previously by scholars and there is no evidence that any conscious principle of selection was applied in determining what was kept and what was discarded. A large proportion of the 22,716 items is fragmentary, that is, a few individual service records, rather than complete volumes for an agency. Sometime in the nineteenth century, another substantial group of records was taken from the original agency volumes and arranged in alphabetical order by surname. For purposes of the present study, only volumes that included an entire agency for a given year were used, and either data on all of the officials or on all of the officials at specific rank levels was recorded, thus eliminating problems of "sample bias" within the agency. However, the data in this study is presented largely in terms of two broad categories, "central" and "provincial." One must ask how representative of those broad categories in general the agencies used are. The selection of agencies was determined almost entirely by availability of complete volumes. Although it is impossible to be certain because of the limited catalogue for Collection No. 1,349, the author is convinced that virtually all of the available complete agency volumes were examined and used. A full list of agencies covered is included in Appendix I. For the Central Agencies, the major domestic civilian policy-making and administrative agencies, or at least some of their major subdivisions, are included. For the mid-nineteenth century the selection is extensive, for the beginning of that century, less so. The major omissions are offices dealing with the Army, Navy, and Foreign Affairs. The exclusion of such agencies presumably has decreased the proportion of officials with prior military careers, of noble origin, and possibly of those with substantial wealth. The provincial agencies are drawn from the central Great Russian area, both north and south of Moscow, but do not include the Ukraine or other minority or frontier regions.

The addition of more agencies to those included, if it had been possible, would have made the data more complete but the author is convinced it would not change the basic picture presented below, except as already noted. The concern in this discussion is only with substantial and consistent differences and the direction of changes over time. There are differences among the agencies aggregated under "central" and "provincial," but these differences are not inconsistent with the general trends presented. For example, there are differences among agencies in the percentage of nobles serving at different rank levels, but these differences are not great and in all agencies there are more nobles in higher ranks than in lower ranks. There seems to be no reason to believe that data from additional agencies would change the general picture with regard to the distribution of nobles by rank.

The amount of data recorded in the service records increased substantially from the 1790s to the 1850s. The earlier records lack information on religion and education, and property holding data is unsatisfactory.

a. Includes 12 officials of unknown rank.

TABLE VIII-4

Social Origin of Provincial-Agency Officials, Early Nineteenth Century

Rank Level	Noble	Junior Officer	Civil Service	Ecclesiastical	Merchant	Lower	Foreign	Non-Russian	N =
Top									
N =	28	0	1	0	0	0	1	2	32
%	88	0	3	0	0	0	3	6	
Upper middle									
N =	220	18	8	18	4	14	13	4	299
%	74	6	3	6	1	5	4	1	
Lower									
N =	417	66	176	421	53	97	21	24	1,275
%	33	5	14	33	4	7	2	2	
Total									
N =	665	84	185	439	57	111	35	30	1,612[a]
%	41	5	12	27	4	7	2	2	

SOURCE: Service records in *TsGIA* collected by the author.

a. Includes 6 medical workers and one other official of unknown rank.

TABLE VIII-5

Social Origin of Central-Agency Officials, Mid-Nineteenth Century

Rank Level	Noble	Junior Officer	Civil Service	Ecclesiastical	Merchant	Lower	Foreign	Non-Russian	N =
Top									
N =	386	23	7	36	16	10	17	5	500
%	77	5	1	7	3	2	3	1	
Upper middle									
N =	492	120	52	91	65	53	32	3	908
%	54	13	6	10	7	6	3	0.3	
Lower									
N =	378	268	97	126	27	79	14	0	989
%	38	27	10	13	3	8	1	0	
Total									
N =	1,256	411	156	253	108	142	63	8	2,397
%	52	17	6	11	4	6	3	0.3	

SOURCE: Service records in *TsGIA* collected by the author.

TABLE VIII-6

Social Origin of Provincial-Agency Officials, Mid-Nineteenth Century

Rank Level	Noble	Junior Officer	Civil Service	Ecclesiastical	Merchant	Lower	Foreign	Non-Russian	N =
Top									
N =	36	2	1	3	0	1	0	1	44
%	82	4	2	7	0	2	0	2	
Upper middle									
N =	160	49	26	58	6	26	9	0	334
%	48	15	8	17	2	8	3	0	
Lower									
N =	576	464	123	627	23	56	11	1	1,881
%	31	25	6	33	1	3	0.6	0.1	
Total									
N =	772	515	150	688	29	83	20	2	2,282[a]
%	34	22	7	30	1	4	1	0.1	

SOURCE: Service records in *TsGIA* collected by the author.

a. Includes 23 unranked medical officials (78% noble).

true, we must try to look beyond the formal legal labels used in the service records and attempt to understand what "noble" and "non-noble" meant in terms of other aspects of life. We know that the civil service was expanding and many aspects of Russian society were changing in the course of the century, so one is inclined to suspect that something did happen that has not yet been squeezed out of the data.

One obvious question is, What kind of noble? Perhaps what has happened is that different sorts of nobles came to occupy positions in the civil service over the years. Was an old aristocratic landed elite replaced by a new, nearly landless "service nobility"? Although the data are not entirely complete, it is possible to answer the question, at least with respect to the ownership of serfs, the primary form of wealth independent of government service.

In 1755 high-ranking central-agency officials (fifth rank and above) usually owned serfs and about 40 percent were large holders (500 or more). Overall, 70 percent of all officials had at least one serf. One hundred years later the situation had changed substantially, but perhaps not as much as one might expect. In the 1850s, over 40 percent of top officials had no serfs, but over 20 percent were still large holders. At lower levels the proportion of serfless officials had risen but both groups are still represented in significant numbers at all levels. Thus the development over the century is in the direction we would expect, toward a bureaucracy staffed by men legally noble but divorced from the land and the values of the traditional gentry. But it can hardly be called a drastic transformation of the economic character of the bureaucracy (Tables 7–10).[6]

It is difficult to estimate how many men of nonnoble origin achieved hereditary nobility by rising through the ranks in the civil service between the 1750s and the 1850s. It was, however, not an insignificant number. According to Troitskii, in 1755, 25 percent of the men who

6. In *Pravitel'stvennyi apparat*, pp. 129–78, Zaionchkovskii presents 1853 data on social origin, age, education, serfholding, and other variables for virtually all officials in certain high positions (the State Council, Committee of Ministers, the deputy-ministers, the Senate, ambassadors, governors and vice-governors, and the chief provincial agents of the Ministries of Finance, State Domains, and Justice). In summary, the data indicate that about 40 percent of these top central officials had over 500 serfs and 30 percent had none. Among the top provincial officials about 10 percent had over 500 serfs and 40 percent none. Among the central officials 25 percent had higher education and 50 percent home education, and in the provinces 30 percent had higher and 35 percent home. These data are for an older and higher ranking group (especially in the center) than that in the "top" category in Tables 9 and 10 or in Table 2 in Chapter 9. The group is therefore richer but has less formal education. In other respects Zaionchkovskii's data and ours are consistent.

TABLE VIII-7

Serfholding by Central-Agency Officials, 1755

Rank Level	None	1–20	21–100	101–500	501 or More	No Data	Total (N =)
Number of Male Serfs							
Top							
N =	10	5	8	12	29	9	73
%	14	7	11	16	40	12	
Upper middle							
N =	27	21	40	73	16	3	180
%	15	12	22	41	9	2	
Lower							
N =	263	189	127	50	4	15	648
%	40	29	20	8	1	2	
Total							
N =	300	215	175	135	49	27	901
%	33	24	19	15	5	3	

SOURCE: Troitskii, *Russkii absoliutizm*, pp. 298–99.

TABLE VIII-8

Serfholding by Provincial-Agency Officials, 1755

Rank Level	Number of Male Serfs Owned						
	None	1–20	21–100	101–500	501 or More	No Data	Total (N =)
Top							
N =	4	1	6	15	5	6	37
%	11	3	16	40	13	16	
Upper middle							
N =	31	59	104	102	7	14	317
%	10	19	33	32	0.2	4	
Lower							
N =	167	114	85	21	1	5	393
%	42	29	22	5	0.2	1	
Total							
N =	202	174	195	138	13	25	747
%	27	23	26	18	2	3	
Below *chin*							
N =	2,709	534	82	3	0	0	3,328
%	81	16	2	0.1	0	0	

SOURCE: Troitskii, *Russkii absoliutizm*, pp. 298–99.

TABLE VIII-9

Serfholding of Central-Agency Officials, Mid-Nineteenth Century
(arranged according to rank held)

	Number of Male Serfs Owned					
	None		1–20		21–100	
Rank Level	All Officials	Nobles Only	All Officials	Nobles Only	All Officials	Nobles Only
Top						
N =	214	124	27	23	51	41
%	44	33	5	6	10	11
Upper middle						
N =	571	227	61	44	84	59
%	67	50	7	10	10	13
Lower						
N =	622	203	22	18	30	21
%	84	66	3	6	4	7
Total						
N =	1,407	554	110	85	165	121
%	67	49	5	7	8	11

SOURCE: Service records in TsGIA collected by the author.

had reached at least the ennobling eighth rank in central agencies were of nonnoble origin (Table 1). In 1845 the rank level that bestowed hereditary nobility was raised from the eighth to the fifth and in 1856 to the fourth, presumably because too many commoners were making the grade as the civil service expanded. The proportion of former commoners at the fifth rank or above in the early 1850s was 33 percent, only slightly more than the proportion above the eighth a century earlier, but from the eighth to the sixth nearly half were of nonnoble origin and undoubtedly many of them failed to achieve nobility because of the change in the law in 1845 and 1856 (Table 5). The only absolute figures available are that between 1836 and 1843 a total of 4,685 commoners achieved the eighth rank and were ennobled, an average of 669 per year, or about 7 percent of the total number of civil servants with rank eight or above (10,671 in 1847). Compared to the

Number of Male Serfs Owned					
101–500		500 or More		Total (N =)	
All Officials	Nobles Only	All Officials	Nobles Only	All Officials	Nobles Only
87	80	111	106	490	374
18	21	23	28		
97	87	41	40	854	457
11	19	5	9		
36	34	33	33	743	309
5	11	4	11		
220	201	185	179	2,087	1,140
11	18	9	16		

total population of male nobles, 113,093 in 1858, the annual accretion is negligible (0.6 percent). A. P. Korelin suggests that as many as 20,000 men were ennobled through civil service between 1825 and 1845. The estimate may be high, but it does suggest the cumulative effect of a steady annual addition to the nobility.[7]

Foreigners have been conspicuously present in Russian affairs for

7. PSZ II, 1845, Vol. 20, No. 19,086; 1856, Vol. 31, No. 31,236. A. P. Korelin, "Rossiiskoe dvorianstvo i ego soslovnaia organizatsiia (1861–1904 gg.)," Istorii SSSR, No. 5 (1971): 60. Korelin's figure of 20,000 for the years 1825–45 appears to be an estimate based on the rate of ennoblement from 1836 to 1843 and may include all officials who reached the eighth rank, noble and nonnoble. Total size of officialdom in 1847 is from Zaionchkovskii, Pravitel'stvennyi apparat, p. 67. Total size of nobility 1858, from V. M. Kabuzan and S. M. Troitskii "Izmeneniia v chislennosti, udel'nom vese i razmeschenii dvorianstva v Rossii v 1782–1858 gg.," Istoriia SSSR, No. 4 (1971): 167.

Walter M. Pintner

TABLE VIII-10

Serfholding by Provincial-Agency Officials Serving in the
Mid-Nineteenth Century (arranged according to rank held)

	None		*1–20*		*21–100*	
Rank Level	*All Officials*	*Nobles Only*	*All Officials*	*Nobles Only*	*All Officials*	*Nobles Only*
Top						
N =	16	12	4	2	8	8
%	36	33	9	6	18	22
Upper middle						
N =	153	43	93	46	54	38
%	46	27	28	29	16	23
Lower						
N =	1,479	229	189	144	138	128
%	79	40	10	25	7	22
Total						
N =	1,648	284	286	192	200	174
%	73	37	13	25	9	23

SOURCE: Service records in TsGIA collected by the author.

centuries, and their role has been controversial at least from the time
of Ivan III's marriage to Zoe Paleologue. The bureaucratic state of
Peter I was denounced as "foreign" or "German," and Nicholas I
supposedly had a special liking for his Baltic German subjects despite
the proclamation of "Nationality" as one of the three main principles
of his regime. Throughout the eighteenth and nineteenth centuries it is
easy to point to leading figures in the Russian government who were
either foreign-born or imperial subjects of non-Russian background.
The quantitative significance of non-Russians in the civil service is
another matter and far more difficult to deal with. The service records,
surprisingly, do not call for place of birth or nationality. Officials
classified their fathers socially, in most cases without reference to nationality. Using the data provided on religion it is possible, however,
to make a reasonable estimate of the proportion of non-Russians in

Number of Male Serfs Owned					
101–500		*500 or More*		*Total* ($\text{N} =$)	
All Officials	*Nobles Only*	*All Officials*	*Nobles Only*	*All Officials*	*Nobles Only*
11	9	5	5	44	36
25	25	11	14		
26	25	8	8	334	160
8	16	2	5		
63	61	13	13	1,882	575
3	11	0.7	2		
100	95	26	26	2,260	771
4	12	1	3		

service in the mid-nineteenth century. Assuming that Lutherans are German, that Roman Catholics are Poles, and adding these to officials who do specify foreign origin produces a total of about 15 to 20 percent non-Russian officials for central agencies (Table 11). In the provincial agencies studied, all in the Great Russian core of the empire, the number of non-Russians is insignificant, under 5 percent. During earlier periods, information on religion was not supplied, so the only indication of change over time is supplied by using year-of-entry categories. These suggest that the proportion of non-Russians among officials entering service may have increased significantly; however, the data for the pre-1800 years is not sufficiently extensive to be relied on.[8]

8. Non-Christians were excluded from state service. Any Jews or Muslims who did

Walter M. Pintner

TABLE VIII-11

Nationality and Social Origin of Mid-Nineteenth Century Central-Agency
Officials (arranged according to years of entry into service)

		To 1800 (N = 84)	1800–19 (N = 444)	1820–55 (N = 956)	Total (N = 1,484)	Total[d] (N = 2,377)
Russian, noble	N =	57	214	455	726	1,021
	%	68	48	48	49	42
Russian, nonnoble	N =	17	156	304	477	981
	%	20	35	32	32	41
German, noble[a]	N =	6	17	80	103	126
	%	7	4	8	7	5
German, nonnoble[a]	N =	0	13	36	49	63
	%	0	3	4	3	3
Polish, noble[b]	N =	0	20	43	63	100
	%	0	5	5	4	4
Polish, nonnoble[b]	N =	0	4	5	9	15
	%	0	1	0.5	0.6	0.6
Other non-Russian[c]	N =	4	20	33	57	71
	%	5	5	3	4	3
Total non-Russian	N =	10	74	197	281	375
	%	12	17	21	19	16

SOURCE: Service records in TsGIA collected by the author.

a. Identified as Lutheran in the sources, assumed to be German.
b. Identified as Roman Catholic in the sources, assumed to be Polish.
c. Includes those who indicate foreign or non-Russian origin in the answer to question "iz kakogo zvania?" Of these 57 men, 24 are Orthodox, and the rest Lutheran or Catholic. This group cannot be broken down in terms of social origin.
d. This larger group includes an additional 883 officials for whom year of entry data is unavailable.

Is a figure of 15 to 20 percent non-Russian large or small? For a multinational empire with a rapidly growing need for officials it would hardly seem a surprising figure. It does not, however, suggest the preponderant or even overwhelming role of foreigners that has sometimes been suggested. It must be noted that the distribution of

serve must have been at least nominally converted. The only presumed convert who identified himself as such was "a Presbyterian of Persian Noble origin" serving in the MVD as a translator. Troitskii, in *Russkii absoliutizm*, reports an overall figure of about three percent foreigners in 1755 (p. 215); however, his figures are not comparable to those based on religion in the mid-nineteenth century because he assigns all foreigners reporting a specific social origin to the social category (p. 209).

non-Russians was by no means homogeneous. There were a few mid-nineteenth-century departments where the percentage of Germans was very high in the upper ranks, reaching 40 percent.[9] The substantial number of Poles in service has traditionally gone unnoticed, attention always falling on the Germans. Clearly the impact of foreigners in service depended on more than their actual numbers.

It would appear on the basis of three conventional characteristics—social origin, serfholding, and nationality—that aside from the marked growth in size, the civil service underwent no fundamental change from the time of Elizabeth to the Emancipation. In actuality, civil officialdom was transformed in a major way between the end of the eighteenth century and the death of Nicholas I in 1855. Major and rapid change occurred not in the pedigree and economic background of officialdom, but in the nature of their service experience and in the training officials underwent as preparation for it.

Put very briefly, what happened was that in the course of the first fifty years of the nineteenth century civil service became a distinct professional career requiring specialized training prior to entry. The life patterns and experience of officials came to be essentially the same as those of the bureaucrats of contemporary Western European states. The change is important because what one does throughout one's life, particularly in the earlier years, is certainly as influential in forming the man as is his legal social status or the ownership of serfs. The wealthy aristocrat may or may not have much in common with the poor noble or even a commoner, depending on the patterns that organized their lives.

In the eighteenth century, although the civil service included men of diverse social and economic backgrounds, the typical service career tended to maintain social and economic segregation. In 1755, civil employment was a lifetime career for no more than about half of the officials in central agencies. The rest were retired military men. In the provinces the proportion of former officers was even greater (Table 12). It is probably safe to assume that in the time of Peter the Great, when there was almost constant war, there was an even greater percentage of civil officials with a military background.

9. Four of the ten top-level men in the Economic Department of the MVD. This large a proportion was exceptional. The complicated question of the degree of assimilation to Russian culture and the role of religion in that process is discussed along with many other important aspects of the role of the Baltic Germans in Russian imperial service in John A. Armstrong, "Mobilized Diaspora in Tsarist Russia: The Case of the Baltic Germans," in *Soviet Nationality Policies and Practices*, ed. Jeremy Azrael, New York, 1979.

TABLE VIII-12

Nature of First Service, 1755

Rank Level	Military N =	%	Civil Agency[a] N =	%	Educational Institution N =	%
	Central Agency Officials					
Top[b]	34	49	3	4	23	33
Upper middle	66	39	46	27	52	31
Lower	90	15	353	58	160	26
	Provincial Agency Officials					
Top	25	68	1	3	9	24
Upper middle	250	84	13	4	31	10
Lower	128	40	141	44	48	15

Source: Troitskii, *Russkii absoliutizm*, pp. 276–79.

Note: Troitskii's fourth category—those starting at the imperial court—is not included here.

a. "Civil" does not include boys in the "Junker" program, which is considered an educational institution by Troitskii. Shifting the Junkers to "Civil" and out of Educational Institutions does not produce any important changes.

b. Those not accounted for started in imperial court service, an insignificant number, except at top level where it was 14 percent (N = 10).

If civil service was to become a fully separate career, populated by men with a common background and tending to have a common outlook, the proportion of former military men would necessarily have to decline; otherwise civil employment would remain part of a more general pattern of state service, inevitably dominated by the more numerous and prestigious military. As long as half or more of the important civil positions were filled by former officers the civil bureaucracy could only be regarded as a place for army men to go when they were no longer able or inclined to undertake military duty. Furthermore the military men who transferred to civil service were, at all periods, predominantly nobles, and the massive transfer to rela-

TABLE VIII-13

Percentage of Nobles among Officials
with Prior Military Service, Compared to
Those Entering Service Directly
(central and provincial agencies)

Year of Entry	Noble	Nonnoble	N =
With Prior Military Experience[a]			
Through 1794	79	21	692
1795–1814	89	11	186
1815–34	87	13	268
1835–55	87	13	60
Entering Civil Service Directly[b]			
Through 1794	21	79	1,374
1795–1814	37	63	966
1815–34	36	64	1,340
1835 on	40	60	1,336

SOURCE: Service records in TsGIA collected by the author.

a. Percentages of nobles for those entering central and provincial service are virtually identical.
b. Percentage of nobles tends to be slightly higher in central agencies and lower in provincial agencies.

tively high civil posts helped to maintain noble predominance in the bureaucracy (Table 13).

If the data on officials serving in the early and mid-nineteenth century are grouped according to the year each man entered service, the pattern of 1755 holds until the end of the eighteenth century. Only with the cadres entering between 1795 and 1814 does the proportion of ex-military men decline sharply, a trend that continues in subsequent years down to the 1850s. The proportion of military men is always greater at higher ranks and it remains about 25 to 35 percent at grades five and above (Table 14).

Thus the military is by no means gone from positions of influence

TABLE VIII-14

Nature of First Service, According to Year of Entry

Rank Level	Central				Provincial			
	Military		Civil		Military		Civil	
	N =	%	N =	%	N =	%	N =	%
				To 1794				
Top	47	58	34	42	28	85	5	15
Upper middle	78	42	106	58	222	73	82	27
Lower	27	11	226	89	283	24	900	76
				1795–1814				
Top	55	34	104	66	8	44	10	56
Upper middle	21	15	121	85	23	22	82	78
Lower	8	2	465	98	50	31	111	69
				1815–34				
Top	49	25	148	75	10	52	9	48
Upper middle	45	15	255	85	39	24	176	76
Lower	10	5	180	95	76	12	543	88

SOURCE: Service records in TsGIA collected by the author.

by 1855, but in the course of fifty years they have ceased to be predominant in numbers even at the top where they were once most heavily concentrated. It was a development that began in the decades after the death of Catherine II (1796), but because of the time required for men to rise to high positions the proportion of former officers actually in high posts at the beginning of the nineteenth century was still close to what can be called the "eighteenth-century level" (Table 15).

Throughout the entire period from 1750 to 1850, provincial agencies have a substantially higher proportion of officials with a military background than do central agencies, but this proportion drops sharply

TABLE VIII-15

Nature of First Service, According to Agency of Current Employment

	Military		Civil	
	N =	%	N =	%
Early Nineteenth Century, Central Agencies (1798–1824)				
Top	25	43	33	57
Upper middle	89	36	159	64
Lower	33	4	720	96
Early Nineteenth Century, Provincial Agencies (1795–1805)				
Top	28	85	5	15
Upper middle	223	73	82	27
Lower	318	25	973	75
Mid-Nineteenth Century, Central Agencies (1840–55)				
Top	131	30	311	70
Upper middle	77	13	514	87
Lower	35	7	433	93
Mid-Nineteenth Century, Provincial Agencies (1840–53)				
Top	18	47	20	53
Upper middle	62	21	235	79
Lower	124	7	1,522	93

SOURCE: Service records in TsGIA collected by the author.

among the lower ranking officials in the years 1815–34. By the mid-nineteenth century the overwhelming majority of minor officials in the provinces was composed of lifetime civil servants, while the very small group of high officials in the provinces still included a slightly higher proportion of military men than did the central agencies in the same period. In the eighteenth and very early nineteenth centuries the provinces were administered at all levels, insofar as they were administered at all, largely by retired military men. Only in the post-Napoleonic era does the career *chinovnik* come to predominate, presumably due in part to the increase in the number of posts available; but the change is too dramatic for that fully to account for it. Military men, and to a large extent nobles, obviously dropped out of provincial service, and one must assume that they did something else instead.[10]

That nobles had ever been in provincial service at all is testimony to the desperate economic position of the lower nobility in the eighteenth century. These posts offered negligible pay, little prestige, and even the opportunity to engage in the proverbial corrupt practices cannot have been very attractive. The expanded educational system that developed in the early nineteenth century gave the opportunity to many poor nobles to meet the entrance requirements for better positions in central agencies (paying much more at comparable rank levels). On the other hand, the more rigorous standards for admission to service established in 1827 and 1833 may have excluded some of the least qualified from positions that their ancestors could have filled in the eighteenth century.[11] The law of 14 October 1827, for example, specified that all new recruits be able to show not only that they could read and write correctly, but that they had mastered the basic elements of grammar and arithmetic.

The change from a civil service staffed at the top and in the provinces predominantly by ex-military men of noble status, to one of career civil officials of somewhat more diverse background, is one important aspect of the professionalization of the imperial bureaucracy. There is, however, much more involved. Retired officers came to civil employment with whatever skills and attitudes they had acquired in service. They were generally too old to undergo formal

10. See the following chapter, "Civil Officialdom and the Nobility in the 1850s," for a full discussion of the major differences between central and provincial officialdom.
11. Harold A. McFarlin, "Recruitment Norms for the Russian Civil Service in 1833: The Chancery Clerkship," *Societas—A Review of Social History*, 3, No. 1 (1973): 66, 69; McFarlin, "The Extension of the Imperial Russian Civil Service to the Lowest Office Workers: The Creation of the Chancery Clerkship, 1827–1833," *Russian History* 1, Pt. 1 (1974): 7; PSZ II, 1827, Vol. 2, No. 1,469, *chast'* 5; *Svod zakonov*, 1833, Vol. 3, art. 12.

training for their new careers. The youth, however, who entered civil service directly might, or might not, have prior formal training and there was also the possibility of "in-service" training for the newly hired official.

It is precisely in this area of preparation for the civil career that the second dramatic change took place in the years from 1800 to 1850. In 1755 the low level, indeed the general lack, of formal education among officials is startling even to one familiar with the limited development of Russian education. At the highest levels in central offices 67 percent (forty-seven men) of all officials had attended no educational institution, civil or military (Table 16). Only 9 percent (six men) of the high officials of 1755 had a university education, of necessity obtained abroad since the first Russian university was only founded in that very year. Fourteen others (20 percent) attended institutions probably above the elementary level, three attended military primary schools and the rest, some 67 percent, attended no school whatever. At lower levels in the central agencies, and at all levels in the provinces, the picture was essentially the same. That three-quarters of the Russian civil service in 1755 had no formal education whatever cannot be considered other than remarkable. Presumably at least most of them learned to read and write at home before they entered service, civil or military, in their mid-teens, essentially as apprentices to learn their profession on the job.[12] Certainly a few wealthy nobles could and did afford their sons a more extensive education in the hands of tutors, but those that fortunate were far more likely to elect an elite regiment rather than an office as the place to launch their career.

"On-the-job" training was formally recognized in law at least as early as Peter the Great's "*Generalnyi reglament*" of 1720, which provided that in the colleges and chancelleries the sons of nobles would be trained in office procedures as "junkers" and would advance step by step to higher ranks. It specifically decreed that civil service was not to be regarded as degrading for distinguished families, so we may presume it was so regarded.

The "junker" training program was exclusively for young nobles and was an attempt to prevent the civil service from becoming dominated by members of nonnoble groups: sons of clerks, priests, or

---

12. There were, however, some illiterate civil servants. In February 1831, the Senate, citing the case of illiterate Titular Councilor (Rank 9) Fedorov, ordered all government agencies to adhere to the law of a century earlier, 23 November 1731, forbidding the promotion of illiterate soldiers and noncommissioned officers to officer status. PSZ II, 1831, Vol. 6, No. 4,342, PSZ I, 1731, Vol. 8, No. 5,888.

TABLE VIII-16

Level of Education of Officials, 1755

Rank Level	Junker Program		Elementary & Secondary		Foreign University		Military Schools	
	N =	%	N =	%	N =	%	N =	%
	Central Agencies							
Top	2	3	6	9	6	9	7	10
Upper middle	9	5	1	0.5	4	2	37	22
Lower	78	12	8	1	3	0.5	55	9
	Provincial Agencies							
Top	1	3	3	8	0	0	5	13
Upper middle	2	0.6	1	0.3	2	0.6	26	8
Lower	9	2	5	1	5	1	24	7

SOURCE: Troitskii, *Russkii absoliutizm*, pp. 276–77.

townsmen. Thus the only significant measure taken in the eighteenth century to train senior civil officials was directed as much at maintaining or raising the class character of the bureaucracy as it was at preparing it to render more effective service. No provisions were made for the majority of officials, either through organized on-the-job training or the requirement of formal education prior to entering service. Men, or rather boys, were simply signed on as needed, straight from their homes or, in the case of higher posts, from military service. The specifically social purpose of the junker program was reemphasized in 1737 when it was decreed that the junkers attached to the Senate must come from families with at least 100 serfs, that those in colleges and chancelleries have at least 25. This minimum level of independent economic support must have tended to separate the young nobles from their fellow office workers who were dependent on their small salary alone (plus bribes and other illegal income). The program began when a trainee was sixteen, a "registrar" of the four-

Church Schools		Total Educated at Institutions		Total Officials Serving
N =	%	N =	%	N =
Central Agencies				
2	3	23	33	70
1	0.5	52	30	172
16	2	160	25	635
Provincial Agencies				
0	0	9	24	37
0	0	31	10	306
5	1	48	13	357

teenth rank, the lowest rank in the table, and ended after five years when the successful candidate became a "secretary" and advanced to higher ranks (usually rank twelve). Those found unsatisfactory were to be dispatched to the army to be enrolled as common soldiers, a rather unlikely outcome in view of the limited demands made on the trainees and the difficulty the state had in filling the available places.[13]

It is difficult to estimate the impact of the junker system on the civil service. In 1755 only two alumni had reached top-rank positions (2 percent of the total). They comprised 5 percent (9 men) of the middle level and 12 percent (78 men) of low-level officials. However, even though the enrollment of 95 in 1755 is only about half of the authorized strength this figure suggests an annual class of 19 which, if continued to the program's end in 1763, would have produced over 200 graduates in all, a substantial group in a central civil service that

13. PSZ i, 1737, Vol. 10, No. 7,201.

totaled about 1,000 in 1755 (rank fourteen and above).[14] The available data do not permit us to trace the careers of the ex-junkers in the second half of the eighteenth century. It is likely, however, that they provided a significant portion of the upper-middle and higher officials in those years. They were largely nobles with some property, and it was official policy to favor such men, when they were available, over those of less elite background. Nevertheless the military certainly remained the largest single source of recruits for the upper ranks.

In 1763 Catherine II abolished the junker program, because (according to the decree) there was insufficient participation by young nobles, and because the training was confined "largely to paperwork" and did not give them the knowledge they really needed. The remaining junkers of noble birth were directed to the Infantry or Naval Cadet Corps and the nonnobles to Moscow University.[15] Unfortunately the number of nonnobles is not indicated in the decree, but their mere presence shows that the junker program, initially designed exclusively for nobles, had been unable to compete with more attractive military schools and careers and had had to admit others. Catherine, however, was not satisfied with the status quo and ordered that courses in Russian jurisprudence be established at the Infantry Cadet Corps, socially the most influential educational institution of the day, and at Moscow University. Furthermore she noted a lack of competent clerks in official agencies and ordered that classes be established for *raznochintsy* and junior officers' sons to provide instruction in writing, arithmetic, geometry, and geography at Moscow University, the Academy of Sciences in Petersburg, and at the gymnasium in Kazan; funding was authorized for a total of 180 students.[16] Paul reestablished the junker program in 1797 with a class of 27 trainees. A number of senior officials of the 1850s were products of this program, but it was too small to have a major effect, even on the highest levels of the bureaucracy. With the establishment of the Lyceé at Tsarskoe Selo in 1811, the first full-time institution for training civil officials, the junker system was permanently abandoned.[17]

What can we make of this scattered data on the education and training of civil officials in the latter eighteenth and nineteenth centuries? The earlier service records provide little or no information on

14. Troitskii, *Russkii absoliutizm*, pp. 172–73 for total size (the figure includes court officials), p. 276 for junker school figures.

15. PSZ I, 1763, Vol. 16, No. 11,989, art. 23.

16. Eighty in Moscow, 40 in Petersburg, and 60 in Kazan.

17. PSZ I, 1810, Vol. 21, No. 24,325; 1811, Vol. 21, Nos. 24,580 and 24,001.

the educational background of officials, and legal and institutional sources cannot provide an adequate picture of the actual educational experience of civil servants as a group. We do not know how important, for example, Catherine's classes for clerks turned out to be. However, a very simple but remarkably helpful approach is to ask the age officials were when they began their careers, information that can easily be calculated from almost any service record.

The age of entrance into service is available for roughly 6,000 of the officials studied. The overall average is about 17 or slightly below that of a typical high school graduate today (Table 17). In the second half of the eighteenth century it was substantially lower, rising from 14.5 before 1770 and only reaching 16 by 1801. The average for those who first entered military service tends to be slightly lower than that for those going directly into civil service. Even among officials who eventually achieved the highest ranks, and would presumably be the most likely to have substantial formal education, the age of entrance for lifetime civil servants was 14.4 as late as 1800–1809 (Table 18). Men who transferred from the military had an even lower average entrance age, but that is undoubtedly due to the practice among influential families of registering their sons in elite guard regiments while they were still actually living at home, something not done on the civil side.[18]

These data on age of entrance confirm the legislative and memoir material on the training of civil servants in the eighteenth century. One learned little more than the "three R's" at home or in some sort of elementary school, and as a teenager one was apprenticed in an office. The most favored were the Collegial Junkers, who were supposed to have some formal instruction as well as practical experience; this was a small program, however, and the instruction provided tended to be highly erratic. Catherine did indeed order an expanded program of formal training for bureaucrats, but it does not appear to have had any significant impact on the usual age of entrance into civil service, which remained below 16 until the end of the eighteenth century, no matter what rank or agency the recruit was eventually to serve in.

The age of entrance shows no real change until the decade 1810–19 when, for the first time, the average exceeds 17 years for all central

18. Men who reached only lower levels in the civil service but had started in the military tended to enter service at about the same age as those entering civil service directly. Nominal service via the registration of children in prestigious regiments was a practice confined to the elite.

Walter M. Pintner

TABLE VIII-17

Officials' Average Age at First Entrance into Service (civil or military),
Arranged According to Nature of First Service, Education, and Year of Entry

Years	All Officials		Civil Service Directly		Military Service First		Directly after Higher Education	
	Age	N =	Age	N =	Age	N =	Age	N =
Through 1769	14.3	226	14.5	91	14.1	135	. . .	. . .
1770–79	14.5	534	15.3	288	13.6	246	. . .	. . .
1780–89	15.5	847	15.9	642	14.1	205	. . .	. . .
1790–99	15.9	511	15.5	387	17.1	124	16.1	23
1800–1809	15.9	469	15.9	396	16.0	72	17.5	43
1810–19	17.0	617	17.2	472	16.3	144	20.7	90
1820–29	17.8	769	17.9	632	17.2	129	20.4	174
1830–39	18.4	920	18.5	835	17.8	84	21.6	198
1840–49	20.0	824	20.0	801	18.0	22	22.1	226
1850 on	22.1	64	22.1	64	. . .	. . .	21.4	30
All years	17.1	5,781	17.5	4,608	15.4	1,161	21.0	784

Source: Service records in TsGIA collected by the author.

Note: For years without entries, data for less than twenty officials was available.

agencies and 16 for provincial agencies. From then on the average age level rises steadily a year per decade until, in the 1840s, it reaches about 20 in both central and provincial agencies, and for men reaching the upper-middle ranks (eight through six) nearly 22.[19]

The rising age of new officials was not due exclusively to the increased importance of secondary and higher education. If officials are grouped according to the type of education they received—home, primary, secondary, or higher—the average age of entrance tends to rise for all categories in an essentially parallel fashion, though, of course, those with more education tend to be older at any given time

19. Scattered data for the 1850s suggest that the average continued to rise.

Directly after Secondary Education		Directly after Primary Education		Directly after Home Education	
Age	N =	*Age*	N =	*Age*	N =
. . .	. . .	. . .	. . .	. . .	. . .
. . .	. . .	. . .	. . .	. . .	. . .
. . .	. . .	. . .	. . .	. . .	. . .
17.9	22	. . .	. . .	. . .	. . .
16.6	46	13.8	21	14.2	37
17.1	89	16.4	51	14.1	56
19.0	140	16.7	99	15.6	87
19.0	220	16.6	235	17.9	60
20.4	322	17.5	180	18.4	37
22.4	29	. . .	. . .	. . .	. . .
19.3	868	16.7	586	16.0	277

(Table 19). For example, in the 1840s, men with only primary education entered service at an average age of 17.5 years while those with higher education were 22. In the first decade of the century, the corresponding averages had been 14 and 17.5 years.

The rise in average age of entrance precedes the institution of minimum age and education requirements for service. Only in 1827 was 14 set as the lowest age at which a boy could enter the civil service, and he was to receive no seniority credit until he reached 16 years. This was the same law that required candidates to demonstrate not merely literacy but knowledge of grammar and arithmetic as well.[20] Another

20. PSZ II, 1827, Vol. 2, No. 1,469.

TABLE VIII-18

Officials' Average Age at First Entrance into Service (civil or military),
Arranged According to Current Rank Level, Nature of
First Service, and Year of Entry

Years	Top *Ranks Entering Civil Service Directly*		Upper Middle *Ranks Entering Civil Service Directly*		Top *Ranks Entering Military Service First*		Upper Middle *Ranks Entering Military Service First*	
	Age	N =	*Age*	N =	*Age*	N =	*Age*	N =
Through 1769	. . .	. . .	15.1	34	13.2	25	14.1	75
1770–79	. . .	. . .	15.8	55	. . .	. . .	13.4	119
1780–89	. . .	. . .	15.8	61	9.1	25	14.0	67
1790–99	13.5	33	15.1	43	. . .	. . .	17.1	29
1800–1809	14.4	64	15.8	129	15.1	32	17.5	24
1810–19	18.1	74	16.8	211	16.7	61	15.5	54
1820–29	19.7	104	18.6	220	18.1	22	16.5	60
1830–39	20.3	40	21.4	173	. . .	. . .	17.2	21
1840–49	. . .	. . .	21.9	103	. . .	. . .	. . .	. . .
1850 on	. . .	. . .	. . .	. . .	. . .	. . .	. . .	. . .
All years	17.7	315	18.1	1,029	14.9	165	14.9	449

SOURCE: Service records in TsGIA collected by the author.

NOTE: For years without entries, data for less than twenty officials was available.

statute issued in 1831 specified that all Russian youth between the
ages of 10 and 18 should be educated, preferably in "domestic public
institutions" or, failing that, in their homes "and under no circumstance abroad." The main thrust of the measure was to discourage
foreign study by young members of the upper classes. However, it did
exclude from state service those who failed to conform and, at least in
theory, established both compulsory education and a minimum entrance age of 18 for all aspiring bureaucrats or military men.[21] Perhaps
of more practical importance was the provision in the 1828 law on
primary and secondary schools that gave graduates of district (*uezd*)
primary schools preference over others in application for civil posts.
Graduates of gymnasiums received higher preference, and if they

21. PSZ II, 1831, Vol. 6, No. 4,364.

TABLE VIII-19

Education of Officials Serving during 1840–1855
(arranged according to year of entry into service)

Year of Entry	N =	Percentage Receiving					
		Home	Elementary	Secondary	Pages	Lycée	Higher
Top Officials							
To 1799	37	35	8	32	5	0	19
1800–1809	56	27	4	48	7	0	14
1810–19	99	11	1	25	9	3	50
1820–29	123	2	0	9	2	14	72
1830–39	45	0	0	13	7	13	67
1840–55	5	0	0	0	0	20	80
All years	365	12	2	23	6	7	51
Upper Middle Level Officials							
To 1799	13	31	23	46	0	0	0
1800–1809	60	30	25	32	0	0	13
1810–19	148	20	14	44	1	0	22
1820–29	214	12	6	44	1	1	37
1830–39	180	1	1	18	2	3	74
1840–55	108	1	0	3	2	13	82
All years	723	11	7	30	1	3	47

SOURCE: Service records in TsGIA collected by the author.

knew Greek they could enter at the fourteenth rank directly.[22] Even
greater advantages were given to graduates of the universities and the
Lyceé according to the statutes of each institution. In a system where
seniority was the primary criterion for promotion, level of entrance
played a key role in ultimate success.

22. PSZ II, 1828, Vol. 3, No. 2,502, arts. 133, 234–35.

Looking at the data on average age of entrance into service and the relevant legislative history one is forced to conclude that in 1810, many years before it was required to in 1827, the civil service was accepting most entrants only after extended periods of preservice training in the new educational institutions that were opened early in the reign of Alexander I. The legislation of the late 1820s and early 1830s seems only to have regularized and possibly further accelerated the process.

Thus the expansion of educational facilities in the early nineteenth century, which was of course tiny in terms of the total population of the empire, had a major impact on the career experience of the bureaucracy at all levels, particularly on the higher officials in the central agencies. The newly recruited official no longer spent his early youth in an office where the only people he had contact with were fellow officials. Now he spent his teens in some sort of an educational institution exposed to a wider range of subjects than simply office routine, and in many cases to a student body more socially diverse than the fifteen-year-old apprentice would ever have met in an eighteenth-century chancellery. The development was certainly most important for those who went to the universities, but it was certainly not confined to them.

Thus in addition to growth in size, two fundamentally important changes in the Russian civil service occurred at very nearly the same time—in the first decade of the nineteenth century. First, the shift from a pattern of mixed military and civil service for senior officials to one of lifetime civil careers. And second, full-time formal education at a relatively advanced level came to be a prerequisite for a successful civil career at anything but the very lowest level of service. The change the civil service underwent in the first half of the nineteenth century was a revolution not in social recruitment but in socialization.

APPENDIX: LIST OF AGENCY PERSONNEL RECORDS USED

I. Early Nineteenth-Century Central Agencies

Department of Manufacturing and Trade, 1810
Imperial Court (civil officials), 1802
Ministry of Finance (various departments), 1817, 1824

Ministry of the Interior (various departments), 1810, 1818, 1819
Office of State Control, 1812, 1814
St. Petersburg Mint, 1802
Senate (various departments), 1798, 1800–1803, 1805, 1806,
    1809–1815, 1822
State Agency for the Inspection of Accounts, 1815
State Agency for Revenues, 1812
State Assignat Bank, 1803
State Loan Bank, 1804
Temporary Survey Office, 1802

*II. Late Eighteenth-Century and Early Nineteenth-Century
Provincial Agencies*

Gatchina (city administration), 1812
Iaroslavl', 1807
Kostroma, 1806
Kursk, 1802
Novgorod, 1796
Penza, 1802
Tobolsk, 1791
Vladimir, 1801
Vologda, 1802
Assignat Bank (provincial offices), 1803

III. Mid-Nineteenth-Century Central Agencies

Committee of Ministers (Chancellery), 1850, 1851
Department of Appanages, 1851
His Imperial Majesty's Own Chancellery, 1843, 1853
Main Administration of Transport (various departments), 1849,
    1850, 1854
Ministry of Education (School and Censorship administrations),
    1850, 1852
Ministry of Finance (General Chancellery, Special Chancellery
    for the Credit Section, Department of Foreign Trade) 1846, 1851
Ministry of the Interior (Department of General Affairs,
    Economic Department), 1852
Ministry of Justice, 1851
Ministry of State Domains (Chancellery, Second Department,
    Department of Agriculture), 1850

Office of State Control, 1847
Senate (various departments), 1850, 1851, 1853, 1856, 1857
State Chancellery, 1851
State Council, 1850
State Commercial Bank, 1847
State Loan Bank, 1853

IV. Mid-Nineteenth Century Provincial Agencies

Kharkov (Ministry of Justice), 1851
Kostroma (major civil agencies), 1850, 1853
Kursk (major civil agencies), 1847, 1851
Moscow (major civl agencies), 1846, 1848, 1849, 1850, 1851
Penza (major civil agencies), 1849
Vladimir (major civil agencies), 1850
Vologda (major civil agencies), 1847
Voronezh (major civil agencies), 1847, 1849, 1851
Department of Appanages, provincial offices (Orel, Perm, Saratov, Orenburg), 1841
Ministry of State Domains, Department of Agriculture, Commission for the Administration of Revenues from State Peasants, provincial offices (Kursk and Orel), 1847

NOTE: *In all cases where files for more than one date were available for a given agency, care has been taken to prevent duplication of information on individual officials. All of the above records are in* Fond 1,349 *of the Central State Historical Archive in Leningrad (TsGIA).*

CHAPTER NINE

CIVIL OFFICIALDOM AND THE NOBILITY IN THE 1850s

Walter M. Pintner

From its very origin the Russian nobility was closely tied to the state through service. Despite the abolition of compulsory service in the mid-eighteenth century, the tie remained close. Pintner's essay shows that the Table of Ranks, the statutes creating a uniform ministerial structure, and the development of formal-educational requirements did not transform officialdom by introducing a mass of nonnobles into civil service. Rather, the serving nobility adopted a new life pattern, that of the formally trained career official. By the 1850s this process was well under way, but civil officialdom was by no means a homogeneous group, even at comparable rank levels. High officials with great estates apparently were socially apart from the increasing proportion of their colleagues without land. Inevitably, however, the careers of at least some of them had come to be similar: as the number of offices in general grew so, of course, the elite offices expanded in number providing increasing opportunities for landless nobles to reach exalted heights.

Provincial service was, as always, the least desirable alternative; but it was now staffed with the least educated and least privileged elements of career officialdom rather than the local landlords who had retired from military service. The "amateur" civil official had been largely eliminated from both central and provincial service by the 1850s—even in advance, that is, of the changes in local government which followed emancipation of the serfs in the 1860s. However, the kind of official to be found in the center as contrasted with those in the provinces could hardly have differed more radically. The provincial variety were inadequately, even haphazardly, trained, and their compensation and status reflected their level of preparation and probably their contribution to the state administration. Still, as much as their colleagues in the capitals, they represented the ascendency of bureaucratization of officialdom and the displacement of the landlord in roles of local administration. What Pintner shows is a state administration in the process of being wrested from whatever political and social control had been exercised by the traditional Russian landowning elites of the eighteenth century and, simultaneously, being disciplined to the principles of bureaucratic form and function. [THE EDITORS.]

The argument in the preceding chapter was that although there was, at most, modest change in the socioeconomic characteristics of the civil service over the course of the century prior to 1855, there was a transformation in the nature of the civil career and in the preparation demanded for it. The direction of these developments is clear, toward a career service requiring advanced training prior to entry with an increasing proportion of landless nobles as well as commoners present at all levels

A nation, however, is not governed by a tendency but by men on the job, pen in hand. This chapter considers the officials who were actually governing Russia on the eve of the "Great Reforms" of the 1860s. The data for this period is extensive, and it is possible to consider aspects of service that could not be discussed for earlier periods.[1]

Russian officialdom as it existed in the 1850s is too large and too diverse to permit meaningful overall description. Detailed analysis presumes division according to two basic and overlapping criteria: (1) noble and nonnoble status, and (2) central and provincial service. In terms of the first, noble versus nonnoble status, we are interested in why nobles continued to predominate in the higher levels of service despite the emergence of new career patterns and educational requirements that might appear to open the way for members of other social groups. What kinds of advantages did nobles have and how did they operate in the context of the civil service? In view of the enormous diversity of the group defined in law as nobles we must also determine whether all nobles or only certain types of nobles enjoyed advantages over nonnobles in service and how significant those advantages were.

When asking these questions, it is impossible to lump both central and provincial officials together and obtain a meaningful result. Although there was legally only one civil service, in fact most men served one or the other, and the entire character of the two career alternatives differed drastically. Education, noble status, high rank, superior (if not always adequate) pay, were common attributes of central officialdom, while the opposite in each case characterized the provinces in a truly Gogolian picture of backwardness and neglect. To ask, for example, how great an advantage higher education gave to a man in provincial service is largely irrelevant, because there simply were no men with higher education in the provinces except the handful at the top sent out from the center.

1. The discussion is based on data for about 4,700 officials who served in various agencies between 1841 and 1855, all but a few in the years 1846–55. (See the full list of agencies at the end of the preceding chapter.)

The relationship of nobles and nonnobles and the nature of the noble group itself cannot be divorced from the new patterns of career training and education that marked the early nineteenth century, because both groups had to adjust to the new requirements and opportunities. The fact that the changes were relatively recent in the 1850s meant that different age groups serving at that time represent various types of career experience, the younger men, of course, reflecting the new emphasis on formal education.

Among the highest ranking officials, the three basic career patterns can be designated as "court-elite," "standard military," and "bureaucratic-technical." The first, consisting of training in the Imperial Corps of Pages, elite regiments, or other institutions associated with the imperial court, was characteristic of the older generation of high officials around Nicholas I. Younger officials in the same rank group usually had followed the bureaucratic-technical path, involving formal higher education and a lifelong civil career. In the 1850s these men were concentrated in the top executive positions in the operating departments of the ministries.[2]

Men with higher education holding top ranks averaged forty-nine years of age, those who had attended the Lycée at Tsarskoe Selo or the Imperial School of Jurisprudence forty-two years, while men with the traditional home education averaged sixty-one years, and those with only secondary education fifty-five years (Table 1). Comparable differences exist at all rank levels. In general, Lycée graduates were fifteen to twenty years younger than those with home or secondary education, and men with university training were about ten years younger. The large difference in the educational background of the age groups reflects two separate influences: (1) the "bonus" in rank given by law to graduates of the Lycée, School of Jurisprudence, and, to a somewhat lesser extent, the universities, and (2) the overall growth of formal higher education as the first step in a civil career. Men of older generations were less prone and less able to attend these schools, many of which did not exist in the early years of the nineteenth century.[3]

2. These career patterns are discussed at length in my article, "The Russian Higher Civil Service on the Eve of the 'Great Reforms,'" *Journal of Social History* (Spring 1975): 55–68.

3. Except for the University of Moscow, established in 1755, all of the institutions involved date from the nineteenth century: Universities at Dorpat (1802), Kazan and Kharkov (1804), and St. Petersburg (1819); the Lycée at Tsarskoe Selo (1810), and the School of Jurisprudence (1835). See also Richard Wortman, *The Development of a Russian Legal Consciousness*, Chicago, 1976, Chap. 2; Patrick Alston, *Education and the State in Tsarist Russia*, Stanford, 1969, pp. 9–13, 23–30; and Allen A. Sinel, "The Socialization of

Walter M. Pintner

TABLE IX-1

Average Age of Officials Serving during 1840–1855
(arranged by rank and type of education)

Rank Level[a]	All Types	N =	Home	N =	Elementary	N =	Secondary	N =
Top	52	366	61	42	62	6	55	83
Upper middle	43	723	50	79	52	53	46	218
Lower middle	38	698	44	108	40	184	38	267
Bottom	30	991	34	121	30	371	29	451

SOURCE: For this and all subsequent tables, service records in TsGIA collected by the author.

a. In this and all subsequent tables, "top" rank level refers to ranks 1–5, "upper middle" to 6–8, "lower middle" to 9–11, and "bottom" to 12–14. In practice, rank 1 was held only by the Foreign Minister (Nesselrode, who is included). Rank 11 was never used and rank 13 seldom.
b. "Higher" includes universities and technical institutes.

Table 2 shows the growing importance of education in a different way. At the same rank level the lower age groups show a greater proportion of men with advanced education and fewer with home or elementary education (except, of course, at the bottom level when there are very few with advanced training). Thus in the lower-middle ranks 61 percent of those age twenty to twenty-nine have Lycée, School of Jurisprudence, or higher education, but of men forty to forty-nine years at that rank level, only 5 percent have education beyond secondary school.

To point out that formal training had an increasingly important effect on success in civil service is not to suggest that there were no other factors of significance. Legal restrictions and economic disadvantages made access to education far from equal for the various groups in Russian society. The schools that gave the greatest preference on entering service, the Lycée and the School of Jurisprudence, were restricted by law to nobles. Admission to the universities was open to all nontaxed (free) classes until late in the reign of Nicholas

the Russian Bureaucratic Elite, 1811–1917: Life at the Tsarskoe Selo Lyceum and the School of Jurisprudence," *Russian History* 3, Pt. 1 (1976): 1–31.

Pages School	N =	Lycée or School of Jurisprudence	N =	Higher[b]	N =
53	21	42	33	50	177
36	10	29	56	41	301
28	3	23	40	31	95
0	0	22	5	30	42

when restrictions were imposed, but they were never fully closed to commoners.[4]

What did the introduction of educational requirements for preferential entry mean for the relative position of nobles and nonnobles in service? For men in comparable age groups who started work at the same rank level, nobles rise about one rank level higher than nonnobles (Table 3). The difference remains about the same regardless of the age group involved. There is certainly no tendency for nonnobles to overcome their disadvantages in the course of their service career. Advanced education of any type reduces the advantage of noble over nonnoble only very slightly. If the Lycée and the School of Jurisprudence, which were restricted to nobles and gave greater rank preference on entrance than did graduation from the universities, are eliminated, leaving only the universities and technical institutes, the

4. In the late 1840s, sons of nobles *and officials* comprised 63 percent of all university students. At Kazan and Moscow Universities in the same year, nobles' sons, excluding officials' sons, were in a minority, comprising 44 percent. These data probably are subject to some question, but it is absolutely clear that there were substantial numbers of nonnobles in Russian universities in the mid-nineteenth century. See V. R. Leikina-Svirskaia, "Formirovanie raznochinskoi intelligentsii v Rossii v 40-kh godakh XIXv.," *Istoriia SSSR*, No. 1(1959): 86–87.

Walter M. Pintner

TABLE IX-2

Highest Level of Education Reached by Officials Serving during 1840–1855 (in percentage, by age and rank)

Age	Home	Elementary	Secondary	Pages School	Lycée, School of Jurisprudence	Higher	N =
				Top Rank			
Through 39	0	0	19	5	27	49	37
40–49	4	0	12	6	15	63	136
50–59	15	3	26	7	2	47	105
60 or more	24	3	37	5	0	31	88
Total, all ages	11	2	23	6	9	49	366
				Upper Middle			
Through 29	0	0	2	4	63	31	54
30–39	2	2	22	2	9	63	30
40–49	15	7	39	1	1	37	245
50–59	17	11	40	1	0	31	22
60 or more	24	24	27	0	0	25	49
Total, all ages	11	7	30	1	8	43	723
				Lower Middle			
Through 29	5	9	24	2	30	30	128
30–39	11	28	45	0.3	0.3	15	43
40–49	23	31	41	0	0	5	186
50–59	23	40	35	0	0	2	68
60 or more	72	14	14	0	0	0	14
Total, all ages	15	26	38	1	6	14	698
				Bottom			
Through 29	8	36	50	0	1	5	588
30–39	12	43	41	0	0	4	291
40–49	37	29	32	0	0	2	89
50–59	33	22	45	0	0	0	18
60 or more	0	20	60	0	0	20	5
Total, all ages	12	37	46	0	1	4	991

SOURCE: See Table 1.

TABLE IX-3

Difference in Rank Level Achieved by Noble and Nonnoble Officials, 1840–1855
(arranged according to entrance level, location, and current age)

Age	*Provincial Agencies Entered Below Rank 14*		*Central Agencies Entered Below Rank 14*		*Central Agencies Entered Ranks 14–12*		*Central Agencies Entered Above Rank 12*	
	N =	*Difference*	N =	*Difference*	N =	*Difference*	N =	*Difference*
All Officials								
20–29	576	.6	50	.9	25	1.7	93	.9
30–39	557	.9	98	1.0	66	.6	86	.9
40–49	356	.8	135	1.4	75	1.0	56	1.5
50–59	176	1.7	102	1.8	44	1.3	11	.1
60 or more	55	1.0	50	1.1	25	3.9	0	. . .
Officials with Lycée, School of Jurisprudence, or Higher Education								
20–29	13	2.7	14	.7	15	1.0	92	.8
30–39	15	0.0	11	−.3	51	.3	83	.8
40–49	7	.9	9	1.9	58	1.3	53	1.5
50–59 [a]	0	. . .	6	.6	20	1.2	11	.1
Officials with Higher Education								
20–29	13	2.7	13	.4	8	1.6	25	.7
30–39	15	0.0	11	−.3	49	.3	57	.5
40–49	7	.9	9	1.9	57	1.2	36	1.3
50–59 [a]	0	. . .	6	.6	20	1.2	10	.2

SOURCE: See Table 1.

NOTE: The difference is that between the arithmetic mean of the ranks (14–1) held by the noble and that held by nonnoble officials. Of the 864 men who began service in the military, 95 percent were noble. Of the 193 who began as teachers or medical men, 79 percent were nonnoble. These two categories are excluded from this table.

a. Insufficient data for 60 years of age or more.

difference is further reduced, but not much. The same problem can be examined in terms of the average age of nobles and nonnobles in comparable rank groups (Table 4). The difference varies with different rank levels and levels of entrance. Occasionally it is negligible (or in a few cases even favoring the nonnoble), but it generally favors the noble by several years, but in every case the nobles' advantage is less than would be expected if they had actually benefited to the maximum extent possible under the law. If level of education is held constant the differences remain, but are even less pronounced.[5]

It was certainly better to be a noble than not to be one in terms of service advancement, but the nonnoble who did get into civil service operated in the same basic framework as the noble. Both had a real chance of substantial success and some commoners would do better than many nobles of the same age and starting point. For example, in the agencies included in this study 128 nonnoble officials aged fifty to fifty-nine entered service at the very bottom, below the fourteenth rank in the provinces, and 64 nonnobles entered at the same level in the center. These were men who began in the most menial jobs; nevertheless 41 of them reached the fifth rank, which entitled the holder to hereditary noble status.[6] Another 148 reached the eighth rank, which

5. The small difference in rank achieved between nobles and nonnobles is particularly noteworthy in view of the advantages afforded by law to nobles. The system was complex, dividing officials first according to their level of education, and then within each educational level by social origin. The advantage afforded nobles was greater in the less-educated categories. For example, for men without primary education, nobles were required to serve two years as office workers before achieving rank fourteen, nonnobles, four to seven years depending on the social group they belonged to. Promotion from the ninth to the eighth rank required five years service for nobles and ten years for nonnobles. Men with higher education were treated equally until the crucial ninth to eighth step was reached where nobles had to serve four years and nonnobles six years (PSZ II, 1834, Vol. 9, no. 7224, arts. 22, 39, 40). Prior to 1834, a less detailed statute to 1790 required that nobles serve three years prior to receiving the eighth rank and nonnobles twelve (PSZ I, 1790, Vol. 23, No. 16,930; reaffirmed in PSZ I, 1799, Vol. 25, No. 19,159). Speransky's famous law on examinations (PSZ I, 1809, Vol. 30, No. 23,711) did not change the advantage of nobles in promotion to the eighth rank. Although the law of 1834 gave increased preference to nobles, there seems to have been no measurable impact on the average rank level achieved by nobles and by nonnobles. In fact, the difference in average rank level achieved by men in each group who entered service after 1834 tends to be lower than for those who entered service prior to that year. This remains the case regardless of age or length of service.

6. From the establishment of the Table of Ranks (in 1722) until 11 June 1845, hereditary nobility was achieved with the eighth rank; then the requirement was raised to the fifth rank (PSZ II, 1845, Vol. 20, No. 19,086). On 9 December 1856, the requirement

TABLE IX-4

Average Age of Officials (arranged by rank, social origin, and level of entry into service)

Entrance Level and Place	Nobles		Nonnobles		Difference in Average Age (Nonnobles minus Nobles)
	Avg. Age	N =	Avg. Age	N =	
Top Rank					
Military	56.8	142	53.5	10	−3.3
Provincial, below rank 14	55.5	22	55.2	10	−.3
Central, below rank 14	54.8	41	60.7	20	5.9
Central, ranks 14–12	52.5	71	48.8	14	−3.7
Central, ranks 11 and up	43.0	61	48.3	10	.3
Teaching and Medicine	48.6	14	53.6	39	5.0
Upper Middle					
Military	45.8	151	54.4	21	8.6
Provincial, below rank 14	48.1	95	51.8	141	3.7
Central, below rank 14	45.2	83	50.3	132	5.1
Central, ranks 14–12	40.3	62	43.8	58	3.5
Central, ranks 11 and up	30.9	94	38.6	27	7.7
Teaching and Medicine	40.6	23	45.3	84	4.7
Lower Middle					
Military	41.2	80	46.5	20	5.3
Provincial, below rank 14	37.9	147	40.3	371	2.4
Central, below rank 14	32.6	46	39.5	65	6.9
Central, ranks 14–12	30.4	13	33.0	6	2.6
Central, ranks 11 and up	23.7	48	27.1	10	3.4
Teaching and Medicine	26.3	3	35.8	22	9.5
Bottom					
Military	33.3	37	39.2	11	5.9
Provincial, below rank 14	28.8	228	30.7	710	1.9
Central, below rank 14	24.8	26	30.9	47	6.1
Central, ranks 14–12	23.2	9	27.3	7	4.1
Central, ranks 11 and up	. . .	. . .	. . .	. . .	. . .
Teaching and Medicine	31.0	3	36.8	13	5.8

SOURCE: See Table 1.

(after 1846) conferred personal (lifelong) noble status, leaving only 30 who remained in the very lowest levels of the service. That the nobles did rather better on the average does not negate the fact that nonnobles could do very well; it was one of them who reached rank two, the highest that anyone could expect to reach.[7]

It is impossible, however, to explain the predominance of nobles over nonnobles in high-level positions on the basis of the modest advantage they enjoyed in speed of promotion once they entered service. Nor was it that the nonnoble who managed to get on the civil-service ladder at a reasonably high level was blocked by discrimination when he got near the top. That may have happened at times, but the really important factor was that, except at the lowest provincial levels, more nobles entered service and they entered at a higher level than nonnobles (Table 5). Thus the pool from which the top positions were filled was composed largely of nobles. Level of entry was crucial to the achievement of high rank in a service where seniority counted heavily. Of 469 top officials serving in the 1850s, only 20 percent had started below rank fourteen. The rest, including virtually all of the younger men, entered at a high rank after advanced education or had transferred from the military, teaching, or medicine. Most of these means of gaining entrance at an advanced level favored the nobility. The Lycée and the School of Jurisprudence were reserved exclusively for nobles, and their graduates filled from 17 to 28 percent of the top jobs. Another 30 percent were held by former military officers who were over 80 percent noble. Nonnobles could gain preferential admission to civil service only through the universities or technical schools, either directly or via lateral transfer following a career in teaching or medicine, a route that accounted for 37 percent of the nonnobles in top positions.[8]

The conclusion to be drawn from this extensive discussion is that the changes in education and career patterns discussed in the preceding

---

was raised again to the fourth rank (PSZ ɪɪ, 1856, Vol. 31, No. 31,236). The rights of hereditary nobility could be passed on only to those children born after the noble status was achieved, a major caveat for the man who gained the status late in life. It was possible to petition the tsar on behalf of one son born prior to the achievement of nobility.

7. In effect rank two, actual privy councilor, was the top of the scale, since rank one was reserved exclusively for the minister of foreign affairs.

8. The use of a statistical technique called multiple classification analysis supports the above conclusion that education and social origin were of paramount importance in

TABLE IX-5

Social Origin and Level of Entry
into Service of Officials, 1840–1855

Entrance Level and Place	Noble %	Nonnoble %	N =
Military	86	14	539
Provincial, below rank 14	29	71	1,730
Provincial, ranks 14–12	60	40	114
Provincial, ranks 11 and up	72	28	18
Central, below rank 14	43	57	464
Central, ranks 14–12	65	35	240
Central, ranks 11 and up	81	19	251
Teaching and Medicine	22	78	204
			3,560

SOURCE: See Table 1.

career success (as measured by rank). The technique, in effect, enables one to hold age constant and ask what variables have the greatest impact on rank achieved. The results are summarized in the table. (The level of significance in all cases is .001.)

	% of Variance Explained		
	Central Ministries	Central Advisory Agencies	Provincial Agencies
Social Origin	7	28	20
Education	33	29	30
Serfholding	14	16	7

As one would expect, social origin is less important and education more important in the ministerial agencies than in the advisory agencies around the tsar, and serfholding least important in all three groups. Two other variables can be added to the analysis, chapter certainly did not produce an open or democratized civil service, but rather one in which nobles, as a group, continued to have great advantages, although, as before, others were not excluded. The way the training system worked had changed, but the result with respect to social composition was not markedly different from the past.

More important than the question of noble versus nonnoble is the nature of the noble group itself. The impoverished, ill-educated noble clerk in the provinces, making 150 rubles a year and owning no property at all, and the sophisticated minister in St. Petersburg with salary and expense allowance of many thousands of rubles, and sometimes owning estates with thousands of serfs and a grand townhouse, were legally members of the same estate, the hereditary nobility, and formally their rights were identical.[9] Since the civil service in the 1850s was predominantly a body of nobles, albeit with significant participation by other groups, it is essential to refine the concept of noble as much as possible.

The nobility had developed over many centuries, although its formal definition did not begin until the time of Peter the Great. Some families traced their origins back to the retinue of the early Muscovite princes or even to Rurik, supposed founder of the first Russian state. Most, however, were descended from the mass of sixteenth- and seventeenth-century servicemen who formed the army of that period. By the mid-nineteenth century there was certainly a substantial group whose origin was even more recent, men whose immediate ancestors had been ennobled through the operation of the Petrine Table of Ranks. The service records do not permit any exact determination as to the origin of an individual's noble status. They simply indicate whether or not the official's father was a member of the hereditary nobility at the time of the official's birth. The father may have acquired noble status through service, or the family might trace its ancestry back through many generations of nobles.[10]

---

religion, and nature of first employment. However, religion has little impact, and first employment is so closely tied to education (through level of entrance legislation) that the effect is simply to divide the influence between the two. The statistical procedures followed above are described in Norman H. Nie et al., *SPSS: Statistical Package for the Social Sciences*, 2d ed., New York, 1975, pp. 410–21.

9. Participation in the organs of noble self-government in the rural areas did depend on ownership of property (land and usually serfs).

10. No attempt has been made to use personal names and genealogical sources because of the large number of cases involved and the major uncertainties inherent in the procedure.

We can, however, say a good deal about an official's economic status on the basis of the information provided about family serf-ownership.[11] In the mid-nineteenth century independent and secure wealth, wealth that did not depend on having official favor or official position, could by enjoyed only by inheriting large and well-populated estates. Legally, only a member of the nobility could own land with serfs. Owning land or serfs was however, by no means a prerequisite for membership in the nobility. Among our officials, those most likely to own serfs were the holders of top ranks in advisory agencies where 81 percent had at least one serf and 42 percent had over 500 male souls.[12] At lower ranks and in less prestigious agencies the number of officials with serfs is lower, and very few have large holdings (Table 6). The most striking general feature is the presence everywhere of totally serfless Russian noble officials, even at the highest levels, in the councils of the tsar (21 percent), and in much larger numbers in important positions in the ministries where there was much de facto power. German nobles were much less likely to own serfs (see note 11) than Russian nobles. Polish nobles were intermediate, but closer to the German than the Russian pattern. The other social groups in the civil service held virtually no serfs at all even if their rank entitled them to do so.

Clearly, independent wealth was by no means a prerequisite for a successful career, although it was almost certainly helpful. It is likely that the sons of wealthy nobles tended to prefer military careers, since civil officials who began their careers in the military were far more likely to own serfs than those who began in civil work, even at advanced rank (Table 7).

Land with serfs and service to the state were the two traditional elements in the life of the Russian noble. Originally, of course, the land and serfs were received in exchange for service. In later years service came to be part of the landholders' way of life, both for economic and

11. The service records indicate real property holdings of the official, his wife, and his parents and break it down in terms of serfs inherited and acquired (by purchase and gift). Urban houses (stone, wood, or wood on stone foundations), uninhabited rural land, and urban lots were also recorded. Serf owners rarely indicated their landholdings or the number of rural houses owned. The size of estates was expressed in terms of the number of "male souls." Acreage was not specified unless forests were of special value. Early in the nineteenth century the serfs in the Baltic provinces were emancipated; therefore the data may understate the wealth of Lutheran nobles, since data on landholdings without serfs were not collected.

12. Officials with only a few serfs probably used all or most of them as domestic servants in the city and in an economic sense should be considered landless, whether or not they had some small rural property.

TABLE IX-6

Serfholding of Russian Noble Officials (arranged by type of agency)

Male Serfs Held	Central Ministries[a]		Central Advisory Agencies[a]		Provincial Agencies	
	%	N =	%	N =	%	N =
			Top Rank			
None	36	55	21	23	31	12
1–100	25	39	12	13	28	11
101–500	24	37	25	27	23	9
over 500	15	23	42	46	18	7
			Upper Middle			
None	52	107	44	31	27	52
1–100	22	44	19	13	47	91
101–500	16	32	23	16	21	41
over 500	11	22	14	10	6	11
			Lower Middle			
None	66	73	41	12	35	87
1–100	12	13	0	0	50	125
101–500	14	15	28	8	13	32
over 500	9	10	31	9	2	4
			Bottom			
None	56	22	no officials		49	152
1–100	13	5	at this level		44	137
101–500	10	4			6	19
over 500	21	8			1	4

SOURCE: See Table 1.

a. Central Ministries include Finance, Interior, Justice, and State Domains. Central Advisory Agencies include The Committee of Ministers, The State Council, The Senate, and His Imperial Majesty's own Chancellery. For a complete list see the appendix to the previous chapter.

TABLE IX-7

Serf Ownership and Nature of First Employment
of Officials in Service, 1840–1855

Entrance Level and Place	Percentage with One or More Serfs	N =
Military	66	539
Provincial, below rank 14	20	1,714
Provincial, rank 14 and up	39	193
Central, below rank 14	20	463
Central, ranks 14–12	44	257
Central, above rank 12	48	252
Teaching	22	130
Medicine	23	74

SOURCE: See Table 1.

NOTE: Totals include all officials entering, not just nobles.

social reasons. Our data on officials permits us to deal with a related problem: What was the significance of estate ownership for men as *officials*, rather than as nobles? If estates were prized as a source of status and prestige, one would expect successful officials to acquire them if they could.[13] It turns out, however, that the men most likely to acquire serfs are those who already had some, and particularly those who already had many. Men with no serfs in the family were unlikely to acquire any regardless of their rank or social background. In the highest rank levels only 16 percent of officials without inherited serfs acquired any. For other groups and rank levels the figure is even lower (Table 8). The category most likely to acquire serfs was the Russian noble who already had 500 or more. Fifty-one percent (27 men) of those officials bought (or were given) at least one serf and 21 percent (11 men) acquired over 500.[14]

13. It is theoretically possible that the purpose of estates was an economically rational goal. It is, however, most unlikely in view of what is known about the rural economy of Russia in the mid-nineteenth century.

14. These questions of estate ownership and acquisition are discussed more exten-

Similarly there seems to have been no tendency for successful officials without estates to marry women with substantial estates; on the
contrary it is the men who were already endowed with substantial
landed property who were most likely to marry heiresses. The pattern
is the same for officials of all ranks and for men at the highest level
only. Seventy-nine percent of married top-rank Russian noble officials
who had no serfs in their own families married women with none and
only 2 percent married women with over 500 (Tables 9 and 10). However, 30 percent of those who were already large landlords married
women with similar holdings.

In other words a successful bureaucratic career would give a man
power, prestige, sometimes a large salary and expense allowance, and
legal membership in the hereditary nobility, but there is no indication
that there was any significant economic or social blending at the top.
There was an elite of career officials and an elite of traditional landed
wealth, some of whom held high civil posts and the younger generation among them had had a career experience essentially the same as
that of their fellow officials with a nonlanded background.

If the civil service is examined in terms of its component agencies,
instead of the personal attributes, the fundamental distinction, as noted
at the start of this essay, is clearly to be found in the differences between central and provincial service.[15] In the provinces, posts at rank
five or higher hardly existed, amounting to only 1 to 2 percent of the
total number of positions. They included only the governor, vice-
governor, and two or three top aides. In St. Petersburg agencies, 15
percent or more were at this level. Except at the highest rank level,
provincial salaries were much lower.[16] At the lower-middle and upper-
middle rank levels, officials in the provinces were five to six years

---

sively with respect to top rank officials in: Pintner, "The Russian Higher Civil Service
on the Eve of the 'Great Reforms,'" pp. 58–60.

15. There are, of course, differences among the central agencies. High-level advisory
bodies such as the Senate and State Council had a much higher proportion of older men
with the "court-elite" career pattern than did operating ministries. However, it has
proven impossible to isolate any further degree of occupational specialization among
central agencies or other significant socioeconomic differences among them. In the
provincial/central dichotomy, Moscow agencies are intermediate in many respects. In
the data that follow they are grouped with the other provinces. The discussion that
follows is based on much more extensive data than that in my article, "The Social
Characteristics of the Early Nineteenth Century Russian Bureaucracy," *Slavic Review*
29, No. 3 (1970): 433–35.

16. Salaries depended on the job a man held, but rank and job tended to go together,

TABLE IX-8

Acquisition of Male Serfs by Officials Who Inherited None
(arranged by social origin)

	0 Serfs		1–100 Serfs		101–500 Serfs		Over 500 Serfs	
	%	N =	%	N =	%	N =	%	N =
Top Ranks								
Russian Noble	83	76	11	10	5	5	1	1
German Noble	83	24	7	2	3	1	7	2
Polish Noble	83	10	8	1	8	1	0	0
Other Non-Russian	90	27	3	1	3	1	3	1
Nonnoble Russian	83	38	13	6	4	2	0	0
Total	84	175	9	20	5	10	2	4
Upper Middle Ranks								
Russian Noble	83	146	13	23	3	6	0	0
German Noble	98	39	0	0	2	1	0	0
Polish Noble	91	21	4	1	4	1	0	0
Other Non-Russian	96	54	4	2	0	0	0	0
Nonnoble Russian	92	258	7	21	1	3	0	0
Total	90	518	8	47	2	11	0	0
Lower Ranks								
Russian Noble	87	83	10	9	2	2	1	1
German Noble	100	4	0	0	0	0	0	0
Polish Noble	100	4	0	0	0	0	0	0
Other Non-Russian	100	5	0	0	0	0	0	0
Nonnoble Russian	99	414	1	2	0	0	0	0
Total	97	510	2	11	0.4	2	0.2	1

SOURCE: See Table 1.

although rank by no means guaranteed the holder a job of comparable rating and pay. At the upper-middle level (eight to six), salaries in central agencies averaged about 850 rubles a year (including expense allowances); at the same level in the provinces the average was about 500. In both places individual salaries might range two or three hundred rubles above or below the average depending on the job held. Data for salaries at lower levels in the center is scanty but suggests that a similar differential existed at these ranks as well. Average annual salaries in the provinces were certainly low, 260 rubles for men with lower-middle (ten to nine) ranks and 130 at the bottom (fourteen to twelve). Many provincial clerks at rank fourteen received only 80 rubles a year. Salaries (including expense allowances) for men with top ranks were comparable in central and provincial agencies but the spread among jobs was great. The overall average was about 2,500, but for a group of eight men with ministerial positions it reached 13,236.

Walter M. Pintner

TABLE IX-9

Percentage of All Married Officials of All Ranks
Whose Wives Inherited Serfs (distributed according to
the number of serfs the official inherited)

Serfs Inherited by Officials	Serfs Inherited by Wives				
	0	*1–100*	*101–500*	*Over 500*	N =
0	91	6	3	0.5	779
1–100	75	15	9	1	114
101–500	63	14	18	5	56
Over 500	59	2	15	25	53
All Officials	86	7	5	2	. . .
N =	860	72	49	21	1,002

SOURCE: See Table 1.

TABLE IX-10

Percentage of Married Top-Rank Russian Noble Officials
Whose Wives Inherited Serfs (distributed according to
the number of serfs the official inherited)

Serfs Inherited by Officials	Serfs Inherited by Wives				
	0	*1–100*	*101–500*	*Over 500*	N =
0	79	6	14	2	52
1–100	60	10	27	5	22
101–500	50	18	27	5	22
Over 500	49	3	19	30	37
All Officials	62	8	20	10	. . .
N =	83	10	26	14	133

SOURCE: See Table 1. This is a refinement of the data presented in
Pintner, "The Russian Higher Civil Service," pp. 59–60.

older on the average than in central agencies. Average age at the top and at the bottom level was about the same. Evidently men started at about the same age everywhere and advanced more slowly in the provinces.[17]

Most striking, perhaps, is the contrast in levels of education (Table 11). Only 13 percent of provincial officials had had an advanced education (university, Lycée, or School of Jurisprudence) compared to nearly 50 percent in central agencies. Even at equal rank levels provincial officials were usually less well educated than their counterparts in St. Petersburg. In the center the lower-middle ranks were staffed with many graduates of the university, the Lycée, or the School of Jurisprudence who were expecting to rise to higher posts. In the provinces there were almost none of these, and 92 percent of officials at that level had only elementary or secondary education, for there was little chance of further advancement. The few high-level officials that were in the provinces had the "court-elite" pattern of training rather than the "bureaucratic-technical" that characterized the younger officials in the central ministries.

Provincial service was indeed a separate world with a substantially different pattern of advancement than in the central agencies (Table 12). The lower levels were almost exclusively filled with men who started work in a provincial office, most frequently below the fourteenth rank. Almost all the few top-level officials were transfers from the military or central services. The best that a man who started in the provinces and who remained there could look forward to was an upper-middle-level post, but even there 60 percent of those positions were filled by men who began in the center or the military. Transfer from provincial to central posts was possible, but only about 20 percent (10 percent at the very top) of central positions were held by men who began in the provinces. Thus the provinces were not the place for an ambitious young man to start—most of those who did never left and never rose very high. On the other hand the successful central official might be sent to the provinces, but at a relatively high level and probably not permanently. That there was a social cleavage between the "locals" and the men from the center seems all but certain.

17. One measure of the slower advance of provincial officials is the number of years served in the positions below the fourteenth rank. In central service over 50 percent of those starting below rank fourteen reached that level by the end of their fourth year. In provincial service that point was not reached until the fifth year. Even more important was the fact that many entered service in the central agencies well up the Table of Ranks after extensive formal education. Relatively few with these advantages chose provincial service as the place to start their careers.

TABLE IX-11

Level of Education Achieved by Officials in Central
and Provincial Agencies (arranged by rank, in percentage)

| | Central Ministries | | | | |
	All Ranks	Top	Upper Middle	Lower Middle	Bottom
Higher	44	60	46	38	10
Lycée & School of Jurisprudence	11	11	9	18	7
Pages school	3	5	3	1	0
Secondary	33	21	33	32	66
Home & elementary	9	5	9	11	17
N =	729	208	296	151	76

SOURCE: See Table 1.

Finally it should be noted that the proportion of nonnobles in the lower ranks was 10 to 20 percent higher in the provinces than in the center. As one would expect, the more advantaged element in society was more frequently able to gain the better (central) positions (Table 13). The nobility however was not so uniformly advantaged that it abandoned provincial service. Even at the bottom ranks nearly 30 percent of the officials were nobles. Some of them might hope for significant advancement, but most would never leave their miserable jobs in the provincial backwaters of the empire. In the absence of any private demand for their limited skills, what else could the numerous minimally educated noble *chinovniki* in the provinces do?[18]

Russia entered the second half of the nineteenth century with a cadre of officials significantly changed from that at the beginning of the century. High officials were far more likely to be totally divorced

18. Of the nobles in provincial bottom ranks, 49 percent had only elementary or home education, 45 percent secondary. The situation is similar at the lower-middle level, while further up the number of positions is much smaller and the proportion with higher education reaches one-third. In the absence of substantial transfers to the central agencies, the obvious conclusion is that most of the poorly educated nobles did not

Central Advisory Agencies					Provincial Agencies				
All Ranks	*Top*	*Upper Middle*	*Lower Middle*	*Bottom*	*All Ranks*	*Top*	*Upper Middle*	*Lower Middle*	*Bottom*
35	38	39	23	13	13	46	43	8	4
15	6	26	17	0	0.8	7	2	1	0
4	8	1	0	0	0.2	4	0	0.2	0
22	24	18	17	47	41	24	31	42	44
25	24	17	43	40	45	20	23	49	52
288	123	103	47	15	1,821	46	311	540	924

from the land and entirely dependent on the state for their economic livelihood and social prestige than they had been fifty years earlier. Even more significant was the new requirement that they study at institutions established and controlled by the state if they were to hope for anything better than the most menial of posts. The growth of higher education was one of the factors that produced an increasingly large and vocal dissenting intelligentsia whose activities have been extensively chronicled.[19] On the other hand, the role of the "new officialdom" has just begun to be studied in terms of its impact on policy making, yet it is already clear that their influence was a complex one, neither unequivocally "reformist" or "conservative."[20]

---

advance beyond rank nine, at best. This conclusion is supported by the higher average age (by five to ten years) of nobles in provincial service.

19. The relationship of educational institutions and dissent is dealt with specifically in Daniel R. Brower, *Training the Nihilists: Education and Radicalism in Tsarist Russia*, Ithaca, 1975.

20. Influence in a "reformist" direction is discussed in: Wortman, *The Development of a Russian Legal Consciousness*, especially Chap. 9; and W. Bruce Lincoln, "The Genesis of an 'Enlightened' Bureaucracy in Russia, 1825–1856," *Jahrbücher für Geschichte Osteuropas* 20 No. 3 (1972). For the possibility of a "conservative" impact, see Helju Aulik Bennett,

Walter M. Pintner

TABLE IX-12

Nature of First Employment, Rank,
and Current Agency of Employment

	Current Employing Agency					
Current Rank Level	Central Ministries		Central Advisory Agencies		Provincial Agencies	
	%	N =	%	N =	%	N =
Top						
1st Job Military	28	76	38	55	42	22
1st Job Central	47	128	45	65	30	16
1st Job Provincial	10	26	14	21	17	9
1st Job Teaching						
or Medicine	15	42	2	3	11	6
Upper Middle						
1st Job Military	16	68	8	9	21	91
1st Job Central	57	250	72	83	25	106
1st Job Provincial	18	81	16	18	40	170
1st Job Teaching						
or Medicine	9	38	4	5	14	59
Lower Middle						
1st Job Military	8	17	14	6	14	91
1st Job Central	65	142	68	39	3	17
1st Job Provincial	24	53	18	8	80	509
1st Job Teaching						
or Medicine	3	7	0	0	3	18
Bottom						
1st Job Military	11	10	12	2	5	51
1st Job Central	68	65	65	11	1	13
1st Job Provincial	21	20	23	4	92	960
1st Job Teaching						
or Medicine	0	0	0	0	2	16

SOURCE: See Table 1.

In the longer run the significance of the link between state service and higher education may be found to lie not in education's impact on the handful of elite officials who made or influenced decisions, but in terms of an increasing imbalance between the expectations of univer-

---

"The *Chin* System and the *Raznochintsy* in the Government of Alexander III, 1881–1894," Ph.D. dissertation, University of California, Berkeley, 1972, and the chapter by Daniel Orlovsky below.

TABLE IX-13

Social Origin, Rank, and Agency of Employment

Rank Level	Central Ministries		Central Advisory Agencies		Provincial Agencies	
	%	N =	%	N =	%	N =
Top						
Noble	74	202	82	134	77	43
Nonnoble	26	71	18	30	23	13
Upper middle						
Noble	60	308	60	85	44	208
Nonnoble	40	206	40	56	56	270
Lower middle						
Noble	47	183	50	34	35	253
Nonnoble	53	208	50	34	65	473
Bottom						
Noble	31	70	39	7	28	326
Nonnoble	69	157	61	11	72	838

SOURCE: See Table 1.

sity students and the opportunities actually open to them. For the impoverished young noble, the official's son, and the ambitious youth from lower strata of society, the university was the best hope for improving one's status because of its link to preferment in civil service. Yet as the century progressed, a tension developed between the values of an increasingly self-conscious, even radical, student body and the narrow and restrictive character of the civil-service career that most of them would of necessity enter on completing their studies.[21] It is a dilemma familiar to many developing societies in our own day. As happens so often, a set of institutions devised for one purpose may contribute to developments far from the thoughts of its designers.

21. Samuel D. Kassow, "The Russian University in Crisis: 1899–1911," Ph.D. dissertation, Princeton University, 1976.

CHAPTER TEN

HIGH OFFICIALS IN THE MINISTRY OF INTERNAL AFFAIRS, 1855–1881

Daniel T. Orlovsky

O rlovsky adopts a perspective already used in this book—that of defining a group of officials according to rank and office and examining them both as a group and as individual members of a group. Thus his approach is less like that of Pintner, Menning, or Givens, who examine large populations—societies, really—and more akin to that of Crummey and Meehan-Waters, who focus on relatively small groups of elites. If the officialdom examined by Crummey and Meehan-Waters—the noble bureaucrat, to use Meehan-Waters's term—are an elite and a super-elite, the officials studied by Orlovsky are a sub-elite. Meehan-Waters's population consists in about 180 officials who held ranks four through one in the eighteenth century, and Orlovsky's consists in about 90, holding ranks five through three or possibly two in the nineteenth century, or some four generations later.

To summarize briefly what has happened to Russian officialdom between the end of the seventeenth century and the end of the nineteenth, one might simply say that, like much of Russian society, it has been bureaucratized. That is, just as the ratio of officials to population has increased and just as the range of social activities falling under bureaucratic aegis has expanded, so the impact of bureaucratization on the elite officialdom has intensified. The result of this process of bureaucratization of officialdom—ever enlarging the range of tasks before them, further compartmentalizing their functions, further subordinating individuals of even high rank to increasing layers of hierarchic control—can be seen in a comparison of Orlovsky's sub-elite with the eighteenth century and earlier elites.

The Ministry of Internal Affairs in 1880 would probably have accounted for a large portion of the entire civil government of the early eighteenth century. Orlovsky's elite (87), contained within one ministry, is almost half the size of the entire generalitet (179) studied by Meehan-Waters.

The factor of birth, the genetic element mentioned earlier, is still significant here but not nearly as much as it was with the tighter, more intimate group of 1730. Orlovsky shows here (as will Rowney in the following chapter) that the nobility as a social class dominates the ranks of the sub-elite until the end of *the empire. The nature of this domination, however, has changed markedly. No longer do a few families and clans exercise a firm grip on the prestige and prerogatives of high office as they did in the seventeenth and eighteenth centuries.*

Socialization, the preparation of the child and adolescent for the roles of adulthood, has changed dramatically, of course, as Pintner has already shown. Again, the family and clan have been removed as significant factors, and for them we see substituted the relatively impersonal institutions controlled by the bureaucracy itself (such as the universities, through the Ministry of Education) or the Imperial Court.

Specialization is not yet a factor of prime importance in explaining career success in Orlovsky's sub-elite. Indeed, Orlovsky shows that as in other places in Europe the specialist in Russia is held in contempt. Still, by comparison with the seventeenth- or even the eighteenth-century patterns of preparation for elite careers this is a relatively specialized group. No longer is literacy plus a background of military command accepted as an adequate preparation for any high office in the realm. The largest single group of elite officials (49 percent) identified by Orlovsky were educated in Russian universities and lycées and relatively few of the whole group had had extensive military service, or anything but service in the civil administration.

Finally, it seems evident that rank itself is no longer what it was in the eighteenth century. Most of those who held elite ranks in Meehan-Waters's group also held elite offices such as president of an administrative college, governor of a province, or commander of a large military or naval formation. One effect of the expansion of governmental structures and functions has been to produce a kind of "rank inflation." Relatively high rank now may be associated with offices whose purview and prestige are narrow by comparison with those of roughly similar rank three or four generations earlier. Orlovsky will observe that the average age on attaining the threshold of elite status (rank five; age 36.5) is substantially lower in Russia than in other European countries. It is also lower than the age of attaining first elite rank in the Crummey and Meehan-Waters groups (c. 42 years for each). This would seem to be associated with moving increasing numbers of young candidates into threshold positions in the expanding bureaucracy; it also suggests a kind of devaluation of the rank itself which is now increasingly common in the higher offices of individual ministries.

The process of bureaucratization, in which the bureaucracy expands its own principles of organization and operation throughout the official society of Russia, was not achieved without some realignment of the relationship between the bureaucracy and the upper-class society. Meehan-Waters's "noble bureaucrat" and the landowning military grandee of the seventeenth and eighteenth centuries can hardly be found in the largest and most important civil ministry of 1880. If they still remain in the more exalted offices of the Senate, the Council of State, and the General Staff, they are now, together with the Royal Family itself, an isolated phenomenon in an immense bureaucratic sea. [THE EDITORS.]

The Ministry of Internal Affairs (MVD) was prerevolutionary Russia's most powerful ministry of domestic administration and politics. By the mid-1860s the ministry's functions included police, local administration, censorship, public services, and a variety of economic and social matters that affected all citizens of the empire. Although much has been written about the ministry's role in the formulation and implementation of the Great Reforms and post-Crimean War government policy, historians have yet to examine the institution itself and its personnel.[1]

This essay considers the biographical characteristics and career patterns of a group of high officials (87 men) who held office in the MVD during the reign of Alexander II. "High officials" here means civil servants who reached positions of responsibility and influence within the regular hierarchy of the ministry's central organs. Generally, at the time they held these offices, the officials held ranks five, four, or three on the Table of Ranks. The offices they held that corresponded to these ranks were assistant minister (*tovarishch ministra*), director and vice-director of the various departments, and positions in the highest ministry collegial organs (the Council of the Minister, Main Directorate of Press Affairs, etc.). These men were "successful" career officials—highly educated, professional administrators, who served below the rank of minister but far above the army of petty scribes and others who never attained even the lowest (fourteenth) rank, or who remained mired at the lowest levels of the Table-of-Ranks hierarchy engaged in menial and mechanical tasks. This kind of career civil servant began to emerge in the ministry during the 1840s and 1850s under the impact of earlier government educational reforms, the rapid growth of the ministerial system, and the increasingly complex administrative tasks faced by this apparatus.

The concentration here on a smaller group of officials serving in one

1. There have been two official histories of the Ministry of Internal Affairs: N. V. Varadinov, *Istoriia ministerstva vnutrennykh del, 1802–1855*, 8 parts in 3 vols., St. Petersburg, 1858–61; and S. Adrianov, *Ministerstvo vnutrennykh del: Istoricheskii ocherk*, 3 vols., St. Petersburg, 1901. See also Daniel T. Orlovsky, "Ministerial Power and Russian Autocracy: The Ministry of Internal Affairs, 1802–1881," Ph.D. dissertation, Harvard University, 1976.

central government organ offers an approach somewhat different from the preceding essays in this volume that treat either social elites (Crummey, Meehan-Waters, Givens) or give overviews of "official-dom" for specific time periods (Plavsic, Pintner). This institutional focus uses demographic materials not only to shed light on Russia's governing elite as a social group, but also to explore connections between the background and experience of that elite on the one hand and their ideas (or ethos) and performance as officials on the other. In the case of the Ministry of Internal Affairs during Alexander's reign, my hypothesis is that the history of changes in the nature of the min-istry's personnel is closely related to the kinds of policies the ministry adopted during the 1860s and 1870s.

The study of officials in this ministry was conceived as one approach toward answering the following question: What was the role of per-sonnel in the ministry's evolution from its position as the leading instrument of the peasant emancipation and as haven for "progres-sive" bureaucrats, to that of conservative supporter of immutable autocracy, of a static society dominated by the landed nobility and the principles of administrative and police power?

The analysis is based largely on personnel records (*formuliarnye spiski*) located in Soviet archives.[2] In addition, a variety of published sources were used that provide more information about promotions and the officials' own views of career prospects than do the personnel records. Although the records have many shortcomings, their use permits a much more complete coverage of the holders of the offices considered (only about 30 percent of the eighty-seven men have any

---

2. All the personnel records were located in the Central State Historical Archive of the Soviet Union in Leningrad (hereafter cited as TsGIA SSSR). Most of the material was located in the *fond* of the Department of General Affairs of the Ministry of Internal Affairs, the ministry organ concerned with personnel, or in the *fondy* of the ministry departments in which the officials worked. The following *fondy* were used: Fond 1,284, Department of General Affairs MVD; Fond 776, Main Directorate of Press Affairs; Fond 821, Department of Religious Affairs of Foreign Faiths; Fond 1,162, State Council; Fond 1,349, Personnel records gathered for the Heraldry Office of the Governing Sen-ate. The records were only located with considerable difficulty. After 1857, the Senate no longer kept personnel records for the entire civil service. The Ministry of Internal Affairs had responsibility for keeping its own records, and was particularly disorganized in carrying out this task. The inventories (*opisi*) for the Department of General Affairs do not include personnel records. An excellent discussion of the history and meaning of *formuliarnye spiski* is found in Z. I. Malkova and M. A. Pliukhina, "Dokumenty vyshikh i tsentral'nykh uchrezhdenii XIX–nachala XXv. kak istochnik biograficheskikh svedenii," Glavnoe Arkhivnoe Upravlenie SSSR, *Nekotorye voprosy izucheniia istorich-eskikh dokumentov XIX–nachala XXv.: Sbornik statei*, Leningrad, 1967, pp. 204–8.

published biographical material).[3] The sample of eighty-seven men represents approximately 80 percent of those holding departmental directorships and the office of assistant minister during Alexander's reign. The archivists at TsGIA SSSR in Leningrad were unable to locate the records of the remaining 20 percent. In some cases, such as assistant minister or director of the Department of State Police the representation is 100 percent. For the lower offices (vice-directors and members of collegial bodies) the representation is lower—50 to 70 percent, depending on the office.[4]

Marc Raeff and Hans-Joachim Torke have drawn attention to the dissimilarities between the Russian civil service during the first half of the nineteenth century and the bureaucracies of Western Europe.[5] They single out the nature of Russian officialdom itself as one of the clearest manifestations of the Russian "deviation" from classic Weberian norms. In education, ethos, and efficiency, the Russian official seemed a poor, distant relative to the specialized, ethically charged, rational *Fachmänner* of the West. Raeff emphasizes the use of court favorites—often military men—"to fill important bureaucratic posts or to expedite major policy decisions or reforms."[6] Below these commanding heights, he sees the mass of Russian officialdom, which was separated from the top level by an unbridgeable gulf,[7] and concludes that "while Russia had a host of minor executive clerks busily writing papers they never fully understood, it had no homogenous, efficient, alert and politically conscious policy-making bureaucracy comparable to the Prussian, French, or even Austrian."[8] Torke, while sharing many of these views, at least saw an evolutionary process, a movement closer to the western standard, which resulted in noticeable improvements beginning after the Crimean War.[9] Torke sees the Great Reforms in part as a result of the process of the bureaucracy's emanci-

3. Apart from memoirs and diaries, etc., the best source for career information is the incomplete *Russkii biograficheskii slovar'*, 25 vols., St. Petersburg, 1896–1918 (hereafter cited as RBS). Often the biographies in RBS are taken from the official *spiski*.

4. My search for the personnel records at TsGIA SSSR began with a complete list of the officeholders in question. The sample was limited by the number of records the archivists could locate in the time alloted for the project.

5. Marc Raeff, "The Russian Autocracy and Its Officials," *Harvard Slavic Studies IV: Russian Thought and Politics*, Cambridge, Mass., 1957, pp. 77–91; Hans-Joachim Torke, "Das russische Beamtentum in der ersten Hälfte des 19. Jahrhunderts," *Forschungen zur osteuropäischen Geschichte*, Vol. 13, Berlin-Wiesbaden, 1967, pp. 7–345.

6. Raeff, "The Russian Autocracy and Its Officials," pp. 87–88.

7. Ibid., p. 68.

8. Ibid., pp. 90–91.

9. Torke, "Das russische Beamtentum," pp. 7–48, 285–309.

pation from the tsar. This emancipation paralleled the earlier (circa 1800 for Torke) and equally important emancipation of the bureaucracy from the *dvorianstvo*.[10]

In recent years the work of American and Soviet scholars has shown that Imperial Russian bureaucratic realities were more complex than the above views suggest.[11] We now accept the existence by mid-century of an increasing number of nonlanded, career civil servants, primarily of *dvorianstvo* origin, who occupied middle- to high-level positions in the hierarchies of ranks and offices. These men viewed themselves more and more as bureaucrats, as servants of the state (*dolzhnostnye litsa*) rather than as members of their hereditary legal estate. Their political views and career concerns began to diverge noticeably from those of other members of the *dvorianstvo*. While there was surely a great distance between the notables at the top of the earlier nineteenth-century government apparatus and the Gogolian scribes at the bottom, by mid-century there was something substantial in between. A great deal of the substantive legislative and administrative work of the Russian government was now conducted by a new generation of men occupying the many key positions in the ministries and other central government organs. The trend is evident in the figures offered by P. A. Zaionchkovskii for 1853 (Table 1).[12]

In the category of assistant minister and department director there was a substantial decrease in property ownership, titles, and even of *dvorianstvo* origin. Furthermore, 79.5% were younger than sixty, and

10. Ibid., pp. 300–309.

11. See especially Walter M. Pintner's contribution to this volume and the same author's "Social Characteristics of the Early Nineteenth Century Russian Bureaucracy," *Slavic Review* 29 (September 1970): 429–43. P. A. Zaionchkovskii has recently published another analysis of mid-nineteenth-century officialdom, "Vysshaia biurokratiia nakanune krymskoi voiny," *Istoriia SSSR*, No. 4 (July–August 1974): 154–65. Similar material for the eighteenth century is found in S. M. Troitskii, *Russkii absoliutizm i dvorianstvo v XVIIIv.: Formirovanie biurokratii*, Moscow, 1974, pp. 155–295. For the second half of the nineteenth century, see also V. R. Leikina-Svirskaia, *Intelligentsiia v Rossii vo vtoroi polovine XIX veka*, Moscow, 1971, pp. 71–91; for the early twentieth century, Don Karl Rowney, "Higher Civil Servants in the Russian Ministry of Internal Affairs: Some Demographic and Career Characteristics, 1905–1916," *Slavic Review* 31 (March 1972): 101–10. More complete references to recent works on Russian officialdom may be found in my article, "Recent Studies on the Russian Bureaucracy," *The Russian Review* 35 (October 1976): 448–67.

12. Zaionchkovskii, "Vysshaia biurokratiia," p. 164. Zaionchkovskii has also located in the archives of the First Section reliable figures for the growth of the bureaucracy during the Crimean War period. The following figures represent the number of officials possessing *chin* (p. 55): 1847—61,548; 1850—71,819; 1856—82,352.

Daniel T. Orlovsky

TABLE X-1

The Composition of the Bureaucratic Elite (by percentage)

Office	Land and Serf Owners	Born Nobility	Titled
Committee of Ministers	94.4	100.0	66.6
State Council	92.2	98.2	53.7
Senate	72.7	95.4	13.3
Assistant ministers and directors of departments	63.6	86.3	5.2
Ambassadors and special envoys	52.6	100.0	47.3

SOURCE: See note 12.

71.8% were educated at home.[13] This departed significantly from the profile of the older men sitting in the highest governing institutions. In the State Council, 67.2% were over sixty years of age (23.6% over seventy), 69% were educated at home, and 49% were military generals.[14] The corresponding figures for the Committee of Ministers were 77.7% over age fifty-five, 61.9% educated at home, and 55.5% military generals.[15]

W. B. Lincoln has even noticed among the younger career officials a small group of "enlightened" bureaucrats: men unselfishly serving more abstract notions of the state and willing to speak for and act in the interests of society.[16] These were men who looked to West European ideas and experience and who might have qualified for in-

13. Ibid., pp. 162–63.
14. Ibid., pp. 156–58.
15. Ibid., pp. 159–60.
16. W. Bruce Lincoln, "The Circle of the Grand Duchess Yelena Pavlovna, 1847–1861," *Slavonic and East European Review* 48 (July 1970): 373–87; Lincoln, "The Genesis of an 'Enlightened' Bureaucracy in Russia, 1825–1856," *Jahrbücher für Geschichte Osteuropas* 20 (September 1972): 321–30; Lincoln, "N. A. Miliutin and the St. Petersburg Municipal Act of 1846: A Study in Reform Under Nicholas I," *Slavic Review* 33 (March 1974): 55–68; Lincoln, "Russia's 'Enlightened' Bureaucrats and the Problem of State Reform, 1848–1856," *Cahiers du monde russe et Soviétique* 12 (October–December 1971): 410–21. See also Richard Wortman, "Judicial Personnel and the Court Reform of 1864," *Canadian Slavic Studies* 3 (Summer 1969): 224–34; and Wortman, *The Development of a Russian Legal Consciousness*, Chicago, 1976.

clusion in the Hegelian "universal class"—the theoretical formulation of the Prussian bureaucratic ideal.[17] The influence of these men on the Kiselev Reform of the State Peasantry, the St. Petersburg Municipal Reform, and at least three of the Great Reforms, the 1861 Emancipation of the Proprietary Serfs and 1864 Judicial and *zemstvo* Reforms has already been demonstrated.[18]

In the Ministry of Internal Affairs, such men constituted a small, though influential, minority that first gained prominence during L. A. Perovskii's tenure as minister (1842–52).[19] These officials, perhaps best exemplified by N. A. Miliutin, reached the summit of their power during the legislative process leading to the 1861 Emancipation. Shortly thereafter, Miliutin (then assistant minister) was eased out of office. A similar fate awaited Ia. A. Solov'ev, head of the *Zemskii otdel*,* two years later. Others preferred to transfer to institutions where their particular skills and opinions might be more appreciated. Thus, A. K. Giers, a specialist in financial matters, transferred to the Ministry of Finance under M. Kh. Reutern—himself a former colleague of the reformist Grand Duke Konstantin Nikolaevich at the Naval Ministry.[20] Of the eighty-seven men in this sample, very few then (perhaps six to eight) can be included definitely in the subgroup

---

*That section of the Ministry created in 1857 to deal primarily with affairs of the "land" or peasant matters.

17. G. F. W. Hegel, *The Philosophy of Right*, trans. T. M. Knox, Oxford, 1942, pp. 145–60, 188–93. See also Shlomo Avineri, *Hegel's Theory of the Modern State*, Cambridge, 1972, pp. 155–61 especially; Z. A. Pelczynski, ed., *Hegel's Political Philosophy: Problems and Perspectives*, Cambridge, 1971; and Hans Rosenberg, *Bureaucracy, Aristocracy, and Autocracy: The Prussian Experience, 1660–1815*, Cambridge, Mass., 1958, *passim*.

18. See, for example, Terence Emmons, *The Russian Landed Gentry and the Peasant Emancipation of 1861*, Cambridge, 1968; Daniel Field, *The End of Serfdom: Nobility and Bureaucracy in Russia 1856–1861*, Cambridge, Mass., 1976; P. A. Zaionchkovskii, *Otmena krepostnogo prava v Rossii*, Moscow, 1954; V. V. Garmiza, *Podgotovka zemskoi reformy 1864 goda*, Moscow, 1957; S. Frederick Starr, *Decentralization and Self-Government in Russia, 1830–1870*, Princeton, 1972; Friedhelm Barthold Kaiser, *Die russische Justizreform von 1864: Zur Geschichte der russischen Justiz von Katharina II bis 1917*, Leiden, 1972; and Wortman, *Development of a Russian Legal Consciousness*.

19. A. D. Shumakher, "Pozdnyia vospominaniia o davno minuvshikh vremenakh," *Vestnik Evropy* 196 (1899): 89–128; W. Bruce Lincoln, "The Daily Life of St. Petersburg Officials in the Mid-Nineteenth Century," *Oxford Slavonic Papers*, Vol. 8, Oxford, 1975, pp. 82–100; and Lincoln, "N. A. Miliutin"; see also, Sidney Monas, "Bureaucracy in Russia under Nicholas I," in M. Cherniavsky, ed., *The Structure of Russian History: Interpretive Essays*, New York, 1970, pp. 269–81.

20. Jacob Walter Kipp, "The Grand Duke Konstantin Nikolaevich and the Epoch of the Great Reforms, 1855–1866," Ph.D. dissertation, The Pennsylvania State University, 1970; also S. M. Seredonin, *Istoricheskii obzor deiatel'nosti Komiteta ministrov*, 3 vols., St. Petersburg, 1902, Vol. 1, *passim*.

of "enlightened" bureaucrats. The majority of new career civil servants in the sample first entered the Ministry as appointees of P. A. Valuev, minister of internal affairs (1861–68), and A. E. Timashev, minister of internal affairs (1868–78). They did not share the theoretical and political concerns of the "enlightened" minority, preferring instead to view society more and more as an adversary.[21] In their unequivocal support of the regime, they adopted a kind of bureaucratic statism that was at once less articulate and more conservative than might be expected from reform-era officials.

These men, and not the more transitory "enlightened" bureaucrats, are indicative of the evolution of high Russian officialdom in the ministry after the Emancipation. The existence of a new generation in Russia by mid-nineteenth century of highly educated career officials is an important fact of social and institutional history. But this fact taken alone does not permit assumptions about the impact of such men within a specific institutional context. To determine in what sense, if any, these administrators brought "rationalization" to the ministry one must move beyond the information contained in personnel records and learn as much as possible about the ideas and labors of the men while members of the ministry staff. Only by combining demographic data with more traditional types of historical evidence can one arrive at a balanced assessment of the officials' impact on the Ministry of Internal Affairs.[22] With this in mind, the various types of biographical data and the career patterns of the officials can be examined as a prelude to some generalizations on the role of these men in the history of the ministry during Alexander's reign.

The age of the ministry officials brings into sharp focus the question of generational change in the Russian bureaucracy. The ministry officials fall into three distinct age groups. The first or oldest group consists of men whose careers peaked during the late 1840s or 1850s and extended no further than the early 1860s. The second group is the majority of the sample, and includes most occupants of the high min-

21. Many examples could be cited here from the memoirs, memoranda, and other writings of the men included in this sample. For a classic statement of this point of view by one of the ministry officials, see B. Obukhov, *Russkii administrator noveishei shkoly: Zapiska pskovskogo gubernatora i otvet na nee*, Berlin, 1868; also D. N. Tolstoi, "Zapiski grafa Dmitriia Nikolaevicha Tolstogo," *Russkii arkhiv*, 23, No. 2 (1885): 5–33.

22. Michel Crozier emphasizes the importance of analyzing the "bureaucratic experience" within the institutional and historical context in which officials lived and worked. I follow Crozier in viewing bureaucracy as first of all a national experience, the historic product of a specific culture and society—but equally important as an institutional experience. See Crozier, *The Bureaucratic Phenomenon*, Chicago, 1967, pp. 1–9, 145–269.

istry offices during the reign of Alexander II. The youngest group includes men who generally did not attain high positions until the very end of the reign, and who often went on to play leading roles in the ministry in the decades after 1881 (Table 2).[23] The average age of the officials upon promotion to the fifth rank (*Statskii sovetnik*—equivalent of a military rank between colonel and general) was 36.5 years. This remarkable figure compares most favorably with the age span of 43–52 offered by John Armstrong as a general guideline for the attainment of high office by the European administrative elite (England, France, Germany, and Russia) over several centuries.[24]

The emergence of a new generation of bureaucrats (signified by group II of Table 2) shows the pivotal nature of the reign of Alexander II in Russia's institutional and social history from 1825 to the October Manifesto of 1905. This twenty-five-year period (1855–81) saw the rise and decline of "enlightened" bureaucrats, the attainment of high office by their more conservative contemporaries, as well as the formative early careers of such later ministry conservative nobles as V. K. Plehve and P. D. Durnovo (represented in group III of Table 2). That progressive bureaucrats had their formative career experience under Nicholas I, while reactionaries had theirs under Alexander II, suggests that developments within the bureaucracy were more complex during both reigns than is often implied by uncritical periodizations and labels.

The high officials of the Ministry of Internal Affairs were predominantly the sons of hereditary members of the *dvorianstvo*. Of the eighty-seven men, seventy-seven (88.5%) were born into the *dvorianstvo*, four men (4.6%) were born into the merchant class, three men (3.4%) were sons of clergymen, one (1.1%) was the son of a non-commissioned officer, one (1.1%) the son of a low-ranking *chinovnik* who had not attained hereditary noble status, and one (1.1%) the son of a foreigner who later took Russian citizenship. As far as can be ascertained, only three men were born with titles, although another three earned titles (as counts) during their careers.

That so many of the men were born into the *dvorianstvo* may mean that they were only second-generation noblemen. Or it may mean that their ancestors had acquired hereditary nobility status as a result of service at any time during the preceding three centuries. The information is difficult to trace because it is not provided in the personnel

23. All tables are derived from the *formuliarnye spiski* discussed in Note 2 above, RBS, and memoirs.

24. John A. Armstrong, *The European Administrative Elite*, Princeton, 1973, p. 239.

TABLE X-2

Age of Ministry of Internal Affairs High Officials,
1855–1881

	I	II	III
Year of birth	1785–1815	1815–35	1835–50
Number of officials	16	62	8
%	18.6	72.1	9.3

SOURCE: See note 23.

records. A check of several genealogies (*rodoslovnye knigi*) reveals that only a relatively small percentage (perhaps 15%) of the family names are traceable back before 1600. And among these, direct ancestral links can only be established in a handful of cases. Another modest group (10%) has identifiable ancestors who acquired hereditary status after 1600. Approximately two-thirds of the men have family names that do not appear in the various genealogies.[25] This indicates that many of the ministry officials descended from families which acquired their hereditary status as recently as the eighteenth or nineteenth centuries. The ennoblement of most of these families was therefore a function of the continuous expansion of the service nobility in the eighteenth century beginning with the policies of Peter the Great.[26]

Memoir literature reveals that some of these men came from provincial families of small or medium landowners or local officials.[27] These men were imbued at an early age with the need to attain *chin*, to

25. See for example, P. Dolgorukov, *Rossiiskaia rodoslovnaia kniga*, 4 parts, St. Petersburg, 1854–57; A. Bobrinskoi, *Dvorianskie rody vnesennye v obshchii gerbovnik vserossiiskoi imperii*, 2 parts, St. Petersburg, 1890; and *Russkaia rodoslovnaia kniga izdanie "Russkoi stariny"*, 2 vols., St. Petersburg, 1873 and 1875.

26. On the history and expansion of the service nobility in the eighteenth century, see especially, Troitskii, *Russkii absoliutizm, passim*; and Brenda Meehan-Waters, "The Russian Aristocracy and the Reforms of Peter the Great," *Canadian-American Slavic Studies* 8 (Summer 1974): 288–302; also Robert E. Jones, *The Emancipation of the Russian Nobility, 1762–1785*, Princeton, 1973.

27. V. A. Insarskii, "Zapiski Vasiliia Antonovicha Insarskogo," *Russkaia starina* 81 (January 1894): 4–20; Tolstoi, "Zapiski," pp. 5–10; [signed A. K.], "Mezhdu strokami odnogo formuliarnogo spiska 1823–1881," *Russkaia starina* 32 (1881): 817–55; B. N. Chicherin, *Vospominaniia Borisa Nikolaevicha Chicherina, Moskva sorokovykh godov*, Moscow, 1929, *passim*.

pursue their educations and to make a successful career in the state apparatus, preferably in St. Petersburg. With a few exceptions, even the officials whose direct lineage can be traced as far back as the thirteenth century, men such as P. A. Valuev, shared the financial problems and career ambitions of the offspring of the more recently ennobled service *dvorianstvo*. In a society marked by its lack of corporate institutions, professional associations, and employment opportunities in private enterprise, both the older and newer hereditary *dvoriane* were dependent on state service for livelihood and status. This fact helps explain the enduring statism of many bureaucrats and their willingness to sacrifice on specific issues the interests of some members of their legal class.

If 100 souls or 500 *desiatiny*, the amount required to gain voting rights in the Provincial Assemblies of the Nobility, are taken as a standard of what was required for the maintenance of an extremely modest life style on income from the land, two-thirds of the officials may be considered as falling below that standard, or landless. Table 3 shows the breakdown of property holdings of the ministry officials.[28] In a number of cases a small amount of property was later acquired either by purchase or award, and a very small number married women possessing small amounts of property. As Walter Pintner has shown for the mid-century civil service as a whole, there is no correlation between landownership and the attainment of either high office or rank or conversely between the holding of high office and the subsequent acquisition of land.[29] Not only were most of the men not tied to economic interests based on property ownership, but these officials could and did attain any of the highest posts in the ministerial hierarchy.

The religious affiliation of the officials was solidly Russian Orthodox. Seventy-six (88.3%) were of this faith, and the remainder were predominantly Lutheran—nine men (10.3%). One man was listed as a member of the Uniate Church and one as a member of the Armenian-Gregorian Church. Though telling us nothing of the depth of the men's religious feeling, the figures do reflect the existence of an important German-Lutheran group in the Russian bureaucracy as well

28. Assessing the significance of the property holdings listed in the *spiski* is difficult because of the absence of uniform categories in the listings. Sometimes the number of serfs is listed and other times amounts of land. It is not clear whether officials with only land listed did not actually own serfs as well. If in fact those with landholdings did not own serfs, it would imply that the civil servants were even less well off than my table indicates.

29. Pintner, "Social Characteristics," p. 440.

Daniel T. Orlovsky

TABLE X-3

Property Holdings of Ministry of
Internal Affairs Officials

Hereditary Property	Officials (N = 71)	%
None of any kind	44	61
Less than 100 souls or 500 *desiatiny*	4	5.6
100–500 souls or 500–2,000 *desiatiny*	14	19.4
Over 500 souls or 2,000 *desiatiny*	9	12.9

SOURCE: See note 23.

as the discrimination against other minority religions in the service statutes.[30]

By the end of the Crimean War, the formal educational attainments of Russia's civil servants had been radically transformed.[31] High officeholders of the first four decades of the nineteenth century would most likely have been educated in private institutions, in the military, or at home. Their formal education consisted of the most basic and general subjects, and their preparation for administrative work was developed through experience on the job. This situation was a hold-over from the late appearance in Russia of a developed system of higher educational institutions and the seventeenth- and eighteenth-century Russian tradition of "on-the-job training" that has been ad-

30. Zaionchkovskii gives the following number of "Germans" in the highest government organs for 1853: State Council, 16.3%; Senate, 10.8%; Committee of Ministers, 11.1%; assistant ministers and directors of departments, 15.2%. Thus, the number of Lutherans seems to have decreased slightly at the assistant-minister and department-director levels during the Reform Era. Rowney finds only 6% Lutherans among high MVD managers in 1905. Zaionchkovskii, "Vysshaia biurokratiia," pp. 157, 159, 161–62; Rowney, "Higher Civil Servants," p. 103.

31. See James E. Flynn, "The Universities, the Gentry and the Russian Imperial Services, 1815–1825," *Canadian Slavic Studies* 2 (Winter 1968): 486–503 and Walter Pintner's analysis in this volume. Also, Patrick L. Alston, *Education and the State in Tsarist Russia,* Stanford, 1969; Torke, "Das russische Beamtentum," pp. 137–73; and Allen Sinel, *The Classroom and the Chancellery: State Educational Reform in Russia under Count Dmitry Tolstoi,* Cambridge, Mass., 1973, pp. 1–33; Also, Wortman, *Development of a Russian Legal Consciousness,* pp. 35–50.

mirably described in the recent work of S. M. Troitskii.[32] As Walter Pintner has shown, with the various educational reforms accomplished during the reign of Nicholas I, the situation began to change rapidly. New universities, such elite institutions as the Imperial Lycée at Tsarskoe Selo and the Imperial School of Jurisprudence, and a system of state secondary schools were established. The goal was to provide educated servitors for the rapidly growing state apparatus—both at the center and in the provinces,[33] and by the 1840s the new system was already bearing fruit for the Ministry of Internal Affairs, as can be seen from Table 4. The figures indicate that approximately 75 percent of the officials were graduates of higher, nonmilitary institutions of learning, and that a very small percentage, about 6 percent, had only received secondary educations.

The statutes on state service in the Digest of Laws provided the legal mechanism for rich and poor noblemen alike to launch their careers with advantages largely unavailable to the other estates in Russian society.[34] The state needed officials, and *dvoriane* had both the legal right to enter the service and either a monopoly or high priority on admission to the state institutions of higher education. Graduates of these institutions were immediately given the twelfth, tenth, or ninth *chin* depending on their standing in the graduating class.[35] These graduates thus began their careers at levels barely, if ever, attainable in a lifetime for most *chinovniki*.

From a formal point of view, Russia seemed to be emulating the experience of Prussia, where the state universities and particularly the juridical faculties were producing a professional class of technically competent civil servants.[36] Yet the Russian institutions of higher education were not wholly successful in instilling either the technical

32. Troitskii, *Russkii absoliutizm*, pp. 267–95. For the seventeenth century, see B. Plavsic's discussion in this volume.

33. Functionally, the educational reforms of the early nineteenth century played a role similar to that of the eighteenth-century reforms. In both cases the state viewed the educational experience as the first step on the service ladder. Thus, the junker schools of the eighteenth century may be seen as a more primitive version of the later universities in terms of their function as preparatory schools for officials.

34. *Polnyi svod zakonov rossiiskoi imperii*, 16 vols., St. Petersburg, 1857, Vol. 3, Pt. 1, *Ustav o sluzhbe grazhdanskoi po opredeleniiu ot pravitel'stva* (hereafter cited as *Svod zakonov*, 1857), arts. 1–87 (*o priniatii v grazhdanskuiu sluzhbu i opredelenii k dolzhnostiam*). Also, Torke, "Das russische Beamtentum," pp. 97–102.

35. *Svod zakonov*, 1857, Vol. 3, arts. 88–351. These articles discuss the service rights pertaining to all the empire's educational institutions, including the rights to enter service and to receive rank upon graduation.

36. Torke, "Das russische Beamtentum," pp. 1–48; Rosenberg, *Bureaucracy, Aristocracy and Autocracy*, pp. 46–74, 137–228.

Daniel T. Orlovsky

TABLE X-4

Educational Attainments of the MVD Officials

Education	Officials (N = 85)	%
Imperial Lycée, Tsarskoe	13	15.3
University (Russian)	39	45.9
Imperial School of Jurisprudence	6	7.1
Other elite Lycées or schools	2	2.3
Military schools	15	17.6
Religious Institutions	2	2.3
Institute of the Corps of Engineers	2	2.3
Privately educated	2	2.3
University (foreign)	1	1.2
Other (secondary education only)	3	3.5

SOURCE: See note 23.

competence or the ethos of their Prussian counterparts. This is not the place to analyze Russian higher education in the nineteenth century. Hans-Joachim Torke has already shown that the Russian system in the first half of that century, for several reasons, failed to produce bureaucrats on the Prussian model.[37] First, beginning with Speranskii's early reforms there was an overemphasis on general education as opposed to specialization. The curricula were unfocused and aimed at providing a smattering of general knowledge; juridical and other subjects relevant to future administrators were either ignored or underemphasized. But even more telling was the nature of Russian juridical education during this period. While the establishment of juridical education came to be regarded as an important goal of the state, and separate faculties and schools were created, the quality of the training itself proved to be formalistic, dry, and uninspiring, largely unsuited to the creation of a class of critically thinking jurists, the backbone of the classic *Rechtsstaat*, Prussian bureaucracy.[38]

Memoirs of student life at the universities and the Imperial School

37. Torke, "Das russische Beamtentum," pp. 102–73.
38. This view differs from Wortman's, *Development of a Russian Legal Consciousness*, in

of Jurisprudence offer a stark picture of Russian legal training, which consisted often of learning sections of the Digest of Laws by rote.[39] In the words of the art critic V. V. Stasov, a graduate of the Imperial School of Jurisprudence, the students were mainly concerned with their career prospects as opposed to substantive legal issues and how these might apply to Russia.[40] Although some recipients of Russian legal education are counted among the "enlightened" bureaucrats of the reform era, it is a mistake to view the fact that Russia had more civil-servant graduates of juridical faculties as a sign of any overall increase of progressive views within the bureaucracy or of any trend toward a "jurist monopoly."[41] Some of the most notorious upholders of the autocratic principle, statism, and various traditional views were, as shall be shown, not only graduates of these same faculties, but men who worked for a time in the same new judicial organs created in 1864 that they later tried so diligently to undermine.

Although a small number of Ministry of Internal Affairs positions required specialized or technical education (e.g. medical degrees for work in the Medicine Department or Council, engineering training for construction and public works, formal academic training for geographical surveys, statistical work, and certain kinds of censorship), the majority of high ministry officials must be considered generalists.[42] Only within that broad category can further distinction be

---

that he finds, at least within the judicial organs, such a class of jurists to have emerged by the Reform Era from Russia's institutions of higher learning (particularly from the Imperial School of Jurisprudence and the universities). These different interpretations only underline the difficulties inherent in applying generalizations based on the experience of one institution to the bureaucracy as a whole or to other institutions.

39. See, for example, Chicherin, *Vospominaniia- Moskva sorokovykh godov*, pp. 1–70 and *passim*; K. K. Arsen'ev, "Vospominaniia K. K. Arsen'eva ob Uchilishche Pravovedeniia 1849–1855" *Russkaia starina* 50 (April 1886): 199–220; V. V. Stasov, "Uchilishche Pravovedeniia sorok let tomu nazad 1836–1842," *Russkaia starina* 29 (1880): 1015–42; 30 (1881): 393–422, 573–602; 31 (1881): 247–62. Also Charles and Barbara Jelavich, *The Education of a Russian Statesman: The Memoirs of Nicholas Karlovich Giers*, Berkeley and Los Angeles, 1962.

40. Of course, one could argue that careerism among law students is hardly an unusual phenomenon. See Stasov, "Uchilishche Pravovedeniia," pp. 1030–31, 1035–36; and Arsen'ev, "Vospominaniia," pp. 215–17.

41. Again, Wortman, *Development of a Russian Legal Consciousness*, convincingly shows for the judicial organs a significant increase in officials with higher legal education by the late 1850s. These men seem to have differed in ethos from many of their contemporaries with similar educations who worked in other sectors of the bureaucracy. Leikina-Svirskaia, *Intelligentsiia v Rossii*, p. 77, shows that by 1869, 50.7 percent of the students of Russia's eight universities were enrolled in juridical faculties.

42. In some respects, the Russian experience in the mid-nineteenth century may be compared to Britain's historical reliance upon generally educated civil servants. For an

made. There is little evidence that the formal education of these men imparted either expertise or technical competence, or that they were seen by their service superiors as having such skills. The tradition of on-the-job training continued in what was essentially a generalist ministry. Officials became "expert" on certain kinds of administrative problems later in their careers after they had acquired working experience. V. I. Insarskii, one of the young, successful career officials from the provinces, whose rise began in the Ministry of State Domains under Count P. D. Kiselev, and who later served as director of the Moscow Post Office and in the Council of the Minister of Internal Affairs, summarized the situation well. In his view, "what was required (in the Russian bureaucracy) was able men (*sposobnye liudi*), not experts or specialists, that is, people who could get things done whatever they might be and however necessary."[43] For Insarskii, the specialists who did exist within the ministry were largely incompetent when it came to "affairs," and he thought that they should by all means be kept from both current matters and anything outside their own narrow fields of competence. The Ministry of Internal Affairs with its diverse and growing functions and general police and administrative responsibilities would become more and more a suitable home for this kind of "talented" official.

P. A. Valuev (minister of internal affairs, 1861–68) once wrote that the laws on promotion in the Digest of Laws were "outworn arithmetic formulas," largely responsible for the low quality of the Russian civil service during the first half of the nineteenth century.[44] According to Valuev, the system instituted by Peter the Great was called forth to meet specific historical requirements and factors, such as the persistence of *mestnichestvo*, no longer relevant for Russia as a European state.[45] For him, the only result of the "time-in-grade" requirements was that the highly talented no longer held any advantage over the incompetent—"who remain in their positions by that unlimited indulgence which pervades the spirit of all Russian administrative chiefs (*nachal'niki*)."[46]

---

enlightening discussion of the educational background of the English, French, and German administrative elites, see Armstrong, *The European Administrative Elite*, pp. 127–251.

43. See Insarskii, "Zapiski" (second installment), pp. 10–11; Shumakher, "Pozdnyia vospominaniia," pp. 109–22; Lincoln, "Daily Life," *passim*.

44. P. A. Valuev, "Otryvki iz zamechanii o priadkoi grazhdanskoi sluzhby v Rossii (1845?)," TsGIA, Fond 908, op. 1, d. 24, fol. 26.

45. Ibid., fols. 26–31.

46. Ibid., fols. 26–31.

Valuev's claims were echoed by other contemporaries, and have been generally accepted by today's historians as one of the pervasive weaknesses of the Russian administration.[47] The problem may be formulated as follows. Did the so-called man of talent find insurmountable legal obstacles to the rapid attainment of either rank or responsible positions in the civil service hierarchy? The evidence for the Ministry of Internal Affairs, at least, indicates that this was not the case. The personnel records of the ministry officials reveal a pattern of rapid promotion, often in contravention of the laws, beginning in the earliest stages of their careers. This trend may be observed in the administration as a whole throughout the 1840s and 1850s, but it becomes even more pronounced in the ministry after the 1861 Peasant Emancipation during Valuev's tenure as minister.

   According to law, promotion from rank fourteen through five (collegiate assessor to state councilor) was to be governed by time-in-grade intervals (*vysluga*) applied "equally for all servitors."[48] (See Table 5.)[49] All promotions to rank four (actual state councilor) and above were to be awarded without reference to time-in-grade and were subject to the tsar's approval.[50] According to these rules, if a man entered service at rank fourteen, it would have taken twenty-four years to reach the fifth rank (state councilor), the rank that prior to 1856 secured hereditary noble status and which by the Tables of Organization (*shtaty*) was the prerequisite for holding a position at the vice-director level of a ministerial department. As noted above, most of the ministry officials, by virtue of their education, entered service at ranks twelve, ten, or nine. Assuming most officials began service at age twenty, we see that higher civil service positions were theoretically

47. For an excellent discussion of rank, see Torke, "Das russische Beamtentum," pp. 48–96. Also Richard Pipes, *Russia Under the Old Regime*, New York, 1974, pp. 135–37. Pipes's analysis is on the whole correct, but he overemphasizes the idea of automatic promotion for time in grade, and underestimates the possibilities, in certain institutions at least, of very rapid promotion. Helju Aulik Bennett, in "The *Chin* System and the *Raznochintsy* in the Government of Alexander III, 1881–1894," Ph.D. dissertation, University of California, Berkeley, 1971, pp. 50–80, also overemphasizes obstacles to rapid promotion.

48. *Svod zakonov*, 1857, Vol. 3, art. 664. It must be remembered that time-in-grade intervals differed according to social class and educational attainment. The discussion here concerns only members of the highest *razriad*, that is, individuals who had completed institutions of higher education. Members of the *dvorianstvo* and others with only secondary or primary educations had, theoretically, to endure even longer time-in-grade intervals.

49. Ibid., arts. 664–68.

50. Ibid., art. 669.

TABLE X-5

Time-in-Grade Intervals for Table of Ranks

From Rank	To Rank	Interval	(years)
14	12	3	
12	10	3	
10	9	3	
9	8	3	
8	7	4	
7	6	4	
6	5	4	

SOURCE: See note 49.

not attained until a man was in his late thirties or early forties after as much as two decades of bureaucratic labor.[51] As mentioned earlier, even this figure compares favorably with the experience of Western Europe.

The Russian service statutes provided opportunities for "skillful people" or outright favorites to be propelled up the service ladder at a much faster rate, however. The most important legal alternative to time in grade was that of meritorious promotion "for excellence" (*za otlichie*). By this concept (*zasluga* as opposed to *vysluga*) the law allowed the time-in-grade intervals in specific cases to be "shortened by one year" for *chinovniki* "distinguished by their special labors and talents" (*darovaniia*).[52] The mechanism by which such promotions were made was petition of the immediate hierarchical superior listing specific cause followed by approval of the main chief of the institu-

51. It seems that even the full time-in-grade requirement would have placed Russian officials in high posts at ages equivalent to Armstrong's estimate of forty-three to fifty-two years of age for European administrative elites. However, fulfilling the time-in-grade requirement did not automatically mean promotion—that is, there were no doubt many "unsuccessful" *chinovniki* who remained "eternal titular councilors." On the other hand, as the data reveal, there was an acute shortage of capable men at the top, and ministers could not afford to wait out time-in-grade intervals to raise men to responsible positions.

52. *Svod zakonov*, 1857, Vol. 3, art. 665.

tion.[53] This gave ministers considerable powers to promote men more rapidly than prescribed by the *vysluga* intervals. Personal relationships with one's superiors were often decisive in influencing the course of a career. The evidence reveals a pattern of continuous intervention by superiors and ministers to promote men in this way. The possibilitiy of such intervention, of course, could only invite abuses as well as the rapid advancement of genuinely talented men.

To illustrate the rapidity of promotions and how the laws were both used and circumvented and how these ministry officials reached high positions beginning in the early 1840s, the rates of their promotion may be examined. Let us assume rank nine (titular councilor, equivalent to military captain) to be the takeoff point for a successful career. This was the rank given to the highest graduates of the elite schools as they entered the service. For those beginning at ranks ten, twelve, or fourteen (eleven and thirteen were never used) attainment of rank nine meant the end of one's apprenticeship and the opening up of possibilities similar to those open to men beginning at that rank. As mentioned earlier, rank five (state councilor, equivalent to military rank between colonel and brigadier general) was the legal prerequisite for the class of Ministry of Internal Affairs office under consideration here. According to the *vysluga* system of promotion, the time-in-grade intervals for the four promotions between ranks nine and five add up to fifteen years. Assuming that each of the four promotions was "for excellence" (the *zasluga* principle), one year can be subtracted from each interval resulting in a period of eleven years. By law it was thus possible for a man to reach rank five at quite an early age, especially if his career began at rank nine. The *average* period between these two ranks for sixty-two officials for whom data exist was 10.9 years. In addition, almost all of the men received the next highest rank (four—actual state councilor—outside the *vysluga* system by definition) within another two or three years. Of the four promotions necessary in each case to attain rank five, anywhere from two to four were recorded "for excellence." What is even more striking is that the 10.9 figure, already less than the minimum legal interval, is only an average. There were no less than twenty-four examples of men progressing from rank nine to five in even shorter periods, ranging from six to ten years (Makov six years, Barykov seven years, Zaika eight years, Palen eight years, Shumakher nine years, etc.).

These rapid promotions were not peculiar to the Ministry of Internal Affairs, since some men served elsewhere early in their careers. How-

53. Ibid.

ever, the increasing pressures on the state apparatus and particularly on the ministry after the Crimean War (and Emancipation) are reflected in a marked increase in rapid promotions during the years of the Valuev ministry (1861–68). The chronic Russian shortage of capable administrators could not be solved alone by the gradual influx of the generation of highly educated men. The demands made upon the ministry were increasing almost geometrically, and ministers chose to adhere selectively to the formal aspects of the service statutes.

There were two other important points in the service statutes that permitted ministers a degree of freedom from the excessive formalism of the law requiring equivalence of rank and the class of office (*klass dolzhnosti*). First an individual could hold an office (*dolzhnost'*) the class of which could be up to two ranks higher than his *chin*.[54] This decision was left to the minister "on the basis of current needs" within the ministry.[55] In addition, a man could be promoted one rank above the class of his office, thus setting up the possibility of his being given an even higher office should the "need" arise.[56] Furthermore, one did not have to be the legally confirmed (*utverzhdennyi*) occupant of an office in order to carry out its functions. The personnel records offer many instances of appointments as "acting" holder of a given office. These features of the service statutes help account for the dynamism in career patterns of the successful ministry officials. Men moved temporarily up the functional ladder, and kept moving upward rather than either stagnating at middle-level posts or moving back down one step in the hierarchy. In short, in the Ministry of Internal Affairs at least, "temporary needs" were a permanent condition.

And this was not all, because the records contain examples of promotions that seem to defy even these elastic rules. There are instances of men receiving as many as five rank promotions in the short period of five years. This circumvention of Russia's legal formalism was hardly a paradox to the ministers involved. In order to attain any desirable degree of efficiency or even simply to have "reliable" men as the executors of his will, the minister, whose own position was precarious, had to promote men in the ways described above. "Skillful and trustworthy" men were promoted quickly in the hope that they would facilitate the realization of the minister's own political goals. This was the only alternative to a massive structural transformation

54. Ibid., art. 360. See also arts. 361–69.
55. Ibid., art. 360.
56. Ibid., art. 556.

of the Russian administrative system, a possibility never considered realistic during the reign of Alexander II.[57]

In addition to the rules on promotions, an elaborate system of awards and gifts was written into the Digest of Laws.[58] There were Orders, each with several degrees and decorations, medals, marks of excellence, monetary awards of various kinds, and other gifts ranging from land to gold snuffboxes. Often in the personnel records there are simple notations of approval or thanks for specific services either in the name of the minister or the tsar himself. Each order carried certain legal privileges, usually of no practical meaning, and the recipients often had to pay sums of money, at times not readily available, to receive the medals and ribbons. From this point of view, cash awards or salary supplements were doubtless more desirable for the already financially pressed officials.

Why then did the nonmonetary awards exist at all, and why are the personnel records of the successful ministry officials littered with perhaps a dozen examples for each person? The answer must be sought in notions of esteem and approval important both to the servitor and the society in which he lived. Awards were constant reminders to the officials and those around him—his colleagues—that he was valued by his superiors. Failure to receive expected rewards would be taken as a sign that something was amiss in one's career. Wearing the dress uniform of the administrative institution, the orders and medals were displayed for all to see, and this, as Lazarevskii suggests, greatly enhanced the individual's self-esteem and sense of belonging.[59] These and other intangibles to some degree made up for the low salaries, the sense of precariousness, and the ever-present curse of domination from above that might profoundly and negatively affect the course of their careers at any moment. In any case, it is clear from personnel records that a constant flow of awards always accompanied a successful career.

For the successful bureaucrat whose career had already been launched during the decades of Nicholas I's reign, a "reputation" for capability

57. N. I. Lazarevskii, *Lektsii po russkomu gosudarstvennomu pravu*, Vol. 2, *Administrativnoe pravo*, St. Petersburg, 1910, pp. 65–137. Apparently the efficacy of the Table of Ranks was discussed in a number of commissions during the second half of the nineteenth century. The system was never altered, however. See also Iu. B. Solov'ev, *Samoderzhavie i dvorianstvo v kontse XIX veka*, Leningrad, 1973.

58. *Svod zakonov*, 1857, Vol. 3, arts. 1154–86. See also Vol. 1, Bk. 6, arts. 1–869.

59. Lazarevskii, *Lektsii*, pp. 113–120; Torke, "Das russische Beamtentum," pp. 173–222; see also Chap. 7 (Bennett) above.

and either personal knowledge or awareness of this reputation by people who mattered were the best guarantees of continued success after the Crimean War. In its extreme forms this was the notorious principle of protection (*pokrovitel'stvo*), which seems to have been always operative in Russian bureaucratic history. The government's mobilization for reform provided new fields for careerism and ever-increasing amounts of work for existing institutions. Protection would be practiced on a larger and less personal scale to provide staff for a ministry that had expanded greatly and accumulated many new functions during the 1850s and 1860s. The personnel records reveal a quickening of pace in the advancement of bureaucratic careers as men were brought into the ministry to work on the Peasant Emancipation and its implementation, to gather statistical information and reliable intelligence on conditions in the provinces, to serve as provincial governors, to work on the multitude of legislative proposals for further reform, and finally to staff such important new institutions as the Main Directorate of Press Affairs. Though the quality of their education may be questioned, there is no doubt that these men had skills which improved the quality of work performed at high levels of the ministry.[60] There is also no doubt that they gave conservative support to the autocratic principle and acted as a brake on the reformist tendencies displayed by ministry officials prior to Valuev's ascendency. The relationship of these men to the political concerns of the Ministry of Internal Affairs and the autocracy can best be explored in conjunction with their career patterns and the appointment policies of the ministers of internal affairs during Alexander's reign.

It is hard to generalize about the extraordinarily diverse career patterns of the ministry officials. Very few men served their entire careers in either the central or provincial organs of this ministry. Frequent transfers from institution to institution within the government were prevalent at the lower and middle levels of the civil-service rank hierarchy. Once a man had reached one of the middle- or higher-level positions in the ministry, however, he usually remained in the ministry for the remainder of his active career. It was normal for men to be enlisted from outside the ministry to occupy such important posts as assistant minister, member of the Council of the Minister, or member of the Council of the Main Directorate of Press Affairs. The best

60. This does not mean, of course, that the dysfunctions peculiar to the ministry and the Russian bureaucracy as a whole disappeared. On the contrary, as I try to show elsewhere ("Ministerial Power and Russian Autocracy"), the Ministry of Internal Affairs continued to have great difficulty coping with its responsibilities after 1861, and was never able to solve certain endemic structural and procedural problems.

examples of longevity and career stability are found within the ministerial departments, where for example N. A. Miliutin (1853–59) and A. D. Shumakher (1859–79) together held the directorship of the Economic Department for a total of twenty-seven years.[61] Yet even in the highly specialized departments, where expertise in particular matters would seem to be of importance, there are examples of outside appointments to directorships and vice-directorships. Although in some cases these outside men had relevant prior experience, it was not unusual for them to have had little knowledge of either departmental responsibilities or procedures.

For most high-level appointments, personal connections, recommendations, prior work with the minister in another institution, or the minister's political motives were of primary importance. For example, P. A. Valuev appointed many men (D. N. Tolstoi—director of the Department of Executive Police, V. I. Fuks—member of the Council of the Main Directorate of Press Affairs, etc.) to high posts on the basis of personal knowledge of their talents and political views gained during periods of joint service in both the Baltic region and in the Ministry of State Domains.[62] Although administrative and drafting skills as well as political reliability were of the utmost importance to Valuev, he also reserved certain appointments for socially prominent members of the *dvorianstvo*. This drew criticism from the progressive minister of education A. D. Golovnin, who accepted the commonly held view of Valuev as defender of *dvorianstvo* interests after the abolition of serfdom in 1861.[63] Golovnin singled out the appointments of several members of the Shuvalov family, Prince A. B. Lobanov-Rostovskii and a large number of provincial governors and vice-governors, and claimed that Valuev "was guided often not by the skills of the individual, but by his court and social connections, position in society . . . and that he tried to create for himself at the court and in the aristocratic section of society a party and support."[64] A. E. Timashev (minister of internal affairs, 1868–78), himself a general and former second-in-command of the Third Section and Corps of Gendarmes, liked to appoint conservative military men to certain high ministerial posts. Similarly, M. T. Loris-Melikov, during his brief tenure as minister of internal affairs (1880–81), appointed trusted sub-

61. For Miliutin's service record, see TsGIA Fond 1,162 op. 6, d. 335, fols. 46–78; Shumakher's record is in TsGIA, Fond 1,284, op. 76, d. 76, fols. 175–232.
62. Material on Tolstoi's career is found in Tolstoi, "Zapiski," pp. 5–33; Fuks's service record is located in TsGIA, Fond 776, op. 3, d. 934, fols. 119–44.
63. TsGIA, Fond 851 (Collection of A. V. Golovnin), op. 1, d. 8, fols. 9–16.
64. Ibid., fols. 14–15.

ordinates from earlier assignments who shared his reformist political conceptions.

The early careers of the ministry officials were marked by frequent transfers from ministry to ministry and between the provinces and St. Petersburg. Once an individual had attained a place in one of the central St. Petersburg organs however, it was very rare for him to return to a provincial post. Any subsequent work in the provinces (and this occurred frequently) would be done as an agent of a central ministry department. Usually, the official would be on a special mission of a supervisory or information-gathering nature. In some cases, the official's early career was spent in the military and a transfer to the civil service arranged because of "poor health" or other personal reasons. An examination of the first civil-service positions held by the ministry officials reveals that the path to the highest posts in the ministry was indeed winding. Aside from a very small percentage (approximately 7 percent) who began service in the central ministry organs, officials started their careers in such diverse places as the chanceries of provincial civil governors and governors-general, the various departments of the Senate, the various sections of His Majesty's Own Chancellery (particularly the Second Section responsible for codification), the central and provincial organs of other ministries (particularly State Domains, Finance, and Justice), the Diplomatic Corps, the State Controller's Office, the State Chancellery, the provincial and district corporate bodies of the *dvorianstvo*, the Corps of Engineers, and the Postal Institutions.

After these initial posts the officials usually made several changes in order to find positions offering the best potential for security and future advancement in the St. Petersburg bureaucratic world. In these early stages, the civil servant had little, if any, responsibility; even with his university or Lycée education he was usually little more than a clerk or copyist, and was not yet trusted to "expedite affairs" (that is, participate in the process of *deloproizvodstvo*). The interests or particular skills of the young official, if indeed he had any at this early stage, were rarely taken into account for work assignments. Memoirs reveal that the young officials often viewed their initial work assignments as a burdensome necessity.[65] It is only later in the career, after several promotions up the ladder of ranks and offices, that any specialization or accumulation of substantive work experience in a given area

---

65. Insarskii, "Zapiski," pp. 13–16; Shumakher, "Pozdnyia vospominaniia," pp. 112–15; [signed A. K.] "Mezhdu strokami," pp. 820–25. Insarskii's service record is found in TsGIA, Fond 1,284, op. 50, d. 260.

of administration may be discerned. Although a reputation for skills in such a subject area was often a decisive factor in further advancement, it was always possible for an official to be shifted to a new subject area in the same or any other ministry.

Although the high officials in the ministry had diverse career experiences, it is possible to categorize these careers by taking into account all the offices held by an official, both in the ministry and elsewhere. Using the information in the personnel records and published materials, one can formulate the following six categories that represent distinct types of career patterns:

1. Career Ministry of Internal Affairs men—The career ministry man usually specialized in a subject area that required either a professional education qualification (such as a medical degree for high-ranking positions in the Medicine Department, etc.) or concentration on certain types of mixed administrative and economic problems involving the social estates, the cities, or even religious sects and non-Orthodox faiths. Most positions were in the Economic Department, the *Zemskii otdel* and the Department of Spiritual Affairs of Foreign Faiths. These men entered the service directly in the central ministry organs, and served their entire ministry careers in those organs. Their service records indicate, however, that they often spent time on missions in the provinces to collect data, conduct investigations, and supervise subordinate provincial officials. Interestingly, these departmental officials never rose above the level of office attained by virtue of their reputation for competence and specialized skills. They never became ministers, although their departmental work and service on legislative commissions often helped shape the content of significant legislation.[66]

2. Administrative generalists—Generalists were highly skilled administrators and personal aides to the minister. They were often brought into the ministry at mid-career to occupy such offices as assistant minister, director of the Department of General Affairs, or

---

66. In addition to Miliutin and Shumakher, F. L. Barykov, who directed the *Zemskii otdel* for a thirteen-year period (1869–82), may be seen as an example of this type. For Barykov, see TsGIA, Fond 1,284, op. 67, d. 186, fols. 19–38. The details of Miliutin's biography are well known and need not be elaborated here. Shumakher was a classic organization man who worked quietly and loyally behind the scenes with great impact on ministry policy. See his defense of Timashev and ministry policies in A. D. Shumakher, "Neskol'ko slov o g.-a. Timasheva i otnoshenii ego k obshchestvennym uchrezhdeniiam," *Vestnik Evropy* 6, No. 12 (1893): 846–57. For further details on the careers of these men and others mentioned in the categories below, see my dissertation, "Ministerial Power and Russian Autocracy," Chap. 5.

secretary of the Minister's Chancellery. In the Department of General Affairs they coordinated the disparate parts of the ministry and acted as the central ministry authority in all personnel matters, finances, and other kinds of record keeping. The secretary of the Chancellery set the minister's agenda and assisted in ordinary and secret matters requiring his personal attention. The assistant ministers acted as troubleshooters for the minister, although in several cases they also became trusted co-workers responsible for generating policy or legislative proposals.[67]

3. Military officers—An insignificant minority in the post-Crimean War Ministry of Internal Affairs, these men rarely worked in the ministry's central organs and therefore were out of the mainstream of ministry administrative work. They were used most often as especially trusted officials of Special Missions or as provincial governors (and of course as military governors-general). Sometimes their early careers involved investigative or police work in either the military or the Corps of Gendarmes.[68]

4. Censors—According to the empire's censorship law of 1865, primary censorship responsibility was shifted from the Ministry of Education to a new Ministry of Internal Affairs organ, the Main Directorate of Press Affairs.[69] The work of the council and its chief were closely supervised by Valuev, who regarded censorship as one of the

67. N. P. Mansurov served as director of the Department of General Affairs from 1866 to 1880. See TsGIA, Fond 1,162, op. 6, d. 313, fols. 193–220. L. S. Makov (TsGIA, Fond 1,162, op. 6, d. 309, fols. 40–67) and V. D. Zaika (TsGIA, Fond 1,284, op. 67, d. 174, fols. 122–140) served as secretary of the Minister's Chancery (1865–76) and as director of the Department of General Affairs (1880–83), respectively. Makov went on to become minister of internal affairs in 1878, an office that was clearly over his head and in which he performed lamentably. See my "Ministerial Power and Russian Autocracy," pp. 215–28. Noteworthy examples of assistant ministers are A. G. Troinitskii (TsGIA, Fond 1,162, op. 6, d. 555, fols. 51–80), who held that office from 1861 to 1867, and M. S. Kakhanov (TsGIA, Fond 1,162, op. 6, d. 230, fols. 78–98), assistant minister during Loris-Melikov's brief tenure as minister during 1880–81. Troinitskii worked on statistical and censorship matters and authored *Krepostnoe naselenie v Rossii po desiatoi narodnoi perepisei*, St. Petersburg, 1861. Kakhanov was one of Loris-Melikov's most trusted aides. He drafted many legislative proposals including the abortive "constitutional" project of 28 January 1881.

68. The best example would be M. R. Shidlovskii (TsGIA, Fond 1,284, op. 67, d. 132, fols. 46–61), who was appointed one of the two assistant ministers by his fellow general, Timashev, in 1871. Shidlovskii held this post for five years to the incredulity of men like Valuev who viewed it as just one more sign of the ministry's decline under Timashev. See P. A. Valuev, *Dnevnik P. A. Valueva ministra vnutrennykh del*, ed. P. A. Zaionchkovskii, 2 vols., Moscow, 1961, 2: 303.

69. See Charles Ruud, "The Russian Empire's New Censorship Law of 1865," *Canadian Slavic Studies* 3 (Summer 1969): 235–45.

ministry's most important functions.[70] The censors had varied service backgrounds and were usually enlisted into the ministry specifically for this work. Transfers between the regular ministry departments and the Main Directorate were rare, but as trusted appointees of the minister, the censors often performed a variety of special missions for him.[71] Also, censors often sat concurrently on the Council of the Minister, or did editorial or supervisory work on the ministry newspaper (*Northern Post*, 1861–68; *Government Messenger*, 1868–1917). The censors' career backgrounds included general administrative work, information gathering, and academic or literary pursuits. Although several had prior experience as censors elsewhere in the government, it is difficult on the whole to discern specific qualifications for these posts.[72] Significantly, Main Directorate censors appointed during Alexander's reign enjoyed great longevity in office and many continued to serve under his successors.[73]

Until the brief ascendancy of Loris-Melikov, the ministers of internal affairs used their censorship apparatus to combat "critical tendencies" among the educated classes. The Main Directorate put at the minister's disposal a number (six to eight) of relatively high-salaried positions guaranteed by the Table of Organization. These could be used to bring into the ministry talented men of known political views who could help the minister enforce his notion of what was permissible in print and what was a violation of the government's interests.[74]

5. Generalists with extended service in state provincial organs or in

70. When Valuev left the Ministry of Internal Affairs in 1868, he included the censorship problem among the four most important issues the government had to face. Valuev, *Dnevnik*, 2: 496–99. He reiterated this theme in many of his other writings.

71. Two exceptions were A. G. Lazarevskii, who served as vice-director of the Department of General Affairs (1863–66), and M. N. Pokhvisnev, who served as director of the Department of Executive Police (1863–66). On the former, see TsGIA, Fond 776, op. 4, d. 419, fols. 1–36; on the latter, TsGIA, Fond 1,284, op. 76, d. 47, fols. 5–34.

72. One might make a case for D. I. Kamenskii, who served early in his career as a censor in Kiev (TsGIA, Fond 776, op. 4, d. 213, fols. 92–101); V. V. Grigor'ev, Professor of Eastern Languages at St. Petersburg University (TsGIA, Fond 776, op. 11, d. 105, fols. 5ob.–32); and N. V. Varadinov, who wrote the official history of the Ministry of Internal Affairs cited above in note 1 (TsGIA, Fond 776, op. 2, d. 134, fols. 39–56).

73. Many, like E. M. Feoktistov and F. P. Elenev, remained in office into the 1880s and 1890s. See E. M. Feoktistov, *Za kulisami politiki i literatury 1848–1896, vospominaniia*, Leningrad, 1923; for Elenev, TsGIA, Fond 776, op. 4, d. 209, fols. 106–8, and Fond 777 (St. Petersburg Censorship Committee), op. 2, d. 134, fols. 39–56.

74. Typical of the censorship appointments made by Valuev and Timashev were V. I. Fuks (appointed in 1865: TsGIA, Fond 776, op. 3, d. 934, fols. 119–44) and D. P. Skuratov (appointed in 1878: TsGIA, Fond 777, op. 2, d. 112, fols. 41–46). One could also include P. D. Stremoukhov and M. R. Shidlovskii here, since both served as

dvorianstvo corporate bodies—These men were brought into the ministry after the Emancipation by Valuev and Timashev in their search for fresh talent and for men with close ties to the provincial *dvorianstvo* who might be willing to subordinate their sympathy for that class to state interests. Their willingness to seek or accept positions in the ministry and their espousal of the ministry's brand of statism that was opposed to both Slavophilism and gentry oligarchism makes them especially important for understanding the ministry's attitudes toward society during the Reform Era.[75]

6. Police and jurisconsult organs—Here the generational changes in ministry personnel and the relationship between personnel and ministry ideology and policy are most strikingly illustrated. Throughout

---

censors, but owing to the career patterns that preceded their becoming censors, I have placed them in other categories.

Fuks had worked with Valuev in the Ministry of State Domains prior to 1861, at which time Valuev brought him into the Ministry of Internal Affairs as an official of Special Missions attached to the Minister. Fuks was Valuev's trusted lieutenant on the commission that prepared the 1865 censorship law and was named an original member of the Main Directorate of Press Affairs. During his long service in the ministry he also worked on questions involving the State Peasantry, reform of the Ministry Table of Organization and Finances, supervision and reform of the St. Petersburg police and prisons, and the introduction of a censorship system in Poland. Later, in 1883, he published *Court and Police*, in which he set forth the pro-administration view of separation of powers and the conflict between the police and the post-1864 judicial system. See V. I. Fuks, *Sud i politsiia*, 2 vols., Moscow, 1889. The close relationship between censorship appointments and the political views of Valuev and Timashev was also apparent during Loris-Melikov's brief ministry. He tried to alter the policies of his predecessors and use the censorship to conciliate society and to aid in the reform process. To this end in 1880 he appointed N. S. Abaza (TsGIA, Fond 1,162, op. 6, d. 2, fols. 70–80) first to membership on the Supreme Executive Commission, and then to the office of chief of the Main Directorate of Press Affairs. Abaza was a man of proven administrative skill and progressive political views—and he was a relative of one of Loris-Melikov's group of "liberal" ministers, A. A. Abaza, the minister of finance. On Loris-Melikov's use of the censorship and the hostile reaction of high officials to his censorship policies, see P. A. Zaionchkovskii, *Krizis samoderzhaviia na rubezhe 1870–1880-x godov*, Moscow, 1964, pp. 262–69; and P. A. Valuev, *Dnevnik 1877–1884*, Petrograd, 1919, pp. 146–47.

75. Although Valuev appointed many socially prominent men of proven loyalty and little talent, he also brought several talented individuals of this category into the ministry. The best examples are B. A. Obukhov (TsGIA, Fond 1,284, op. 67, d. 72, fols. 5–25), and P. D. Stremoukhov (TsGIA, Fond 776, op. 4, d. 224, fols. 119–33). Both cases are instructive since the men served under both Valuev and Timashev (the former as governor of Pskov and assistant minister of internal affairs, and the latter as a member of the Council of the Minister and the Main Directorate of Press Affairs), and both left behind published evidence of their statist ideology held while serving in the government. See, for example, Obukhov, *Russkii administrator*; and P. D. Stremoukhov, "Iz vospominaniia o grafe P. A. Valueve," *Russkaia starina* 116 (November 1903): 273–93.

the 1860s and 1870s the directors of the Department of Executive Police were chosen on the basis of criteria similar to those at work for the other career categories discussed above.[76] General administrative skills, personal connections, political reliability, and experience in police or investigative work gained on the job were most important.[77] These directors might have held any number of high ministry posts, and most did. Their diverse career experiences, ranging from service in the diplomatic corps to the holding of provincial governorships, place these men within the parameters of the ministry career sample. As with the departmental officials discussed above, the police officials were men of narrow political vision. None was ever appointed either assistant minister or minister of internal affairs.

By the end of Alexander's reign however, new men appeared in the police organs who would leave an indelible mark on subsequent ministry history. These were younger men (born in the 1840s) best exemplified by P. N. Durnovo and V. K. Plehve.[78] They received their educations and formative early career experiences entirely during the reign of Alexander II and only attained high ministry office in 1880. Their early careers differed from their predecessors' in that both had juridical training and served as Ministry of Justice prosecutors (*prokurory*) in the regional courts created by the 1864 Judicial Reform. Both had therefore participated in the momentous struggle between

76. The five police directors during Alexander's reign prior to August 1880 were: S. R. Zhdanov (1855–61, TsGIA, Fond 1,349, op. 3, d. 786, fols. 77–86, and Fond 1,405, op. 63, d. 5,733, fols. 23–40); D. N. Tolstoi (1861–63, see Tolstoi "Zapiski," pp. 5–33); M. N. Pokhvisnev (1863–66, TsGIA, Fond 1,284, op. 76, d. 47); Baron I. O. Velio (1866–68 and 1880–81, TsGIA, Fond 1,162, op. 6, d. 77, fols. 55–80); and P. P. Kosagovskii (1868–80, TsGIA, Fond 1,284, op. 67, d. 139, fols. 101–16). Another key figure of this period was the ministry's first jurisconsult, P. T. Kititsyn (1867–80, TsGIA, Fond 1,291, op. 123, d. 102, fols. 42–59), who was appointed by Valuev, but who served in that office until Loris-Melikov came to power in 1880. Kititsyn worked on many legislative matters and authored significant memoranda and projects on administrative and police reform. He also chaired several small commissions that tried to ameliorate the growing conflict between the courts and the administration (especially the police). Kititsyn was unflinching in his support of administrative power as a principle and of the interests of the ministry as well as the government as a whole. On Kititsyn's reform projects of the late 1860s, see Baron S. A. Korf, *Administrativnaia iustitsiia v Rossii*, 2 vols., St. Petersburg, 1910, 1: 312–21. See also such memoranda as "Kratkii soobrazheniia po proektu ob ustroistve uezdnoi politsii," in TsGIA, Fond 908, op. 1, d. 277, and the projects and materials in Fond 908, op. 1, d. 274, d. 371, and d. 375.

77. Tolstoi's appointment resulted from his personal relationship to Valuev, who knew Tolstoi's capabilities well from periods of prior service together.

78. Plehve's service record is found in TsGIA, Fond 1,162, op. 6, d. 419, fols. 163–67ff. For Durnovo see TsGIA, Fond 1,284, op. 51, d. 261, fols. 110–122, 188–189.

the administration and the courts even before entering the Ministry of Internal Affairs, and clearly both sided with the primacy of administrative power.[79] Plehve and Durnovo dominated the ministry police structure during the 1880s and their policies helped solidify the ministry's position as a bulwark of autocracy. Most significantly, their ministry careers extended into the twentieth century and may be seen as a link between the Reform Era autocracy and that which survived the 1905 revolution. Both men were appointed ministers of internal affairs (Plehve in 1902 and Durnovo in 1905), and while holding that office earned reputations as enemies of reform, advocates of police repression, ardent believers in russification, and supporters of landed-gentry interests.[80]

In drawing conclusions about the social profiles and career patterns of the ministry officials, one is struck first by the fact that despite the influx beginning in the 1840s of younger, highly educated men, there is no evidence that there were enough "skilled" men to fill the most responsible positions in the Ministry of Internal Affairs hierarchy. Ministers and their subordinates (departmental directors and section chiefs) had to take an active and personal interest in middle- and high-level appointments in order to ensure a share of loyal and competent young career officials for the key positions. Without an aggressive appointments policy (such as those of Perovskii, Lanskoi, and Valuev), the formalistic promotions laws would have made operations exceedingly difficult.

Also, higher education was less important for imparting knowledge than as a means of controlling entrance to the closed bureaucratic world of those with the potential to reach high office. Neither technical nor professional training was yet a requirement for career success. General ability to get things done within the system, expertise gained from work experience, political reliability, and personal relationships were most important.

The history of ministry officialdom clearly reflects the history of the

79. These attitudes were carried forward into their initial Ministry of Internal Affairs appointments in 1881—Plehve as the director of the new and enlarged Department of State Police, and Durnovo as the head of the newly formed Judicial Section (this combined the old Jurisconsult Sections of the Ministry of Internal Affairs and the Corps of Gendarmes).

80. See, for example, V. I. Gurko, *Features and Figures of the Past: Government and Opinion in the Reign of Nicholas II*, Stanford, 1939, pp. 107–249, 438–58; Howard D. Mehlinger and John M. Thompson, *Count Witte and the Tsarist Government in the 1905 Revolution*, Bloomington, 1972, *passim*; and Wayne S. Santoni, "P. N. Durnovo as Minister of Internal Affairs in the Witte Cabinet: A Study in Suppression," Ph.D. dissertation, University of Kansas, 1968.

ministry as an institution and as a political actor during the reign of Alexander II. In the early 1840s the ministry central departments were managed by members of an older generation who lacked the motivation and skills to cope with the increasing administrative and legislative demands made upon the ministry. At that time a younger, highly educated generation entered the ministry and other state institutions and rose quickly through the ranks. The influx of new men continued throughout the 1850s and 1860s. The ministry's administrative and legislative capabilities increased immediately as these men moved into middle- and high-level departmental positions in the ministry hierarchy. The rise of these men and their successful work in the ministry coincided with, and was related to, the general elevation of the ministry's political role within the autocracy. The most progressive and vocal of these men—the so-called "enlightened" bureaucrats were a small, but influential minority in the ministry that virtually disappeared after 1861.

Under Valuev in the early 1860s the ministry moved from military advocacy of social reform to concern with public order, political crimes, and defense of the autocratic principle against society as well as the rival principles expressed by the new judicial and *zemstvo* institutions.[81] As minister, Valuev became an eloquent advocate of the primacy of administrative and police power and the turn to conservatism in ministry policy was only accentuated by his less talented successors Timashev and Makov.

Loris-Melikov might have reversed the trend toward bureaucratic conservatism and police ideology within the ministry, but the conjunction of forces within the autocracy after Alexander's assassination went against him.[82] After his fall, the ministry was quickly purged of the progressive talent he had assembled and the path cleared for a reassertion of the ministry's latent conservatism.[83]

The ministry high officials examined here were one source of this latent conservatism. Increasingly after 1861 the presence in the ministry of a silent and growing conservative majority can be seen. They

81. See Orlovsky, "Ministerial Power and Russian Autocracy," pp. 161–98.
82. Zaionchkovskii, *Krizis samoderzhaviia*, pp. 300–378.
83. Ibid., pp. 379–472. In addition to the removal of such high-ranking officials as Kakhanov, there is evidence that the new minister of internal affairs, Ignat'ev, purged the ministry of some middle-level officials regarded as politically unreliable. Ironically, it was the reformer, Loris-Melikov, who, in his haste to combat police and administrative arbitrariness in cases of political crime, created an even stronger institutional base (by unifying the Executive Police and the Third Section and gendarmes within the Ministry of Internal Affairs) for the advocates of a police ideology in the ministry.

were ideal *apparatchiki*, loyal supporters of the system, men of muted ambition willing to work behind the scenes to cope with the growing pressures on the ministry of politics and work load. Their official papers and memoirs reveal a natural and inarticulate conservatism quite opposed to the spirit of militant state-initiated change one might expect from Reform Era bureaucrats. As entrenched and willing servants of their institution, these men helped move the ministry during the 1860s and 1870s toward a final commitment to a police-power ideology. Although the social and educational profiles of the Ministry of Internal Affairs officials would include them in the professional bureaucracy described by Pintner, placing the men in their institutional context suggests that the impact of these professionals on Russian history is by no means uniform or predictable.

CHAPTER ELEVEN

ORGANIZATIONAL CHANGE AND SOCIAL ADAPTATION: THE PRE-REVOLUTIONARY MINISTRY OF INTERNAL AFFAIRS

Don Karl Rowney

Rowney's specific focus is on the senior officials of the Ministry of Interior in the early twentieth century, continuing, in many ways, the examination begun by Orlovsky in the preceding chapter. However, in an effort to evaluate the interplay of the social and organizational factors that combine to create the bureaucratic experience, Rowney also looks back at the entire nineteenth century and forward, briefly, to the feverish change of the revolutionary era. Ministerial structure, the gross characteristics of organized bureaucratic procedure, or deloproizvodstvo, changes dramatically in the nineteenth century as bureaucratization is extended. By the early twentieth century, the structural answer to further division and organization of more and more functions is clear: the era of specialization is dawning.

Max Weber described the legal-rational bureaucracy as a kind of culmination of administrative development. Weber's notion was that legal authority required a bureaucratic administrative staff, and while other forms of authority (i.e. nonlegal ones) could be routinized, they were not bureaucratic. Such a legal-rational administration, staffed by an almost priestly body of executives, emerges as the core of the ultimate, orderly, human society, the Rechtsstaat. *In giving a rationale—but little evidence—for such a teleological notion of cultural development of all human society, Weber simultaneously offered a rationale for the "Westernization" model as it applies to administration: namely, that the end and the norm of all development was a legal-rational administration in a* Rechtsstaat.

If Russia is accepted as a significant empirical or historical example of development, our study thus far clearly contradicts the Weberian rationale. In conjunction with population growth, urbanization, and industrialization, the need grew for more extensive, centralized, formal social organization. On the one hand, it is clear that the Russian method of dealing with this problem was no different in principle from that of any other industrial society; it was to create an ever-expanding bureaucracy. On the other hand, it is also clear that

Russia never created a Rechtsstaat, *a system in which nothing, not even politics, the self-interest of powerful social elites, or bureaucratic procedure could contravene the law. In the case of Russia, instead of a mutually reinforcing bureaucratization and rule of law, there is a conjoint bureaucratization of social function and of society itself. Rowney calls attention to the division and redivision of increasingly specialized administrative functions (*deloproizvodstvo*) and to the accompanying specialization of the human participants in this system, and the gradual reduction of the range of choice open to them. What is emerging is not a* Rechtsstaat, *a law-state, but a bureaucratic state in which bureaucratic principles of procedure (*deloproizvodstvo*) gradually displace the significance and the need for law. What also emerges is a system in which bureaucratic rules of career advancement (*chinoproizvodstvo*) displace the traditional preference and even some of the power accorded to both social and political elites.* [THE EDITORS.]

INTRODUCTION

When an effort is made to describe the relations among important persons in a given social, economic, or political situation, historical literature often focuses on the attitudes of the leading personalities toward one another and toward their institutional roles. As a common alternative, historical description may focus on legislation or policy or other expressions of authority relationships in order to evaluate political behavior. While I do not reject these approaches, I wish to argue that it is appropriate to evaluate certain historical phenomena collectively rather than from the perspective of individuals. In this chapter I wish to suggest that there are good reasons for interpreting the development of Russian officialdom as a social group and also that this interpretation must be conducted in the context of institutional structures in which the officials made their careers. This chapter, then, is an attempt to define and partially explain the processes of change experienced by a part of the Imperial Russian bureaucracy—the central higher civil service of the Ministry of the Interior—from the era of Alexander II to 1917.

Since the early twentieth century, a fair amount of the nonhistorical research on large-scale organizations and some elite social classes or castes appears to argue that the most fundamental question about organizational control is not whether this or that individual exercises it and what the sources and objectives of this control are. Instead this literature seems to have raised the question whether *anyone* consciously exercises consistent control. Thus, with reference to social groups, not only Marx but Gaetano Mosca, and Vilfredo Pareto have argued that the patterns of distribution of wealth, power, and social status are subject to control by individuals only to a limited degree because of recurring, impersonal factors. Thus, Mosca wrote:

> What we see is that as soon as there is a shift in the balance of political forces—when, that is, a need is felt that capacities different from the old should assert themselves in the management of the state, when the old capacities, therefore, lose some of their importance or changes in their distribution occur—then the manner in which the ruling class is constituted changes also. If a new source of wealth develops in a society, if the practical importance of knowledge grows, if an old religion declines or a new one is born, if a new current of ideas spreads, then, simultaneously, far-reaching dislocations occur in the ruling class. One might say, indeed, that the whole history of civilized mankind comes down to a conflict between the tendency of dominant elements to monopolize political power and transmit possession of it by inheritance, and the tendency toward a dislocation of old forces and an insurgence of new forces; and this conflict produces an unending ferment of endosmosis and exosmosis between the upper classes and certain portions of the lower. Ruling classes decline inevitably when they cease to find scope for the capacities through which they rose to power, when they can no longer render the social services which they once rendered, or when their talents and the services they render lose in importance in the social environment in which they live.[1]

Similarly, Pareto asserted a class or group quality in the process according to which elites maintained their hold on power, or wealth and, therefore, elite status. The secret, he thought, lay not in the fact that they weren't subject to decay, but rather in the social processes according to which the class, as a class, was continually restored.

> [Over time, the elite] decay not in numbers only. They decay also in quality, in the sense that they lose their vigour, that there is a decline in the proportions of the residues which enabled them to win their power and hold it. The governing class is restored not only in numbers, but—and that is the more important thing—in quality, by families rising from the lower classes and bringing with them the vigour and the proportions of residues necessary for keeping them-

---

1. Mosca, *The Ruling Class*, New York, 1959, pp. 65–66.

selves in power. It is also restored by the loss of its more degenerate members.[2]

Nor have such observations been exclusively theoretical. From the 1930s an increasing number of empirical studies have explicated the processes according to which either specific social subgroups or given organizations have restored their grasp on power and/or wealth, the sources of their status. Philip Selznik in 1949, for instance, described co-optation as the process of absorbing new elements into the leadership or policy-determining structure of an organization as a means of averting threats to its stability or existence.[3]

Thus, over the past century or less, our sophistication in understanding patterns of change within and between social groups or classes has changed as has the fund of our information. Difficulties arise, however, when we look at what may be termed the opposite side of the theoretical coin. In a given period of time—one year, one generation, one century—there is, of course, only so much change to be encountered historically within a given social group or institution. If we argue that large proportions of this change, or variance, are accounted for by class, or group, or systematic phenomena, are we not arguing simultaneously, that a relatively small proportion, the residual, is accounted for by the action of powerful and authoritative individuals? Naturally, I do not wish to suggest that class, or systematic, changes are not the result of many individual actions. Instead I want to call attention to the fact that such changes, to the extent they are the result of collective behavior, are independent of the conscious, premeditated effort of one individual to produce change. Thus, if we account for change collectively or systematically, it seems to me that some change cannot be attributed to the action of a specific individual, whatever his power and authority. This does not mean, I think, that there are no powerful persons in history, if power means the ability to achieve an effect that one has set out to achieve. It does mean that powerful persons may be fewer than we (or they) imagine and that their "powerful" actions are likely to be limited to a very few, especially when we speak of effecting change in social groups or classes.

With these observations about the relative unimportance of individuals in group or class change, it now becomes necessary to note that in modern societies (say, for instance, Western, politically centralized societies from the seventeenth century on), social status and

2. Pareto, *The Mind and Society: A Treatise on General Sociology*, New York, 1935, 3: 1430–31.
3. Selznik, *TVA and the Grassroots*, Berkeley, 1949, p. 259.

social change are, more often than not, combined with institutional structures. Status, thus, is measured in part by position in the institution. To be sure, this combination of statuses—one determined by birth, upbringing, and the like; the other by the position held in an institution—has been a major preoccupation of social theorists and social managers alike for more than two centuries. Max Weber was not the first to attempt to clarify these two statuses when he wrote,

> The effectiveness of legal authority rests on the acceptance of the validity of the ideas [that] the person who obeys authority does so . . . only in his capacity as a "member" of the corporate group and what he obeys is only "the law." He may in this connexion be a member of an association, of a territorial commune, of a church, or a citizen of a state. . . .
>
> . . . [and that] the members of the corporate group, insofar as they obey a person in authority, do not owe this obedience to him as an individual, but to the impersonal order. Hence, it follows that there is an obligation to obedience only within the sphere of the rationally delimited authority which in terms of order has been conferred upon him.[4]

Of course, the interactions of individuals, corporate groups, and impersonal orders are not invariate but tend to change from one society to another and over time. In a recent major study, John A. Armstrong traces the patterns according to which the administrative elites of four European countries experienced changes in the source and nature of their status, a process involving reorganization of social groups and long-term modification of "impersonal orders."[5] Armstrong's analysis is rendered the more interesting in that it is explicitly comparative and historical and focuses on adaptation to administration in increasingly technical and economically centralized societies. These are phenomena that also concerned Weber, Marx, Pareto, and Mosca. While its total implications are very broad, I think this literature is arguing in the narrow sense that patterns according to which large, complex organizations operate are the function of collective, rather than individual, behavior; that institutional, as well as social, function is the outcome of ten thousand actions by a thousand individuals, the ultimate consequences of which are often difficult to anticipate[6] or to control;

---

4. Weber, *The Theory of Social and Economic Organization*, trans. A. M. Henderson and Talcott Parsons, ed. Talcott Parsons, London, 1947, pp. 329–30.

5. Armstrong, *The European Administrative Elite*, Princeton, 1973.

6. George Yaney, *The Systematization of Russian Government: Social Evolution in the*

and that neither the elites which dominate these institutions nor the institutional structures themselves can be meaningfully considered independently of one another.

In 1973, three major studies appeared, each of which argued convincingly that the political and economic environments in which the administrative organs of Russian government operated changed dramatically in the nineteenth century. George Yaney and S. Frederick Starr both concentrated on political-administrative change in the nineteenth century, while John A. Armstrong focused on change in technical-economic administration.[7] I shall not attempt to recapitulate or elaborate these studies. Instead while fully accepting their view of change in the Russian social environment, I shall try to call attention to the systematic regularity with which the bureaucracy, primarily as a social entity, operated over a very long period of time; I shall also argue that the effect of this regular behavior was to preserve certain social and institutional values in an environment which threatened to change them dramatically. It seems to me that, within a pattern of both social and institutional co-optation (to use Selznik's term), there remained, in one ministry at least, a core of stability fairly consistent from the founding of the ministry to its dissolution at the time of the Revolution of 1917. In choosing to concentrate more or less on one ministry—the Ministry of Internal Affairs or MVD—I am focusing on the largest and most important agency for domestic administration in pre-Revolutionary Russia. In addition it is also the case that this ministry, combining as it did a large number of diverse functions of the MVD at the central level, will illustrate the contrasts of institutional and social change and stability better than other agencies.

The first part of this study defines what I mean by a "core of stability," in this case a continuing dominance by the gentry of ministerial organs in the face of dramatically changing institutional conditions. The second part attempts to elaborate an explanation of the adaptation that evidently occurred—both in the social groups that controlled it and in the organization. The adaptation of social groups may be identified with Selznik's "co-optation" if we note that this means not only adding new people ("from the lower classes" as Pareto saw it) but also adding new skills to those available to the "ruling"

Domestic Administration of Imperial Russia, 1711–1905, Urbana, 1973, repeatedly cites examples of unanticipated, i.e. systematically induced, consequences of individual actions or of policies formulated on high. See pp. 174–75, 190–91, 234–44.

7. Ibid., chaps. 5 to 9; Starr, *Decentralization and Self-Government in Russia, 1830–1870*, Princeton, 1973. See especially, Chaps. 4 and 5; Armstrong, *The European Administrative Elite*, especially Chaps. 12, 13, and 14.

classes. The adaptation of the organization is more complex and can only be briefly sketched. It is what I have called elsewhere[8] the establishment of traditional bureaucracy—i.e. a large organization that combines technologically sophisticated agencies with traditional ones and in which technologically sophisticated agencies and professionally or technologically trained persons are subordinate to persons with no such training or experience.

CONTROL AND STABILITY:
AN ILLUSTRATION FROM 1905-1917

The Russian government, for our purposes, has to be considered in the light of the effective control of its leaders over the complex organizations set up to serve as means to achieving policy ends. Two specific aspects of the problem will be considered: (1) Did the laws give the minister a formally powerful position with respect to his ministry? and, (2) Did the minister in fact actually exercise that formal authority?

Answers to these questions, given the organizational structure of Russian politics, ought to provide some clue to the amount and kind of resources available to a minister to carry out his policy objectives and the degree to which the sociopolitical amalgam over which he presided behaved independently. What we want to evaluate then is whether, and to what extent, the minister controlled the system (i.e. his bureaucratic subordinates) and, conversely, the extent to which the system was independent of the minister. In this effort we will adopt a case-study approach. That is, we will choose the ministry of one man—presumably very powerful—P. A. Stolypin, who held office as minister from 1906 to 1911. In order to evaluate the authority and power of the minister over the MVD, we will examine a specific detail of ministerial operation, "turnover" or the selection of high-level personnel to fill the managerial and submanagerial offices of the ministry: Is there reason to believe that the minister exercised such control?

Essentially, "high-level" offices are defined here as the most organizationally prominent official positions in the central apparatus (*uchrezhdenie*) of the MVD in St. Petersburg.[9] They include deputy

8. Don Karl Rowney, *The End of Traditional Bureaucracy in Pre-Revolutionary Russia: Central Administration of the Ministry of Internal Affairs*, in preparation.

9. For a brief description, see my "Higher Civil Servants in the Russian Ministry of Internal Affairs: Some Demographic and Career Characteristics, 1905–1916," *Slavic Review* 31 (March 1972): 101–10.

ministers, members of the Council of the Minister, heads of departments and their deputies, and members of special ministerial councils (such as the Statistical Council or the Council for the Main Administration for Affairs of the Press). In all, these positions number roughly one hundred out of the one thousand to twelve hundred positions allocated for "ranking servitors" (*chinovniki*) in the central MVD.[10] The incumbents of these positions were defined, in Russian bureaucratese, as higher ranks, and their names were listed in a special annual publication of the MVD called *Spisok vysshikh chinov* (*A List of High Ranks*) together with details of their social backgrounds, careers, and current positions.[11] As both the structure of the central administration and the offices that were filled or left vacant from year to year varied slightly, the total number of persons listed varies; but, on the whole, they account for about 10 percent of the MVD ranking servitors in the central administration.[12] Occupying what appear to have been the most prestigious offices in the central ministry, these men were presumably in positions of some importance, at least in their respective organizational spheres (which extended from police administration to veterinary medicine). The selection of incumbents into these offices would seem to constitute an important source of real power for the man who exercised it. By the same token, failure to control the process of selection would imply that the minister was willing—or obliged—to accept the personnel who, in effect, were given him by a process that he did not control. What we want to ask here, then, is whether turnover among incumbents in the higher civil service offices was within the minister's sphere of authority to control and whether there is evidence that the minister exercised this authority or whether the turnover system, as part of a larger bureaucratic system, appears to have operated independently of him. This analysis rests on several assumptions:

1. That the formal structure of the central MVD remained reasonably stable during the period under examination
2. That the career and biographic data as reported in the *Spiski* are reasonably complete and accurate

10. "Ranking Servitors" (*chinovniki sluzhiteli*) as distinct from lower-grade "chancellery servitors" (*kantseliarskie sluzhiteli*).

11. *Spisok vysshikh chinov*, normally published annually in two parts, of which the first dealt with central agencies and their incumbents.

12. A list of all ranking incumbents (i.e. not just the *higher* civil servants) will be found in *Sobstvennaia Ego Imperatorskaia Velichestva Kantseliaria. Adres kalendar'. Obshchaia rospis' nachal'stvuiushchikh i prochikh dolzhnostnykh lits po vsem upravleniem v Rossiiskoi Imperii na 1905 god*, St. Petersburg, annually.

3. That it was important to the scheme of Russian political practice whether a minister controlled his ministry or exercised relatively little power over it

4. That turnover among higher civil servants is an index of this control if it is further assumed that the nature of personnel change or stability is reflected in the biographic and career data analyzed below.

Let us first turn our attention to a definition of the minister's authority over the higher civil service personnel in his ministry.[13] The most direct way to describe the role of the minister is to say that he was responsible for applying the law through the channels which were constituted by his ministerial agencies. One partial exception to the rule on working through channels was the minister's authority over the staff of his own ministry's central administration.[14] It was the minister's right to present for appointment and dismissal by the "supreme power" (*verkhovnaia vlast'*) officials in his ministry of the third and fourth classes. In practice, this meant heads of departments and members of the Council of the Minister, with higher authority also receiving recommendations for deputy ministers. Officials of the next lower levels (fifth and sixth classes) were appointed and dismissed by the minister directly. Officials of still lower levels were dependent on the head of their agency. Similarly, the minister exercised a right of suspension over all his subordinates up to a maximum of four months. This authority applied to everyone in the ministry without exception and, presumably, could be used in response to a request from the civil servant or as a disciplinary measure.[15]

Throughout the legislative code which defines the authority of the minister it is clear that the ideal state of affairs would be one in which the minister and his subordinates in both the central government and its local counterparts were always guided in their actions by the law, merely executing the decisions clearly specified by existing legislation. There is nothing exceptional in this. Political decision makers, if not the bureaucrats themselves, have maintained in theory a separation of functions between themselves and their administrative servitors since the advent of modern central governments. Indeed, this objective is the very basis for the terminology that separates political *makers* of decisions from professional bureaucratic *administrators* of decisions.

13. The principal corpus of relevant legislation is found in *Polnyi svod zakonov Rosiiskoi Imperii*, 1906, Vol. 1, Pt. 2, Bk. 5, "Uchrezhdenie ministerstv."

14. Ibid., arts. 36–105 and 152–56.

15. For a fuller description of these procedures, see Chap. 7 in this book by Helju Aulik Bennett, "*Chiny, Ordena,* and Officialdom."

Thus the legislation concerning personnel, or the minister's authority over hiring and firing, stands out in some relief. The minister, even if he was obliged to consult sometimes with higher-ups, would appear to have had a fair amount of latitude in his choice of civil servants. The question which must now be raised is whether there is evidence that the minister—in this case the decision maker—exercised his power of choice over who would serve with him in his ministry. The procedure we shall use to evaluate this problem is described in the next paragraphs.

Biographic and career data were gathered on the higher civil servants of the central MVD who were listed in the *Spiski vysshikh chinov* of 1905, 1911, and 1914. These years are chosen because the cohort of 1911 is likely to display the maximum effect (whatever that was) of Stolypin's tenure in office; 1905 should be free of those effects entirely (Stolypin took office in 1906); and 1914, two years after Stolypin's death, should also be free of these effects, provided we place certain additional constraints on the data. In order to throw the influence of the decision maker into the highest possible relief, except for 1905, only those civil servants were studied who were new to the ministry in the year in question. Thus, for 1911, we look only at those civil servants who were *not* listed in 1905. Similarly, in 1914 we study only those who were not listed in 1911. For the cohort of 1905 the problem is slightly different; that is the first year studied, therefore we do not know who the newcomers were. On the other hand we do know who was present in the 1905 *Spisok* but absent from the 1911 edition—i.e. who departed. Although there are many reasons why this may not have been so, let us hypothesize that these 1905 departees were people of whom Stolypin wished to be rid and that except for Stolypin's presence in the ministry after 1906, they would have stayed.

By now the thrust of our analysis will be clear. We have one cohort that we hypothesize to represent people Stolypin did not want (1905); a second that we hypothesize as composed of people Stolypin did want (1911); and a third (1914) composed of people whom somebody else (N. A. Maklakov, the minister then?) wanted. If our hypotheses are correct, we will expect maximum disparity between the 1905 cohort (departees) and the 1911 cohort (arrivees). As to the 1914 cohort, it should exhibit characteristics that, perhaps, return to the patterns of 1905 or trace some new direction of change. In any case they are expected to be noticeably distinct from the 1911 (Stolypin) cohort. The three turnover cohorts include sixty-nine departing civil servants in 1905, fifty-eight incoming civil servants in 1911, and thirty-nine incoming in 1914. The variables chosen for study are nine in all. Four describe general background, or biographic, characteristics: social class of birth; date of birth; whether the subject received higher education; whether the subject was a landowner. Five variables describe career characteristics: date of entry in the civil service; the rank (*chin*) of the subject; the level at which an appointment was made in the MVD (ranging from 1 for the minister and his deputies to 4 for a deputy section head); monetary compensation; area of operation (i.e. general administration, police-censorship, technical-professional areas).

It should finally be noted that some variables are defined slightly differently in Tables 1 and 3, on the one hand, and Table 2, on the other. Thus, in order to make year-to-year comparisons more obvious, several dichotomous or summary measures are used in Tables 1 and 3; but in order to take advantage of the sensitivity of correlational statistics to distribution, the data in Table 2 are left in close-to-natural order. For example, in Tables 1 and 3 "date of birth" and "date of entry" are summarized using the mean, the earliest year recorded, and the latest year recorded. In those same tables, other variables—"legal class," "higher education," "position level" (i.e. the level of appointment), and "compensation" have been reduced to dichotomies. By contrast, "compensation" in Table 2 is the actual amount in rubles awarded to each civil servant annually and these data were correlated, for instance, with the actual amount of land held (in *desiatiny*). In the same table, "class" ranks each subject depending on whether he was (1) born to the gentry (*iz dvorianstva*), (2) was the son of an official or an officer, (3) was the son of a cleric, or (4) was the son of a burgher (*meshchanin*). "Education" in Table 2 ranks each subject depending on whether he attended university (1), left after secondary school (2), or left after primary school (3). "Specialization" in Table 2 is assigned depending on whether a man's position involved one of the professions or some technical work such as medicine, engineering, or animal husbandry (3), police and censorship administration (2), or some other area of more general administration (1). Association was measured in Table 2 by the Pearson product-moment coefficient of correlation.

The trends reflected in Table 1 seem reasonably clear even if the rate of change is not dizzyingly rapid. By 1914 a few more civil servants received some higher education, less land was held, there were fewer landholders, fewer nobles, and those entering the MVD were slightly younger than those who left. It is clear that as time passed the MVD higher civil service as a whole was becoming slightly less the preserve of traditional social elites and more open to those without such cre-

Don Karl Rowney

TABLE XI-1

Demographic Characteristics of Turnover: Higher Civil Servants
in the MVD, 1905–1914

Variable	Civil Servant Group		
	Departing From 1905 Cohort	Joining 1911 Cohort	Joining 1914 Cohort
Date of birth			
Mean	1849	1861	1865
Maximum–minimum	1824–69	1845–75	1849–80
N =	68	56	38
Legal class			
Noble (%)	88	80	77
Nonnoble (%)	12	20	23
N =	67	49	39
Landholdings			
Landed (%)	45	44	23
Not landed (%)	55	56	77
Mean holdings			
of landed (*desiatiny*)	1,936.6	649.5	392.7
N =	69	58	39
Higher education			
Higher education (%)	75	82	82
No higher			
education (%)	25	18	18
N =	63	55	39

SOURCE: *Spiski vysshikh chinov Ministerstva vnutrennikh del na 1905, 1911, 1914 gg.*,
Pt. 1 (St. Petersburg).

dentials.[16] Is this a result of increasing pressure for "democratization"
or advancement of the "third element" (i.e. neither peasant nor landholding noble) in Russian professional and *zemstvo* organizations after
the turn of the century? Perhaps. But what must be noted as most
important for our purposes here is that Stolypin appears to have had
relatively little to do with the changes. The data appear to argue that

16. Similar conclusions have been reached by both Daniel Orlovsky and Walter M.
Pintner in this book. See Chaps. 8 to 10.

this is a pattern of change which *may* have emerged clearly when he took office in 1906 (but may just as well have preceded him—we do not know), but which certainly extended beyond the waning of his political influence and his death.

As we move from the biographic data in Table 1 to more explicit career or organizational data in Table 3, the analysis grows slightly more complex. For one thing there are more variables to take account of and, sometimes, more categories. In partial consequence of this, the patterns of change are not as clear-cut here as they are for the biographic data. Additionally there are, perhaps, more alternative interpretations we can impose on the changes we do observe. Thus, the meaning of a rise in the proportion of arrivals on a given level of position in the organization (Table 3, variable 3) obviously depends upon whether the structure of the central administration of the MVD remained relatively stable. If the structure were significantly changed so that there was a larger number of high offices, say, in 1914 than in 1911, then we have an explanation for the increased figure. Since the structure remained stable,[17] then we must look elsewhere for an explanation. Similar remarks could be made about the distribution of values for the variables "compensation" and "specialization" (4 and 5, respectively, in Table 3).

An even more complex issue is raised concerning the interrelation—or "interaction"—of the variables being studied. We are treating them here as though they were all independent of one another. It can be easily shown, however, that this is not the case—that compensation is obviously related to position level and even that biographic variables are related to organizational variables. Table 2 consists in two correlation matrices of all the variables for the 1911 and 1914 cohorts. From these matrices it will be easily seen that date of birth, date of entry, and rank (*chin*) are all strongly associated with one another; this should not be surprising to anyone familiar with the legislation on appointment to the civil service and advancement through it.[18] Similarly these sta-

---

17. Changes in scope of ministerial authority are not considered here. Of structural changes in the central apparatus, the legislation from 1906 through 1916 indicates only six. See *Gosudarstvennyi Senat. Sobranie uzakonenii i rasporiazhenii pravitel'stva izdavaemoi pri Pravitel'stvuiushchem Senate na _____ god*, St. Petersburg, annually, Pt. 1: art. 1,268; art. 652; 1909, art. 603; 1914, arts. 1,854 and 1,880; 1916, art. 1,633. In 1908 the Chancellery for Affairs of the Nobility was absorbed by the Chancellery of the Minister with staff and budget intact. In 1909 the Administration for Military Responsibility was reorganized and given a substantially increased budget. All other changes were relatively minor and involved quite small alterations in staff authorizations.

18. See Helju Aulik Bennett, Chap. 7, and Daniel Orlovsky, Chap. 10.

Don Karl Rowney

TABLE XI-2

Association among Career and Demographic Characteristics of
Arriving Higher Civil Servants in the MVD, 1911–1914

	Class	Level	Entry	Land	Position	Rank	Compensation	Specialization
					1911			
Date of birth (N =)	.14 (47)	−.11 (51)	.86 (56)	−.01 (48)	−.03 (51)	.67 (51)	.03 (43)	.05 (51)
Class ("highest" = 1)		−.04 (47)	.15 (47)	−.13 (44)	−.003 (47)	.35 (47)	−.07 (39)	.19 (47)
Education ("highest" = 1)			−.17 (53)	.04 (49)	.04 (53)	.05 (53)	−.09 (45)	−.12 (53)
Date of entry				.06 (49)	.04 (56)	.70 (56)	−.05 (48)	.05 (56)
Land					−.38 (49)	−.17 (49)	.59 (43)	.04 (49)
Position ("highest" = 1)						.04 (56)	−.62 (48)	−.16 (56)
Rank ("highest" = 1)							−.27 (48)	−.04 (56)
Compensation								−.02 (48)
					1914			
Date of birth (N =)	−.01 (38)	−.04 (38)	.86 (38)	−.25 (36)	−.19 (38)	.46 (38)	.18 (36)	−.25 (38)
Class		−.20 (38)	.18 (38)	−.17 (38)	.24 (38)	−.06 (38)	−.10 (36)	.08 (38)
Education			−.23 (38)	0 (36)	−.03 (38)	.02 (38)	.18 (36)	.02 (38)
Date of entry				−.30 (36)	−.18 (38)	.48 (38)	.16 (36)	−.09 (38)
Land					.13 (36)	.04 (36)	−.22 (34)	−.24 (36)
Position						−.07 (38)	−.56 (36)	−.20 (38)
Rank							−.18 (36)	−.08 (38)
Compensation								.01 (36)

SOURCE: *Spiski vysshikh chinov na 1911, 1914, gg.*, Pt. 1.

TABLE XI-3

Career Characteristics of Turnover: Higher Civil Servants
in the MVD, 1905–1914

	Civil Servant Group		
Variable	Departing from 1905 Cohort	Joining 1911 Cohort	Joining 1914 Cohort
Date of entry			
Mean	1871	1884	1886
Maximum-minimum	1847–91	1865–99	1866–1902
N =	69	56	38
Rank (*chin*)			
3rd (%)	36	29	26
4th (%)	46	54	53
5th (%)	15	14	13
6th (%)	3	4	3
7th (%)	0	0	5
N =	69	56	38
Position level			
1st & 2nd (%)	26	36	54
3rd & 4th (%)	74	64	46
N =	69	58	39
Compensation			
Upper 1/2 (%)	33	33	51
Lower 1/2 (%)	67	67	49
N =	69	58	39
Work area or specialization			
General administration (%)	71	62	59
Police and censorship administration (%)	19	24	21
Professions or technical specialization (%)	10	14	20
N =	69	58	39

SOURCE: *Spiski vysshikh chinov na 1905, 1911, 1914 gg.*, Pt. 1.

tistics indicate a strong association between a civil servant's position in the central MVD and the salary (compensation) he commanded. Somewhat unexpected, by contrast, is the rather important role which Table 2 argues for landholding in the 1911 group of appointees. For the higher civil servants selected under Stolypin, the larger one's land-holdings the more likely it was that one would hold a relatively high office. As we have already seen, the number of landowners in the MVD higher civil service was on the decline as was the mean amount of land held; in spite of this it seems clear that the diminished number of landowners commanded access to the relatively more prestigious offices. We can examine this relationship more easily if we compare the holders of the most prestigious 10 percent of offices in the MVD with their colleagues on the basis of landholding (Table 4). These data highlight the pattern according to which landholding declined among MVD higher civil servants after 1905. In addition they argue that the MVD elite were not only organizationally elite but also socially elite in a traditional sense of the word. Their tendency to be landholders is considerably greater than that of the MVD higher civil service as a whole, emphasizing the traditional social qualities required for organizational eliteness.

It will be recalled from Table 2 that the one clearly dramatic difference about the data of the Stolypin cohort is to be found not in the biographic and career tables but in the correlational statistics. The amount of land held, it will be recalled, varied directly with the level of one's office. Does this statistic, when combined with our other observations, mean that Stolypin simply let whatever selection processes were already operating in the MVD continue to operate— except that he loaded the highest offices with country squires like himself? It is quite possible, although there are some important caveats to keep in mind here. Of the ten or so *highest* positions in the 1911 central MVD, seven were held by noble landowners. They were: P. A. Stolypin, minister; A. I. Lykoshin and P. G. Kurlov, deputy ministers; A. V. Bel'gard, head, Main Administration for Affairs of Press; S. N. Gerbel', head, Main Administration for Affairs of Local Economy; G. E. Rein, president of the Medical Council; and N. A. Troinitskii, president of the Statistical Council. Three of these seven were in their offices before Stolypin assumed his office (Bel'gard, Gerbel', Troinitskii). Of the remaining four, one (Rein) was a professor and a physician with a long academic career and one (Lykoshin) a careerist in the central and provincial procuracy. Of the last two, one (Kurlov) spent a fair number of years in the military and, then, the civil pro-

TABLE XI-4

MVD Higher Elite and Nonelite Civil Servants'
Landholding Characteristics

	Landed	Landless	Landed	Landless
	1905		*1911*	
Elite	7	3	7	3
	(70%)	(30%)	(70%)	(30%)
Non-elite	26	68	17	66
	(28%)	(72%)	(20%)	(80%)
	1914		*1916*	
Elite	5	5	6	7
	(50%)	(50%)	(46%)	(54%)
Non-elite	16	65	23	90
	(20%)	(80%)	(20%)	(80%)

SOURCE: *Spiski vysshikh chinov na 1905, 1911, 1914, 1916 gg.*,
Pt. 1.

curacy; at length he became a vice-governor, governor, and then moved to St. Petersburg, where he eventually became deputy minister in charge of the gendarmes. The last, Stolypin himself, was also a governor, of course; but he seems to have spent more time in the provinces and to have been more deeply involved with provincial politics than any of the others. In any case, the idea that these—the highest ranking landowners—held high offices because they were all old cronies of Stolypin from the provinces doesn't appear to hold up. On the other hand it does seem likely that these were men committed to a special social order (because of their backgrounds) in the capital city as well as in the countryside, men who, whatever the explanation of their personal career successes, had a stake in avoiding another debacle such as 1905 and who had special interests such as land and houses to protect. In the event of another revolution, both land reform and political reform must have seemed certain. In the former case such men as composed the MVD elite would have lost landed wealth to be sure. But, more importantly perhaps, they would certainly have lost social standing and local influence. In the case of political reform these men would have lost organizational standing and its accompanying power.

Going back to the MVD higher civil service in general, what do the data in Table 3 suggest about change in the group and about Stolypin's role specifically? If we assume that budget, compensation, and authorization for personnel were relatively fixed between 1905 and 1914, only two of the variables—specialization and date of entry—would lend any credence at all to the notion of exceptional quality of the 1911 cohort. Among the three specialization groups (Table 3, variable 5), the first and third reflect tendencies to change that are consistent throughout the entire period. For example, a large proportion of administration specialists were departing from the 1905 cohort, a somewhat smaller proportion arriving in 1911, and a smaller proportion still in 1914. Similarly—but in the reverse direction—professional and technical groups were relatively stable in 1905 and then increased as a proportion of replacements in 1911 and 1914. By contrast, however, the police-censorship groups display the greatest tendency to turnover in the 1911 cohort, a possible indication that this group was more subject to scrutiny and evaluation—and, therefore, turnover—by Stolypin. The data on date of entry also suggest a slightly atypical experience in 1911. Seniority (i.e. date of entry subtracted from the year in question) is lowest for the 1911 cohort, suggesting a slight tendency in the Stolypin ministry for civil servants to move into these positions a little earlier in their careers than usual.

The other three sets of career data displayed in Table 3 all exhibit different degrees of variance. Position level (variable 3) shows turnover increasing at the higher levels and decreasing at the lower levels. Rank shows turnover decreasing at the highest (privy counselor) level, increasing somewhat at the next lower level and at the lowest levels. The point to keep in mind, however, is not the change itself but rather that the pattern of change does not appear to single out the 1911 cohort as exceptional. Because we already know there is a fairly strong association between compensation and position level (variables 3 and 4), we should expect compensation to follow, roughly, the pattern of change of variable 3, position. The direction of change, in fact, is the same but it is less clear-cut in the case of compensation and delayed until the last of the three periods studied: in 1914 it was somewhat more likely that those with higher salaries would be replaced than those with lower salaries.

What, on balance, do our data argue about turnover patterns for the three periods under examination? The biographic data argue that through the decade the MVD higher civil service was becoming slightly less noble, less landed, perhaps slightly younger and more highly educated. Possibly, therefore, what was emerging in the period following the Revolution of 1905 was a higher civil service both less traditional and more professional, if we are correct in associating characteristics such as noble status and landholding with traditional behavior, and increasing education with increasing bureaucratic professionalism; but we will want to reevaluate these observations after looking at data from earlier periods. In any case it is clear that the Stolypin cohort of 1911 was not unique with respect to any of these characteristics. Similarly the career or organizational characteristics of the civil servants involved in turnover between 1905 and 1914 do not underscore the uniqueness of the 1911 cohort. There is some tendency for the level of turnover among police and censorship specialists to be high in 1911, but on the whole the patterns of change manifested tend to carry through to the 1914 cohort in a fashion which strongly suggests that the 1911 cohort is *different* from 1905 and 1914 but that it is not *unique* in that difference. On the other hand it will be recalled that the law gave the minister—any minister—a strong hand in choosing and dismissing the civil servants who were employed in "his" ministry. Judging from the law at least, we might have expected not only differences but unique patterns of change for 1911 as compared to 1905 or 1914. The data, however, do not make a strong case for Stolypin as an administrator who used the law to affect sudden or dramatic change in a bureaucracy that was central to his administrative objectives. On the other hand, the data do appear to argue that there were patterns of change emerging in the bureaucratic system independently of the minister.

It would seem that any discussion of Stolypin's relationship with "his" ministry is obliged to take account of several factors. It is important to recognize, for instance, that there was some question whether the powers which the law accorded the minister in dealing with his staff and, possibly, in other affairs, were exercised. Similarly it should be borne in mind that whatever patterns of change were manifest among the higher civil servants of the central MVD following the Revolution of 1905, they may have been responding to forces entirely beyond the minister's control. This is not to assert that Stolypin, Goremykin, Bulygin, Maklakov, or any of the other relevantly "important personages" were opposed to the manifest changes; but neither does it argue that they were in favor of them, and certainly there is no clear evidence that they were responsible for them whatever the law may have said.

An obvious question which arises in the context of this analysis is whether the observed patterns of change were limited to the post-1905 era or whether they went beyond that date into the past. If we can argue that these changes occurred independently of a given minister (in this case, Stolypin) it is tempting to see them as the products of a certain "democratization and modernization" of the era of 1905. On the other hand, if it should emerge that the changes took their origin at an earlier point in time or that they were but a single iteration in a longer, more complex series of changes in the MVD higher civil service, then we must seek alternative explanations. Certainly our perspectives on the social and institutional dimensions of the system would require redefinition.

Even a cursory examination of available data will cause us to re-evaluate. Table 1 showed the higher civil service of the MVD as composed of an overwhelming majority of individuals whose legal class of origin was the nobility: 88% in 1905 declining to 77% in 1914. Data collected by Pintner for the highest ranking (i.e. ranks 1 to 5) higher civil servants in central ministries in the early nineteenth century indicated about 80% nobility[19]—a figure identical to our findings for 1911 and not greatly different from those for 1905 and 1914. Similarly, data presented by Troitskii in his *Russkii absoliutizm i dvorianstvo*[20] show a heavy majority—88%—of nobility in a similar population for the year 1755. While I may repeat that both Pintner's and Troitskii's figures are for the whole higher civil service in central offices of the bureaucracy, I must assume that there is at least a rough correspondence between these figures and those for the early nineteenth century MVD only. Unfortunately, we cannot be certain, since the MVD data do not happen to be available for the early nineteenth century and the MVD didn't exist in 1755. On the other hand Pintner's data for mid-nineteenth century (1852) do give figures for the central MVD as well as other top ranks at the center. For the central higher civil service as a whole, the proportion of nobility was about 85%. For the MVD alone, it was 87%.[21] Finally, to complete the picture for the nineteenth century, Orlovksy finds a closely similar figure (88.5%) in the preceding chapter.

Of course, as Pintner and Orlovsky have already pointed out, the simple denomination "noble" concealed a great amount of variation in social and economic standing. Still, two conclusions emerge rather

19. Taken from Walter M. Pintner's machine-readable data file on Russian civil servants.
20. Subtitled *Formirovanie biurokratii*, Moscow, 1974.
21. Pintner, data file.

clearly. First, men who were born into the relatively privileged legal-social category of "noble" managed to retain a position of dominance in the central higher civil service as a whole and in the MVD in particular for a very long time. This position was maintained, it should be noted, in spite of considerable social and economic change in Russian society, and in spite of change in the status of nobility itself. Second, it seems likely that the decline in proportion of nobility in the MVD higher civil service which we noted among the 1905 and 1914 cohorts was no more than a temporary fluctuation in the overwhelming and consistent tendency of the nobility to dominate the central higher civil service and the MVD with it. Neither the Revolution of 1905, nor the post-Revolutionary period, nor Stolypin appear to have had any significant impact on this situation.

Thus, instead of a civil service changing in the direction of greater openness to nontraditional elites, we seem to have a civil service more or less consistently dominated by traditional elites for a century or a century and a half. This is not an especially surprising finding in one sense. We know that Russian society before 1917 tended to be dominated both socially and politically by the nobility. However, we also know that the consensus among historians for many years has been that that dominance was on the wane. With emancipation of the serfs, for instance, the nobility ceased to play some of their traditional roles in local governance. This is the underlying theme, at least, of the major studies by Starr and Emmons.[22] True, each of these studies makes clear that traditional roles for the nobles were replaced by nontraditional roles for the same class. The nobles, in other words, were obliged to adapt, as a class, to changing political and economic environments, and though they were less successful in certain spheres— say economics[23]—than in others—say, *zemstvo* politics—in the first two post-emancipation generations, the nobility seem to have retained much of their traditional status, with its attendant privileges if not their traditional roles. I wish to suggest that the social class data on the civil service and the MVD in particular argue similarly that rather than submitting to replacement by new, or nontraditional, elites, the Russian nobility successfully adapted themselves to changing institutional environments. I am proposing that even though changes, such as Mosca described and Pareto implied, were occurring in Russia be-

22. Starr, *Decentralization and Self-Government in Russia*; Terence Emmons, *The Russian Landed Gentry and the Peasant Emancipation of 1861*, Cambridge, 1968.

23. As argued many years ago, for instance, by G. T. Robinson, *Rural Russia under the Old Regime*, New York, 1932, Chap. 8.

tween, say, 1855 and 1914, the result was not replacement (à la Mosca) but adaptation—or co-optation—(à la Pareto and Selznik) not of persons so much as of new skills and experiences. In the final section of this study, I will try to substantiate these assertions by evaluating one particular form of adaptation, the changing formal educational experiences of the MVD higher civil servants in a changing organizational environment.

SOCIAL ADAPTATION

In the preceding chapter, Orlovsky shows that about three-fourths of high MVD officials had attended higher educational institutions. According to data gathered by Armstrong for his study of European administrative elites, a total of 82.1% of a sample of higher civil servants serving in the MVD before 1881 had attended the equivalent of a higher educational institution.[24] Using somewhat more stringent criteria (i.e. the individual had to finish in order to be counted as attending an institution), I found that higher educational experience varied for the MVD higher civil service in 1905–16 between 74% and 81%, with a mean for the aggregate (280 higher civil servants) closer to 80% than to 74%. For the whole central higher civil service (i.e. "top" ranks 1 to 5) Pintner found that in 1852, 71% had attended higher educational institutions.[25] On the other hand, while the figures from 1852 forward seem reasonably stable (varying from about 70% to 80%), Pintner has convincingly shown that, for the whole higher civil service at the center, the situation with respect to education changed significantly in the late-eighteenth-, early-nineteenth-century period. In a recently published study he presented data which showed that higher civil servants who entered service between 1799 and 1839 were increasingly likely to have attended a higher educational institution. Before 1799, for example, the figure was only 18%. For the cohorts entering between 1810 and 1819, however, it had risen to

---

24. Taken from a machine-readable data set on 1,417 higher civil servants, 1762–1881. Armstrong's principal source was the *Russian Biographic Dictionary*. Armstrong furnishes detail on the data set in *The European Administrative Elite*, "Appendix on Quantitative Data," pp. 319ff. and in his "Old-Regime Governors: Bureaucratic and Patrimonial Attributes," *Comparative Studies in Society and History* 14 (1972): 2–29. In the present study I am using the following educational categories, as recorded by Armstrong, as equivalent to higher education: engineer, medical, Tsarskoe Selo Lyceum, university, pedagogical.

25. Pintner, data file.

49%. And for the 1830–39 cohorts it was 68%.[26] It seems clear, thus, that the fundamental social characteristics and the major qualification for entering the higher civil service were both fixed by the 1830s and tended not to change significantly until after 1917. The central higher civil service was the preserve of a more or less well-educated traditional elite right up to the Revolution of 1917.

Adaptation of the nobility through education is more complex than I have already indicated, however. When the ministerial offices expanded during the nineteenth century[27] a great deal of the expansion occurred in areas of professional and technical specialization. Thus, there were added in the MVD statistical agencies, veterinary agencies, medical administrations, research agencies, and so on.[28] In every case professionally and technically trained staff were required. Thus, by the end of, say, the reign of Alexander II, the central MVD had become what I will call a traditional bureaucracy—a combination of agencies, some of which were professional-technical in orientation, some of which were much less specialized, like the police and higher administrative agencies. These latter, of course, required general education and perhaps training in the law, but not the highly specialized training of a statistician. The question that remains, in this light, is, Did the nobility and the ministry adapt themselves uniformly to these changes as they did to the more general requirement for higher education? The answer, as the data suggest it to me, is somewhat complex. First, it has to be based on records of educational experience. For all practical purposes, this means the data collected by Armstrong, Pintner, and Orlovsky, since the official records of the early nineteenth century do not include educational details. Thus, we look at these data to learn what proportion of higher civil servants received technical training and whether this proportion changed as the MVD (and other ministries, presumably) established agencies that dealt with technical matters in the nineteenth century.[29]

26. See Pintner, "The Russian Higher Civil Service on the Eve of the 'Great Reforms,' " *Journal of Social History* (Spring 1975), Table 4.

27. In 1811 the MVD consisted in some half a dozen major agencies; see PSZ I, Manifesto of 25 June 1811, No. 24,687. In 1905 there were some 27 agencies managed by 104 higher civil servants and about 1,000 subordinates; see *Spisok vysshikh chinov ministerstva vnutrennikh del na 1905 g.* The *Adres kalendar'* for that same year lists the more than 1,000 *chinovniki* who were attached to the MVD central apparatus.

28. In 1905 the complement included nine agencies with a higher civil servant staff of thirteen. See my "Higher Civil Servants," Tables 4 and 5.

29. As noted above, Armstrong's data classify civil servants according to *type* of educational institution attended. I chose "engineer" and "medical" categories as the

If we cross-tabulate the variables education and the date at which certain offices were attained in each data set, a rough pattern begins to emerge for the period between 1801 and 1881. This pattern will be described shortly, but it should also be observed that these same data make it possible to show whether technical education was more or less common among "lower" higher civil servants or "higher" ones—i.e. among heads and assistant heads of departments as opposed to ministers, deputy ministers, department heads, and the like. We ask, in other words, whether MVD higher civil servants were sufficiently adaptable to changing times to acquire the special technical skills necessary to serve as medical or veterinary specialists or as civil engineers.[30] We also ask, however, whether the system of which both the agencies and the civil servants were a part was as likely to promote persons of technical training to the highest ministerial posts as it was to promote persons of nontechnical background.

The reason for this approach is, I think, straightforward. It comes down to wanting to know how far or how much the dominant nobility in the MVD were capable of adapting and how much adaptation the bureaucracy actually demanded of them. While it may be reasonably argued that literacy and ciphering were abilities necessary for the socialization of eighteenth-century nobility into the bureaucratic system, I think it equally plausible that algebra, trigonometry, immunology, internal medicine, and animal husbandry were increasingly necessary as socialization devices in the nineteenth century. Did the bureaucracy demand this of its higher civil servants? Did they respond to the demand? The answer to both questions is yes, up to a point; beyond that point it significantly changes to no.

Armstrong's data are most interesting, if not wholly satisfying, for our purposes. During the long stretch of time encompassing the first three reigns of the nineteenth century, approximately 34 percent of MVD higher civil servants were trained in medicine or engineering— some 25 out of the 74 for whom such data were collected. During the same period (i.e. 1801–81) some 39 out of a recorded 201, or 19 percent, of the higher civil servants in the other large ministries were so educated. Thus, specific adaptation took place *somewhere*—either in the nobility, in the organization, or in both. Presumably, if we went

---

most specifically professional-technical educational experiences. In the case of Pintner's data I chose the similar categories of "medical" and "technical."

30. By mid-nineteenth century, or at least the end of Alexander II's reign, the MVD included several agencies specializing in these areas as noted above. In 1810 or 1820 they either didn't exist or they existed in much reduced form.

back far enough before 1801, we would discover a time when smaller and smaller proportions of higher civil servants were technically educated; so some organizational adaptation may be presumed. We do not know, however, whether this also represents adaptation on the part of the nobility, since it is at least conceivable that the great bulk of these technically educated could have been from other classes. Moreover, we do not yet know as much as we would like about organizational adaptation. The controlling departments in the MVD (such as the office of the minister, his deputies, the Council, and the Department of General Affairs) were nontechnical. Were their incumbents nontechnicians? Or did the technically trained have as much opportunity for upward promotion into controlling positions as anyone else?

To begin, in Armstrong's data as summarized in Tables 5–7, the ratio of technically trained to nontechnically trained in the MVD higher civil service gradually increased over the first eighty years of the nineteenth century. According to these data the proportions of technically trained gradually increased from 25% in 1801–25 to 37% in 1856–81. On the other hand, if we look at Pintner's data from 1851–52, the figures are different. Of a recorded 78 MVD officials in ranks one to five only 10, or 13%, were technically trained (Table 8). What does it mean? I think these data are beginning to define for us the limits of both social and organizational adaptation in the pre-Revolutionary, or traditional, Russian bureaucracy. Pintner's data were based on officials in the Department of General Affairs (1852) and the Department of Economy (1852) as well as the Statistical Section of the Council of the Minister (1851). The selection, in other words, emphasizes controlling departments and deemphasizes areas that might specifically demand specialized training in the 1840s and 1850s such as medicine. Armstrong's data, on the other hand, were not based on a selection from specific departments, but on notables—included in the *Russian Biographical Dictionary*—from throughout the ministry. The findings from Pintner's data are significant, I think, to the extent that they focus on controlling areas in the ministry such as the Council of the Minister and the Department of General Affairs. In such areas professionally-technically trained higher civil servants tended to be found in small numbers if at all. This argues a joint response to technology on the part of both the noble society and the bureaucracy—a response that said, in effect, to the educational innovations and innovators, "This far you shall encroach upon our traditions and perquisites and no farther." This finding, of course, fits well with Orlovsky's characterization of MVD officials as generalists in a gener-

Don Karl Rowney

TABLE XI-5

Educational Background of MVD and
Non-MVD Higher Civil Servants:
Central Higher Civil Service Cohorts
Holding Office between 1801 and 1825

Education	MVD	Non-MVD
Professional-Technical	2 (25%)	5 (24%)
Nonprofessional-Technical	6 (75%)	16 (76%)

SOURCE: Data file, "Russian Imperial Bureaucracy: 1762–1881" created by John A. Armstrong and on file with the Social Science Data and Program Library Service, University of Wisconsin, Madison, Wisconsin.

TABLE XI-6

Educational Background of MVD and
Non-MVD Higher Civil Servants:
Central Higher Civil Service Cohorts
Holding Office between 1826 and 1855

Education	MVD	Non-MVD
Professional-Technical	11 (32%)	15 (18%)
Nonprofessional-Technical	23 (68%)	68 (82%)

SOURCE: See Table 5.

TABLE XI-7

Educational Background of MVD and
Non-MVD Higher Civil Servants:
Central Higher Civil Service Cohorts
Holding Office between 1856 and 1881

Education	MVD	Non-MVD
Professional- Technical	12 (37%)	19 (20%)
Nonprofessional- Technical	20 (63%)	78 (80%)

Source: See Table 5.

TABLE XI-8

Educational Background of MVD and
Non-MVD Higher Civil Servants:
Central Higher Civil Service Cohorts
Holding Office between 1851 and 1852

Education	MVD	Non-MVD
Professional- Technical	10 (13%)	16 (12%)
Nonprofessional- Technical	68 (87%)	114 (88%)

Source: Data file, created by Walter M. Pintner
from service records in TsGIA.

alist ministry if it is remembered that he focuses on high-level officials and offices. This view is further substantiated by more Armstrong data and by data from my own analysis of the MVD after 1900.

First Armstrong. If we subdivide the higher-civil-servant population not only into cohorts attaining office in each of the first three reigns but into a group that attained managerial position at the department level and another that attained ministerial or deputy ministerial office, the comparisons are most instructive. Armstrong's data suggest that no one with technical training was likely to attain the highest ministerial offices in the MVD between 1801 and 1881.[31] The same data suggest, equally, that no one in ministerial or deputy-ministerial office throughout the government was likely to have had professional-technical training: of twenty cases recorded by Armstrong between 1801 and 1881, only one had had engineering or medical training.

Education in general may well have been a crucial means for attainment of civil-servant status in nineteenth-century Russia. As state requirements for formal education were imposed, so did the incidence of higher education among higher civil servants increase. Pintner observed, however, that this had much to do with the fact that the nobility, already dominant in the bureaucracy, enjoyed preferred access to educational institutions as well.[32] Thus, rather than a means of social levelling of the civil service, the education requirements preserved the traditional advantage of the nobility. When we look at specific types of education, however, important differences emerge. In an increasingly technological age—indeed, in an increasingly technical-organizational environment—the higher civil service both as organizational and social entity seems to have held the line against incursions by the technologically specialized as well as against technical requirements for the highest organizational offices. The noble servitors of 1870 certainly had to know how to read, write, make sense of a column of figures, perhaps interpret the law, display familiarity with the intellectual and social environments of their educational experiences. They did not have to bother, however, with higher mathematics, zoology, organic chemistry, or epidemiology even though they controlled offices that relied increasingly on these disciplines.

As we know, the industrial revolution did not strike Russia with full force until the era of Alexander III and after. Perhaps, therefore, our

31. The data show that, in fact, there was no case in which a technically trained higher civil servant achieved MVD minister or deputy-minister status. Nevertheless, it is not certain that such an event never occurred since every case has not been recorded.
32. Pintner, "The Russian Higher Civil Service," pp. 61ff.

inquiry is premature. What about the post-1881 civil service? Unfortunately, Armstrong's data do not extend much beyond 1881, Pintner's stop at 1852, and Orlovsky, too, limits his interest to Alexander II's reign. I can, however, offer some observations based on the time and place from which this study departed—the MVD higher civil service from 1905 to 1916.

If we subdivide the MVD higher civil service between 1905 and 1917 into an elite and a sub-elite (the same subdivision as in Table 4), it will be possible to estimate the likelihood of attaining elite status according to educational experience, as well as to identify certain other factors related to elite status. During 1905 and 1914 two of the ten elites received their final education in professional-technical schools.[33] In 1911 only one out of ten received such an education.[34] In 1916, finally, none of the elites graduated from a professionally-technically oriented institution. During each of the four years, the balance of the elites were civil servants who attended one of the universities, the Lycée, one of the law schools, or one of the military schools. Of course this doesn't mean that such persons were totally ignorant of specialized technical matters; but it is noteworthy that the professional-technical graduates were a smaller proportion of the MVD elites than higher civil servants of similar background in the Armstrong data. Moreover, there is only one case of a man with professional-technical training attaining the post of minister or deputy minister.[35] We thus conclude that, in spite of the fact that some 35 percent or more of ministerial offices were professionally or technically oriented,[36] persons with training especially suited to such positions were not likely to be promoted to elite status.

INSTITUTIONAL ADAPTATION

The meaning of the social change just described here will emerge more clearly if we see it in the context of a very brief survey of institutional or structural change in the MVD from the time of its creation in 1802 until 1917. At the time of its creation by Alexander I the MVD was assigned the dual objectives of maintaining law and

33. The institutions included a Veterinary Institute and a Building School and the St. Petersburg Medical-Surgical Academy.
34. Also the Medical-Surgical Academy.
35. V. F. Dzhunkovskii, deputy minister in 1914, attended the Veterinary Institute.
36. Some eleven out of twenty-nine offices between 1905 and 1916. See my "Higher Civil Servants," Tables 4 and 5.

order, on the one hand, and securing the peace and welfare of the population, on the other.[37] This alignment of responsibilities continued as the base of the ministry's grant of authority as it grew in size and complexity during the next ten decades. Keeping the peace through police administration was the earliest responsibility, but this was combined, for example, with maintenance of postal communications. After emancipation of the state and landlord serfs in the 1860s, the ministry became principally responsible for their welfare even as it undertook the administration of military conscription. As time passed, the welfare obligations increased not only in number, but—to deal with increasingly technical functions of an increasingly complex society—they also waxed strong in technological and even scientific sophistication. The gathering and interpretation of ever-more statistical data and the growth of the administration of public and animal health are, perhaps, the most obvious examples of this development.

By 1905 the ministry consisted of some twenty-five separate agencies and, as noted above, the number of ranking civil servants in the central ministry totalled more than 1,000. The annual budget of the ministry exceeded 125 million rubles. Perhaps the single most impressive group of additions from the nineteenth century concentrated in the professional-technical areas. Thus, the legal responsibility of the ministry for maintaining the well-being of society in the nineteenth century took several specific forms. The small Medical Board (*Meditsinskaia ekspeditsiia*), for example, had, by mid-century, become a rudimentary public-health organization including the Medical Council (*Meditsinskii sovet*) and the Medical Department. After the turn of the century the public-health administration—now called the Administration of the Main Medical Inspector—was full-blown and from it had sprung another, by then separate, group of agencies for animal health and husbandry, the Veterinary Administration. The expansion of the Central Statistical Committee[38] is similarly traceable to the nineteenth century, when the changing nature of the economy and society required increasingly accurate and comprehensive information on commerce and agriculture. With the development of such institutions there arose in the ministry a cadre of professionally qualified specialists in fields of expertise which, prior to the nineteenth century, didn't even exist or existed in embryo only. In some measure the Ministry of

37. PSZ I, 1802, Vol. 27, no. 20,406.

38. It was attached to the MVD in 1834 as the Statistical Division (*Statisticheskii otdel*); in 1857 it was reorganized with the title of Central Statistical Committee (*Tsentral'nyi statisticheskii komitet*). In 1863 the Statistical Council (*Statisticheskii sovet*) was added to the ministry.

Internal Affairs, like other Russian ministries, directly developed such expertise, establishing its own training and research institutes in medicine, civil engineering, communications technology (or, as it was then called, electro-technical science), and statistics.

Between 1850 and 1900, extensive changes had swept over the traditional Russian economy and society. Similarly, in the same period, extensive change had overtaken the ministry that was responsible for the "good order and well-being" of that society. We thus conclude that in the second half of the nineteenth century, at least two patterns of institutional adaptation to a changing social environment were evident. First, the ministry retained and augmented its position as the bureaucratic organization primarily responsible for domestic order. This primacy was evidenced by the ministry's acquisition of more and more functions, bureaucratically organized and subordinated to the central ministry authority. In addition to this trend, however, we find another—that of professionalization and specialization: many of the newly identified functions required expertise unnecessary and unknown in the eighteenth or early nineteenth century. Nor was this latter development confined to the pro forma establishment of institutes and agencies; our data confirm that increased professionalization and specialization were reflected in the educational and career experiences of many of the MVD higher civil servants—up to, but not including, the most prestigious and authoritative offices. It is this combination of factors that forms the basis of our description of the MVD as a traditional bureaucracy.

Ordinarily it is thought adequate by historians simply to record the fact that the MVD was abolished immediately after the Revolution of 1917. But this bald statement conceals a great deal of importance. In fact, few, if any, of the pre-Revolutionary *functions* of the MVD were abolished. Instead, they were relocated into other organizations or given independent bureaucratic status. The Main Medical Inspectorate, the Central Statistical Council, and the Statistical Administration are examples of technical agencies that became independent. In a matter of months following the October Revolution each was on its way to independent existence and vigorous future growth. Similar observations could be made about other former MVD agencies from the Institute of Experimental Medicine to the censorship and police administrations, all of which exist in the contemporary Soviet Union under altered conditions but still carrying out many of the same pre-Revolutionary functions.

Thus the history of the imperial MVD ends in 1917 not in annihilation but with a transformation of traditional bureaucratic structures and functions into more highly subdivided and rationalized twentieth-century structures. Essentially what began to emerge were specialist organizations run by specialists who were simultaneously professional bureaucrats.

CONCLUSION

I will conclude this somewhat complex survey by summarizing observations already made under three general heads. The first pertains to the organization; the second to the social group composing the higher civil service; the third to the amalgam created by the two. Clearly, the organization expanded and, as it did so, became more technically and professionally oriented from the early nineteenth century to the early twentieth century. This expansion involved a combination of technical and nontechnical agencies such that, among other things, the technical agencies were subordinated to nontechnical ones. This process created what I termed the traditional bureaucracy and, lest it should seem all too obvious and necessary that this development should occur, I ought to point out that the alternative is for technical agencies to be controlled by technical agencies and technologically-professionally trained bureaucrats. Thus, in the twentieth century, it is uncommon for a public-health administration to be controlled, in an industrial-urban society, by anyone other than a physician trained in public health. Such groups of agencies are typically organized into separate ministries or are at least not subject to day-to-day administration by nonprofessionals. The traditional bureaucracy was only logical and obvious given the historical tradition, the political dynamics out of which it grew. Functionally—and this, I think, is very important—it made less and less sense as the expertise and numbers of technocrats grew in the nineteenth century.

The society we have been examining in context of the institutional MVD was the Russian nobility. It held its own, remarkably I think, in face of considerable institutional and broader social changes. Moreover, traditional values appropriate to this society—i.e. that high status was a function of landholding—survived in the institutional context right on into the twentieth century. Thus the organizational elite tended to be a social elite in the traditional sense as well. Finally promotions into the organizational elite and sub-elite reflected a pattern of social adaptation to changing times of considerable vitality. Judging from other research, it seems evident that general adaptation in the form of rising educational standards took place. Nevertheless, this adaptation was not unlimited or universal in the sense that it avoided certain types of education necessary to the development of the organization. The traditional elites continued to dominate the organization precisely because of the development of the organizational structure that was termed traditional bureaucracy.

The organizational-social amalgam, finally, appears to have responded to a complex set of influences rather than to the influence of any one individual, however powerful. Such "causation" of events may be thought of as impersonal, since it is clear that no single individual was responsible for them. This is so in spite of the fact that law and custom give the illusion of great personal or individual power and that students of these events—including historians—cooperate in the illusion by emphasizing the role of individuals and ignoring more complex phenomena. On the other hand it is equally clear that the social, economic and educational characteristics of any group of people together with the patterns according to which they change *are* the result of the interaction of many individual choices. In this sense there are neither impersonal causes nor impersonal effects in social and political history.

CHAPTER TWELVE

ADMINISTRATION FOR DEVELOPMENT: THE EMERGING BUREAUCRATIC ELITE, 1920–1930

Stephen Sternheimer

incorporate into part on State or statistical data Bel

Some aspects also relate to intelligentsia (Ch 1)

new cadres took over quickly

The Revolution of 1917 is the most famous landmark of modern Russian history. Sternheimer grapples with the complex problem of how it affected Russian officialdom and how officialdom embodied and expressed the revolution. Society's tasks, most of them more or less the same, had to be performed under new political auspices and often with new objectives. Who was to do the job? The familiar question of how many tsarist officials kept their old jobs under new titles is only a small part of the more general problem of how any revolutionary government can achieve the promised transformation of society using only the human and material resources that that society was endowed with before the revolution. According to Sternheimer, the actual officials of the Old Régime were rapidly reduced to a small proportion of the new officialdom; even among technical specialists, the new cadres overwhelmed the old with surprising speed. Looking at the early Soviet experience from a broader perspective, Sternheimer's analysis suggests, however, that the institution of officialdom—the bureaucracy, really—emerged unchanged in principle. The new regime was unable to reduce administrative costs or numbers for long. The priority that was placed on preservice training, a tradition which began with Alexander I, was reemphasized. Very importantly, moreover, the expansion of bureaucracy, as a means of securing reliable patterns of social behavior, was reasserted with the revolution. In spite of the bold promises of Lenin and the Bolshevik leadership to create a classless, lightly administered society, the formal organization and subordination of greater segments of society proceeded rapidly from 1917. Thus, if one simply looks at the categories of administrative organization and functions that Sternheimer deals with, it becomes immediately apparent that whole new areas of social life have been incorporated under the official, governmental, bureaucratic aegis: heavy industry, economic planning and development, and, although Sternheimer does not discuss it, even most political behavior itself through the highly bureaucratized apparatus of the Communist party. In addition, areas of bureaucratic function that before the revolution were small parts of other ministries have now become independent, further subdividing, and *specializing and enlarging, the official role in social and economic functions such as health, trade, transport, communications, and labor. The Revolution of 1917 gave* deloproizvodstvo *a new meaning, in effect, by raising it to a new order of magnitude, encompassing much larger areas of social behavior than before.* [THE EDITORS.]

It has been a matter of considerable interest for students of social and political change whether 1917 marked a radical disjuncture or merely a temporary aberration in the historical evolution of the Russian state and its officialdom. One group of scholars, loosely defined, has opted for the argument that the failure of the traditional imperial state to adapt itself to new social demands and economic forces in its domestic as well as international environment was what precipitated the process of its demise. When viewed from this vantage point, the history of the Russian state bureaucracy (at least for the latter half of the nineteenth century) reduces to a chronicle of aborted attempts at either administering reform or reforming administration. Rejecting both the determinism of a rigid Marxist approach and the disguised voluntarism implicit in Soviet theories of the modernization process, the writings of this group tend to describe the role of Russian state servitors in political change in terms of the colorations of bureaucratic politics, court intrigues, idiosyncratic viewpoints, or simply as a series of historically inappropriate choices. These factors, singly and in combination, are read as dooming all major attempts at "modernization from above" to failure.

A second school of writings on the collapse of the imperial state approaches the problem from a more Marxian perspective and discounts the will as well as the ability of the traditional autocracy to reform itself. Contradictions in the economy, the subsequent mobilization of social forces, and the growth of new wants and expectations are described as depriving the imperial state of significant support, either in the linear fashion of classic theories of revolution or along the lines described by James Davies's J-curve model of revolutionary situations.[1] From this perspective, the imperial state first lost its eco-

---

1. Crane Brinton provides the "classic model" for understanding the dynamics of a revolutionary situation in *The Anatomy of Revolution*, New York, 1965, pp. 236–64. James Davies's J-curve model stresses the importance of a variable, curvilinear relationship between satisfaction and demands over time. See James Davies, "Revolution and the J-Curve," in *Revolution and Political Change*, ed. C. Welch and M. Taintor, Belmont, California, 1972, pp. 122–53. Neither focuses on the behavior of revolutionary actors themselves; see Ted Robert Gurr, *Why Men Rebel*, Princeton, 1969.

nomic raison d'être and then found itself isolated against a number of different forces, groups, and organizations dedicated to its overthrow.

Both approaches concur in treating the state bureaucracy as something of a historical constant, as a force which, in its attachment to dominant landed interests, its low level of technical ability, its highly conservative socialization patterns, and its operation as a closed status system, had changed little in the centuries preceding October 1917. The essays in this volume have provided a critical reexamination of such conventional assumptions, relying on quantitative as well as qualitative data. One question, however, remains, What happens to the nature of "Russian" (or Soviet) state bureaucracy after 1917?

It is the contention of this essay that as in previous centuries, the state bureaucracy simultaneously developed as a leading agent for change and forced socioeconomic transformation even as it was substantially shaped and altered by new forces in its environment after 1917. Contrary to the general picture painted by much of the theoretical literature dealing with bureaucracy and development, Soviet state administration in the 1920s and 1930s was not, we hypothesize, a purely dependent variable whose strengths, weaknesses, and overall organizational capacity were simply the product of either historical legacies, "iron laws," or pressures outside its control.[2] Nor can we assume that the state bureaucracy no longer "mattered" after 1917, turning our attention instead to the growth of Party organs and to the political struggles within the Party's elite as the most suitable "handles" for understanding the choices and policy outcomes of the decades following October.[3] Even granting that the Party made all policy and set the overall political direction for Russian society after 1917, we are left with the fact that the implementation of Party pro-

2. See, for example, Joseph LaPalombara, "Political Science and the Engineering of National Development," in *Political Development in Changing Societies*, ed. Monte Palmer and Larry Stern, Lexington, 1971, pp. 48–49; Joseph LaPalombara, "Public Administration and Political Change: A Theoretical Overview," *Empathy and Ideology*, ed. Charles Press and Alan Arian, Chicago, 1966, pp. 74–78, 87–95; Gabriel Almond, *Political Development*, Boston, 1970, pp. 181–222, 273–331; Fred von der Mehden, *Politics of the Developing Nations*, Englewood Cliffs, 1969; David Apter, *The Politics of Modernization*, Chicago, 1965; Joseph LaPalombara, ed., *Bureaucracy and Political Development*, Princeton, 1963.

3. See, for example, Barrington Moore, Jr., *Soviet Politics: The Dilemmas of Power*, New York, 1965, pp. 58–158; Merle Fainsod, *How Russia Is Ruled*, 2nd ed., Cambridge, Mass., 1963. John Armstrong's *European Administrative Elite*, Princeton, 1974, and Olga Narkiewicz's *The Making of the Soviet State Apparatus*, Manchester, Eng., 1970, represent two efforts to fill this gap. Unfortunately, Armstrong limits his purview of "development interventionist" administrators to Party officials, while Narkiewicz concerns herself solely with the local level and institutional developments.

handwritten margin note: bureaucrats responsible for implementation of Soviet party policy

nouncements still remained the preserve of a vast number of Soviet state officials. These served, much like their tsarist forerunners, in one or another of the traditional state agencies. For this reason—and because the distinction between "policy making" and "policy administration" in other contexts has long since been shown to be an analytic fallacy—the question, Who were the Soviet servitors of the 1920s? remains an important (and altogether neglected) area for empirical investigation.[4]

In the interest of drawing comparisons with earlier periods in the development of Russian bureaucracy, this essay has deliberately eschewed reliance upon formal policy statements and descriptions of the development of the Soviet state during its early years. It seeks instead to follow and isolate some of the same threads of analysis and data utilized in the other studies. Considerations of the kinds of data available, coupled with the longitudinal framework within which the entire volume was conceived, suggest that our picture of the emerging Soviet state officialdom must deal with such issues as size of the state apparatus, its fiscal resources, the distribution of rewards, the bureaucracy's political complexion, the careers (and socialization) of its members (holdovers versus new recruits), and servitors' qualifications for administrative posts. Did Soviet bureaucrats by 1930 represent a new kind of state servitor, one who possessed different kinds of competencies, higher levels of formal training, more political cohesiveness, and greater generational solidarity than had been evident among his tsarist predecessors? Did the kinds of incentives and reward system used in the 1920s suggest that notwithstanding Lenin's perennial fulminations against red tape and bureaucratism, the Party leadership already accorded a traditional kind of state bureaucracy a prominent place in its schemes for building a new social and economic order? Or did the Party leadership regard state officialdom as genuinely dispensable, therefore striving to minimize rather than redirect its influence over Russian life?

To be sure, answers to questions regarding *who* was involved in Soviet political life in the 1920s will not tell us *what* was done at a particular time. Nor will they fully explain *why*, as Walter Pintner has so aptly noted. But they should shed important light on certain aspects of the Soviet "model" (strategy) for social change and economic

4. George Yaney's study of the role of local state officials in Soviet agricultural administration in the 1920s represents a notable exception to this assertion. See Yaney, "Agricultural Administration in Russia from the Stolypin Land Reform to Forced Collectivization," in James Millar, ed., *The Soviet Rural Community*, Urbana, Ill., 1971, pp. 3–35.

development, aspects that have previously been overlooked. Given the prominent role played by state officialdom in many developing nations today, the answers to these questions have contemporary as well as historical relevance.

No simple answer to the question What constitutes a revolutionary state bureaucracy? was readily available to the Bolshevik leadership when it seized power in 1917. Despite a long tradition of attacks on the tsarist "feudal-capitalist" bureaucracy as the source of Russia's political backwardness and economic stagnation, neither the Bolsheviks nor their socialist or liberal opponents ever developed a coherent picture of the kind of political and administrative order they would put in the place of the imperial autocracy.[5] But the experience of stubborn bureaucratic resistance to the takeover, coupled with Lenin's own predisposition to regard state servitors as largely dispensable, dictated that one of the Party's first objectives would be to reduce the size and importance of the bureaucracy as a whole. The ideological arguments outlined in *State and Revolution*, coupled with quite concrete political and economic calculations on the part of an unstable revolutionary elite, combined to push the Party leadership in this direction.

A large state bureaucracy necessarily consumed a substantial portion of available resources while leaving control in the hands of non-Bolshevik officials who had already registered their hostility to the fledgling Soviet state.[6] In the language of the time, questions of staff inflation and deflation translated into the traditional Leninist formula of *kto-kogo* (literally "who defeats whom"). They were seldom regarded simply as questions of improving administrative efficiency.

The Party's initial efforts at administrative cutbacks, however, met with little real success. This stemmed in part from the time-honored tradition in all administrative reform of achieving purely fictional results by elimination of "dead souls"—positions that in any case had not been filled for years. As a result, according to one estimate, the official figures of a 10 to 13 percent reduction in Soviet administrative staffs between 1922 and 1923 in fact masked real decreases of only 4 to

[handwritten margin note: hostility on part of bureaucrats]

5. S. Sternheimer, "Administration and Political Development: An Inquiry into the Tsarist and Soviet Experiences," Ph.D. dissertation, University of Chicago, 1974, pp. 339–48.

6. M. P. Iroshnikov, *Sozdanie sovetskogo tsentral'nogo gosudarstvennogo apparata*, Moscow, 1966, pp. 156–63, 180–205, 255–59; Isaac Steinberg, *In the Workshop of the Revolution*, New York, 1953, *passim*.

5 percent.[7] More generally, the Party's call for a reduction in the 852,000-man bureaucracy for 1926 went unheeded, so that by 1927, the number of administrative posts officially recorded had risen by over 49,000.[8] Much of the blame for such personnel increases attaches to the leadership's own mania for checking and control, especially its penchant for instituting a new bureaucracy to curtail old ones (as Lenin described it in his writings on Rabkrin and its reorganization). The result, as Ordzhonikidze warned in 1928, was that the regime threatened to suffocate itself under a new mountain of paper and under the combined weight of the officials needed to process it.[9]

Some progress, to be sure, was registered. According to Rabkrin's figures (undoubtedly somewhat inflated), overall staff reductions of 28.5 percent were achieved in the state apparatus between 1923 and 1925.[10] But as soon as the pressure was released again in 1925, the

7. *Piatnadtsataia konferentsiia VKP (b). Stenograficheskii otchet* (hereafter *15th Conference*), Moscow, 1927, pp. 239–40 (Figatner), 470 (Zatonskii), 479–80 (Kotov). In the years immediately following the Revolution, a massive inflation apparently occurred. Whereas the tsarist bureaucracy employed 432 thousand officials according to the 1897 census (which included a large proportion of the empire's medical, educational, and sanitary personnel), the Soviet bureaucracy of 1920 had 416 thousand officials *in Moscow and Petrograd alone*. Whereas about 19 percent of the employed population of both capitals in the 1910–1912 period was in positions later included in the category "Soviet state employee," this proportion had risen to 46 percent in the case of Moscow and 50 percent in the case of Petrograd by 1920. See *Gosudarstvennaia biblioteka imeni Lenina*, Fond 358 (N. Rubakin), karton 138, No. 20, p. 1; S. S. Maslov, *Rossiia posle chetyrekh let revoliutsii*, Paris, 1922, p. 87.

8. G. K. Ordzhonikidze, *Stat'i i rechi*, Moscow, 1957, 2: 4.

9. Ibid., pp. 8–9, 11–13, 15. The cost of paper alone consumed by the state apparatus rose from 444 thousand rubles during the final years of the tsarist autocracy to 1.3 million rubles by 1926 (both values in 1914 rubles). For Lenin's original warning that the Revolution might yet drown itself in a sea of paper, see V. I. Lenin, *Polnoe sobranie sochinenii* (hereafter *PSS*), 5th ed., Moscow, 1958–65, 44:364 (letter to Tsiurpa, 24 January 1922). A 1927 study of administrative procedure conducted by Rabkrin revealed that the county executive bodies (and their departments) for Moscow and Saratov provinces and for the Ukrainian republic processed from ten thousand to thirty thousand reports annually, compared to three thousand for the old tsarist village organs (*volost'*). At a lower level, each village soviet received fifteen questionnaries a year "with hundreds of thousands of questions" from the central administration. Much of the paperwork originated in the multiplicity and sheer magnitude of control structures. By the time of Lenin's death in 1924, Vsenka (the Council of the National Economy) had one controller per productive employee, while the Commissariat of Communications had one for every two. See Maslov, *Rossiia posle chetyrekh let revoliutsii*, pp. 85–86, 98.

10. S. N. Ikonnikov, *Organizatsiia i deiatel'nost' RKI v 1920–1925 gg.*, Moscow, 1960, pp. 136–37.

numbers rose rapidly. It was only as a result of a concerted effort in 1927–28 and a clear directive at the Fifteenth Party Congress (1927) that the total size of the state bureaucracy was at last brought back down to the 1924 levels.[11]

Despite the ideological vehemence of the Party's attack on what it termed the grossly inflated and politically dangerous staff increases in state officialdom, a closer look at the 1927–28 reductions indicates that the political leadership set about its task by wielding the scalpel rather than the axe. The cutbacks of this period, deliberately or otherwise, resulted in a well-targeted strategic mobilization of administrative resources so as to contribute substantially to the Party's overall "model" for political development.[12] The model stressed increased control and penetration of rural society by capital-city modernizers; reliance on structural and institutional mechanisms (rather than the transformation of values) for purposes of control; heavy investments in the building of an educational-technical infrastructure to provide expertise; and the use of coercion rather than reeducation to eliminate opposition.

Seen in this light, the aggregate staff reductions, while seemingly contrary to the bureaucratic expansionism usually associated with social modernization and economic development, in fact concealed substantive rationalities. These appear once the figures for staff reduc-

---

11. The data on which these conclusions is based is drawn from *Gosudarstvennyi apparat SSSR*, Moscow, 1929, p. 12 (Table 4). According to one source, on 1 July 1924 there were 112 institutions included in the category "central administration" with 22,132 employees and 17,978 local administrative units with 258,725 servitors. On 1 May 1926, there were 31,925 employees in the central administration and 306,345 in local bodies. And in January 1927, there were 33,900 employees in central administration and 305,000 at the local level. Real reductions did not occur until the year 1927; by 1928 there were 28,000 employees in all-union bodies and 268,800 in local offices. See *Narodnoe khoziastvo SSSR v tsifrakh*, Moscow, 1925, p. 480; *Statisticheskii spravochnik SSSR za 1927*, Moscow, 1928, p. 282; *Statisticheskii spravochnik SSSR za 1928*, Moscow, 1929, p. 527. The 1924 figures exclude Armenia, Georgia, and the Far Eastern Autonomous Region, while the 1926 figures do not include civil servants in Irkutsk ASSR, the Kamchatka and Sakhalin regions, or others in the Far East. With respect to the 1927 staff cuts, Ordzhonikidze claimed (at the Eighth All-Union Congress of Trade Unions in 1928) that for every commissariat and main board (with the exception of the Postal Service and Transportation), personnel cuts of approximately 12.6 percent had been effected in the course of 1927. For the two exceptions, the claimed reductions were larger, 21.2 and 28 percent respectively. See Ordzhonikidze, *Stat'i i rechi*, 2: 125.

12. The concept of public administration as a resource that can be mobilized for development objectives (political as well as economic) and as a resource that acquires an "exchange value" derives from a political-economy approach to the study of change. See Warren Ilchman and Norman Uphoff, *The Political Economy of Change*, Berkeley, 1969, pp. 209–20, 244–47.

tions are disaggregated and the results are interpreted against the background of the overall Bolshevik strategies for development. Far from contributing to a "public-administration gap" or an underadministered polity, the Party's attack on staff size probably left it with *increased* resources to pursue its goals of economic growth and social transformation.[13]

The most severe cutbacks affected personnel performing generalist "administrative-management" functions, while the organs of police administration and judicial administration were hardly touched. In view of the conflict then raging within the Party, the need to repress opposition members and to guard against peasant unrest would have made any cutbacks in staffs used for legal control and police repression extremely risky. Similarly, the regime's commitment to the creation of a Soviet intelligentsia to replace tsarist holdovers and bourgeois specialists dictated practically unchecked expansion of the educational and cultural bureaucracies (Table 1). Such data suggests that Soviet administrative policy in the late twenties emerged basically as the product of decisions, strategies, and considerations of a primarily political nature.

The recorded impact of overall staff size reductions masked dramatic shifts both in the proportional distribution of state officials among the various levels of the bureaucratic hierarchy and in the distribution between various branch agencies of the central apparatus. Such shifts also included a redistribution of officials from urban to rural posts. This was a move that was to have tremendous significance for increasing the Party's capacity to effect rural transformation starting in 1929. Data on levels of personnel concentration reveal that in commissariat after commissariat, all-union, republican, and provincial offices lost staff members while the *okrug* (circuit) and *uezd* (county) posts gained. With the sole exception of the Commissariats of Welfare (8.3 percent reduction) and Finance (35.3 percent reduction, chiefly through the elimination of excise officials), all local branches of central agencies increased their staffs (Table 2). Moreover, when

---

13. The concept of a "public administration gap" is taken from Gur Ofer, *The Service Sector in Soviet Economic Growth*, Cambridge, Mass., 1973, pp. 31–36. The argument for personnel reductions as a positive force for development rests on a number of considerations relevant to the Soviet experience. As Ordzhonikidze noted at the Fifteenth Party Conference of Moscow province, salaries and overhead for superfluous officials consumed scarce capital resources and depleted the sums available for investment; see Ordzhonikidze, *Stat'i i rechi*, 2: 23–44. And in the USSR as in other developing polities, an overblown bureaucracy promised to monopolize scarce managerial skills needed more urgently in factories and enterprises. See B. Richman, *Industrial Society in Communist China*, New York, 1969, esp. pp. 209–19, 443–57.

TABLE XII-1

Size of Administrative Staffs, July 1924 through December 1927
(by types of institution)

	Percentage and Absolute Increases (1924 = 100)						
	%	*1924*	%	*to 5/1/25*	%	*to 5/1/26*	%
Admin. Judicial	100	589,442	101.3	7,377	108.7	51,031	111.4
State executive bodies [a]	100	451,394	96.6	−15,345	104.1	+18,565	105.1
Courts & juridical posts	100	28,622	128.3	8,102	135.9	10,267	138.9
Police	100	109,426	113.3	14,620	120.3	22,199	130.1
Social-Cultural	100	731,332	113.5	98,603	129.8	218,084	145.1
Scientific & educational	100	465,600	113.5	62,912	125.2	117,261	141.0
Theaters, studios, movie houses	100	12,852	114.1	1,816	139.7	5,107	193.4
Publishing	100	6,571	197.9	6,430	245.1	9,534	238.7
Health & medical	100	230,911	111.4	26,419	135.2	81,262	148.2
Social welfare	100	(3,894)	100	0	97.3	−97	100
Social insurance	100	11,504	108.9	1,026	143.6	5,017	156.3
State-owned economic institutions	100	157,766	117.6	27,813	132.4	51,042	127.0
State trading bodies	100	96,452	123.7	22,860	168.0	65,548	162.2
Credit institutions	100	21,127	137.8	7,996	181.2	17,145	168.3
Communications	100	76,548	107.7	5,884	123.0	17,643	123.4
Others	100	116,078	105.5	6,421	102.4	2,836	107.0
Total	100	1,788,745	. . .	. . .	. . .	. . .	. . .

SOURCE: Data drawn from *Gosudarstvennyi apparat*, Tables 3, 4, 5, 15, pp. 12, 14, 23.

a. Refers to personnel attached to the All-Union Central Executive Committee, republican Central Executive Committees, Councils of Peoples' Commissars at all levels, and the various organs of the Supreme Economic Council.

to 5/1/27	%	to 5/1/28	Total Increase/ Decrease 1924–28		1924–28 Increase as % of Total Increase
67,218	107.3	42,836	+7.3	+42,836	7.4
+23,162	96.9	−13,874	−3.1	−13,874	−2.4
11,121	135.9	10,277	+35.9	+10,277	1.8
32,935	142.4	46,433	+42.4	+46,433	8.0
329,593	159.6	435,615	+59.6	+435,615	74.9
190,672	154.8	255,247	+54.8	+255,247	43.9
12,005	220.9	15,542	+120.9	+15,542	2.6
9,117	230.8	8,598	+130.8	+8,598	1.4
111,328	165.4	150,925	+65.4	+150,925	26.0
+2	98.1	−75	−1.9	−75	.01
6,473	146.7	5,378	+46.7	+5,378	.9
42,544	117.5	27,606	+17.5	+27,602	4.7
59,951	136.6	35,285	+36.6	+35,285	6.1
14,427	156.5	11,933	+56.5	+11,933	2.1
17,950	124.0	18,400	+24.0	+18,400	3.2
8,073	108.5	9,858	+8.5	+9,858	1.7
...	132.5	581,533	+32.5	+581,533	100.1

(handwritten margin note:) aggregate increases in various fields of administration

Stephen Sternheimer

TABLE XII-2

Personnel Shifts, 1926–1928 (by territorial unit)

Commissariat	Central (USSR) Organs % Incr./Decr.	Republic Organs % Incr./Decr.	Provincial Organs (oblast'-guberniia) % Incr./Decr.	County Organs (okrug-uezd) % Incr./Decr.
Central Executive Committee	−5.4	−30.6	−30.5	−27.9
Interior		−47.1	−33.8	+9.9
Foreign Affairs	−22.3			
Justice		−19.0	−13.5	+16.9
Labor	+10.4	+12.5	−10.1	+18.0
Workers–Peasants' Inspectorate	+6.3	−16.8	−27.7	+13.4
Supplies		−31.2	−51.2	−8.3
Education		−30.8	−30.9	+14.3
Health		−23.5	−17.9	+7.4
Agriculture		−33.6	+1.2	+127.1
Finance	−39.5	−37.7	−37.1	−35.3
Trade	−26.4	+18.3	−51.5	+9.2
Transport	−26.9		−17.0	insufficient data
Communications	−17.6		−46.9	
Supreme Economic Council	−50.0	−21.6	−17.1	+15.2
Central Statistical Board	+31.8	+126.3	+144.7	+40.6

SOURCE: Calculations from *Gosudarstvennyi apparat*, p. 28 (Table 18).

figures from May 1925 are employed as a base, the proportional increases in local administrative personnel resources by May 1928 appear quite dramatic (Table 3).

In many instances, local placement also meant a rural one. Even as personnel were shifted downwards, they were also being moved out of urban posts (Table 4). To be sure, neither the size of the shift nor our confidence in the accuracy of the statistical reporting are sufficient to conjure up a convincing image of a new group of well-qualified, ideologically zealous bureaucrats who willingly waded through the mud of the Russian countryside to help (force) the peasantry into a new, socialist order. As this essay subsequently indicates, few of these "downward transfers" were former tsarist officials.[14] But like their tsarist predecessors, they too were probably loathe to leave com-

---

14. The major exceptions were the technicians and other officials administering land reform as Yaney describes. But these were not "downward transfers" in any sense, having always served in the provinces.

TABLE XII-3

Growth of Personnel, Local Level, 1925–1928
(circuit and county, by agency)

Commissariat	5/1/25	5/1/28	% Increase/ Decrease
Interior	18,037	27,133	+50.4
Foreign Affairs	. . .	. . .	. . .
Justice	2,177	4,302	+97.6
Labor	1,866	3,586	+92.2
Workers–Peasants' Inspectorate	389	813	+109.0
Supplies	778	1,072	+37.8
Education	2,488	4,778	+92.0
Health	2,721	5,036	+85.1
Agriculture	13,839	23,486	+69.7
Finance	29,311	24,076	−17.9
Trade	778	1,173	+50.1
Transport	. . .	119	+100.0
Communications	. . .	. . .	. . .
Supreme Economic Council	778	1,348	+73.3
Central Statistical Board	2,721	5,834	+114.4

SOURCE: Ia. Bineman and S. Kheinman, *Kadry gosudarstvennogo i koop-erativnogo apparata SSSR*, Moscow, 1930, pp. 104–5 (Table 6).

fortable urban posts. One can only assume, lacking evidence to the contrary, that they therefore did so with great reluctance.

Even an imposed shift, however, meant that the Party leadership successfully executed a major reallocation of scarce administrative resources. This allocation was aimed at the rural sector, where speedy execution of programs was now deemed critical. As such, this administrative policy formed an important element in the Party's gradually evolving plan for making the power and authority of the new state felt throughout Russia's vast rural hinterlands. Seen through the lens of

Stephen Sternheimer

TABLE XII-4

Urban-Rural Redistribution of Administrative Personnel,
1925–1928

	Urban as % *of Total Staff*		*Rural as %* *of Total Staff*	
Type of Personnel	*1925*	*1928*	*1925*	*1928*
Administrative-judicial	61.7	59.6	38.3	40.4
Administrative	57.6	53.3	42.4	46.7
Judicial	65.3	60.5	34.7	39.5
Social-cultural institutions	58.4	56.2	41.6	43.8
General education	33.8	31.3	66.2	68.7
Medical personnel	69.5	67.7	30.5	32.3
Trade	92.1	86.8	7.9	13.2
Communications	75.8	74.7	24.2	25.3

SOURCE: *Gosudarstvennyi apparat*, pp. 29, 30 (Tables 19, 20).

historical hindsight, the data suggest that by 1929 the Party had *already* succeeded in laying the kind of administrative foundation which might make the forced transformation of rural Russia a practical goal rather than a utopian aspiration.

Staff reductions and redeployments in turn reflected favorably on administrative costs at the national level. According to figures compiled by G. Ia. Sokolnikov (Soviet commissar of finance during the period under review), administrative costs in the 1920s steadily decreased as a proportion of the unified state budget: 14.6 percent in fiscal 1922/23; 13.6 percent in 1923/24; 11.8 percent, 1924/25; 11.2 percent, 1925/26; 9.3 percent, 1926/27 and 8.5 percent, 1927/28.[15]

15. Gregory Y. Sokolnikov et al., *Soviet Policy in Public Finance, 1917–1928*, Palo Alto, 1931, p. 322. These figures agree generally with those that R. W. Davies, the British economist, has produced from a variety of alternative sources for the combined administrative-defense expenditures of the period. Unfortunately, the open-source documents produced by the Central Statistical Board for the period—chiefly the statistical handbooks for 1923–24, 1927 (which covers 1926 as well), and 1928 (which has projections for 1929)—do not include "administrative expenditures" as a separate category under the various tables dealing with finances. Only aggregate outlays (including operating expenses and investment) for each commissariat are given. In the text of this essay, the term "unified budget" includes all-union and republican administrative costs

During the same period, absolute ruble outlays increased, from 213.6 million rubles (current rubles in 1922–23) to 563.3 million in 1927/28. Nevertheless, Sokolnikov argued, a comparison of administrative costs for the Russian Empire of 1913 and the Soviet Union in 1927/28 suggested that the new regime had indeed achieved real economies both in its total outlays during the 1920s (measured in prewar rubles) and in its per capita administrative expenditures.[16] Unfortunately, the rapid shifting of administrative functions back and forth between state-supported, *khozraschet* (cost-accountable), and economic organs during the NEP era, coupled with considerable fuzziness in both tsarist and Soviet budgets as to precisely what kinds of costs were included in the category "administration," invariably renders conclusions on this score highly tentative.

Despite the actual administrative economies achieved by 1925, traditional Marxist prejudices regarding the noncritical nature of administrative and managerial functions continued to color the Party leadership's thinking. In 1926, a new campaign for economy was launched. The initial demand for a 10 percent reduction in administrative outlays was quickly followed by a call for a 20 percent reduction by 1929.[17] The projected savings of 300–400 million rubles annually would have had a significant impact on Soviet development goals; the amounts involved almost equalled the planned investments in agriculture, retail trade, education, or cities during the First Five-Year Plan.[18]

In terms of the regime's ability to stabilize administrative expenditures, economies were partially realized. While the combined administrative and defense expenditures rose from 936.8 million rubles in

but excludes the expenditures borne by local budgets. For a brief explanation of Soviet budgeting terminology, see R. W. Davies, *The Development of the Soviet Budgetary System*, Cambridge, 1958, p. 84, n. 1. According to official Soviet statistics, the trend toward the reduction of administrative expenses resumed once the initial push for industrialization was completed. In 1940, administrative outlays accounted for 3.9 percent of the state budget, for 3.4 percent in 1950, for 1.5 percent in 1960, for 1.3 percent in 1965, and for 1.1 percent in 1970. Absolute costs figured in current rubles have continued to rise. See *Narodnoe khoziastvo SSSR*, 1922–72, Moscow, 1972, pp. 481–82.

16. Sokolnikov, *Soviet Policy in Public Finance, 1917–1928*, pp. 301–2.

17. *Kommunisticheskaia partiia sovetskogo soiuza v rezoliutsii i reshenii s"ezdov, konferentsii, i plenumov (1917–1931)* (hereafter *KPSS v Rez.*), Moscow, 1970, 4: 18–19, 22–24, 35–37, 39; Akademiia obshchestvennoi nauki pri TsK KPSS, *Rabochii klass v upravlenii gosudarstvom, 1926–1937 gg.*, Moscow, 1968, pp. 127–28; *Piatnadtsatyi s"ezd VKP (b) oktiabria 1927 goda. Stenograficheskii otchet* (hereafter *15th Congress*), Moscow, 1961, 1: 596–600.

18. For investment figures for the plan, see E. H. Carr and R. W. Davies, *Foundations of a Planned Economy*, London, 1969, 2: 979 (Table 47).

1924/25 to 1,621.2 million rubles in 1928/29, the total outlay (as a proportion of the state budget) decreased from 30.6 percent to 18.5 percent. (Apparently much of the absolute increase can be attributed to a rise in defense costs.) Of equal significance, the ruble increase for the combined categories was more than offset by increased expenditures on economic investment. These accounted for only 29.9 percent of the "traditional" budget of 1924/25 but rose to 42.0 percent in the "growth" budget of 1928/29. Finally, while the state budget in toto expanded at a faster rate than the national economy, administrative-defense expenditures remained the sole item that did not rise proportionately.[19] From another perspective, administrative expenditures represent only 10.5 percent of state budgetary outlays for economic investment by 1929/30, as compared to 48.8 percent of these outlays some three years earlier.[20]

Administrative economizing (relative only to total budget outlays, however) continued on into the era of collectivization and industrialization. Even as absolute amounts expended increased, they accounted for a steadily dwindling proportion of the unified state budget:

8.5 percent in 1928/29 (741.4 million rubles)
6.8 percent in 1929/30 (903.7 million rubles)
4.5 percent in 1931 (1,124.1 million rubles)
4.2 percent in 1932 (1,576.1 million rubles).[21]

19. Davies, *The Development of the Soviet Budgetary System*, pp. 129–30 and Table 25. While the budget grew by some 125 percent, administrative expenses increased only 73 percent.

20. A. Alymov and S. Studenikin, "Rekonstruktsiia gosapparata," in *Piatnadtsat' let sovetskogo stroitel'stva*, ed. E. Pashukanis, Moscow, 1931, p. 252. The contribution such economizing may have made to Soviet economic development becomes apparent when we remember that development depends upon maximal use of extremely scarce resources. By way of cross-national comparison, the choices and resources of contemporary statesmen in the Third World are limited precisely by administrative costs that are excessive by any standard. In some states of Francophone Africa, administrative salaries still consumed as much as 67 percent of the national budgets in the early 1970s. In Anglophone Africa (Ghana, Nigeria), the recent trend has been to increase rather than decrease the income of civil servants as opposed to those of the rural masses of the population (Ghana, 29:1 to 31:1, 1960–70; Nigeria, 58:1 to 65:1, 1960–70). See William T. Levine, "Dilemmas of African Development," unpublished manuscript, University of North Carolina, Chapel Hill, Department of Political Science, 1973, pp. 20, 21.

21. Insofar as all figures are given in current rubles, they are not comparable; see Davies, *The Development of the Soviet Budgetary System*, p. 238. For 1933–37, no figures are available; in 1938–39, the figures again hovered around the 4 percent mark. See ibid., p. 296 (Table 43).

Much of the savings achieved could be attributed to reductions in personnel; some efforts to economize in overhead, however, were also registered. In theory at least, the transfer of expenditures from administrative categories to operations categories was strictly forbidden.[22]

Such measures were not without an impact, at least at the upper levels of the bureaucracy. When costs for *all-union* bodies (excluding the branch commissariats) are factored out of the aggregate budgetary data, it appears that these outlays first rose and then shrank dramatically. By 1928/29, such outlays were actually below 1924/25 levels in absolute as well as relative terms. And while the cost of *local* administration rose steadily throughout 1927/28, even here some economies were achieved in 1928/29.[23]

Viewed from another perspective—that of the actual structure of rewards and punishments set up to control the behavior of individual bureaucrats—the fluctuations in aggregate administrative costs appear preeminently rational. At least part of the initial inflation was due to the regime's early concessions in favor of large wage differentials for the state bureaucracy, particularly with respect to bourgeois-specialist "holdovers," political controllers, and military executives. Lenin himself supported such differentials in 1918 and 1919.[24] But starting in 1924, the regime began to turn its attention to the reduction of such differentials, demanding across-the-board cuts at the top of the pay scale and substantial raises for lower-level (and local) officials. Such a move was designed to reduce the historical venality of Russian officialdom and to provide incentives for executing Party policies. Salaries rose in 1923 and 1924, partially as a result of the staff cuts effected.[25]

22. Ibid., pp. 132–33.

23. G. Ia. Sokolnikov, ed., *Osnovy finansovoi systemy SSSR*, Moscow, 1930, pp. 252–53, 274. This apparently did not hold true for administrative costs in the branch economic organs. At the local level, the overall increase in the combined costs of administration, police protection and judicial operations was 128.2 percent for 1923–29. These aggregate figures conceal wide disparities between the republics: 1.78 rubles per capita for the RSFSR; 2.02 rubles for the Transcaucasus; 1.87 rubles for Uzbekistan; and 2.14 rubles for Turkmenistan. In general, administrative costs for peripheral republics were higher than in the core areas.

24. V. M. Lesnoi, *Sotsialisticheskaia revoliutsiia i gosudarstvennyi apparat*, Moscow, 1968, p. 50. For Lenin's drafts of decrees supporting wage differentials, see Lenin, *PSS*, 35: 105; 38: 63–64, 218, 382. See also A. Barmine, *One Who Survived*, New York, 1945, p. 58, for the Civil War period.

25. T. Sapronov, *Ocherednye voprosy sovetskogo stroitel'stva*, Moscow, 1923, p. 46; *KPSS v Rez.*, 3: 134. Salaries rose between 1923 and 1924 as evidenced by the fact that the total wage fund recorded more than doubled (from 16 million rubles to 33 million), while the

And, as Table 5 indicates, the 1924 decision of the Central Committee to upgrade local posts substantially improved the material position of line officials. The historical gap between the average monthly wages for administrators located in the capitals and those serving in the provinces and countryside soon diminished noticeably.

Other patterns also surfaced. The wages of administrators charged with control functions within the bureaucracy remained relatively high, so that a substantial spread between rewards for bureaucratic controllers and other bureaucrats whom they supervised persisted. A comparison of such wage-gap differentials at various levels indicates that this spread, on the whole, remained consistently greatest locally where political penetration was probably weakest (Table 6). At the same time, the average monthly wages of administrators at all levels (see Table 5) remained substantially higher than the average monthly wage in large-scale industry (1925–28). Salaries of top-level personnel—from 140 to over 250 rubles a month in the case of more than half of all economic specialists, department heads, legal consultants, and procurators—set them apart as a definite economic elite.[26]

Toward the end of the twenties, the regime's administrative policy began to shift in the direction of greater wage levelling within the state apparatus. The 20 percent staff reduction decreed by a joint Central Committee–Central Control Commission plenum in August 1927 affected chiefly the high-paying positions of the state bureaucracy. Savings were utilized to raise the wages of line personnel.[27] Thus, by the close of the decade, the middle-level Soviet official was relatively indistinguishable by virtue of his income level from either his administrative superior or his proletarian client—certainly less so than had

---

number of employees *decreased* by 12–14 percent. See *Trinadtsatyi s"ezd VKP (b), mai 1924 goda; stenograficheskii otchet* (hereafter *13th Congress*), Moscow, 1963, pp. 282, 284.

26. The raw data for these calculations is drawn from the breakdown of job classifications by salary range (the percentage of officials in each position within a given range) developed by Ia. Bineman and S. Kheinman, *Kadry gosudarstvennogo i kooperativnogo apparata SSSR*, Moscow, 1930, pp. 122–23 (Table 16). During the same period, the average wage in large-scale industry stood at 47.6 rubles per month (1925–26), 52 rubles per month (1926–27), and 58.6 rubles per month in 1928. By 1929, the average wage for a male industrial worker was 83 rubles per month and for a female 56 rubles per month. See Margaret Delwar, *Labor Policy in the USSR, 1917–1928*, London, 1956, p. 139; Alexander Baykov, *The Development of the Soviet Economic System*, New York, 1947, p. 148; Harry Schwartz, *Russia's Soviet Economy*, New York, 1950, p. 460. Naum Jasny, however (*Soviet Industrialization, 1928–1952*, Chicago, 1961, pp. 44–45), suggests that wages in large-scale industry in the USSR during 1927–28 were relatively the highest in the entire economy with administrators earning much less.

27. A. I. Chugunov, *Organy sotsialisticheskogo kontrolia RSFSR 1923–1934 gg.*, Moscow, 1972, p. 198.

TABLE XII-5

Soviet State Administrators and Industrial Workers:
Average Monthly Wages (*chervonetz* rubles)

Occupation	1925/26	1926/27		1927/28		1928/29
Administrative						
Central administration	124.85	136.45		140.99		144.58
Provincial (*krai, oblast'* and						
guberniia) administration	77.24	88.14		96.71		103.22
Departments, county-circuit (*okrug*) soviets	59.73	77.77	70.85	86.75	81.69	
Departments, county (*uezd*) soviets		62.39		75.68		
Workers						
All industrial workers	55.29	61.63		67.81		71.28
Machine-building	67.39	76.84		86.92		92.70
Oil	52.16	57.92		61.21		64.47
Metal-processing	66.82	73.01		81.09		84.95
Textiles	46.78	53.16		57.27		58.36
All Administration	76.53	85.80		91.27		
Wage spread, administration (central administration to county administration)	65.12	65.60		59.30		insufficient data

SOURCE: Bineman and Kheinman, *Kadry gosudarstvennogo i kooperativnogo apparata SSSR*, p. 112 (Table 10); *Statisticheskii spravochnik SSSR za 1928*, pp. 546, 548, 551 (Tables 16, 18, 19).

been true for his tsarist counterpart. In 1913, the salary differential between the lowest-level tsarist line official and an industrial worker stood at 7:1. By 1929, however, the differential between industrial worker and Soviet civil servant had been reduced to approximately 2:1.[28]

The administrative purge of 1929–30 continued the process of staff reduction while upgrading the matrix of material incentives within which the Soviet official was expected to operate. Perhaps its most significant "rationalizing" aspect stemmed from the fact that the purge yielded further salary increases for local line officials. Local administrative budgets initially fell (369.9 million rubles, 1926–27; 344.3 million rubles, 1927–28) and then rose rapidly (369 million rubles

28. For the raw data and calculations on which these ratios are based, see Sternheimer, "Administration and Political Development," pp. 389–90, n. 1 (tsarist data); pp. 394–95; n. 3; p. 395, n. 1; N. Rubakin, "Gosudarstvennaia sluzhba," *Entsiklopedicheskii slovar'*, ed. A. and I. Granat, Moscow, n.d., 16: 10–15 (supplementary insert); A. I. Vainstein, *Narodnyi dokhod Rossii i SSSR*, Moscow, 1959, pp. 57–59.

Stephen Sternheimer

TABLE XII-6

Percentage Wage Differentials, Administrators versus Control Staff,
1925–1928 (central and local offices)

	Central Offices			Local Branches		
Commissariat	1925–26	1926–27	1927–28	1925–26	1926–27	1927–28
Interior	60.9	65.0	67.0	43.5	52.1	56.8
Foreign Affairs	67.2	65.3	67.0	. . .	. . .	. . .
Justice	69.5	71.0	70.3	61.4	60.5	64.0
Labor	73.3	75.1	77.3	70.6	79.1	79.3
Supplies	59.7	60.9	65.2	58.4	60.3	64.1
Education	70.9	74.9	77.1	64.6	66.1	71.8
Health	70.2	73.5	71.6	68.3	70.1	73.7
Agriculture	79.0	83.4	86.7	62.9	71.7	73.7
Finance	78.7	80.8	82.2	55.5	62.0	68.5
Trade	90.5	92.5	91.3	77.8	80.9	82.1
Transport	125.5	122.7	110.8	. . .	. . .	. . .
Communication	100.7	94.8	92.3	. . .	. . .	. . .
Supreme Economic Council	103.6	105.9	99.1	67.2	76.6	85.0
Central Statistical Board	55.8	57.1	53.0	49.1	51.6	48.2

SOURCE: Bineman and Kheinman, *Kadry gosudarstvennogo i kooperativnogo apparata SSSR*, p. 112 (Table 10).

NOTE: Percentage differentials = $\dfrac{\text{average monthly wage of commissariat}}{\text{average monthly wage of Rabkrin officials (controllers)}}$

1928–29; 437 million rubles, 1929–30). For the entire period (1926–30), the economies achieved by administrative cutbacks at the national level (81.8 million rubles) were largely offset by the increases that registered in local administrative budgets (67.9 million rubles).[29] Later, during the purge years of 1929–30, the size of administrative staffs at the province and village levels held constant, while salary expendi-

29. *Shestnadtsatyi s"ezd VKP (b). Stenograficheskii otchet*, Moscow, 1930 (hereafter *16th Congress*), p. 317. Other sources for the years 1926–28 also indicate that the average monthly salaries of administrative personnel in the county and village levels rose during a somewhat shorter time period. See *Gosudarstvennyi apparat SSSR*, pp. 124–25 (Table 17).

tures rose in both instances (31.8 percent for the provinces, 64 percent for the villages, 1929–30). Given that the deflationary policies of the First Five-Year Plan had not yet decisively faltered, increments to administrative costs still meant real increases in prevailing wages.[30]

A similar process was at work in the offices of the all-union (national) bureaucracy as Table 7 reveals. In commissariat after commissariat, reductions in the size of staffs consistently outran the reductions in aggregate wage costs. Given a deflationary economy, the real incomes of individual administrators rose significantly and remained high until at least January 1931.[31]

On the one hand, this process represented the logical culmination of that practice of purchasing the political commitment and technical skills from a group of professional state servitors which had been growing apace in Russia since at least the middle of the eighteenth century. On the other, we should note the steady (and deliberate) erosion of alternative institutional modes of access to wealth (e.g. inheritance or accumulation of private property). This fact, when coupled to the growing insecurity attendant upon occupancy of positions of control or management, meant that the overall significance of salaries as a source of income and status rose proportionately. For these reasons, we argue, the power of the Soviet state over the livelihood (and lives) of its servitors increased dramatically after 1917, striving for an intensity of commitment previously unknown in Russian history. Conversely, seldom in Russian history had the lives and fortunes of those occupying lower-level posts in the outer reaches of the state's far-flung bureaucratic network so visibly improved. Thus, under the guise of concessions to a purely technical rationality, the regime in fact tried to purchase both administrative skills and

---

30. Avilov, "Deiatel'nost' RKI v oblasti uluchsheniia sovetskogo apparata, 1929–1930 gg.," *Ezhegodnik sovetskogo stroitel'stva za 1931*, Moscow, 1931, pp. 297–98. Jasny (*Soviet Industrialization, 1928–1952*, pp. 80–81) notes that while the precise date when inflation superseded deflation in the Soviet economy cannot be pinpointed with any great accuracy, it seems to have set in only after May 1930. Thus, while the momentum in salary increases for officials continued until 1932, inflation later wiped out many of the earlier gains. The 1928–32 inflation rate approached 200 percent, while 1932 administrative salaries were only 158 percent of the 1928 base. See Alymov and Studenikin, "Rekonstruktsiia gosapparata," p. 261.

31. In actual fact, real wages were probably even higher than those recorded, since Soviet state agencies during this period were continually criticized for inflating their staff requirements while leaving redundant positions unfilled. These "dead souls" produced additional increments to a bureau's wage fund that never showed up in any official censuses or personnel charts. See Alymov and Studenikin, "Rekonstruktsiia gosapparata," p. 261.

TABLE XII-7

Average Annual Administrative Salaries (in current rubles),
Central Administrative Organs, RSFSR, 1926–1932

Institutions and Commissariats	1925/26	1926/27	1927/28	1928/29	1929/30	Jan. 1931	Jan. 1932
Central Executive Committee	947.7	1,154.2	1,191.8	1,188.1	1,880.0	2,070.7	1,678.8
Council of Peoples' Commissars	1,454.5	1,563.6	1,538.7	2,179.6	2,482.5	2,357.1	2,194.0
State Planning Commission	2,230.1	2,334.4	2,295.9	2,370.8	2,486.9	2,330.5	2,304.1
Justice	1,482.6	1,469.8	1,575.9	1,455.5	1,269.6	2,178.4	2,442.4
Finance	1,469.1	2,727.7	2,048.9	2,163.2	2,514.9	2,349.6	2,758.8
Supplies	1,667.9	1,905.6	2,047.0	1,847.7	2,124.3	2,282.8	2,161.5
Health	1,293.2	1,646.3	1,674.9	1,832.0	1,763.2	1,893.4	2,004.1
Education	1,454.2	1,713.1	1,748.3	1,815.1	1,873.7	2,398.1	2,334.7
Agriculture	1,454.9	1,805.2	1,919.4	1,928.7	1,915.3	2,758.6	2,759.8
Workers–Peasants' Inspectorate	2,150.2	2,436.7	2,265.0	2,311.6	2,278.3	2,642.0	2,827.0
Supreme Economic Council	1,882.9	2,821.8	2,523.8	2,545.3	2,729.4	2,766.2	2,591.7
Social Welfare	1,488.9	1,450.5	1,561.6	1,560.0	1,560.0	2,005.9	1,870.0
Labor	1,735.0	1,909.7	2,073.2	1,909.1	2,111.8	2,427.3	2,480.4
Total annual average	1,432.4	1,676.8	1,795.5	1,860.7	2,038.4	2,385.3	2,391.8

SOURCE: Alymov and S. Studenikin, "Rekonstruktsiia gosapparata," p. 253 (Table I). Calculated as the ratio of the total wage fund to the total number of personnel employed.

political loyalty. It did so, moreover, in a far more determined and systematic fashion than had its tsarist predecessor of the early twentieth century.[32]

The gradual transformation of the political profile of Soviet officialdom emerged as yet another outcome of the administrative policy pursued by the Party and the government in the 1920s. During the Civil War and the early years of NEP, the Party framed its political staffing objectives in terms of a "commanding heights" strategy whereby Bolshevik control was confined to critical administrative positions. The remainder of the posts were left in the hands of non-Bolshevik personnel. These were not, however, necessarily drawn from the

32. For the eighteenth century, as Brenda Meehan-Waters has demonstrated, the administrative elite acquired both wealth and status as a function of service and personal fealty to the ruler. By the twentieth century, however, this flexible system of incentives manipulated to stimulate performance had long since given way to a rigid (and costly) system of sinecures and pensions for the upper elite coupled with grossly underpaid line officials in the provinces. See Sternheimer, "Administration and Political Development," pp. 389–90, n. 1.

ranks of former tsarist officials or from executives from Russia's pre-
Revolutionary private sector.

As a result, early achievements in the overall politicization of the
Soviet state bureaucracy remained relatively unimpressive. By 1924,
only 14 percent of all commissars, deputies, department heads, and
collegium members in central agencies were registered as Party members or candidates.[33] As Table 8 suggests, matters may have been
somewhat brighter at the local level even as early as 1922. For lower-
level *ispolkomy* (executive committee of local soviets, which included
leading administrative personnel), the proportions of Party members
ranged from 40 percent in the large villages (*volosty*) to 91.2 percent in
provincial-level (*oblast'*, *guberniia*) bodies.

Efforts undertaken to distribute scarce Party cadres more efficiently
altered this profile somewhat by 1927. Party control at the lowest
levels visibly increased, apparently at the expense of the concentration of Red administrators in upper-level bodies (provincial, county,
municipal). Between 1927 and 1931, the percentages of Party members
in the executive-administrative organs at the local level rose across the
board. In the territorial (*krai*) and provincial bodies, the Party cohort
increased from 69.8 to 76 percent. In cities and villages, Party control
also grew, from 51.3 to 64.3 percent in municipal administration and
from 7.8 to 13.6 percent in rural executive bodies. The most decisive
increases, however, occurred in what were soon to become the main
control points of Soviet rural administration, the *raion* (regional) staffs.
Here the percentage of Party cadres among administrators rose from
45 percent in 1926 to 64 percent in 1931.[34]

At the top levels of the administrative hierarchy, the politicization of
Soviet officialdom continued apace after Lenin's death.[35] From 1924
until 1928, the Party-Komsomol component of the central commissariats grew at a rate ranging from 1.0 to 4.3 percent annually (Table
9). But by 1928, Communists still accounted for only 18 percent of all

33. T. H. Rigby, *Communist Party Membership in the USSR, 1917–1967*, Princeton,
1968, p. 420. According to Kuibyshev at the Thirteenth Party Congress, the correct
figure was only 13 percent. See *13th Congress*, p. 282. And even this figure may err on
the high side, for the 1926 census of Soviet officialdom lists only 49,878 Party members
in "Soviet and administrative work," barely 10 percent of the total number recorded for
1926. See *Gosudarstvennyi apparat*, p. 15; *Kommunisty v sostave apparata*, Moscow, 1929,
p. 9, and Table 1.

34. B. Levin and I. Suvorov, "Sovety i stroitel'stvo sotsializma," in Pashukanis, ed.,
Piatnadtsat' let sovetskogo stroitel'stva, p. 493.

35. *Kommunisty v sostave apparata*, Tables 5–7; *Ten Years of Soviet Power in Figures,
1917–1927*, Moscow, 1927, pp. 14–15 (Table 5).

Stephen Sternheimer

TABLE XII-8

Party Penetration of Local Administrative Apparatus, 1922–1930

Level of Administrative Body	1922 (%)	1926 (%)	% Increase/ Decrease		1930 (%)
Small-village soviets (selsovet), deputies	6.1	12.9	+6.8		16.4
Small-village soviets (selsovet), chairmen	20.1[a]	23.8	+3.7	+45.2	39.6 (all ispolkom members)
Large-village soviets (volost'), deputies	11.0	31.0	+20.0		. . .
Large-village soviets (volost'), executive committee	40.0	54.7	+14.7		59.8 (raion-volost' ispolkom)
County soviets (uezd), executive committees[b]	81.2	67.2	−14.0		71.3 (okrug-uezd ispolkomy)
Municipal soviets (gorsovety), executive committees	69.8	52.0	−17.8	−51.1	. . .
Provincial soviets, executive committees	91.2	71.9[c]	−19.3		75.5[d]

SOURCE: *Ten Years of Soviet Power in Figures, 1917–1927*, Moscow, 1927, pp. 14–15 (Table 5); G. S. Gurvich, et al., *Sovetskoe gosudarstvennoe ustroistvo: Lektsii dlia rabotnika nizogo sovetskogo apparata*, Moscow, 1930, appendix, n.p., Tables 1, 3.

a. Figure for 1924.
b. There is no data for county soviets (*uezd*), deputies.
c. Figure for 1925.
d. Russian Republic only.

state officials working in the central organs (Table 10). In retrospect, it may well have been alarm at the regime's singular inability to Bolshevize the state apparatus to a meaningful degree that led Stalin and his aides to introduce a wholesale purge of the state bureaucracy in 1929. Simple projections reveal that if the average rate of politicization achieved between 1924 and 1928 had continued, the Party would not have been able to call any commissariat "ours" before at least 1933.[36] And for the majority of the commissariats for which data is available, no Communist majority would have emerged before 1947. Given the

36. The base in the Commissariats of Justice, Agriculture, and Interior was so small that from ten to twenty years would have been required for the Party to dominate the agencies numerically. But as a result of the 1929–30 purge, Agriculture (which had only 14.4 percent Party members in 1927) had over 51 percent in 1933. See *15th Congress*, 1: 446–47; Rigby, *Communist Party Membership in the USSR*, pp. 421–22.

TABLE XII-9

Central Commissariats: Average Yearly Increase,
Party Penetration, 1924–1927

Commissariat	% Increase in CPSU Members
Trade	4.1
Finance, USSR	1.5
Finance, RSFSR [a]	. . .
Foreign Affairs	2.3
Supreme Economic Council, USSR	4.3
Supreme Economic Council, republic branches [b]	. . .
Transport	4.6
Agriculture	1.1
Labor, RSFSR	3.3
Justice	2.6

SOURCE: *15th Congress*, 1: 446–47.

a. Finance, RSFSR: Owing to a purge of 27% of all its cadres in 1924–25, the *Narkomfin* component of CPSU members dropped from 18% to 14%. From 1925 to 1927 it rose again slowly to 17%, yielding a yearly increase of 1.6%. This, however, did not persist long enough to produce any consistent pattern.
b. Percentage of change negligible.

additional fact that the political sympathies of many administrators (Bolshevik and otherwise) lay with the Right Opposition, such an administrative cadre hardly provided a suitable staff for implementing Stalin's "revolution from above."[37]

By the end of 1929, the levels of bureaucratic politicization had risen markedly. More than ever before, a state bureaucrat was likely to wear a second hat as either Party or Komsomol member. But whether this resulted more from the aggressive co-optation of those already em-

37. Sternheimer, "Administration and Political Development," pp. 404–15; A. Avtorkhanov, *Stalin and the Communist Party*, New York, 1969, pp. 25–26, 35, 92–93; Ordzhonikidze, *Stat'i i rechi*, 2: 174; T. Seibert, *Red Russia*, New York, 1932, pp. 93–95.

TABLE XII-10

Party Membership in Commissariats, 1927

Commissariat	Number of Staff	Number of CPSU Members	% CPSU
Trade, USSR	1,090	265	24.3
Finance, USSR	1,040	189	18.2
Interior	410	72	17.8
Supreme Economic Council, USSR	2,034	422	20.2
Supreme Economic Council, republic branches (1926)	3,214	434	20.2
Transport	1,599	350	22.0
Agriculture	1,538	221	14.4
Justice	295	60	22.4
Labor, RSFSR	136	38	28.0
Finance, RSFSR	563	96	17.0
Total	11,919	2,143	18.0

SOURCE: *15th Congress*, 1: 446–47. For military administration, the Party component rose from 10.5% in 1920 to 22.5% in 1922, 31.3% in 1924, 47.0% in 1926 and 54% in 1927.

ployed or from the elimination of non-Party personnel (including holdovers) is impossible to determine from available data. Whatever the reason, Party loyalists in the state bureaucracy now accounted for about half of all controllers, one-quarter of all specialists, and slightly less than a third of all general executives (Table 11). In local offices, the Party's direct control of these posts was equally marked. In each case, the sole exceptions to this transformation remained the technical specialists. These, like their counterparts working in the Soviet industrial establishment, proved impervious to the Party's threats and blandishments.

Once the upheavals of the administrative purges had subsided in the early thirties, the political physiognomy of the Soviet state bureaucracy had altered visibly. By January 1932, 31.1 percent of all officials in the sixteen commissariats of the Russian Republic were Party or

TABLE XII-11

Party Membership and Educational Levels,
Soviet State Bureaucracy, 1929

Level of Post	% of Bureaucracy CP Members	% of Bureaucracy Experts	Red Experts as % of All Experts
All-union, general & departmental executives	28.6	32.7	19.1
All-union, controllers	48.1	46.3	28.3
All-union, specialists	23.7	62.6	16.1
Union-republic, general & departmental executives	27.2	25.8	20.1
Union-republic, controllers	49.7	35.7	31.4
Union-republic, specialists	21.1	62.6	15.0
Province (oblast'), general & departmental executives	23.7	17.0	14.1
Province (oblast'), controllers	50.8	26.6	23.8
Province (oblast'), specialists	11.3	42.1	6.1
Circuit (okrug), general & departmental executives	34.5	6.9	12.1
Circuit (okrug), controllers	71.2	8.3	24.0
Circuit (okrug), specialists	9.43	42.1	4.5
County (raion), general & departmental executives	38.8	4.3	19.5
County (raion), controllers	80.6	6.5	40.0
County (raion), specialists	12.7	33.9	5.0

SOURCE: Bineman and Kheinman, *Kadry gosudarstvennogo i kooperativnogo apparata SSSR*, pp. 202–7 (Table 14).

Komsomol members.[38] In other republic-level organs, the proportion of card-carrying officials rose to 61 percent and in the departments and boards of provincial bodies to 62.6 percent. The regional apparatus, however, remained the administrative unit within which the transformation was most dramatic; by 1933, Party and Komsomol mem-

38. Alymov and Studenikin, "Rekonstruktsiia gosapparata," pp. 258–60. In some commissariats, Party membership was even higher: education, 42 percent; Agriculture, 31.4 percent; Supplies, 33.1 percent.

bers accounted for 92.1 percent of all personnel at this level.[39] The political homogenization of local administrators advanced within the village and *volost'* as well, albeit at a somewhat slower pace.[40] By the end of the same year, *all* middle-level officials of the central commissariats (department heads, bureau chiefs) were Party members as were their counterparts within provincial and regional bodies.[41]

Such structural monolithism and ideological homogenization, to be sure, could hardly have eliminated bureaucratic politics as a permanent feature of the Soviet political landscape. Many policy decisions continued to emerge as the product of both administrative and personal rivalries. Nevertheless, we argue, such conflict was substantially tempered by the overall success the Party enjoyed in its attempts to impose a single set of values and commitments on the group of officials charged with executing its programs. In this respect, Soviet state officialdom of the thirties differed markedly from its tsarist counterpart, especially as it had operated for the decade or so preceding the Revolution.[42]

Despite the importance of political staffing in shaping the Soviet administrative apparatus, it never acted as the sole criterion. Political considerations in Soviet administrative policy were consistently tempered by a sober recognition of the need for technically qualified officials who were able to execute schemes for the transformation of Russia's social and economic structure.

Like many contemporary African and Asian regimes for which development is a much sought-after commodity, the Bolshevik leadership was faced with a clear dilemma. To staff on the basis of educational qualifications and other indicators of technical proficiency (achievement criteria) invariably meant the utilization of a considerable number of "holdovers." These were individuals whose values, role expectations, and (presumably) political loyalties were anchored to a now-discredited political order. But to avoid such political risks by staffing solely on the basis of new modes of ascription (political rectitude as measured either by Party affiliation or class origin) meant

---

39. Rigby, *Communist Party Membership in the USSR*, pp. 421–22 (Table 46), 181–83, 198–200; Avtorkhanov, *The Communist Party Apparatus*, New York, 1968, p. 77 (Table 4).

40. G. S. Gurvich, *Sovetskoe gosudarstvennoe ustroistvo: Lektsii dlia rabotnikov nizhnogo sovetskogo apparata*, Moscow, 1930, Tables 3 and 7; Akademiia obshchestvennoi nauki pri TsK KPSS, *Rabochii klass v upravlenii gosudarstvom, 1926–1937 gg.*, p. 99.

41. Rigby, *Communist Party Membership in the USSR*, pp. 420, 423–24.

42. See Sternheimer, "Administration and Political Development," pp. 142–202, 503–16.

to ignore the very real problems of Russian backwardness.[43] And
Lenin himself had admonished the Party to "learn from the capitalists,"
to build on the technology and skills of the bourgeois world rather
than to destroy them. In the end, the regime pursued an administrative
policy that minimized the political significance of holdovers while
replacing them with "Red specialists" as rapidly as possible.

An accurate assessment of either the size or the strategic importance
of the holdover cohort is rendered difficult by a number of circumstances. Predictably, the issue of the holdovers quickly became en-
meshed in the ideological debates regarding strategy and tactics that
engulfed the Party in the twenties. Once the issue became a political
football, such a tangle of charges and countercharges emerged that
distinguishing statements of fact from politically inspired rhetoric (or
statistics!) becomes extraordinarily difficult.[44]

As the tumult and confusion of the first years after 1917 abated, it
gradually became clear that Lenin's gloomy prognostications of hundreds of thousands of former bureaucrats slowly strangling the revolutionary state amounted to little more than a rhetorical flourish. Two
censuses of the state bureaucracy, one from 1926 and another from
1928, revealed that holdovers accounted for no more than 27.8 percent
of all administrative personnel.[45] Moreover, the label itself tended to
be highly misleading. The numbers of bureaucrats identified as "holdovers" and the number of officials who actually had held a rank (*chin*)

43. For a discussion of this issue in various national settings, see A. R. Tyagi, *The
Civil Service in a Developing Society*, Delhi, 1969, pp. 158–208; A. L. Adu, *The Civil
Service in New African States*, New York, 1965; Tamar Golan, *Educating the Bureaucracy in
a New Polity*, New York, 1968.

44. The holdovers formed a major bone of contention between Lenin and the Left
Communists in 1918–19. Some years later, the debate over utilizing the "former
people" (*byvshie liudi*) would surface once again. This time it formed a major—but
largely fictitious—point of dispute between Stalin and the two oppositions. For estimates of holdovers serving after 1917, see S. I. Liberman, *Dela i liudi (na Sovetskoi
stroike)*, New York, 1944, p. 90; V. I. Lenin, *Sochineniia*, 4th ed., Moscow, 1941–52, 33:
391 (speech at the Fourth Comintern Congress, November 1922); *13th Congress*, p. 283.
The military bureaucracy, the judiciary, financial organs, and agricultural administration were singled out for providing "safe nests" for former *chinovniki*. See Ikonnikov,
Organizatsiia i deiatel'nost' RKI v 1920–1925 gg., pp. 138–39; Carr and Davies, *Foundations of a Planned Economy*, 2: 734 (nns. 3–5); Z. Grishin et al., *V borbe s nedostatkami
gosapparata*, Moscow, 1931, pp. 109–10.

45. *Gosudarstvennyi apparat*, pp. 59–62 (Tables 45–48). Unfortunately, the calculation
of holdovers by Soviet statisticians excludes those who might have entered the tsarist
civil service between 1913 and 1917. It also fails to account for those Soviet officials who
may not have belonged to the Union of Soviet White-Collar Employees. The records of
this union provided the basis for the 1925–28 calculations.

in the Russian civil service diverged rather sharply. The latter group (who would have constituted a cadre of holdovers in the strict sense of the word) amounted to only 4 percent of all Soviet state employees. The remainder of the 200-thousand-odd individuals so labeled had in fact been employed in private enterprise under the ancien régime (manufacturing, trading, banking, credit institutions). Or else they had worked in agencies (*zemstvos* and municipal bodies) which, as likely as not, had been at odds politically with the central government. Thus, applying the label "holdover" to the aggregate mass clearly exaggerates the commitment of this group to a political status quo ante. Indeed, the Party's willingness to accept the benefits of the hold-overs' technical skills was made far easier by the relatively insignificant nature of the political risks involved—excluding, of course, those the leadership deliberately chose to manufacture.

Analysis of the distribution of holdovers among the various offices of the Soviet state bureaucracy confirms that it was indeed the regime's need for specialist and clerical skills that shaped its decision to employ officials from the tsarist regime.[46] For almost all of the individuals involved, earlier patterns of occupational and wage stratification were preserved intact. Retention seldom produced mobility for holdovers, and colorful images of a revolutionary regime wooing disgruntled bureaucrats and technicians with the promise of high pay and new career opportunities lack any real foundation. Technicians and managers once again occupied comfortable and remunerative posts, while the clerks and service personnel of the Soviet state apparatus continued to struggle along in working conditions little changed since the days of Gogol's hero Akakii Akakievich.

As a rule, the holdovers gravitated into the same kinds of posts they had occupied before 1917. Individuals from the tsarist business world went into Soviet trade organs, those from the old central ministries into the new commissariats, and former *zemstvo* and municipal personnel into the departments and boards of the local soviets. In the Finance, Trade, and Control Commissariats, the proportion of holdovers exceeded the national average (Finance, 37.3 percent; Trade, 29.7 percent; Workers-Peasants' Inspectorate, 38.5 percent). This picture changed hardly at all prior to 1929. For certain kinds of administrative posts—general management, control, and specialist positions in the all-union commissariats—the proportion of holdovers stood above the average until the end of the decade. Only in circuit and regional

---

46. Ibid., pp. 61–62 (Tables 47–48); Alymov and Studenikin, "Rekonstruktsiia gos-apparata," p. 255 (figures for 1929).

divisions did the holdovers' collective weight diminish somewhat over time.

In other ways, however, the combined political and psychological pressures to which the regime subjected the holdovers (while utilizing their skills) left their mark. As a direct result of a campaign to bind the holdovers irrevocably to the new political order, fully one-quarter of the group had joined the Party by 1929 (Table 12). Among those holdovers occupying checking-and-control posts, the percentage who were politically co-opted appeared especially great. Only those who could be labeled "bourgeois specialists" in the strictest sense—pre-Revolutionary engineers, economists, and technicians employed in a specialist capacity—turned a deaf ear to the Party's call. Apparently the technocratic weltanschauungen that initially pulled many specialists to the side of the Bolsheviks, coupled with their passionate belief in the democratizing tendencies of scientific progress, precluded even pro forma acceptance of the Party's political values.[47] Notwithstanding such holdouts, the Party's ability to effect the political conversion of the holdovers constituted an important part of its effort to combine partocracy and technocracy in a new kind of administrative formula.

In the final analysis, the administrative policies the Bolshevik regime pursued during the twenties aimed at more than simply reducing the number of holdovers or politicizing the administrative staff. The development of a new cohort of "Red experts"—rather than a mixture made up of Bolsheviks in some posts and non-Party specialists in others—remained the leadership's eventual goal. Lenin had argued in *State and Revolution* that traditional ascriptive criteria for administrative recruitment (membership in the nobility) should be turned on their head to create a proletarian bureaucracy. But the regime could not long ignore the real problems of technical preparation and pre-entry training for its pool of administrative recruits. Its ideal remained a Soviet official with as much specialist expertise as commitment to Party orthodoxy.[48]

As of 1926, Party policy had not yet produced a large number of Red-expert officials to staff state posts. In those central agencies for which data is available, an inverse correlation between levels of technical proficiency (measured by educational grade completed) and levels

47. See Jeremy Azrael, *Managerial Power and Soviet Politics*, Cambridge, 1966, pp. 28–53.

48. V. A. Vlasov, *Sovetskii gosudarstvennyi apparat*, Moscow, 1959, pp. 143–45; Lenin, *Sochineniia*, 33: 199–200, 447; 35: 444, 459–61; 32: 46–47; Lenin, *PSS*, 44: 368–69; 38: 141–42; 54: 277–78.

Stephen Sternheimer

TABLE XII-12

Holdovers, Political Co-optation, and Party Penetration of
Soviet State Administration, 1929

Level of Posts	Total administrative Personnel	Personnel with Administrative/Executive Careers, pre-1917		
		Total Holdovers	Co-opted Holdovers (CP members)	Co-opted Holdovers as % of Holdovers
All-union, general admin. & dept. executives	10,828	5,208	1,286	24.7
All-union, leading controllers	2,348	1,445	613	42.4
All-union, specialists	3,299	1,824	317	17.4
Union-republic, general & dept.	13,476	5,598	1,414	25.3
Union-republic, leading controllers	3,399	1,878	872	46.4
Union-republic, specialists	2,705	1,367	207	15.1
Province (oblast'), general & dept.	30,857	12,076	2,805	23.2
Province (oblast'), leading controllers	8,571	4,380	2,051	46.8
Province (oblast'), specialists	5,018	2,054	129	6.3
Circuit (okrug), general admin.	15,407	6,134	2,016	32.9
Circuit (okrug), leading controllers	4,216	2,071	1,462	70.6
Circuit (okrug), specialists	1,325	630	34	5.4
County (raion), general admin. & dept. executives	58,925	16,902	4,037	23.9
County (raion), controllers	17,129	6,092	3,350	55.0
County (raion), specialists	7,856	2,218	70	3.2

SOURCE: See Table 11.

Personnel with Unknown Date of Entry into State Service or Admin. Careers	Party Members Among Administrative Personnel	Co-opted Holdovers as % of All CP Members in State Bureaucracy
566	3,095	41.6
203	1,130	54.2
182	782	40.4
687	3,667	38.6
217	1,689	51.6
203	570	36.3
1,521	8,033	34.9
545	4,353	47.1
352	568	22.7
597	5,319	37.9
283	3,001	48.7
32	125	27.2
2,279	18,110	22.3
826	11,671	28.7
348	952	7.4

of politicization persisted.[49] Among all Party members serving in the Russian republic's administrative posts in 1926, the overwhelming majority (71.6 percent) barely had more than a primary education (four grades). Matters appeared even worse once officials at all levels and in every branch were taken into account; here the percentage with only four years of education stood at 78.5 percent (Table 13). Unfortunately, no breakdown of the educational data with reference to the kind of post occupied by Party-member officials is available for this period.

By the end of 1929, however, the fusion of ascriptive and achievement criteria in administrative recruitment produced a somewhat altered picture (see Table 11). On the one hand, the educational qualifications of the administrative elite as a whole seem to have risen. Administrators with specialized secondary or some form of higher education accounted for 33 percent of all executive personnel and department heads at the national level, 46 percent of the controllers at this level, and 25 percent of republic-level executives. Over half of all "specialists" and "scientific workers" had qualifications appropriate to their responsibilities. On the other hand, the inverse relationship between Party membership and technical proficiency that prevailed as late as 1926 at last showed signs of diminishing. Party members now accounted for 10 to 20 percent of all those who could be labeled "experts" by virtue of their educational backgrounds. In control positions, the proportion of Red-experts ranged from 24 to 30 percent depending on the administrative units surveyed. Only among those distinctly charged with specialist tasks did the Red-expert cohort still figure insignificantly (5 to 16 percent). Projections for the future, however, looked more promising; among those already employed in the Soviet state bureaucracy in 1929 but still attending school (the future "experts"), over 50 percent had already enrolled in either the Party or Komsomol.[50]

The administrative purges that stretched on into 1930 did little to impair steady progress toward the creation of an official both Red and expert. To be sure, the purge sharply reduced the influence of the holdovers within the administrative ranks. While the rate of removal stood at one in ten for the bureaucracy as a whole, for holdovers con-

49. Akademiia obshchestvennoi nauki pri TsK KPSS, *Rabochii klass v upravlenii gosudarstvom, 1926–1937 gg.*, p. 139.

50. Bineman and Kheinman, *Kadry gosudarstvennogo i kooperativnogo apparata SSSR*, pp. 202–38 (Table 14).

TABLE XII-13
Educational Levels of Party Members in
State Bureaucracy, 1926 (percentage)

Higher education	0.8
Secondary education	7.0
Primary education	78.5
Domestic education	13.6
Illiterate	0.1
Total	100.0

SOURCE: *Kommunisty v sostave*, Table 15, n.p. (N = 23,495). The N does not include candidate members of the Party. According to the same source, there were 31,033 Party members and 18,345 candidate members within the state bureaucracy in 1926. The N, therefore, represents a large sample and not the total universe of bureaucrats *cum* Party members.

sidered as a separate category, the purge rate was one of every two.[51] Once the dust of the campaign had settled, holdovers accounted for only 10.9 percent of the Soviet state apparatus. Quite predictably, the purge breathed new life into the Party's efforts to consolidate its political control over the state apparatus. By 1933, all leading posts in the central commissariats were occupied by Bolsheviks—as were 60 percent of such posts at the republic and province levels, and over 90 percent in the regions.[52]

At the same time, the Party took some care to protect the specialists serving in the state bureaucracy so as not to endanger steady progress toward a fusion of Red and expert by precipitate action on the part of a few political radicals. Unfortunately, quantitative data on the scope of

51. Avilov, "Deiatel'nost' RKI v oblasti uluchsheniia sovetskogo apparata 1929–1930 gg.," p. 303.
52. Bineman and Kheinman, *Kadry gosudarstvennogo i kooperativnogo apparata SSSR*, pp. 36–37, 42–43, 48–49. By 1933, according to one source, 89.3 percent of all Soviet executive committee employees (down to the level of the city) were Party members. See Akademiia obshchestvennoi nauki pri TsK KPSS, *Iz istorii Sovetskoi intelligentsii*, Moscow, 1966, p. 179.

such a commitment to protect specialists is presently lacking. But during the 1929–30 purges the leadership did warn all local units of the Central Control Commission and Rabkrin (the two agencies conducting the administrative purge) not to remove a single specialist without prior notification *and approval* of either republican or all-union bodies. Across-the-board attacks on experts, particularly in rural areas, were frowned upon.[53] Even those commissariats whose personnel were politically most suspect (Finance) continued to expand programs for training new recruits during the height of the purge.[54]

Further evidence of the importance the leadership continued to attach to specialist skills is provided by a joint decree of the Central Executive Committee and the Council of Commissars in the Russian Republic that created six new university-affiliated "departments of Soviet state development." These aimed to prepare professional administrators for local posts. In addition, six independent "institutes of Soviet state development" operated from 1930 until 1936, and the "divisions of Soviet state development" (operating within the framework of Communist universities) were simultaneously being upgraded.[55] Indeed, throughout the administrative purge years—at the Sixteenth Party Conference in 1929, the November 1929 Central Committee plenum, and the Sixteenth Party Congress in 1930—the Party elite continually emphasized the importance of staffing the Soviet state bureaucracy with individuals who were technically proficient as well as politically loyal.[56] Taken in toto, these facts suggest that the Red-expert continued to represent the ideal Soviet official.

Analysis of aggregate data on Soviet officialdom during the 1920s suggests that consciously or otherwise, the political leadership pursued policies in the administrative sector which had as their outcome the development and transformation of the administrative resources of the fledgling Soviet state. To be sure, policies that shaped Soviet administration not infrequently pursued conflicting objectives. In some cases, decisions that vitally affected the state apparatus on the surface were aimed at other kinds of targets (e.g. the push to economize in

53. L. F. Morozov and B. V. Portnov, *Organy TsKK–NK RKI v borbe za sovershenstvovanie sovetskogo gosudarstvennogo apparata (1923–34 gg.)*, Moscow, 1964, pp. 128, 134.

54. Alymov and Studenikin, "Rekonstruktsiia gosapparata," p. 262.

55. Ibid., p. 263; N. Cheliapov, "Sovetskii apparat i zadachi ego uluchsheniia," in Pashukanis, ed., *Piatnadtsat' let Sovetskogo stroitel'stva*, pp. 31–32.

56. Morozov and Portnov, *Organy TsKK–NK RKI v borbe za sovershenstvovanie sovetskogo gosudarstvennogo apparata*, p. 134; *Itogi noiabr'skogo plenuma TsK VKP (b): 10–17 noiabria 1929 goda*, Moscow, 1929, pp. 15–19; *16th Congress*, pp. 361–62.

the state budget as a means of capital accumulation for economic development).

Out of this tangled network of forces and counterforces, a distinctly "Soviet" officialdom slowly but inexorably emerged. While the political qualifications of the group initially outstripped its economic skills, by the end of the decade such a gap had narrowed visibly. At the same time, the erstwhile competitors of the new servitors—former tsarist officials—were either absorbed into the new cohort via political recruitment or, alternately, were eliminated from the administrative ranks altogether. Meanwhile, the system of rewards and incentives within which Soviet officials operated was manipulated to render administrative posts the regime deemed most vital the most attractive from a material point of view. In this fashion, regime policy worked to bind officials more firmly to the Party's development goals.

In light of such evidence pointing to the transformation of Soviet officialdom, it remains puzzling that the Party leadership continued to express serious reservations regarding the actual performance of the Soviet state bureaucracy throughout the twenties. Lenin's initial gloomy prognoses set the tone for much of the rest of the decade. In 1922 he wrote to Krupskaia that administrative red tape and bungling threatened Party programs with wholesale sabotage. And for these reasons he recommended a series of show trials of "bureaucratic saboteurs" to bring the bureaucracy to heel.[57] The October 1924 Central Committee plenum explored various remedies for dealing with what Party speakers termed "the complaints of administrative distortion, self-serving careerism and general incompetence," which threatened the execution of Party programs. The Fifteenth Congress in 1927 and the Sixteenth Conference in 1929 continued to echo these negative evaluations of administrative performance.[58]

For a variety of reasons, such evaluations take on the cast of reliable historical evidence only when they have been placed in the proper analytic perspective. In the absence of independent verification or aggregate statistical confirmation, episodic data remains inadequate as a source of hard and fast conclusions. Bolshevik politicians of the 1920s, like their counterparts in the Third World faced with development tasks, constantly confronted the problem of allocating their scarce resources economically in order to achieve social and political goals. In short, they confronted all the dilemmas associated with political economizing: assessing the costs and benefits of alternative

57. *15th Congress*, 1: 465 (cited by Ordzhonikidze).
58. *KPSS v Rez.*, 3: 138, 255–58, 367–68.

policies, estimating the comparative advantage of one or another choice, developing a clear hierarchy of goals.[59]

In the process, these leaders frequently imposed contradictory demands upon the state bureaucracy. While trying to simultaneously remake it into a "socialist bureaucracy"—or to eliminate it altogether —they also required that officialdom radically increase its effectiveness as part of the "organizational weapon" for the building of socialism. Indeed, the imposition of contradictory (and unusually onerous) requirements on the shoulders of a state bureaucracy constitutes one of the general features of modernizing polities everywhere. This in turn gives rise to considerable intrapersonal stress and role ambiguity on the part of bureaucrats as well as the kinds of formalism and goal displacement frequently denounced as dysfunctional. At the same time, such "functional dysfunctionalities" (to use Merton's term) appear to political leaders little concerned with the niceties of administrative dynamics as more evidence of bureaucratic attempts to sabotage otherwise well-conceived programs.[60] From this perspective, therefore, the Bolshevik elite's perception of "successful" program implementation on the part of the state bureaucracy was quite predictably negative. But this tells us little about the amount of real transformation that had occurred in the bureaucratic elite itself.

The nature of the Party leaders' occupation, "politics," also inclined them to view the achievements of the bureaucracy with a jaundiced eye. For politicians, the chief criterion of success consists of the ability to mobilize resources in pursuit of specific goals. Consequently, *any* inability on the part of officials to realize *any* goals ipso facto appeared as evidence of failure.[61] As Max Weber pointed out in his seminal work on political and bureaucratic life, the qualities that distinguish political leaders are fundamentally different from those defining an ideal bureaucrat. Insofar as the political leader is engaged in a constant struggle for power, he must continually demonstrate his capacity for independent action for which he alone takes responsibility. Given that partisanship and personal responsibility comprise the essential features

59. Ilchman and Uphoff, *The Political Economy of Change*, pp. 1–11 *inter alia*.

60. Robert Merton, "Bureaucratic Structure and Personality," in Robert Merton et al., eds., *Reader in Bureaucracy*, New York, 1952, pp. 361–71. For the sources of the intrapersonal stress development administrators experience, see Richard Taub, *Bureaucrats Under Stress*, Berkeley, 1969. The social dimension of this problem originates in the conflicting role systems and value sets in which development administrators operate and which make "effectiveness" in implementing change a highly elusive goal. See Robert Price, *Bureaucracy and Society in Modern Ghana*, Berkeley, 1975.

61. William A. Welsh, *Studying Politics*, Boston, 1973, p. 6.

of his activity, the politician (by virtue of his "calling") is bound to portray the achievements of others, however real, in a negative light.[62]

This universal aspect of politicians' behavior was further compounded in the Soviet setting by the "rachet-principle" mentality. This had surfaced in the thinking of the Party elite regarding domestic policy by 1923–24, and it quickly dominated Soviet economic planning in the 1930s.[63] In light of the leadership's doctrinal inclination toward voluntarism (especially in its thinking regarding modernization), whatever human or bureaucratic effort *had* achieved in the past simply became "evidence" that more *could and should* be achieved in the future. Simply put, success in meeting any kind of targets, rather than serving as a signal to release pressure or reward achievement, instead became a pretext for further inflating indicators of acceptable performance. In this fashion, all forces were to be propelled forward, ratchetlike, toward new and greater efforts for change.

A discussion of the merits and drawbacks of such a strategy lie beyond the boundaries of this essay. But it is important to recognize that this mode of thinking invariably led the Party to criticize the state bureaucracy and to emphasize its shortcomings regardless of the absence of any objective grounds for such an attack. As one member of Stalin's entourage admitted in a rare moment of candor (1930), any and all shifts in the Party's prescriptions for what constituted "development" (e.g., the collectivization of agriculture) would invariably reflect negatively on the bureaucracy's past performance. Each time the political line shifted, he observed, it would appear that the state bureaucracy had once again been derelict in its duties.

Such remarks point to one inescapable truth in any historical setting. As an organization, a state bureaucracy is doomed to aspire to order, routine, and predictability in its operations and projections. Thus it is equally likely to pursue programs and strategies that a forward-looking leadership will eventually brand as politically reactionary.[64]

Seen in this light, support for a claim that no distinctly "Soviet" officialdom emerged in the 1920s appears to lack any substantial foundation. At the same time, a considerable body of quantitative evidence

62. Reinhard Bendix, *Max Weber: An Intellectual Portrait*, Garden City, 1962, pp. 440–41.

63. For a description of the ratchet principle at work in the Soviet economy between 1930 and 1955, see Joseph E. Berliner, *Factory and Manager in the USSR*, Cambridge, Mass., 1957, pp. 78–79, 315. Fainsod (*How Russia Is Ruled*, 2nd ed., pp. 104–8) describes how this modus operandi of the elite affected Soviet society generally under Stalin.

64. *Shestnadtsataia konferentsiia VKP (b). Stenograficheskii otchet*, Moscow, 1929, p. 231 (Iakovlev).

concerning both levels and trends points in precisely the opposite direction: the emergence of a substantially new kind of administrative elite, one increasingly attuned to, and presumably supporting, Party objectives. The claim that former bureaucrats continued to exercise a stranglehold on a revolutionary state finds its credence solely in the eye of the Bolshevik beholder. Just as previous periods of cultural and economic change in Russian history had been both accompanied and preceded by substantial transformation of the state bureaucracy, so this process continued unabated (or, alternately, was revived) during the first decades of Soviet rule. Indeed, there are substantial grounds for arguing that such administrative transformation may have constituted one of the prerequisites for the kind of social and economic changes associated with what is usually termed "the Soviet model of development."[65] If this is the case, then early (and substantial) investments in changing the administrative infrastructure may have been one of the reasons why a small modernizing elite was able to impose its will upon a large—and not altogether unresisting—Russian population.

65. For the Soviet "model" of development, see Charles Wilber, *The Soviet Model and Underdeveloped Countries*, Chapel Hill, 1969; and David Albright, "The Soviet Model: Development Alternative for the Third World," in Henry Morton and Rudolph Tokes, eds., *Soviet Politics and Society in the 1970s*, New York, 1974, pp. 299–339; Alex Inkeles, *Social Change in Soviet Russia*, Cambridge, Mass., 1968, pp. 419–36.

CHAPTER THIRTEEN

EVOLUTION OF LEADERSHIP SELECTION IN THE CENTRAL COMMITTEE, 1917–1927

Robert V. Daniels

D*aniels is concerned with the very highest echelon of Soviet officialdom, those who have reached an official position important enough to entitle them, ex officio, to membership in the Central Committee of the Communist party. These men have worked their way up through the structure described by Sternheimer after receiving the required preservice training. Daniels argues that on reaching the summit of power they enter an institution that is analogous to the advisory bodies of officials with access to the tsar in the pre-Revolutionary period, even though the Central Committee was a truly elective body of political activists in its original form at the beginning of the 1920s. Here, then, we have a kind of apotheosis of the bureaucratic principle, an ultrabureaucratization, in which the political leadership that historically created the bureaucracy to do its bidding is now the product of the bureaucratic principle of* chinoproizvodstvo. *As Daniels writes, "Membership in the Central Committee is with few exceptions a function of the official job assignment of the particular member, and the individual's rank . . . is a reflection of the status imputed to the job he holds."*

The post-1917 ultrabureaucracy is the historical result of the gradual but fairly consistent extension of the professional bureaucratic role both within state officialdom and, through that officialdom, to ever-expanding areas of society. The upper-level official roles, jobs that because of their high status were both political and administrative in nature, were in the seventeenth and eighteenth centuries dominated by elites chosen by genetic accident and socialized in institutions such as the family and the military which were regarded as independent of and superior to the civil administration. As time has passed from the seventeenth century to the twentieth, these elites have been replaced by political-administrative elites chosen by and socialized by the bureaucracy itself. Already in the nineteenth century the superior institutions of the central state administration were coming to be controlled by individuals trained specifically—if not very well—for the civil functions they performed: lawyers, historians, graduates of philosophy and literature faculties of the universities, physicians, and engineers began to rise in importance. Retired captains and colonels, whatever their social background, would no longer do. As more time passed and bureaucratic roles became more extensively and precisely defined, so too did the training and career patterns of the officials themselves. As bureaucratic procedure (deloproizvodstvo) *came to dominate increasing areas of social behavior, so, gradually, the routes traveled by those who would dominate the bureaucracy were defined by the bureaucratic selection* (chinoproizvodstvo).

Bureaucratization is a phenomenon in Russia that overcame both official-dom and society. If deloproizvodstvo *and* chinoproizvodstvo *represented principles of impersonality, replicability, and security which were otherwise absent in pre-Revolutionary Russia because of the weakness of rule by law, then the autocracy and, earlier, the nobility represented the opposite—the personal, arbitrary, and unpredictable. Clearly, as we know both from pre-Revolutionary Russian history and, especially, post-1917 history, this latter element has not been reduced to insignificance, although it now finds expression through very different means. Still, it is clear that the tendency to bureaucratization has continued. In the Central Committee, for example, system and impersonality lay increasingly at the root of member selection in the 1920s and, while the purges drastically interfered with the regular or normal functioning of the selection system, the system itself emerged intact after the purges. Because of the bureaucratization of officialdom, of large segments of social behavior, and, as Daniels shows, of elite politics itself, an enormous, powerful, complex society has been disciplined to the regularities and uniformities of industrial civilization in a fashion quite different from that of similarly large and complex Western societies.* [THE EDITORS].

The Central Committee of the Communist Party of the Soviet Union (CPSU) is an institutionally defined bureaucratic elite, bringing together in the nominally leading body of the Party all the leading figures—currently 287 plus 139 candidate members and 85 members of the Central Auditing Commission—in the central and local echelons of the major functional hierarchies in Soviet society.[1] Membership in the Central Committee is with few exceptions a function of the official job assignment of the particular member, and the individual's rank—Politburo member, Politburo candidate, Central Committee

1. For an analysis of the current principles of Central Committee composition, see Robert V. Daniels, "Office Holding and Elite Status: The Central Committee of the CPSU," in Paul Cocks, Robert V. Daniels, and Nancy Whittier Heer, eds., *The Dynamics of Soviet Politics*, Cambridge, Mass., 1976.

member, Central Committee candidate, Central Auditing Commission—is a reflection of the status imputed to the job he holds. The selection of jobs to be represented is governed by a set of unwritten laws that nevertheless operate with very strict regularity, to specify the proportions of seats from the party apparatus, the civil government, the military, the trade unions, and the miscellaneous "public organizations" that make up the rest of the institutional fabric of Soviet society. Similar rules of status determine representation geographically among the Party and government people, as between the center, the union republics, and the major regional entities.

Two major areas of inquiry arise in considering the distinctive status characteristics of the Central Committee elite in a historical context. One is the intriguing parallel, superficial at least, between the Soviet status system and the rank and status practices of the imperial government before the Revolution. The other area especially inviting inquiry is the historical emergence of the current elite membership rules during the early years of the Soviet regime. Pursuit of this developmental phenomenon may shed some light on the actual process whereby pre-Revolutionary political patterns reemerged, as many authorities hold, under the Revolutionary banner.[2]

From the inception of the Russian Social Democratic Workers' party, ancestor of the Communists, up to the present, the Central Committee has, according to the statutes, been the responsible decision-making organ of the Party. To this extent, the institution was originally unexceptional among Western as well as Russian political party organizations. Elected—at least pro forma—by the party congress—the Central Committee was and is supposed to exercise leadership in the interim between congresses, during which time, according to Lenin's dictates of "democratic centralism," its decisions were binding on all the party membership.

Until well after the Revolution the makeup of the Communist Central Committee was governed by genuine elections at the party congresses, however they may have been influenced by factional controversies and pressure by the leadership (i.e. Lenin). Congress delegates voted for as many individuals as there were seats on the Central Committee, and the appropriate number with the highest votes were declared elected. Candidate members were originally the runners-up,

2. See, e.g., Zbiginiew Brzezinski, "Soviet Politics: From the Future to the Past?" in ibid.

but by 1920 they were being voted on separately after the roster of full members was announced.[3] Under these conditions the membership of the Central Committee was naturally drawn from well-known Revolutionary activists and key figures in the central party leadership.

From the Revolution until Lenin fell ill after the Eleventh Party Congress in 1922, the size of the Central Committee was relatively stable—twenty-one members and ten candidates elected at the Sixth Congress in August 1917, trimmed to fifteen and eight at the Seventh Congress in March 1918, held to nineteen and twelve as late as 1920, then raised incrementally to twenty-seven and nineteen by 1922. Through 1920, at least, the numbers were small enough so that most aspirants were being voted on by the Congress delegates on the basis of personal or direct knowledge. However, or perhaps for this reason, election to the Central Committee was sensitive to personal popularity and the interplay of the factional controversies that freely animated the life of the party during the War Communism period. Some individuals (A.S. Bubnov, for instance) reached, fell, and returned to the Central Committee as many as three times.

In 1921, at the Tenth Party Congress, the first signs appeared of a basic change in the actual manner of selecting Central Committee members. This was the practice of making up a semiofficial slate of aspirants, to be voted on de facto as a group by the Congress delegates. The occasion happened to be the most acute crisis ever experienced by the Soviet leadership, when it came under attack both externally from peasant rebels and the naval mutineers at Kronstadt, and internally from the left and ultraleft factions represented by Trotsky and the Workers' Opposition. Having decisively defeated his critics within the Communist party in the pre-Congress delegate selection, Lenin evidently decided to use his influence not only to oust several key oppositionists from the Central Committee but to expand the body from nineteen to twenty-five, thereby creating in all nearly a dozen openings for new people.

The fact that a slate of recommended official candidates was prepared for the Congress delegates to vote on is made clear by the totals of individual votes announced after the ballot. Lenin was everyone's choice, with 479 votes. But nearly unanimous votes were received by numerous other people, tapering down to 351 for the twenty-fourth member, the newcomer I. Ia. Tuntul. Only F. A. Artem-Sergeev, an incumbent, fell appreciably below the rest of the slate with 283, for the

---

3. *Deviatyi S"ezd RKP (b): Protokoly* (Ninth Congress of the Russian Communist Party [Bolsheviks]: Minutes, Moscow, 1960, p. 398.

last slot, and he was far ahead of the next contender, the deposed Trotskyist party secretary Krestinsky with 161.[4]

Fourteen of the new Central Committee were holdovers, all with outstanding reputations, representing from Lenin down the top posts at the center in government, the Party, and the trade unions.[5] Among the elven members newly elected or promoted from candidate rank, the territorial principle stood out instead: party leaders from Siberia (Yaroslavsky), the Caucasus (Ordzhonikidze), and the Ukraine (Molotov, moving into the national secretariat), plus the government chiefs from the Ukraine (Petrovsky) and Petrograd (N. P. Komarov). Though transitory and overlapping assignments at this early stage make it hard to define some individuals' functions, one of the new members at the center (V. M. Mikhailov) is identifiable as a former Cheka official moving into the party secretariat; two (Frunze and Voroshilov) represented the army; and two (Shliapnikov and I. D. Kutuzov) were added to the trade-union representation in a move to co-opt the Workers' Opposition.[6] (The function of the remaining individual, Tuntul, is unknown.)

Among the candidate members of the Central Committee, only four of the twelve incumbents of 1920 were held over in 1921, probably on grounds of reputation as much as function. Two, the commissar of labor and the Siberian government chief, were former full members; one, the outgoing mine-union chief newly installed as senior deputy people's commissar, was a former candidate. Eight entirely new candidates reflected strongly the territorial principle—two from the Ukraine, one from the Caucasus, one from Turkestan, one from Petrograd, and one from the Urals—plus one more trade unionist and one man (Osinsky) to conciliate the "Democratic Centralist" opposition group. Basically Lenin's slate making to curb the opposition factions that so plagued him in 1921 relied on the award of Central Committee status to loyal but not widely known provincial function-

4. *Desiatyi s"ezd RKP (b): Protokoly* (Tenth Congress of the Russian Communist Party [Bolsheviks]: Minutes), Moscow, 1963, p. 402.

5. Government: Lenin, prime minister; Kalinin, chief of state; Trotsky, commissar of war; Dzerzhinsky, head of the Cheka; Rykov, chairman of The Supreme Economic Council; Kamenev, chairman of the Moscow Soviet; Rakovsky, prime minister of the Ukraine. Party: Stalin, Politburo and Orgburo member; Bukharin, editor of *Pravda* and leading theoretician; Zinoviev and Radek, Comintern leaders. Trade unions: Tomsky, chairman; Rudzutak, secretary; Artem-Sergeev, new head of the miners.

6. Biographical data for this study has been drawn from a variety of sources, but most particularly from the index of names in the Minutes of the Eleventh Party Congress (*Odinnadtsatyi s"ezd RKP (b): Protokoly*, Moscow, 1936) and from *Who Was Who in the USSR* (prepared by the Institute for the Study of the USSR, Metuchen, N.J., 1972).

aries who would have stood little chance in the earlier style contest for a smaller body of stellar personalities.

At the Eleventh Party Congress in 1922 (Lenin's last) balloting for Central Committee members presumably took place in the usual fashion, though no individual vote totals were announced. The membership was increased by two more (from twenty-five to twenty-seven, with a rise in candidates from fifteen to nineteen). There happened to be much less turnover than the year before (mainly involving the elimination of Workers' Opposition members). Individual political distinction seems to have governed most of the new choices. However, among eight men newly installed as candidate members, territorial representation (Petrograd, Turkestan, the Ukraine) prevailed where direct replacement of vacancies (mostly trade unionists) did not.

Nineteen twenty-three was the year of Joseph Stalin's signal breakthrough in setting up a personal political organization in the Party, following his designation as general secretary the year before. Turning Lenin's proposal for an expanded Central Committee to his own advantage, Stalin persuaded the Twelfth Congress to increase the body from twenty-seven to forty.[7] This substantial expansion, together with three vacancies, gave him sixteen slots to fill.

Slate making was in evidence once again when the Twelfth Congress came to the election of the Central Committee, though the mathematics of it were covered up by a motion at the Congress to withhold announcement of individual vote totals.[8] Three of the new candidates of 1921 were now promoted, together with two of the 1922 group (Manuilsky and Mikoyan), and two ex-candidates, while four former members were restored. Among them these eleven represented the party in the Northwest region (Zalutsky), Nizhnii Novgorod (Uglanov), Azerbaidzhan (Kirov), the Ukraine (Manuilsky), the North Caucasus (Mikoyan), and the Urals (Sulimov), plus a second Moscow secretary (Mikhailov), together with the government

7. See Daniels, *The Conscience of the Revolution*, Cambridge, Mass., 1960, pp. 190–97. Stalin wanted to double the membership of the Central Committee, in order to "bring new, fresh, party workers into the work of the Central Committee," individuals whom he qualified in anticipation as "independent people . . . but not independent of Leninism, . . . independent people free from personal influences, from those habits and traditions of struggle within the Central Committee which have been formed among us and which often cause alarm within the Central Committee." Trotsky led the opposition to the proposed expansion, holding out for a small body that could continue to exercise quick day-to-day decision-making authority.

8. *Dvenadtsatyi s"ezd RKP (b). Stenograficheskii otchet* (Twelfth Congress of the Russian Communist Party [Bolsheviks]: Stenographic Report), Moscow, 1968, p. 661.

and trade unions in Petrograd (Komarov and Yevdokimov, Moscow already being represented), and the deputy commissar of War (Lashevich). Some of these selections—the Petrograders and Lashevich—represented politicking by Zinoviev to promote his friends and aides in the same way that Stalin was operating in most other parts of the country. Only Piatakov seems to have been an individual recognized in his own right as a stellar industrial administrator. Of the five noncandidates directly installed as members, two were industrial administrators (Tsiurupa, head of Gosplan, and Ukhanov, head of the electrical industry), while three represented still more regional party organizations—the Far East (Kubyak), Ekaterinburg in the Urals (Kharitonov), and the Ukraine (Kviring).

At the candidate level, promotions and demotions together created fourteen vacancies in 1923, again filled mainly by leaders of territorial Party organizations—Tver, Perm, the Don, Samara, and Siberia, with additional men from Moscow, the Northwest Bureau, and the Ukraine. Four new candidates represented government in Transcaucasia and Turkestan, plus one more from the Ukraine. One—Lazar Kaganovich—was the new head of the Organization and Instruction Department in the Central Secretariat. Stalin—and Zinoviev in his own northwestern area—were clearly bent on making the Central Committee a council of their regional party secretaries. In the course of this effort patterns of precedence were beginning to appear that have held true ever since: priority of party representation over government (more in toto, and more at the full-member level), and higher rank and/or more representation for the key provinces—Moscow, Leningrad, and the Ukraine.

The Thirteenth Party Congress of May 1924, was the first to come after Lenin's demise and the open break between Trotsky and the party leadership. It was the occasion for another substantial expansion in the ranks of the Central Committee, this time from forty to fifty-two. While practically all incumbents were confirmed in office,[9] six candidates were promoted, representing the Don, Ural, and Far Eastern party organizations, the Central Secretariat (Kaganovich), the chief military commissar (Bubnov), and the metal workers union. Nine newcomers directly installed as members included two from the Donets province, two more from Leningrad (Zinoviev's people, one becoming the sole woman on the Central Committee as head of the

---

9. One—Lenin—had died; one was transferred to the Central Control Commission, which ruled out Central Committee membership, and one—Karl Radek—was dropped for his activities on behalf of Trotsky.

Women's division), and one more from the Moscow party organization, plus two trade unionists (Tomsky's central aide Dogadov, and
the miners' chief Shvarts) and two economic administrators (Krzhi-
zhanovsky of Gosplan and Krassin of Trade). These selections rein-
force the picture of a body composed heavily of territorial party chiefs
—mostly the people recently installed by Stalin—together with top
functional administrators—party, governmental, industrial, military,
and trade union—at the center.

Twenty-one new Central Committee candidate members introduced in 1924 to fill the vacancies created by promotion and expansion
continued to fit the same pattern. Among them were a host of additional provincial party leaders, including Tula, Samara, Ivanovo,[10]
Kharkov and Podolia in the Ukraine, Belorussia, two more from the
Urals, three from Turkestan, and one more each from Moscow and
Petrograd. Three central party functionaries were the heads of Agit-
prop and the Komsomol, and the deputy chief of the Women's Division. Three more trade unionists were included, two representing the
Moscow Province unions specifically and one the national teachers'
union. One industrial administrator, heading the machinery industry,
was added, and one candidate (K. A. Rumiantsev) cannot be identified
in terms of his employment but may have come from the central party
apparatus.

At the Fourteenth Party Congress, in December 1925, when Zinoviev broke with Stalin and went down to defeat, the Central Committee was once again substantially enlarged—this time by eleven
men, from fifty-two to sixty-three. In this manner Stalin continued to
build his power base while minimizing the head-on confrontations
that would be implied in removing his leading opponents. These new
slots, combined with one death (War Commissar Frunze), three drops
(of lesser Zinovievists), and two demotions to candidate status (the
Zinovievists Lashevich and Nikolaeva), opened up seventeen membership positions. Nine were filled from the candidate ranks and
eight from outside. Administrators (the commissar of labor, Shmidt,
the deputy Gosplan chairman Smilga, the machinery industry chief
Tolokontsev, the Northwest Industrial Bureau head Lobov, along
with Foreign Commissar Chicherin) figured prominently in this expansion, while party leaders were included from Tula and the Donetsk
regions, together with second-line secretaries from Moscow and the
Ukraine, and the new head of the Women's Division of the Secretariat
(Artiukhina). Others brought in were the deputy Leningrad govern-

10. Presumed from incomplete data.

ment chief, the new head of the Ukrainian trade unions, and the chief army commissar for the Russian Republic (Shvernik), plus a leading party journalist (Stepanov-Skvortsov). Three cannot be identified as to job.

At the candidate level, expansion (from thirty-five to forty-three), promotions, and drops opened up an even larger number of new slots than the year before, a total of twenty-five (after allowing for the three demotions). These openings were filled by a very mixed crew—eight regional party officials (including Andrei Zhdanov of Nizhnii Novgorod), a functionary from the Institute of Party History, and another from the Comintern, four regional government officials (the prime minister of Azerbaidzhan and the number two people for Moscow, Leningrad, and the Transcaucasia federation), two oil-industry officials, two more trade unionists (textiles and another Ukrainian leader), the chief of the nascent Kolkhoz movement, and the deputy commissar of war (Unshlikht, recently shifted from the GPU). Three new candidates are not identifiable as to position. The breadth of selections at both levels suggests that Stalin was now broadening his political basis, or that he was temporarily heeding the wishes of Rykov and Tomsky to stress industrial and trade-union appointments.

The Fifteenth Party Congress, held in December 1927, a year later than the rules called for, saw the dramatic expulsion of the Left Opposition headed by Trotsky and Zinoviev. The unprecedented number of eight Central Committee members were dropped for oppositionist activity, which together with two deaths (Dzerzhinsky and Krasin), a transfer to the Central Control Commission (Ordzhonikidze), and an expansion of eight seats, created nineteen vacancies in all. Most were filled by promoting candidates (twelve) or by transfers from the Central Control Commission (Kuibyshev and Piatnitsky, and Lenin's widow, Krupskaya, enjoying honor without influence). Direct appointments included such specialities as the party leader of Belorussia, the head of the GPU (Menzhinsky), the new head of the Ukrainian trade unions, and a leading party intellectual (Stetsky). Twenty-four candidate vacancies were created by expansion, promotion, and drops, and these were filled by a wide variety of party, governmental, and trade-union functionaries: new party secretaries from the Don, Donetsk province, Lugansk province in the Donbas, Azerbaidzhan, the Tatar Autonomous Republic, two additional men from Moscow, and the secretary of the Red Trade Union International (Lozovsky); also the government chiefs of Georgia and the Far East region, together with the commissar of finance, the head of the metal industry, and the chairman of the Ukrainian economic council; the chief of the air force; and the leader of the agricultural workers union. Eight new candidates remain unidentified as to function.

With the seventy-one members of 1927, the Central Committee had reached a level that was to hold constant through the postpurge Eighteenth Congress of 1939, although the candidate roster continued to creep up marginally. Therefore, 1927 is a logical stopping place to review systematically the personnel structure of the Central Committee as it had evolved up to that time.

The 121 members and candidate members of 1927 break down into functional groups as follows: party apparatus, 55; civil government, 36; trade unions, 10; military, 3; police, 1; miscellaneous, 2 (the head of the Kolkhoz Union and, more or less in her own right or as a cultural figure, Lenin's widow, Krupskaya); position undetermined, 1 member and 12 candidate members. In comparison with the ratios of functional representation in the post-Stalin regime, the party and government proportions have remained nearly constant. However, the trade unions were much higher in 1927, and the military distinctly lower, suggesting an interesting shift of imputed prestige from the proletariat to the armed forces since the 1920s. Other evidence of sensitivity about the working-class base of the regime at that time was the heavy representation from the Donets Basin industrial area (both party and industrial administrators) and the status accorded Commissar of Labor Shmidt as full Central Committee (CC) member and candidate member of the Orgburo.

Within the party sector, the 1927 allocation of CC member and candidate seats was: central apparatus (including Comintern representatives), fifteen; Russian Republic, twenty-five; Union Republics, fourteen (including future Central Asian republics). Again the proportions are not radically different from the present distribution. The varying status of particular areas was already clearly reflected, as it has been systematically in more recent times. Considering first the Russian Republic, the Moscow organization had six members and candidates, headed by a candidate member of the Politburo with seats on the Orgburo and Secretariat (Uglanov). Leningrad had three, headed by a candidate member of the Politburo (Kirov). At this time in certain parts of the Russian Republic groups of provinces (*gubernii*) were combined into *oblasti*,[11] (not to be confused with the present use of the

11. See Robert V. Daniels, "The Secretariat and the Local Organizations in the Russian Communist Party, 1921–23," *American Slavic and East European Review* 16 (1957): 44–45.

terms as a province), and these large entities were all represented by their party chiefs—the North Caucasus (Politburo candidate Andreev and two Central Committee candidates), the Urals (Orgburo member Sulimov and two Central Committee candidates), Siberia (one member), and the Far East (one member). In addition, a cluster of *gubernii* surrounding Moscow (Tula, Orel, Ivanovo, Vladimir, roughly corresponding to the present *oblasti*) had full CC membership status for their first secretaries, while another group trailing down the Volga (Nizhnii-Novgorod [Gorkii], the Tatar Autonomous Republic, Samara [Kuibyshev], and Saratov) had candidate status. Among the Union Republics the pecking order was fairly clear: seven member or candidate slots for the Ukraine (headed by Politburo candidate Kaganovich); two for Uzbekistan; one for Belorussia; one for the Transcaucasian Regional Bureau as a whole, and one for Azerbaidzhan in particular. The Central Asian territories yet to become Union Republics had two members as well (who both happened to be Russians).

On the government side the distribution of member and candidate positions was: central (USSR), nineteen; RSFSR (central and local), ten; Union Republics, seven (five from the Ukraine, one from Azerbaidzhan, and one from Georgia). Allowing for the difference in organizational structure, involving in 1927 no great proliferation of industrial ministries, the distribution of central seats among the key commissars and industrial chiefs was essentially similar to the present allocation where every cabinet-level post is included. Local government chiefs included Moscow (Orgburo candidate Ukhanov) and Leningrad (Komarov), each with one deputy; and the regional (*oblast'*) administrations for the Northwest, Siberia, and the Far East (all at the candidate level).

Within its more limited numbers the 1927 trade-union representation followed a similar pattern: central, seven seats (Chairman Tomsky, a Politburo member, Secretary Dogadov, and the union chiefs of four different industries); Russian Republic, two (Moscow, with Orgburo candidate status, and Leningrad); Union Republics, one (the Ukraine). Rank distinctions also figured among the industrial unions: metalworkers, Orgburo candidate; miners, Central Committee member; textiles and agricultural workers, Central Committee candidates.[12]

Further systematic status relations emerge from a comparison of geographical representation between the various functional sectors.

12. This count is one short; an additional trade-unionist (Melnichansky) had been head of the textile union but was probably an assistant to Tomsky by this time.

For any entity, the party apparatus had more representation, at an equal or higher rank, followed by the government and then the trade unions. Geographical units received representation both in numbers and in rank in close proportion to their demographic and economic importance. This held true in the apportionment among Union Republics and among regions within the Russian Republic. All of these hierarchical relationships continue to characterize the post-Stalin leadership, though with a greatly expanded Central Committee the implicit principles of apportionment are able to operate in a considerably more refined way.

Expansion of the party's Central Auditing Commission to nine members in 1927 brings it into the scope of this representational analysis along with the Central Committee. Apart from their new chairman (former head of the Central Control Commission in the Ukraine) and the rector of the Sverdlov party university, the members of the Central Auditing Commission were all leaders of regional party or government bodies in the Russian Republic. The list clearly anticipated the regular practice in the later Stalin and post-Stalin years of making the Central Auditing Commission an honorable-mention category for functionaries in a variety of capacities whose jobs carried a status just below those distinguished by Central Committee membership or candidate status.

The picture of functional apportionment and rank allocation as of 1927 demonstrates very clearly how the leadership institutionalized in the Central Committee had acquired by that time the basic characteristics of status and representation that still prevail under the post-Stalin regime. Within the short span of five years under Stalin's organizational domination the central leadership body (Central Committee members and candidates) was expanded more than two and a half times and almost totally realigned from an elected group of the articulate and politically popular to a body de facto appointed on the basis of bureaucratic constituencies.

There is ample precedent in pre-Revolutionary history for such a status-based bureaucratic leadership body as the Central Committee had rapidly become under Stalin's leadership. Russia had a long tradition of consultative policy sounding-boards, de facto appointed by the man in charge and apportioned among representatives of the key political institutions and social groups. Kerensky used the device in 1917, in the absence of any nationally elected body, when he convened the Moscow State Conference in August 1917, and the Petrograd Democratic Conference in September. In the nineteenth-century empire the

State Council was such a body, appointed by the emperor from among the top figures in the nobility and the bureaucracy, including cabinet ministers and provincial governors-general. As a legislative advisory body whose recommendations the tsar might or might not respond to, it conferred more status than power on its members. Status within the council was further refined by the distinction between the upper group of sixteen, who participated in one of the Council's subcommittees (legislative, police and church, general policy, and economic affairs) and the remainder, who attended only the general sessions.[13] The distinction suggests the Communist differentiation of the Politburo, Orgburo, and Secretariat out of the membership of the Central Committee.

Long before the creation of the State Council by Alexander I and Speransky, basically similar procedures provided for some form of top-status consultative body putting the heads of the various component institutions and interests of the realm in touch with the tsar (but more to underscore their subservience than to limit his arbitrary will). Such were the Boyar Duma and the *Zemskii sobor* before Peter's time, and the Senate as it functioned during the eighteenth century. Peter's Table of Ranks crystallized the old Russian tradition of prescribed status and precedence relationships (especially *mestnichestvo*) in a new, superficially rational and seemingly Western mold. Throughout the subsequent operation of this system the compulsion was evident to equate the status of a function and some badge of personal rank of the individual, in a manner that Western societies observe only in military service. At the uppermost level the most common way of underscoring this consideration of rank was membership at the appropriate grade in those bodies in contact with the tsar.

None of the foregoing is to suggest that Stalin was consciously or specifically guided by a knowledge of imperial practices when he set about expanding and packing the Central Committee of the CPSU. Such knowledge was and is rather esoteric when it comes to the details. But what Stalin does appear to have been guided by was a feel for what would be most acceptable in the Russian milieu for his choice of members to serve in the nominal governing body of the Party. The canons of such acceptability, in turn, seem to be a deeply established traditional expectation that the top body should represent the key institutional functions and geographical areas in some proportion to the importance of the respective functions and areas, and that the

13. *Entsiklopedicheskii slovar'* (Encyclopedic Dictionary), St. Petersburg, 1893, 17: 415–16.

representatives of each functional or geographical unit should be the top appointed functionaries in that unit. These were criteria for inclusion in the Central Committee slate that no one seemed to be able to quarrel with. Conveniently they dovetailed with the circumstance that the top appointed functionaries (especially at the provincial level) in what was emerging as the key national institution were Stalin's own appointees to provincial party secretaryships. Stalin built his own power by paralleling the model of the imperial bureaucratic elite institutions.

Stalin's political tactics exemplify a widespread, though not commonly recognized, mechanism, not only in Russia but in other situations following abrupt social and political change, that serves to explain the "return of the repressed" patterns of behavior from the Old Régime. Pragmatic and opportunistic leadership rising to the surface in the wake of a revolution senses the political steps that will be acceptable because they are familiar and expected within the context of the particular culture, even if they are not particularly liked —and the change of ideological labels can allay some of that last reservation. In Russia this mechanism, broadly conceived, helps account for the Bolsheviks' ability to establish a new autocracy with old, scarcely disguised bureaucratic and police methods, and to have this regime accepted by the Russian nation.

CHAPTER FOURTEEN

OFFICIALDOM AND BUREAUCRATIZATION: CONCLUSION

Walter M. Pintner and Don Karl Rowney

The preceding essays cover a span of over 350 years, from the early seventeenth century to our own times. The changes in virtually every aspect of human activity in the course of those years have been enormous everywhere, and Russian officialdom has not been isolated from them. Within Russia, in fact, officialdom has been a major instrument of change as well as a product of it. The aim of these concluding remarks is to suggest in what ways Russian officialdom has been most affected and what characteristics have tended to remain essentially the same as the Russian state evolved from the premodern era to our own times. Only with both factors in mind can the nature of officialdom and its impact on Russian life at any given time be properly understood. Only if we know what was already well established can we determine what was new and significant. To decide whether or not Peter the Great's Table of Ranks "opened careers to talent," for example, one must know not only what followed the new law, but how things worked before it was enacted. Having identified the constant and very slowly changing aspects of officialdom we can then recognize periods when truly new features were introduced, or first became significant, and attempt to fit them into the general evolution of Russian history.

The most striking constant that emerges from our study is the very fact of the continuous existence of officialdom throughout the period covered. It was an institution that bound generations together; each in turn prepared the way for the next, in the early centuries by training youths on the job and later through the establishment of formal educational institutions to qualify men for service. Where other societies used "collegial" forms of organization (parliaments, town meetings), at least to some extent, Russia used officials subordinate to the sovereign. Power depended on office, and few men had influence solely because of birth or wealth. This general model of official organization permeated every aspect of contemporary Russian life and did not differ very much from that already developed in the seventeenth century, although the writ of the Muscovite *d'iak* (clerk) was far more limited than is that of the contemporary Soviet official. Despite the fact that the sovereign's original intention was presumably to create an official-dom which would effectively carry out his wishes, it is both historically ironic and a measure of the strength of the "official way" in Russia that the official way has become virtually universal in public life. This is one of the reasons why we can speak of the bureaucratization of Russian society.

One can think of the history of Russian officialdom as a rope that spans the 350-year period; few strands will extend the full length but there obviously can be no point where all end and an entirely new set begins. At any point there will be some about to end, some beginning, and some at midpoint; otherwise there could be no rope, no continuity. As just noted, the strand that most clearly goes from the beginning to the end of our period is that of the centralized hierarchy of officials as the mechanism through which those holding power attempted to achieve their objectives. In the very broadest sense this idea of how political decisions should be implemented does not change.

Another consistent pattern, extending throughout the entire period, is that of the tendency to bureaucratize both the officialdom and, through the growth of the official presence, large segments of non-official society. This is a theme that, in numerous ways, is broader than the one to which we address ourselves in this book, yet it is nevertheless inseparable from the officialdom itself. One dimension of bureaucratization is represented by changes in the structures in which officials worked, although it is often difficult to differentiate between changes in name and changes in substance.[1] Seventeenth-century *prikazy* become eighteenth-century colleges, which in turn become nineteenth-century ministries, twentieth-century commissariats, and, again, ministries. To trace the tortured paths that the formal structures of Russian administration take from the seventeenth century is to follow a vague and badly drawn road map of change in official procedure (*deloproizvodstvo*). For all that, it is one of the best guides we have. In the most general terms the thrust of these changes in the structure of official authority, responsibility, and procedure is in the direction of accommodating similar functions together under the

---

1. The structure of Russian administration is discussed in Hans-J. Torke, "Continuity and Change in the Relations between Bureaucracy and Society in Russia, 1613–1861," *Canadian Slavic Studies* 5 (Winter 1971): 457–76; and comments on that article by John Keep, "Light and Shade in the History of Russian Administration," *Canadian-American Slavic Studies* 6 (Spring 1972): 1–9.

same organizational roof (rationalization) and, simply, of accommodating new and ever more functions. Running against this thrust of
rationalization is the tendency of individual organizations to add new
functions, new authorities, to enhance their own status at the expense
of their competitors. There is also another, crossing tendency, that of
groups to enhance their status by breaking off from their controlling
ministries. Structural reorganization in the nineteenth and especially
the twentieth centuries gives political and fiscal scope to increasing
specialization, just as the creation of specialist agencies (e.g. for health
care or statistics gathering) adds the luster of official status to a developing profession.[2] Thus the multiplication of specialized ministries
in the twentieth century is both a consequence of and a stimulant to
the process of bureaucratization that overcomes Russian society and
its officialdom.

Just as they underscore important if not sudden changes, new ministerial names may still obscure one of the most important elements of
continuity, the dramatic difference that has always existed between
service in central and provincial agencies. Despite repeated efforts at
local government reform, provincial reorganization, decentralization,
and so forth, central service remained attractive and provincial service
unattractive. Pay, power, promotion all drew men to the center, at
least down to 1917. A provincial assignment might come after a successful central career (designation as a *voevoda* or governor), and appointment to a central-ministry position might be preceded by several
rapid changes in middle-level provincial offices. Still, the provinces
were a dead end for those who started there near the bottom. The
result has been that the most talented and best-trained men have served
at the center, but generally have had to depend on the least educated
and least ambitious to execute their policies throughout the realm.

The best-known landmark in the history of Russian officialdom is,
of course, Peter I's Table of Ranks (1722). It established the formal
hierarchy of ranks that remained in effect until 1917 and traditions of
hierarchy and precedence that are still obvious in the Soviet Union
today. More important, it became part of a more elaborate series of
rules for career advancement through state office (*chinoproizvodstvo*)
and thus became an instrument of bureaucratization of all officials—
those at the top as well as the lowly clerks. It also provided for a clear
separation of military and civil careers. Nevertheless, it is difficult to
show that, at the time of its publication, the Table marked a major

---

2. The influence of such changes on the legal profession is discussed by Richard S.
Wortman in *The Development of a Russian Legal Consciousness*, Chicago, 1976, pp. 34–88.

break in the development of Russian officialdom. The same kinds of people continued to do the same jobs, and meaningful separation of military and civil careers at any but the lowest levels did not emerge for nearly a century. The Table of Ranks in practice probably had greater initial impact on the nobility as a social group—technically it defined it—than it did on the civil service as a profession. The Table defined membership in the nobility in terms of state service and provided for ennoblement through service, a fact of great symbolic and some practical significance. Over the long run, the impact of the hierarchy of ranks, through which officials came to rise largely through seniority, had great importance for the operation of officialdom, although the parallel hierarchy of offices became increasingly important in the decades prior to 1917. It is striking, however, that none of the threads which have been followed in this volume—the role of family ties, social background, landed wealth, career patterns, and formal versus informal training—seem to have been immediately or sharply affected by Peter's famous statute.

The preparation of officials, like structural change and uniform rules for career advancement, made its own slow contribution to the definition and bureaucratization of officialdom. As apprenticeship, home education and military schools gave way before the universities, the Lycée, and the School of Jurisprudence, the influence of families and individuals alike weakened before the uniform influence of these more impersonal institutions. The fact that entrance at an advanced level and rapid promotion—and, thus, achievement of elite status—depended almost wholly upon acquisition of a degree in the nineteenth century meant that the socially elite as well as the low born were now bound to submit to formation by institutions which themselves were part of the official apparatus. During the nineteenth century, indeed, ministries had sometimes created educational institutions for training specialists of their own, in effect, to their own specifications. In some cases (e.g. the Ministry of Justice and the Ministry of Ways and Communications at the end of the century) a substantial portion of the ministerial elite were products of their own school.[3] The formal education requirement, thus, became an important means of integrating the previously independent, superior high officialdom into a bureaucratized hierarchy of functions manipulated by *chinoproizvodstvo* and disciplined by *deloproizvodstvo*.

An essential part of the bureaucratization of officialdom was simply

3. Again, Wortman, *Legal Consciousness*, pp. 198–233, discusses this point as it bears on the legal administration.

its increasing size over the centuries, paralleling but exceeding the growth of the empire in territory and population. The seventeenth-century clerk worked in a hierarchical and formally described structure doing things that differed little from the tasks of modern officials, aided though they are by telephones and office machines, but he did probably know virtually every other official by name, a situation inconceivable in any large agency much less the whole government today. Similarly, throughout the nineteenth century, if officials in one ministry did not know those in another, they at least understood the subject and thrust of each other's work. In the twentieth century this dimension of what was once unity of officialdom has been seriously if not totally undermined. From the 1920s the problem was not only increasing size—as in the eighteenth century, the sheer number of officials—but also the enormous diversity and narrow specialization of function. What has happened to officialdom, at least in Russia, is similar to the metamorphosis of the classical university into a multiversity. In the eighteenth century, under the aegis of classical education, the university was small, intimate, both in numbers and the distances that separated the information fields of its members. In the twentieth century, it has become enormous in both respects. The community of scholars, like the community of officials, exists only on paper or in small groups created and sustained with difficulty by a few individuals often on an unofficial basis.

It should be kept in mind that the expansion of Russian officialdom is not a recent development. In terms of the transformation of an intimate group into an anonymous and much subdivided mass, one must go back at least to the beginning of the nineteenth century, or even earlier. From time to time there was criticism of officialdom and its growth from such diverse figures as Prince Shcherbatov and Karamzin in the late eighteenth and early nineteenth century and Lenin in the 1920s, but neither the critics outside the government, or Lenin in actual charge could have their way. There were many tasks—always more—to be done, and in the Russian tradition the only way to try to get them done was through officials.

The emphasis in most of the essays in this volume has been on the officials themselves. Who were they? What basic social and economic categories describe them, and what constituted their life experience? It is primarily in these terms that we have traced the evolution of Russian officialdom for 350 years.

Returning to the analogy of the rope, there seem to be two periods in which several strands end and new ones begin: (1) the last years of the eighteenth century and the early decades of the nineteenth, and (2) the early twentieth century, particularly the decade or two immediately following the Revolution of 1917.

At the end of the eighteenth century the traditional importance of family ties, on-the-job training for civil service, and the mixed military and civil career came to an end. These forms of socialization were replaced by a rapidly increasing emphasis on objective criteria, expressed in terms of the completion of specified periods of formal education prior to service, and a drastic reduction in the number of civil officials with prior military service. Civil service became a lifetime career with its own specific entrance requirements.

The Revolution of 1917 ended the importance of noble birth and inherited wealth as factors affecting officialdom, but two threads at least span this early twentieth century period of change. Under the new Bolshevik regime the century-old importance of formal educational credentials became a far more explicit demand for specialized technical training and, of course, officialdom itself has continued to operate and to grow.

That there was some discontinuity following the Revolution of 1917 is hardly surprising, but the early nineteenth century does not have a comparable landmark. It is nevertheless clear that in the course of a generation civil officialdom underwent substantial change. Peter I had certainly emphasized training of the nobility, but not training directed at preparing civil officials in institutions designed for that purpose. Throughout the eighteenth century it was assumed that prior military experience, frequently including education in the Cadet Corps, was adequate preparation for the upper ranks of civil officialdom. For lower-level clerkships, apprenticeship in an office from a tender age was the normal pattern. Beginning in the early nineteenth century, however, qualifications came to be set in terms of reaching specified levels of formal education. The new system did not represent democratization any more than did the Table of Ranks, since the privileged classes had much greater access to the requisite training. Like the Table of Ranks and uniform grades, it was a step toward a more impersonal, bureaucratic system. To be sure there were exceptions, but just as one must travel through the ranks at specified rates and by specified paths, so without the specified degree one could not enter service at an advanced level, no matter what one's social status was.

The second strand that seems to end in the late eighteenth and early nineteenth century is the great importance of family ties. Our picture of seventeenth-century lower-level officials has a strikingly modern ring with its regular procedures, accountability, and so forth, except for the repeated references to the role of family connections among the chancery clerks. Much the same thing seems to have been true among the higher ranks in the seventeenth and eighteenth centuries. Even after the abolition of compulsory service, family connections played a vital part in court politics at the highest level.[4] However, court politics by Catherine II's day were not solely familial in the genetic sense. Even then the older tradition was breaking down.

At the lower levels the official's son who could learn something informally from his father inevitably had a major advantage in a period when there were virtually no facilities to train boys for civil positions. The small caste of professional clerks could not, however, produce enough offspring to staff the growing ranks of civil officialdom in the eighteenth century. As early as the 1750s only 22 percent of lower-level central officials were the sons of office workers. In the provinces, where expansion came later, this proportion was much higher, 71 percent.[5] The combination of growth in size and, in the early nineteenth century, increased emphasis on formal education inevitably produced a more impersonal institution, although family ties, friendship and patronage undoubtedly continued to play a role in appointments and promotions.

The third major thread that ends in the late eighteenth-early nineteenth century is the unity of military and civilian service at the upper level. From the seventeenth century, and possibly even earlier, the lower-level positions in central service were largely filled with lifetime employees and a few of them rose to important posts, but the normal career pattern of high officials in the seventeenth and eighteenth centuries was one that included both civil and military assignments, frequently so intermingled as to preclude designating the official as primarily one or the other. From the early nineteenth century forward to the present day, although ex-military men are still to be found, the characteristic career pattern at all levels increasingly came to be one of purely civil service.

It must be emphasized, however, that civil officialdom was not totally transformed in either the early nineteenth century or the early twentieth. In each instance important aspects of the earlier period continued into the later one. At the beginning of the nineteenth century the training and career pattern of the typical official, particularly of the higher-ranking official, was transformed, but in terms of two important characteristics, social background and landed wealth, there

4. David L. Ransel, *Politics of Catherinian Russia: The Panin Party*, New Haven, 1975.

5. S. M. Troitskii, *Russkii absoliutizm i dvorianstvo v XVIIIv.: Formirovanie biurokratii*, Moscow, 1974, p. 215.

was little change. Nor, as we have noted was there any drastic change in the functions performed. Thus the same kind of men were going into similar jobs, but they were preparing for them in a new way.

It is easy to demonstrate that from the seventeenth century to the Revolution, the higher positions in the civil hierarchy were largely filled by "nobles," men who at any given time can be distinguished fairly easily in terms of their legal status and privileged social position. This most definitely is not the same as saying that Russia was ruled by a small, self-perpetuating upper class for 300 years until it was overthrown by the Bolsheviks in 1917. The Russian nobility was always too ill-defined and diverse to permit such a situation to develop. It was a restricted group, but one that was neither totally closed nor homogeneous. At the very top, where the personal favor of the sovereign was most important, the chance of rapid movement, both upward and downward, was greatest. There were always a very few who moved spectacularly from lowly backgrounds to the highest positions through a combination of talent and good fortune in attracting the attention of powerful people, especially of the sovereign. More significant in a quantitative sense was the relatively open nature of state service at the lower levels. When, during periods of expansion, there were not enough nobles to fill the positions open, formal criteria for entrance, if there were any, were ignored. The close association of state service with the acquisition of legal membership in the nobility gave this avenue considerable significance, particularly for nobility over two or more generations. Mobility beyond one generation is a phenomenon that as yet has defied quantification, except in the case of very small elite groups, because of the elaborate genealogical research required. However, the significant cadre of officials from noble families without land or serfs, at every period, strongly suggests that the process was taking place. Civil officialdom never became the exclusive preserve of the nobility at any level, but the nobility remained the predominant group at the top from the seventeenth century to 1917.

It might be expected that the increasing importance of formal education would have tended to democratize officialdom, since the educational system that developed in the early nineteenth century, particularly in the universities, was a multiclass one. However, as mentioned above, this appears to have been the case only to a very limited degree, if at all. It was certainly true that nonnobles with higher education did nearly as well in service as did nobles. However, the overall proportion of the two groups in service in the nineteenth century changed only moderately compared to earlier periods. The incentive to acquire the necessary educational credentials, and the economic and social realities of doing so, were such that the institution of relatively "objective" criteria for upper-level entrance into service had only limited effect on the makeup of officialdom. This experience is actually very similar to that in major Western and non-Western countries. Applicants who succeed in the most rigorous and "objective" examination and promotion systems turn out to be those from elite backgrounds that give them both the incentive to acquire the needed skills and the realistic possibility of doing so in practice.[6] In the context of nineteenth-century Russia the elements of society outside the legal nobility with these attributes were small.

The second thread that firmly connects the officialdom of the nineteenth century with the seventeenth and eighteenth centuries is the evident but limited role of landed wealth. The nexus of wealth, power, and status is a familiar one in most societies, and certainly it is not absent in the case of Russia. Yet, as we examine the data for any period in our 350-year survey, it is immediately clear that the correspondence is not a simple one. Even though most high officials had substantial estates, there were always a few who did not. Until the late nineteenth century, the Russian landed nobility was the only significant group with wealth independent of government salary, but that wealth was rarely of long standing in the family, and it would be false to suggest that it was truly independent of the state, even in the case of the handful of great magnates. At the highest levels in the seventeenth and eighteenth centuries, service and the retention or loss of estates and imperial favor or disfavor were inextricably intertwined. In the nineteenth century rewards were largely monetary, and although the income from specific state-owned property was sometimes assigned to important officials, outright grants became rare. The well-known Russian tradition of equal division of inheritance effectively prevented the maintenance of large family fortunes over several generations. Thus, even after the abolition of compulsory service in 1762, few could afford not to serve as a way of supplementing income from an estate, if there was one, and retaining prestige and social position. The whole Table of Ranks system was an elaborate device to link status to nonmonetary rewards. The prestige of position came to be as important as, and indistinguishable from, the prestige of independent wealth.

What we find over a period of centuries is not a civil service domi-

6. Ezra N. Suleiman makes the case convincingly for contemporary France and cites other studies to the same effect for Denmark, Great Britain, the United States, Turkey, and India, in *Politics, Power, and Bureaucracy in France: The Administrative Elite*, Princeton, 1974, pp. 72–89.

nated at the top by men of independent landed wealth, that is, men who in some sense could be regarded as representative of an autonomous landed interest, but rather officials who wanted and needed to serve, even when not legally required to, in order to supplement their incomes in most cases, and always to enhance their social status. Certainly social, and in later periods educational, advantages made the achievement of high position easier for sons of the wealthy, but they could never buy a position or claim it by right. Below the highest levels, civil officialdom was filled, down to the Revolution, with nobles who had little or no land and men who were not noble at all, and there was no line above which at least a few of them could not rise if they had the talent and much good fortune. No level was ever the exclusive preserve of a special category of people defined by either heredity or by wealth.

Officialdom was always a body of men oriented to the state's concerns. In the nineteenth century the acquisition of landed wealth through gift or purchase even ceased to be a necessary by-product of the most brilliantly successful careers. In a sense one could argue that the Romanovs had largely eliminated the landed interest from the state service long before the Bolsheviks ever existed, although, of course, men with landed wealth served down to the end in 1917.

The Revolution of 1917 marked the end of the nobility as a distinct social group, and the end of private landholding. As rapidly as possible the new Bolshevik government got rid of politically unreliable administrative generalists and more slowly the tsarist technical specialists. The traditional role of birth and wealth in the formation of officialdom ended in 1917. However, the role of formal education, or impersonal, "objective" criteria as a qualification for official position that dates back to the early nineteenth century continued and became increasingly important in the Soviet period. Initially, of course, the demand for "red," i.e. politically reliable, specialists was a significant one, but by now, after over sixty years of Soviet rule, the demand for political reliability is hardly more significant than the tsarist requirement of professed Christianity. What has been important in the Soviet period is the growing role of technical skills and the related structural subdivision of offices. Formal education when it first became a requirement of advanced level entrance was, in most cases, very general and was not designed to produce technical specialists. As the nineteenth century progressed, the importance of specialized training grew, first in areas such as law and medicine and later in many other subjects, such as engineering, associated with the growth of a modern industrial sector of Russian society. The increasing role of specialists contributed to the decreased importance of rank (*chin*) as a measure of success in civil service, but on the eve of the Revolution of 1917 the tension between specialists and generalists within officialdom was by no means resolved.

With the establishment of the new Soviet government the role of the technical specialist was rapidly and definitively expanded. This occurred at least as rapidly as the changes that were made for purposes of securing politically reliable servitors. Thus with the governmental reorganization of 1917–18, Imperial Ministries and their functions were not so much abolished as they were broken up into their specialized—and often technical—positions. The Imperial Ministry of the Interior, for example, was "abolished" in 1917, but its place was taken by not one but many agencies that were more specialized.

What this reorganization appears to have achieved is the possibility both for expansion of technical roles and their control by the technicians themselves cum bureaucrats. Thus, while in the nineteenth century technocrats often had to be content with subordination in their own ministry to nonspecialists, in the post-1917 period they began to operate in ministries composed more or less exclusively of their own kind. The proliferation of specialized ministries and ministerial-type agencies has continued into the later twentieth century: in 1916 there were thirteen national ministries while in the mid-1970s there were twenty-nine all-union and thirty-one union-republic ministries in the USSR. If the Russian official was a military servitor in the eighteenth century and a legal bureaucrat in the nineteenth century, he is an engineer bureaucrat in the twentieth.

During the past 350 years, Russian officials and their role in Russian society have changed. To some extent the paths followed by Russian administrative development have simply been those already traced by other, especially Western, bureaucracies from the eighteenth century to the present time. This is especially true of formal patterns of bureaucratic organization including the use of ranks, the creation of ministries, the introduction of formal educational requirements, and the like. There are dimensions to this development that mark it as quite distinct from Western patterns and make the creation of parallels misleading. This is especially true of the respective roles played in social organization by the enforcement of formal legislation and of bureaucratic rules of behavior. In effect, the widespread Western assumption that the guide for common social behavior and the protector of the individual was, and ought to be, a legally controlled polity (*Rechtsstaat*) never took root in Russia. Faced with the same demands for social stability and reliable social organization as any other society, Russia responded typically with the extension of officialdom, but an officialdom disciplined and limited only by bureaucratic rules. As we have seen, this extension of officialdom and the accompanying bureaucratization of both officialdom and society have been relentless in Russia since the seventeenth century. By the twentieth century little in the way of social reality existed that was outside its organizing grasp. The apotheosis of this growth came with the transformation of politics and politicians themselves into officials when the unique and unanswerably powerful emperor was replaced by an official and thoroughly bureaucratized Party. The stunning importance of the role assumed by the Party in the 1920s is not that it became a new state religion through fostering a new ideology, but that it integrated political power, irretrievably perhaps, into another institutional tradition. The organization of politics into the society of bureaucratized officials created what we have called an ultrabureaucracy in which bureaucrats are answerable only to bureaucrats.

Do these observations lead us to conclude that policy formation as well as its administration have fallen, in Russia, into the hands of a clique of mandarins who train and choose their own successors and who so dominate society that they are capable of blunting any challenge to their authority? Yes, in a sense they do. But one must also recognize the limits placed on the exercise of power by bureaucratic discipline, enormous size, and specialization. To refer to the Soviet ultrabureaucrats as mandarins calls too much attention to what they share in common (their commitment to officialdom, its careers, and its bureaucratic methods) and too little to their great numbers and the real differences that separate them from each other intellectually and in experience.

It is also important to recognize that in certain respects the patterns of change, especially the generally consistent expansion of the role of the bureaucratized official in Russia, have been harbingers of the developing relations between governments and society worldwide, in both technologically advanced and relatively backward societies. Although the degree of the official presence in Russia and the USSR has been extreme, it nevertheless remains that as centralization continues elsewhere—as the welfare state, and national economic planning grow, for example—the official presence expands and is likely to continue doing so.

Bibliography

This is a highly selective bibliography of works that directly relate to the chapters in the preceding text. Whenever possible, works in Western languages have been given preference. No attempt has been made to cover the general problem of bureaucracy or the development of bureaucracy in countries other than Russia. Since the footnotes are not recapitulated here, the interested reader will find full bibliographic information in the first citation of a given work in each chapter.

Section I. General Works

Amburger, Erik. *Geschichte der Behördenorganisation Russlands von Peter dem Grossen bis 1917.* Leiden, 1966.

Armstrong, John A. *The European Administrative Elite.* Princeton, 1973.

Black, Cyril E. "Japan and Russia: Bureaucratic Politics in a Comparative Context." *Social Science History* 2 (Summer 1978): 414–26.

Crozier, Michel. *The Bureaucratic Phenomenon.* Chicago, 1967.

Eroshkin, N. P. *Ocherki istorii gosudarstvennykh uchrezhdenii dorevoliutsionnoi Rossii.* Moscow, 1960.

Mousnier, R. *Social Hierarchies, 1450 to the Present.* Translated by Peter Evans. Edited by Margaret Clark. New York, 1973.

Orlovsky, Daniel T. "Recent Studies on the Russian Bureaucracy." *The Russian Review* 35 (October 1976): 448–67.

Rowney, Don Karl. "Bureaucratic Development and Social Science History." *Social Science History* 2 (Summer 1978): 379–84.

Weber, Max. *The Theory of Social and Economic Organizations.* Translated by A. M. Henderson and Talcott Parsons. Edited by Talcott Parsons. New York, 1947.

Yaney, George L. *The Systematization of Russian Government: Social Evolution in the Domestic Administration of Imperial Russia: 1711–1905.* Urbana, 1973.

Section II. Prebureaucratic Administration:
The Seventeenth and Eighteenth Centuries

Alexander, John T. *Autocratic Politics in a National Crisis: The Imperial Russian Government and Pugachev's Revolt, 1773–1775.* Bloomington, 1969.

Augustine, Wilson. "Notes toward a Portrait of the Eighteenth Century Russian Nobility." *Canadian Slavic Studies* 4 (Fall 1970): 373–425.

Blanc, S. "La pratique de l'administration russe dans la premiere motié du XVIIIe siècle." *Revue d'histoire moderne et contemporaine* 10 (1963): 45–64.

Bogoiavlenskii, S. K. *Prikaznye sud'i XVII veka.* Moscow and Leningrad, 1946.

Crummey, Robert O. "Crown and Boiars under Fedor Ivanovich and Michael Romanov." *Canadian-American Slavic Studies* 6 (1972): 549–74.

————. "The Reconstitution of the Boiar Aristocracy, 1613–1645." *Forschungen zur osteuropäischen Geschichte* 18 (1973): 187–220.

Givens, Robert D. "Supplication and Reform in the Instructions of the Nobility." *Canadian-American Slavic Studies* 11 (Winter 1977): 483–502.

Got'e, Iu. *Istoriia oblastnogo upravleniia v Rossii ot Petra I do Ekateriny II.* 2 vols. Moscow, 1913, 1941.

Hassel, James. "Implementation of the Russian Table of Ranks during the Eighteenth Century." *Slavic Review* 29 (1970): 283–95.

Hellie, Richard. *Enserfment and Military Change in Muscovy.* Chicago, 1971.

Jones, Robert. *The Emancipation of the Russian Nobility, 1762–1785.* Princeton, 1973.

Kahan, Arcadius. "The Costs of Westernization in Russia: The Gentry and the Economy in the Eighteenth Century." *Slavic Review* 25 (1966): 40–66.

Kliuchevskii, V. O. *Boiarskaia duma drevnei Rusi.* Moscow, 1909.

Kliuchevsky, V. O. *A Course in Russian History: The Seventeenth Century.* Translated by Natalie Duddington. Chicago, 1968.

Kotoshikhin, G. *O Rossii v tsarstvovanie Alekseia Mikhailovicha.* St. Petersburg, 1906.

Longworth, Philip. *The Cossacks.* New York, 1969.

Meehan-Waters, Brenda. "The Muscovite Noble Origins of the Russians in the Generalitet of 1730." *Cahiers du monde russe et soviétique* 12 (1970): 28–75.

————. "The Russian Aristocracy and the Reforms of Peter the Great." *Canadian-American Slavic Studies* 8 (1974): 288–302.

————. "Elites Politics and Autocratic Power." In *Britain and Russia: Contacts and Comparison, 1700–1800,* edited by A. G. Cross. Newtonville, 1978.

Pronshtein, A. P. *Zemlia Donskaia v XVIII veke*. Rostov-na-Donu, 1961.

Rabinovich, M. D. "Sotsial'noe proiskhozhdenie i imushchestvennoe polozhenie ofitserov reguliarnoi russkoi armii v kontse severnoi voiny." In *Rossiia v period reform Petra I*, edited by N. I. Pavlenko et al., Moscow, 1973, pp. 133–71.

Raeff, Marc. *Origins of the Russian Intelligentsia: The Eighteenth-Century Nobility*. New York, 1966.

———. "Pugachev's Rebellion." In *Preconditions of Revolution in Early Modern Europe*, edited by Robert Forster and Jack P. Green, pp. 161–202, Baltimore, 1970.

———. "The Style of Russia's Imperial Policy and Prince G. A. Potemkin." In *Statesmen and Statecraft of the Modern West*, edited by Gerald N. Grob, pp. 1–51, Barre, 1967.

———. "The Well-Ordered Police State and the Development of Modernity in Seventeenth- and Eighteenth-Century Europe: An Attempt at a Comparative Approach." *American Historical Review* 80 (December 1975): 1221–43.

Ransel, David L. "Bureaucracy and Patronage: The View from an Eighteenth Century Russian Letter Writer." In *The Rich, the Well-Born and the Powerful: Elites and Upper Classes in History*, edited by F. C. Jaher, pp. 154–78, Urbana, 1973.

———. *The Politics of Catherinian Russia: The Panin Party*. New Haven, 1975.

Troitskii, S. M. *Russkii absoliutizm i dvorianstvo v XVIIIv. Formirovanie biurokratii*. Moscow, 1974.

Vodarskii, Ia. E. "Praviashchaia gruppa svetskikh feodalov v Rossii v XVIIv." In *Dvorianstvo i krepostnoi stroi Rossii XVI–XVIIIvv.*, edited by N. I. Pavlenko, pp. 70–107, Moscow, 1975.

Section III. The Development of Bureaucratized Administration: The Nineteenth Century

Bennett, Helju Aulik. "The Evolution of the Meanings of *Chin*: An Introduction to the Russian Institution of Rank Ordering and Niche Assignment from the Time of Peter the Great's Table of Ranks to the Bolshevik Revolution." *California Slavic Studies* 10 (1977): 1–43.

Field, Daniel. *The End of Serfdom: Nobility and Bureaucracy in Russia, 1855–1861*. Cambridge, Massachusetts, 1976.

Lincoln, W. Bruce. "The Genesis of an 'Enlightened' Bureaucracy in

Russia, 1825–1856." *Jahrbücher für Geschichte Osteuropas* 20 (September 1972): 321–30.

———. "The Ministers of Nicholas I: A Brief Inquiry into Their Backgrounds and Service Careers." *Russian Review* 34 (July 1975): 308–23.

———. "Russia's 'Enlightened' Bureaucrats and the Problem of State Reform, 1848–1856." *Cahiers du monde russe et soviétique* 12 (October–December 1971): 410–21.

McFarlin, Harold A. "Recruitment Norms for the Russian Civil Service in 1833: The Chancery Clerkship." *Societas—A Review of Social History* 3 (1973): 61–73.

———. "The Extension of the Imperial Russian Civil Service to the Lowest Office Workers: The Creation of the Chancery Clerkship, 1827–1833." *Russian History* 1 (1974): 1–17.

Orzhekhovskii, I. V. *Iz istorii vnutrennei politiki samoderzhaviia v 60–70-x godakh XIX veka.* Gor'kii, 1974.

Pintner, Walter M. *Russian Economic Policy under Nicholas I.* Ithaca, 1967.

———. "The Russian Higher Civil Service on the Eve of the 'Great Reforms.'" *Journal of Social History* (Spring 1975): 55–68.

———. "The Social Characteristics of the Early Nineteenth-Century Russian Bureaucracy." *Slavic Review* 29 (September 1970): 429–43.

Raeff, Marc. "The Russian Autocracy and Its Officials." In H. McLean, M. E. Malia, and G. Fischer, editors, *Harvard Slavic Studies* 4 (1957): 77–91.

———. *Michael Speransky, Statesman of Imperial Russia, 1772–1839.* The Hague, 1957.

Rieber, Alfred J. "Bureaucratic Politics in Imperial Russia." *Social Science History* 2 (Summer 1978): 399–413.

Rowney, Don Karl. "Higher Civil Servants in the Russian Ministry of Internal Affairs: Some Demographic and Career Characteristics, 1905–1916." *Slavic Review* 31 (March 1972): 101–10.

———. "The Ministry of Internal Affairs in the Light of Organizational Theory." In *The Behavioral Revolution and Communist Studies*, edited by Roger Kanet. New York, 1971.

Sinel, Allen A. "The Socialization of the Russian Bureaucratic Elite, 1811–1917: Life at the Tsarskoe Selo Lyceum and the School of Jurisprudence." *Russian History* 3 (1976): 1–31.

Squire, P. S. *The Third Department.* Cambridge, 1968.

Starr, S. Frederick. *Decentralization and Self-Government in Russia, 1830–1870.* Princeton, 1972.

Torke, Hans-Joachim. "Das russische Beamtentum in der ersten Hälfte des 19. Jahrhunderts." *Forschungen zur osteuropäischen Geschichte* 13 (1967): 7–345.

Wortman, Richard S. *The Development of a Russian Legal Consciousness.* Chicago, 1976.

Zaionchkovskii, P. A. "Gubernskaia administratsiia nakanune Krymskoi voiny." *Voprosy istorii* 9 (September 1975): 33–51.

———. *Krizis samoderzhaviia na rubezhe 1870–1880–x godov.* Moscow, 1964.

———. *Pravitel'stvennyi apparat samoderzhavnoi Rossii v XIXv.* Moscow, 1978.

———. "Vysshaia biurokratiia nakanune krymskoi voiny." *Istoriia SSSR* 4 (July–August 1974): 154–65.

Section IV. Soviet Russia, the Ultrabureaucracy

Aleksandrov [A. S. Michelson]. *Kto upravliaet Rossiei?* Berlin, 1933.

Armstrong, John A. *The Soviet Bureaucratic Elite: A Case Study of the Ukrainian Apparatus.* New York, 1959.

Avtorkhanov, Abdurakhman. *The Communist Party Apparatus.* Chicago, 1966.

Azrael, Jeremy R. *Managerial Power and Soviet Politics.* Cambridge, Massachusetts, 1966.

Beck, Carl et al. *Comparative Communist Political Leadership.* New York, 1973.

Cocks, Paul M. "Retooling the Directed Society: Administrative Modernization and Developed Socialism." In *Political Development in Eastern Europe,* edited by Jan Triska and Paul M. Cocks, pp. 53–92, New York, 1977.

Daniels, Robert V. *The Conscience of the Revolution: Communist Opposition in Soviet Russia.* Cambridge, Massachusetts, 1960.

———. "The Secretariat and the Local Organizations in the Russian Communist Party, 1921–1923." *American Slavic and East European Review* 16 (1957): 32–39.

———. "Office Holding and Elite Status: The Central Committee of the CPSU." In *The Dynamics of Soviet Politics,* edited by Paul Cocks, Robert V. Daniels, and Nancy Whittier Heer. Cambridge, Massachusetts, 1976.

Edeen, Alf. "The Civil Service: Its Composition and Status." In *The Transformation of Russian Society: Aspects of Social Change Since 1861,* edited by Cyril E. Black, pp. 274–91, Cambridge, Massachusetts, 1960.

Fainsod, Merle. *How Russia Is Ruled*. 2nd ed. Cambridge, Massachusetts, 1963.

Farrell, R. Barry, ed. *Political Leadership in Eastern Europe and the Soviet Union*. Chicago, 1970.

Gable, Richard W. "Development Administration: Background, Terms, Concepts, Theories and a New Approach." *SICA Occasional Papers* 7 (1976). American Society for Public Administration, Washington, D.C.

Hough, Jerry F. *The Soviet Prefects: The Local Party Organs in Industrial Decision-Making*. Cambridge, Massachusetts, 1969.

LaPalombara, Joseph, ed. *Bureaucracy and Political Development*. Princeton, 1963.

Levytsky, Boris. *The Stalinist Terror in the Thirties*. Stanford, 1974.

Miller, Robert F. "The Scientific-Technical Revolution and the Soviet Administrative Debate." In *The Dynamics of Soviet Politics*, edited by Paul M. Cocks et al., pp. 137–55. Cambridge, Massachusetts, 1976.

Moore, Barrington. *Soviet Politics: The Dilemma of Power*. Cambridge, Massachusetts, 1950.

Rigby, T. H. *Communist Party Membership in the U.S.S.R., 1917–1967*. Princeton, 1968.

Rigby, T. H., and Miller, R. F. *Political and Administrative Aspects of the Scientific and Technical Revolution in the USSR*. Occasional Paper, No. 11, Department of Political Science, Australian National University. Canberra, 1976.

Schapiro, Leonard. *The Communist Party of the Soviet Union*. New York, 1960.

Skilling, H. Gordon, and Griffiths, Franklyn, eds. *Interest Groups in Soviet Politics*. Princeton, 1971.

Sternheimer, Stephen, "Administering Development and Development Administration: Organizational Conflict in the Tsarist Bureaucracy, 1906–1917." *Canadian-American Slavic Studies* 9 (Fall 1975): 277–301.

———. "Local Administration in the USSR: Politicians Without Power?" In *Public Administration and Policy Making in the Soviet Union*, edited by Gordon Smith. Washington, D.C., 1979.

———. "Modernizing Administrative Elites: The Making of Managers for Soviet Cities." *Comparative Politics* 11 (July 1979): 403–24.

Sternheimer, Stephen, and Carol W. Lewis. *Soviet Urban Management: Achievements and Challenges. A Comparison with the United States*. New York, 1979.

Contributors

Helju Aulik Bennett, Department of History, State University of New York at Buffalo, Buffalo, New York.

Robert O. Crummey, Department of History, University of California at Davis, Davis, California.

Robert V. Daniels, Department of History, University of Vermont, Burlington, Vermont.

Robert D. Givens, Department of History, Cornell College, Mt. Vernon, Iowa.

Brenda Meehan-Waters, Department of History, University of Rochester, Rochester, New York.

Bruce W. Menning, Department of History, Miami University, Oxford, Ohio.

Daniel T. Orlovsky, Department of History, Southern Methodist University, Dallas, Texas.

Walter M. Pintner, Department of History, Cornell University, Ithaca, New York.

Borivoj Plavsic, U.S. Department of Labor, Wage and Hour Division, Portland, Maine.

Don Karl Rowney, Department of History, Bowling Green State University, Bowling Green, Ohio.

Stephen Sternheimer, Department of Political Science, Boston University, Boston, Massachusetts.

Index

Accountability: fiscal, 32; for documents, 32

Adaptation, 288–89, 315

Administration: professional, 22; rational, 22; effectiveness of, 30; agricultural, 319n; costs of, 321n, 328–31, 334–35; Marxist view of, 329; purges of, 338, 348; staffing criteria, 342; elimination of tsarist officials, 343–49; burdens on, 352; structural changes in, 370; central vs. provincial, 371. *See also* Bureaucracy; Ministry of Internal Affairs (MVD); Officialdom, civil; Professionalization; Specialization

Age: at entrance into service, 29n, 219–24; of Boyar Duma members, 59–62; of eighteenth-century officials, 91; of provincial officials, 177; of elite, 229; of MVD officials, 255–56, 258–59. *See also* Career patterns; Education and Training

Akakievich, Akakii, 168

Alef, Gustave, 20

Alexander I, 159, 161, 190, 316, 367; and orders, 172; and education, 224

Alexander II, 181, 252–53, 259, 279; MVD under, 281

Alexander III, 188

Alexis Mikailovich (Tsar), 36, 49, 54, 56–58

Anna Ivanovna (Empress), 99, 102, 142, 149

Arakcheev, Count A. A., 6

Armstrong, John, 259, 268n, 287–88, 305–10

Ataman (Cossack chief): selection of, 136–37; and central government, 137; and election of council of elders, 138; growth in power of, 141

Authority: attitude toward, 186; in organizations, 286–87; of minister of internal affairs, 291–92

Azerbaidzhan, 360, 363, 365

Baron, Samuel, 6

Belianinov, Pamfil, 30

Belorussia, 362–63, 365

Bogoiavlenskii, S. K., 35, 39; on social origins of officials, 40n

Bolsheviks: attitude toward bureaucracy, 320

Boyars: sixteenth century, 52

Boyars, Council (Duma) of, 20, 22, 26, 41, 46, 367; ranks in, 48; historiography of, 49; membership of, 49, 51–52, 68–69; "new men" in, 54; "democratization" of, 57; admission to, 59; civil or military service of members, 62–63, 67–68

Bruce, James Daniel, 96

Budget: seventeenth century, 23; adherence to, 24

Bulavin, Kondratii, 140, 142

Bureaucracies: traditional, 289, 310

Bureaucracy: nature of, 9; and the autocrat, 11; and Party leaders, 11; functional subdivision of, 316

Bureaucratic organization: Russian tradition of, 369–70

Bureaucratization, 251, 356; of officialdom, 8, 227; and subordination, 10; Weberian, 10; seventeenth-century, 22; and Cossacks, 130; of nonofficial society, 370; and world-wide development, 380; extension of, 380; of Communist party, 380. *See also* Administration; Officialdom, civil

Bureaucrats: noble, 17; "enlightened," 256. *See also* Officialdom, civil; Nobility

Buturlins, 50

Career patterns, 17–18, 91, 193; seventeenth-century, 27, 33–36; and merit, 35; promotion rate, 35n, 91, 93–94; types of, 47; of Boyar Council members, 59–62, 70, 73–74; during succession crisis, 68; and court service, 85;